Library of
Davidson College

THE VICTORIAN MUSE

Selected Criticism and Parody of the Period

A thirty-nine-volume facsimile set essential to the study of one of the most prolific periods in English literature

Edited by
William E. Fredeman, Ira Bruce Nadel, John F. Stasny

A Garland Series

Victorian Biography
A Collection of Essays
from the Period

Edited by
Ira Bruce Nadel

Garland Publishing, Inc.
New York & London
1986

For a complete list of the titles in this series
see the final pages of this volume.

The facsimile of *Memoirs of the Life of Sir Walter Scott*
is from a copy in the Library of Congress; the remaining
facsimiles are from copies in the libraries of Yale University.

Introduction © 1986 by Ira Bruce Nadel

Library of Congress Cataloging-in-Publication Data

Victorian biography : a collection of essays from the period.

(The Victorian muse)
Reprint of works originally published 1832–1929.
1. English prose literature—19th century—History
and criticism.   2. Biography (as a literary form)
3. Great Britain—Biography.   I. Nadel, Ira Bruce.
II. Series.
PR788.B56V5   1986   820'.9'008   86-7565
ISBN 0-8240-8629-5 (alk. paper)

Design by Bonnie Goldsmith

The volumes in this series are printed on
acid-free, 250-year-life paper.

Printed in the United States of America

Introduction

Nineteenth-century biography remains an often-cited but little-studied discipline. Early works like Waldo H. Dunn's *English Biography* (1916) and Harold Nicolson's *The Development of English Biography* (1927) contained useful summaries, while Richard Altick's *Lives and Letters* (1965) and A.O.J. Cockshut's *Truth to Life, The Art of Biography in the Nineteenth Century* (1974) provided fuller but often uncritical interpretations of the genre. Collections of critical essays have been equally limited, with James L. Clifford's 1962 anthology, *Biography as An Art*, the only representational gathering, although most passages are only excerpts from longer works. The present collection of nineteen complete essays provides an antidote to the lack of primary material by gathering a set of essays that display the panoply of attitudes and approaches to life writing from 1832 to 1911. They also provide an introduction to many of the central issues relating to the content and form of Victorian biography.

Initiating the century's concern with biography and biographical writing is Thomas Carlyle, critic and biographer of Schiller, Cromwell, Sterling, and Frederick the Great. His two essays that open this collection complement one another since the first deals with theoretical matters, the second with practical. In "Biography" (1832) Carlyle claims an essential role for biography in understanding any writer or art form; biography, he declares, is our only record of *"Reality."* But, he complains, "few genuinely-good *Biographies* have yet been accumulated in Literature" and "in England we have simply one good Biography, this *Boswell's Johnson."* To correct that failing and encourage the writing of better biographies is the goal of Carlyle, just as in his essay "Sir Walter Scott" he illustrates, through a detailed critique, what is potentially a notable biography.

"There is no heroic poem in the world but is at bottom a biography, the life of a man," Carlyle announces at the beginning of his essay on Scott and using chiasmus adds, "there is no life of a man, faithfully recorded, but is a heroic poem of its sort, rhymed or unrhymed." Lockhart's *Life of Scott* is not so much a composition as a compilation, Carlyle argues, but it is nonetheless honest and truthful in its presentation. Until now such reticence has been *the* limitation of English biography:

> How delicate, decent is English biography, bless its mealy mouth! A Damocles' sword of *Respectability* hangs for ever over the poor English life-writer (as it does over poor English life in general), and reduces him to the verge of paralysis.

Carlyle attacks such protectiveness in his own biographies, repeatedly criticizing those biographies that make hagiography commonplace. Each man "has to *elbow* himself through the world, giving and receiving offence," he writes, and unless a biography gives all the honest details, it cannot be either truthful or successful.

A biography for Carlyle must provide the blemishes, embarrassments, mistakes, and weaknesses of its subject, as well as his triumphs. According to Carlyle, how a man lived under all circumstances should be the only subject matter of Victorian biography, a principle subsequent biographers had difficulty following. The tradition of praiseworthy lives, often written by relatives, most frequently wives of the deceased (illustrated by Mrs. Richard Burton's or Mrs. Charles Kingsley's biographies of their husbands), met gradual correction in critical biographies like Mrs. Gaskell's *Life of Charlotte Bronte* (1857) or James A. Froude's *Carlyle* (1882, 1884). But in his determination to reform biography by precept and example, Carlyle initiated a fresh approach later biographers could not overlook.

Associated with the new drive for candour in biography was a series of related issues—notably sincerity, ethics, and suppression. A variety of essays such as those by the publisher George Bentley and the novelists Margaret Oliphant and Mrs. Humphrey Ward debate these topics. Of most concern was motive, the reason for writing a biography, especially, as Mrs. Oliphant emphasized, if the biographer was a detractor rather than an enthusiast for his subject. The biographer is always in a position of trust and responsibility, Oliphant asserts, and his use of that power is critical. Furthermore, since "a mere record of facts will not satisfy," the biographer must by the nature of his undertaking interpret. But he must do so without prejudice, although he is "bound to spare no pains in eliciting that truth which is something more and greater than fact, which it is possible even may be almost contradictory in its development, and which is of far greater permanent importance than any mere occurrence." This statement extends the views of Carlyle while it suggests some of the critical positions taken by such twentieth-century biographers as Lytton Strachey. However, Mrs. Oliphant balances this advanced attitude with a firm Victorian conviction: if a biographer should discover any unfavorable facts in events that might undermine the reputation or image of his subject, he should refrain from writing the life. This moral position cancels her earlier commitment to truthful lives but vividly displays the dilemma most Victorian biographers and critics encountered.

The other problem for Victorian biographers was form. Just how should one structure a life? Should it be an omnium-gatherum of undigested facts in two or three volumes (Lockhart's *Scott* was ten volumes in its first edition!), or should the biography be a brief critical interpretation? This debate continued throughout the period as the essays by W. E. Aytoun, George Smith, and Charles Whibley show. During the century there appeared, however, a general move to the condensed life—brief, interpretative, and critical. The emergence of such biographical series as *Lives of the Engineers* by Samuel Smiles, the *English Men of Letters* series, edited by John Morley, and the

Dictionary of National Biography, edited by Leslie Stephen, confirms the acceptance and need for this style that originated in Plutarch and continued in Aubrey's *Brief Lives*. R. H. Christie's 1884 essay "Biographical Dictionaries" provides an extensive discussion of this form supplemented by Leslie Stephen's two articles.

Stephen, the father of Virginia Woolf and founding editor of the *DNB*, was instrumental in shaping the course of nineteenth-century biography and its transition to the twentieth. In his 1893 essay "Biography," he responds to charges that biographies in dictionary form are unsatisfactory by pointing out the overall accuracy, detail, and successful compression of minor as well as major lives. He defends the limitations of biographical dictionaries through a parallel with the writers of sonnets who must deal with fixed parameters. The new biographer must "give nothing but the facts; and yet . . . make the facts tell their own story." The dictionary maker faces a formidable challenge: "he should give the very pith and essence of the case, and, like the skilful advocate, appear to be simply relating a plain narrative, when he is really dictating the verdict." And Stephen again confronts the crux of the biographer that Oliphant, Carlyle, and others have noted: "Is he [the biographer] to give a pure narrative of his own, or to let his hero talk to us face to face?" The main interest is always, he argues, "the development of the man's own character and fortunes"—and the resulting portrait should reveal "the essence of character." Irrelevancies should be cut, redundancies eliminated.

The scholar-journalist Charles Whibley in "The Limits of Biography" continues the drive for concision. He believes that the accumulation of fact is not enough for a successful biography; the facts must also be judiciously presented and interpreted, though there must be limits. The biographer has again to avoid irresponsibility, proving to his readers the absence of indiscretion and avoiding any betrayal of the subject. Whibley still clings to conservative Victorian practices, although he resolves the dilemma of Oliphant and the reform of Carlyle by restating a preference for suppression of the facts if they might harm or misrepresent the subject. But in an effort to establish a "consistent picture" of his subject, the author can fill in the blanks "from an intuitive sympathy" and treat his hero "as he would treat the hero of a romance." Such a compromise, of course, weakens both the resolve to be concise and the need to forestall the use of uncomplimentary facts.

But not all biographers at the opening of the twentieth century were so attached to the nineteenth. Sidney Lee, Leslie Stephen's assistant and then successor at the *DNB*, provides an important coda to the Victorians in his 1911 Cambridge lecture, "Principles of Biography." The essay, a counterpart to Carlyle's 1832 essay "Biography" in its concentration on method, believes that the power of biography lies in its ability to transmit personality, which it cannot do unless the material itself is of interest and is interestingly presented. Subject matter and style must integrate, with Lee preferring an Aristotelian definition of completeness, seriousness, and importance for a successful biography. Furthermore, significant biography must preserve its independence from ethical instruction, history, or anthropological sciences. Lee implies that biography is an art and in this concept frees the genre from the restrictions imposed on it by most Victorian biographers. Biography, he believes, is not inherently moralistic, historical, or scientific but aesthetic. Such an interpretation encourages its development by later innovators like Lytton Strachey, A.J.A. Symons, and Leon Edel.

"A discriminating brevity is a law of the right biographic method," Sydney Lee writes as a kind of summation of the path of biography from Lockhart to Strachey. As the essays in this collection demonstrate, Victorian biography underwent transition and change in its encounter with form and matters of content. In popularity biography never achieved the mass appeal of the Victorian novel but neither did it languish on the shelf unread. Publishers were eager for new lives, and biographers like John Forster, author of lives of Dickens, Swift, and Goldsmith, were soon receiving substantial incomes for their efforts. Most importantly, biography was loosing its tradesman's character and identity as a craft, while gaining new status as art. "The popular idea seems to be," Edmund Gosse wrote in "The Custom of Biography," "that no one is too great a fool, or too complete an amateur, or too thoroughly ignorant of the modes of composition, to undertake the 'life' of an eminent person." The opposite, as Gosse knew and said, was also true, and by 1901 when he published his essay, biography had proven him right. As biographers and critics recognized, biography had left the workshop and entered the study.

Contents

"Biography," *Fraser's Magazine*, 1832
[Thomas Carlyle]

"Memoirs of the Life of Sir Walter Scott," *The London and Westminster Review*, 1838
[Thomas Carlyle]

"Hints for Biographers," *Fraser's Magazine*, 1840
[R. A. Willmott]

"Modern Biography—Beattie's Life of Campbell," *Blackwood's Edinburgh Magazine*, 1849
[W. E. Aytoun]

"Biographia Dramatica," *Blackwood's Edinburgh Magazine*, 1861
[James White]

"A Suggestion for a New Kind of Biography," *The Contemporary Review*, 1870
Robert Goodbrand

"Contemporary Literature," *Blackwood's Edinburgh Magazine*, 1879

"Studies in Biography," *Fraser's Magazine*, 1879

"Sincerity in Biography," *Temple Bar*, 1881
[George Bentley]

"The Ethics of Biography," *The Contemporary Review*, 1883
M.O.W. Oliphant

[Biographical Dictionaries], *The Quarterly Review*, 1884
[R. H. Christie]

"On Biography and Biographies," *Temple Bar*, 1892
[George Smith]

"Biography," *The National Review*, 1893
Leslie Stephen

"Candour in Biography," *The New Review*, 1896
Wilfrid Ward

"On the Ethics of Suppression in Biography," *The Nineteenth Century*, 1896
Edmund S. Purcell

"The Limits of Biography," *The Nineteenth Century*, 1897
Charles Whibley

"National Biography," *Studies of a Biographer*, 1899
Leslie Stephen

"The Custom of Biography," *The Anglo-Saxon Review*, 1901
Edmund Gosse

"Principles of Biography," [1911], *Elizabethan and Other Essays*, 1929
Sidney Lee

FRASER'S MAGAZINE

FOR

TOWN AND COUNTRY.

No. XXVII.   APRIL, 1832.   Vol. V.

BIOGRAPHY.*

Man's sociality of nature evinces itself, in spite of all that can be said, with abundant evidence by this one fact, were there no other: the unspeakable delight he takes in Biography. It is written, "The proper study of mankind is man;" to which study, let us candidly admit, he, by true or by false methods, applies himself, nothing loath. "Man is perennially interesting to man; nay, if we look strictly to it, there is nothing else interesting." How inexpressibly comfortable to know our fellow-creature; to see into him, understand his goings forth, decipher the whole heart of his mystery: nay, not only to see into him, but even to see out of him, to view the world altogether as he views it; so that we can theoretically construe him, and could almost practically personate him; and do now thoroughly discern both what manner of man he is, and what manner of thing he has got to work on and live on!

A scientific interest and a poetic one alike inspire us in this matter. A scientific: because every mortal has a Problem of Existence set before him, which, were it only, what for the most it is, the Problem of keeping soul and body together, must be to a certain extent *original*, unlike every other; and yet, at the same time, so *like* every other; like our own, therefore; instructive, therefore, since we also are indentured to *live*. A poetic interest still more: for precisely this same struggle of human Free-will against material Necessity, which every man's Life, by the mere circumstance that the man continues alive, will more or less victoriously exhibit,— is that which above all else, or rather inclusive of all else, calls the Sympathy of mortal hearts into action; and whether as acted, or as represented and written of, not only is Poetry, but is the sole Poetry possible. Borne onwards by which two all-embracing interests, may the earnest Lover of Biography expand himself on all sides, and indefinitely enrich himself. Looking with the eyes of every new neighbour, he can discern a new world different for each; feeling with the heart of every neighbour, he lives with every neighbour's life, even as with his own. Of these millions of living men each individual is a mirror to us: a mirror both scientific and poetic; or, if you will, both natural and magical;— from which one would so gladly draw aside the gauze veil; and, peering therein, discern the image of his own natural face, and the supernatural secrets that prophetically lie under the same!

Observe, accordingly, to what extent, in the actual course of things, this business of Biography is practised and relished. Define to thyself, judicious Reader, the real significance of these

---

* The Life of Samuel Johnson, LL.D.: including a Tour to the Hebrides: By James Boswell, Esq.—A new Edition, with numerous Additions and Notes: By John Wilson Croker, LL.D. F.R.S. 5 vols. London, 1831.

phenomena, named Gossip, Egotism, Personal Narrative (miraculous or not), Scandal, Raillery, Slander, and such like; the sum-total of which (with some fractional addition of a better ingredient, generally too small to be noticeable) constitutes that other grand phenomenon still called "Conversation." Do they not mean wholly: *Biography* and *Autobiography?* Not only in the common Speech of men; but in all Art, too, which is or should be the concentrated and conserved essence of what men can speak and shew, Biography is almost the one thing needful.

Even in the highest works of Art our interest, as the critics complain, is too apt to be strongly or even mainly of a Biographic sort. In the Art, we can nowise forget the Artist: while looking on the *Transfiguration*, while studying the *Iliad*, we ever strive to figure to ourselves what spirit dwelt in Raphael; what a head was that of Homer, wherein, woven of Elysian light and Tartarean gloom, that old world fashioned itself together, of which these written Greek characters are but a feeble though perennial copy. The Painter and the Singer are present to us; we partially and for the time become the very Painter and the very Singer, while we enjoy the Picture and the Song. Perhaps, too, let the critic say what he will, this is the highest enjoyment, the clearest recognition, we can have of these. Art indeed is Art; yet Man also is Man. Had the *Transfiguration* been painted without human hand; had it grown merely on the canvass, say by atmospheric influences, as lichen-pictures do on rocks,—it were a grand Picture doubtless; yet nothing like so grand as *the* Picture, which, on opening our eyes, we every where in Heaven and in Earth see painted; and every where pass over with indifference,—because the Painter was not a Man. Think of this; much lies in it. The Vatican is great; yet poor to Chimborazo or the Peak of Teneriffe: its dome is but a foolish Big-endian or Little-endian chip of an egg-shell compared with that star-fretted Dome where Arcturus and Orion glance for ever; which latter, notwithstanding, who looks at, save perhaps some necessitous star-gazer bent to make Almanacs, some thick-quilted watchman to see what weather it will prove? The Biographic interest is wanting: no Michael Angelo was He who built that "Temple of Immensity;" therefore do we, pitiful Littlenesses as we are, turn rather to wonder and to worship in the little toybox of a Temple built by our like.

Still more decisively, still more exclusively does the Biographic interest manifest itself, as we descend into lower regions of spiritual communication; through the whole range of what is called Literature. Of History, for example, the most honoured, if not honourable species of composition, is not the whole purport biographic? "History," it has been said, "is the essence of innumerable Biographies." Such, at least, it should be: whether it is, might admit of question. But, in any case, what hope have we in turning over those old interminable Chronicles, with their garrulities and insipidities; or still worse, in patiently examining those modern Narrations, of the Philosophic kind, where "Philosophy, teaching by Experience," must sit like owl on housetop, *seeing* nothing, *understanding* nothing, uttering only, with solemnity enough, her perpetual most wearisome *hoo-hoo:*—what hope have we, except the for most part fallacious one of gaining some acquaintance with our fellow-creatures, though dead and vanished, yet dear to us; how they got along in those old days, suffering and doing; to what extent, and under what circumstances, they resisted the Devil and triumphed over him, or struck their colours to him, and were trodden under foot by him; how, in short, the perennial Battle went, which men name Life, which we also in these new days, with indifferent fortune, have to fight, and must bequeath to our sons and grandsons to go on fighting,—till the Enemy one day be quite vanquished and abolished, or else the great Night sink and part the combatants; and thus, either by some Millennium or some new Noah's Deluge, the Volume of Universal History wind itself up! Other hope, in studying such Books, we have none: and that it is a deceitful hope, who that has tried knows not? A feast of widest Biographic insight is spread for us; we enter full of hungry anticipation: alas! like so many other feasts, which Life invites us to, a mere Ossian's "feast of *shells,*"— the food and liquor being all emptied out and clean gone, and only the vacant dishes and deceitful emblems thereof left! Your modern Historical Restaurateurs are indeed little better than high-priests of Famine;

that keep choicest china dinner-sets, only no dinner to serve therein. Yet such is our Biographic appetite, we run trying from shop to shop, with ever new hope; and, unless we could eat the wind, with ever new disappointment.

Again, consider the whole class of Fictitious Narratives; from the highest category of epic or dramatic Poetry, in Shakspeare and Homer, down to the lowest of froth Prose, in the Fashionable Novel. What are all these but so many mimic Biographies? Attempts, here by an inspired Speaker, there by an uninspired Babbler, to deliver himself, more or less ineffectually, of the grand secret wherewith all hearts labour oppressed: The significance of Man's Life;—which deliverance, even as traced in the unfurnished head, and printed at the Minerva Press, finds readers. For, observe, though there is *a* greatest Fool, as a superlative in every kind; and *the* most Foolish man in the Earth is now indubitably living and breathing, and did this morning or lately eat breakfast, and is even now digesting the same; and looks out on the world, with his dim horn-eyes, and inwardly forms some unspeakable theory thereof: yet where shall the authentically Existing be personally met with! Can one of us, otherwise than by guess, know that we have got sight of him, have orally communed with him? To take even the narrower sphere of this our English metropolis, can any one confidently say to himself, that he has conversed with the identical, individual, Stupidest man now extant in London? No one. Deep as we dive in the Profound, there is ever a new depth opens: where the ultimate bottom may lie, through what new scenes of being we must pass before reaching it (except that we know it does lie somewhere, and might by human faculty and opportunity be reached), is altogether a mystery to us. Strange, tantalizing pursuit! We have the fullest assurance, not only that there is a Stupidest of London men actually resident, with bed and board of some kind, in London; but that several persons have been or perhaps are now speaking face to face with him: while for us, chase it as we may, such scientific blessedness will too probably be for ever denied!— But the thing we want to enforce was this comfortable fact, that no known Head was so wooden, but there might be other heads to which it were a genius and Friar Bacon's Oracle. Of no given Book, not even of a Fashionable Novel, can you predicate with certainty that its vacuity is absolute; that there are not other vacuities which shall partially replenish themselves therefrom, and esteem it a *plenum*. How knowest thou, may the distressed Novelwright exclaim, that I, here where I sit, am the Foolishest of existing mortals; that this my Long-ear of a Fictitious Biography shall not find one and the other, into whose still longer ears it may be the means, under Providence, of instilling somewhat? We answer, None knows, none can certainly know: therefore, write on, worthy Brother, even as thou canst, as it has been given thee.

Here, however, in regard to "Fictitious Biographies," and much other matter of like sort, which the greener mind in these days inditeth, we may as well insert some singular sentences on the importance and significance of *Reality*, as they stand written for us in Professor Gottfried Sauerteig's *Æsthetische Springwürzel*: a Work, perhaps, as yet new to most English readers. The Professor and Doctor is not a man whom we can praise without reservation; neither shall we say that his *Springwürzel* (a sort of magical picklocks, as he affectedly names them) are adequate to "*start*" every *bolt* that locks up an æsthetic mystery: nevertheless, in his crabbed, one-sided way, he sometimes hits masses of the truth. We endeavour to translate faithfully, and trust the reader will find it worth serious perusal:

" The significance, even for poetic purposes," says Sauerteig, " that lies in REALITY, is too apt to escape us; is perhaps only now beginning to be discerned. When we named *Rousseau's Confessions* an elegiaco-didactic Poem, we meant more than an empty figure of speech; we meant a historical scientific fact.

" Fiction, while the feigner of it knows that he is feigning, partakes, more than we suspect, of the nature of *lying;* and has ever an, in some degree, unsatisfactory character. All Mythologies were once Philosophies; were believed: the Epic Poems of old time, so long as they continued *epic*, and had any complete impressiveness, were Histories, and understood to be narratives of *facts*. In so far as Homer employed his gods as mere ornamental fringes, and had not himself, or at least did not expect his hearers to have, a belief that they were real agents in those antique doings; so far did he fail to be *genuine*; so far was he a partially *hollow* and false singer; and sang to please only a portion of man's mind, not the whole thereof.

"Imagination is, after all, but a poor matter when it must part company with Understanding, and even front it hostilely in flat contradiction. Our mind is divided in twain: there is contest; wherein that which is weaker must needs come to the worse. Now of all feelings, states, principles, call it what you will, in man's mind, is not Belief the clearest, strongest; against which all others contend in vain? Belief is, indeed, the beginning and first condition of all spiritual Force whatsoever: only in so far as Imagination, were it but momentarily, is *believed*, can there be any use or meaning in it, any enjoyment of it. And what is momentary Belief? The enjoyment of a moment. Whereas a perennial Belief were enjoyment perennially, and with the whole united soul.

"It is thus that I judge of the Supernatural in an Epic Poem; and would say, the instant it has ceased to be authentically supernatural, and become what you call 'Machinery;' sweep it out of sight (*schaff'es mir vom Halse*)! Of a truth, that same 'Machinery,' about which the critics make such hubbub, was well named *Machinery*; for it is in very deed mechanical, nowise inspired or poetical. Neither, for us, is there the smallest æsthetic enjoyment in it; save only in this way: that we believe it *to have been believed*,—by the Singer or his Hearers; into whose case we now laboriously struggle to transport ourselves; and so, with stinted enough result, catch some reflex of the Reality, which for them was wholly real, and visible face to face. Whenever it has come so far that your 'Machinery' is avowedly mechanical and unbelieved,—what is it else, if we dare tell ourselves the truth, but a miserable, meaningless Deception, kept up by old use and wont alone? If the gods of an *Iliad* are to us no longer authentic Shapes of Terror, heart-stirring, heart-appalling, but only vague-glittering Shadows,— what must the dead Pagan gods of an *Epigoniad* be, the dead-living Pagan-Christian gods of a *Lusiad*, the concrete-abstract, evangelical-metaphysical gods of a *Paradise Lost*? Superannuated lumber! Cast raiment, at best; in which some poor mime, strutting and swaggering, may or may not set forth new noble Human Feelings (again a Reality), and so secure, or not secure, our pardon of such hoydenish masking,—for which, in any case, he has a pardon to *ask*.

"True enough, none but the earliest Epic Poems can claim this distinction of entire credibility, of Reality: after an *Iliad*, a *Shaster*, a *Koran*, and other the like primitive performances, the rest seem, by this rule of mine, to be altogether excluded from the list. Accordingly, what *are* all the rest, from Virgil's *Æneid* downwards, in comparison?— Frosty, artificial, heterogeneous things; more of gumflowers than of roses; at best, of the two mixed incoherently together: to some of which, indeed, it were hard to deny the title of Poems; yet to no one of which can that title belong in any sense even resembling the old high one it, in those old days, conveyed,—when the epithet 'divine' or 'sacred,' as applied to the uttered Word of man, was not a vain metaphor, a vain sound, but a real name with meaning. Thus, too, the farther we recede from those early days, when Poetry, as true Poetry is always, was still sacred or divine, and inspired (what ours, in great part, only pretends to be),—the more impossible becomes it to produce any, we say not true Poetry, but tolerable semblance of such; the hollower, in particular, grow all manner of Epics; till at length, as in this generation, the very name of Epic sets men a-yawning, the announcement of a new Epic is received as a public calamity.

"But what if the *impossible* being once for all quite discarded, the *probable* be well adhered to: how stands it with fiction *then*? Why, then, I would say, the evil is much mended, but nowise completely cured. We have then, in place of the wholly dead modern Epic, the partially living modern Novel; to which latter it is much easier to lend that above-mentioned, so essential 'momentary credence' than to the former: indeed, infinitely easier; for the former being flatly incredible, no mortal *can* for a moment credit it, for a moment enjoy it. Thus, here and there, a *Tom Jones*, a *Meister*, a *Crusoe*, will yield no little solacement to the minds of men; though still immeasurably less than a *Reality* would, were the significance thereof as impressively unfolded, were the genius that could so unfold it once given us by the kind Heavens. Neither say thou that proper Realities are wanting: for Man's Life, now as of old, is the genuine work of God; wherever there is a Man, a God also is revealed, and all that is Godlike: a whole epitome of the Infinite, with its meanings, lies enfolded in the Life of every Man. Only, alas, that the Seer to discern this same Godlike, and with fit utterance unfold it for us, is wanting, and may long be wanting!

"Nay, a question arises on us here, wherein the whole German reading-world will eagerly join: Whether man can any longer be so interested by the spoken Word, as he often was in those primeval days, when, rapt away by its inscrutable power, he pronounced it, in such dialect as he had, to be *transcendental* (to *transcend* all measure), to be sacred, prophetic, and the inspiration of a god? For myself, I (*ich meines Ortes*), by faith or by insight, do heartily understand that the answer to such question will be, Yea! For never that I could in searching find out, has Man been, by Time which devours so much, deprivated of any faculty whatsoever that he in any era was possessed of. To my seeming, the babe born yesterday has all the organs of Body, Soul, and Spirit, and in exactly the same combination and entireness, that the oldest Pelasgic Greek, or Mesopotamian Patriarch, or Father Adam himself could boast of. Ten fingers, one heart with venous and arterial blood therein, still belong to man that is born of woman: when did he lose any of his spiritual Endowments either; above all, his highest spiritual Endowment, that of revealing Poetic Beauty, and of adequately receiving the same? Not the material, not the susceptibility is wanting; only the Poet, or long series of Poets, to work on these. True, alas too true, the Poet *is* still utterly wanting, or all but utterly: nevertheless have we not centuries enough before us to produce him in? Him and much else!—I, for the present, will but predict that chiefly by working more and more on REALITY, and evolving more and more wisely *its* inexhaustible meanings; and, in brief, speaking forth in fit utterance whatsoever our whole soul *believes*, and ceasing to speak forth what thing soever our whole soul does not believe,—will this high emprise be accomplished, or approximated to."

These notable, and not unfounded, though partial and *deep*-seeing rather than *wide*-seeing observations on the great import of REALITY, considered even as a poetic material, we have inserted the more willingly, because a transient feeling to the same purpose may often have suggested itself to many readers; and, on the whole, it is good that every reader and every writer understand, with all intensity of conviction, what quite infinite worth lies in *Truth;* how all-pervading, omnipotent, in man's mind, is the thing we name *Belief.* For the rest, Herr Sauerteig, though one-sided, on this matter of Reality, seems heartily persuaded, and is not perhaps so ignorant as he looks. It cannot be unknown to him, for example, what noise is made about "Invention;" what a supreme rank this faculty is reckoned to hold in the poetic endowment. Great truly is Invention; nevertheless, that is but a poor exercise of it with which Belief is not concerned. "An Irishman with whisky in his head," as poor Byron said, will invent you, in this kind, till there is enough and to spare. Nay perhaps, if we consider well, the highest exercise of Invention has, in very deed, nothing to do with Fiction; but is an invention of new Truth, what we can call a Revelation; which last does undoubtedly transcend all other poetic efforts, nor can Herr Sauerteig be too loud in its praises. But, on the other hand, whether such effort is still possible for man, Herr Sauerteig and the bulk of the world are probably at issue,—and will probably continue so till that same "Revelation" or new "Invention of Reality," of the sort he desiderates, shall itself make its appearance.

Meanwhile, quitting these airy regions, let any one bethink him how impressive the smallest historical *fact* may become, as contrasted with the grandest *fictitious event ;* what an incalculable force lies for us in this consideration: The Thing which I here hold imaged in my mind did actually occur; was, in very truth, an element in the system of the All, whereof I too form part; had therefore, and has, through all time, an authentic being; is not a dream, but a reality! We ourselves can remember reading, in *Lord Clarendon*, with feelings perhaps somehow accidentally opened to it,—certainly with a depth of impression strange to us then and now,—that insignificant-looking passage, where Charles, after the battle of Worcester, glides down, with Squire Careless, from the Royal Oak, at nightfall, being hungry: how, "making a shift to get over hedges and ditches, after walking at least eight or nine miles, which were the more grievous to the King by the weight of his boots (for he could not put *them* off, when he cut off his hair, for want of shoes), before morning they came to *a poor cottage, the owner whereof being a Roman Catholic was known to Careless.*" How this poor drudge, being knocked up from his snoring, "carried them into a little barn full of hay, which was a better lodging than he had for himself;" and by and by, not without difficulty, brought his Majesty "a piece of bread and a great pot of butter-milk," saying candidly that "he himself lived by his daily labour, and that what he had brought him was the fare he and his wife had :" on which nourishing diet his Majesty, "staying upon the haymow," feeds thankfully for two days; and then departs, under new guidance, having first changed clothes, down to the very shirt and "old pair of shoes," with his landlord; and so, as worthy Bunyan has it, "goes on his way, and sees him no more."* Singular enough if we will think of it! This then was a genuine flesh-and-blood Rustic of the year 1651: he did actually swallow bread and butter-milk (not having ale and bacon), and do field-labour; with these hob-nailed "shoes" has sprawled through mud-roads in winter, and, jocund or not, driven his team a-field in summer: he made bargains; had chafferings and higglings, now a sore heart, now a glad one; was born; was a son, was a father;—toiled in many ways, being forced to it, till the strength was all worn out of him; and then—lay down "to rest his galled back," and sleep there till the long-distant morning!—How comes it, that he alone of all the British rustics who tilled and lived along with him, on whom the blessed sun on that same "fifth day of September" was shining, should have chanced to rise on us; that this poor pair of clouted Shoes, out of the million million hides that have been tanned, and cut, and worn, should still subsist, and hang visibly together? We see him but for a moment; for one moment, the blanket of the Night is rent asunder, so that we behold and see, and then closes over him—for ever.

So too, in some *Boswell's Life of Johnson*, how indelible, and magically bright, does many a little *Reality* dwell in our remembrance! There is no need that the personages on the scene be a King and Clown; that the scene be the Forest of the Royal Oak, "on the borders of Staffordshire:" need only that the scene lie on this old firm Earth of ours, where we also have so surprisingly arrived; that the personages be *men*, and *seen* with the eyes of a man. Foolish enough, how some slight, perhaps mean and even ugly incident (if *real*, and well presented) will fix itself in a susceptive memory, and lie ennobled there; silvered over with the pale cast of thought, with the pathos which belongs only to the Dead. For the Past is all holy to us; the Dead are all holy, even they that were base and wicked while alive. Their baseness and wickedness was not *They*, was but the heavy unmanageable Environment that lay round them, with which they fought unprevailing: *they* (the ethereal God-given Force that dwelt in them, and was their *Self*) have now shuffled off that heavy Environment, and are free and pure: their life-long Battle, go how it might, is all ended, with many wounds or with fewer; they have been recalled from it, and the once harsh-jarring battle-field has become a silent awe-inspiring Golgotha, and *Gottesacker* (Field of God)!—Boswell relates this in itself smallest and poorest of occurrences: "As we walked along the Strand to-night, arm in arm, a woman of the town accosted us in the usual enticing manner. 'No, no, my girl,' said Johnson; 'it won't do.' He, however, did not treat her with harshness; and we talked of the wretched life of such women." Strange power of *Reality!* Not even this poorest of occurrences, but now, after seventy years are come and gone, has a meaning for us. Do but consider that it is *true;* that it did in very deed occur! That unhappy Outcast, with all her sins and woes, her lawless desires, too complex mischances, her wailings and her riotings, has departed utterly: alas! her siren finery has got all besmutched; ground, generations, since, into dust and smoke; of her degraded body, and whole miserable earthly existence, all is away: *she* is no longer here, but far from us, in the bosom of Eternity,—whence we too came, whither we too are bound! Johnson said, "No, no, my girl; it won't do;" and then "we talked;"—and herewith the wretched one, seen but for the twinkling of an eye, passes on into the utter Darkness. No high Calista, that ever issued from Story-teller's brain, will impress us more deeply than this meanest of the mean; and for a good reason: That *she* issued from the Maker of Men.

It is well worth the Artist's while to

---

* History of the Rebellion, iii. 625.

examine for himself what it is that gives such pitiful incidents their memorableness; his aim likewise is, above all things, to be *memorable*. Half the effect, we already perceive, depends on the object; on its being *real*, on its being really *seen*. The other half will depend on the observer; and the question now is: How are real objects to be *so* seen; on what quality of observing, or of style in describing, does this so intense pictorial power depend? Often a slight circumstance contributes curiously to the result: some little, and perhaps to appearance accidental, feature is presented; a light-gleam, which instantaneously *excites* the mind, and urges it to complete the picture, and evolve the meaning thereof for itself. By critics, such light-gleams and their almost magical influence have frequently been noted: but the power to produce such, to select such features as will produce them, is generally treated as a knack, or trick of the trade, a secret for being "graphic;" whereas these magical feats are, in truth, rather inspirations; and the gift of performing them, which acts unconsciously, without forethought, and as if by nature alone, is properly a *genius* for description.

One grand, invaluable secret there is, however, which includes all the rest, and, what is comfortable, lies clearly in every man's power: *To have an open loving heart, and what follows from the possession of such!* Truly has it been said, emphatically in these days ought it to be repeated: A loving Heart is the beginning of all Knowledge. This it is that opens the whole mind, quickens every faculty of the intellect to do its fit work, that of *knowing;* and therefrom, by sure consequence, of *vividly uttering forth*. Other secret for being "graphic" is there none, worth having: but this is an all-sufficient one. See, for example, what a small Boswell can do! Hereby, indeed, is the whole man made a living mirror, wherein the wonders of this ever-wonderful Universe are, in their true light (which is ever a magical, miraculous one) represented, and reflected back on us. It has been said, "the heart sees farther than the head:" but, indeed, without the seeing heart, there is no true seeing for the head so much as possible; all is mere *oversight*, hallucination, and vain superficial phantasmagoria, which can permanently profit no one.

Here, too, may we not pause for an instant, and make a practical reflection? Considering the multitude of mortals that handle the Pen in these days, and can mostly spell, and write without glaring violations of grammar, the question naturally arises: How is it, then, that no Work proceeds from them, bearing any stamp of authenticity and permanence; of worth for more than one day? Ship-loads of Fashionable Novels, Sentimental Rhymes, Tragedies, Farces, Diaries of Travel, Tales by flood and field, are swallowed monthly into the bottomless Pool: still does the Press toil; innumerable Paper-makers, Compositors, Printers' Devils, Bookbinders, and Hawkers grown hoarse with loud proclaiming, rest not from their labour; and still, in torrents, rushes on the great array of Publications, unpausing, to their final home; and still Oblivion, like the Grave, cries: Give! Give! How is it that of all these countless multitudes, no one can attain to the smallest mark of excellence, or produce aught that shall endure longer than "snow-flake on the river," or the foam of penny-beer? We answer: Because they *are* foam; because there is no *Reality* in them. These Three Thousand men, women, and children, that make up the army of British Authors, do not, if we will well consider it, *see* anything whatever; consequently *have* nothing that they can record and utter, only more or fewer things that they can plausibly pretend to record. The Universe, of Man and Nature, is still quite shut up from them; the "open secret" still utterly a secret; because no sympathy with Man or Nature, no love and free simplicity of heart has yet unfolded the same. Nothing but a pitiful Image of their own pitiful Self, with its vanities, and grudgings, and ravenous hunger of all kinds, hangs for ever painted in the retina of these unfortunate persons; so that the starry ALL, with whatsoever it embraces, does but appear as some expanded magic-lantern shadow of that same Image,—and naturally looks pitiful enough.

It is vain for these persons to allege that they are naturally without gift, naturally stupid and sightless, and so *can* attain to no knowledge of any thing; therefore, in writing of any thing, must needs write falsehoods of it, there being in it no truth for them. Not so, good Friends. The stupidest of you has a certain faculty; were it but that of articulate speech (say, in the Scottish, the Irish, the Cockney dialect, or even in "Governess-English"), and of physically discerning what lies under your nose. The stupidest of you would perhaps grudge to be compared in faculty with James Boswell; yet see what he has produced! You do not use your faculty honestly; your heart is shut up; full of greediness, malice, discontent; so your intellectual sense cannot be open. It is vain also to urge that James Boswell had opportunities; saw great men and great things, such as you can never hope to look on. What make ye of Parson White in Selbourne? He had not only no great men to look on, but not even men; merely sparrows and cockchafers: yet has he left us a *Biography* of these; which, under its title *Natural History of Selbourne*, still remains valuable to us; which has copied a little sentence or two *faithfully* from the Inspired Volume of Nature. and so is itself not without inspiration. Go ye and do likewise. Sweep away utterly all frothiness and falsehood from your heart; struggle unweariedly to acquire, what is possible for every god-created Man, a free, open, humble soul: *speak not at all, in any wise, till you have somewhat to speak;* care not for the *reward* of your speaking, but simply and with undivided mind for the *truth* of your speaking: then be placed in what section of Space and of Time soever, do but open your eyes, and they shall actually *see*, and bring you real *knowledge*, wondrous, worthy of *belief;* and instead of one Boswell and one White, the world will rejoice in a thousand,—stationed on their thousand several watch-towers, to instruct us, by indubitable documents, of whatsoever in our so stupendous World comes to light and *is!* O, had the Editor of this Magazine but a magic-rod to turn all that not inconsiderable Intellect, which now deluges us with artificial fictitious soap-lather, and mere Lying, into the faithful study of Reality,—what knowledge of great, everlasting Nature, and of Man's ways and doings therein, would not every year bring us in! Can we but change one single soap-latherer and mountebank Juggler, into a true Thinker and Doer, that even *tries* honestly to think and do,—great will be our reward.

But, to return; or rather from this point to begin our journey! If now, what with Herr Sauerteig's *Springwürzel*, what with so much lucubration of our own, it have become apparent how deep, immeasurable is the "worth that lies in *Reality*," and farther, how exclusive the interest which man takes in Histories of Man,—may it not seem lamentable, that so few genuinely-good *Biographies* have yet been accumulated in Literature; that, in the whole world, one cannot find, going strictly to work, above some dozen, or baker's dozen, and those chiefly of very ancient date? Lamentable; yet, after what we have just seen, accountable. Another question might be asked: How comes it that in England we have simply one good Biography, this *Boswell's Johnson;* and of good, indifferent, or even bad attempts at Biography, fewer than any civilised people? Consider the French and Germans, with their Moreris, Bayles, Jördenses, Jöchers, their innumerable *Mémoires,* and *Schilderungen,* and *Biographies Universelles;* not to speak of Rousseaus, Goethes, Schubarts, Jung-Stillings: and then contrast with these our poor Birches and Kippises and Pecks,—the whole breed of whom, moreover, is now extinct!

With this question, as the answer might lead us far, and come out unflatteringly to patriotic sentiment, we shall not intermeddle; but turn rather, with greater pleasure, to the fact, that one excellent Biography *is* actually English; —and even now lies, in Five new Volumes, at our hand, soliciting a new consideration from us; such as, age after age (the Perennial shewing ever new phases as *our* position alters), it may long be profitable to bestow on it;—to which task we here, in this position, in this age, gladly address ourselves.

First, however, Let the foolish April-fool-day pass by; and our Reader, during these twenty-nine days of uncertain weather that will follow, keep pondering, according to convenience, the purport of BIOGRAPHY in general: then, with the blessed dew of May-day, and in unlimited convenience of space, shall all that we have written on *Johnson,* and *Boswell's Johnson,* and *Croker's Boswell's Johnson,* be faithfully laid before him.

ART. II.—*Memoirs of the Life of Sir Walter Scott, Baronet.*
Vol. i—vi. Cadell. Edinburgh, 1837.

AMERICAN Cooper asserts, in one of his books, that there is "an instinctive tendency in men to look at any man who has become distinguished." True, surely; as all observation and survey of mankind, from China to Peru, from Nebuchadnezzar to Old Hickory, will testify! Why do men crowd towards the improved drop at Newgate, eager to catch a sight? The man about to be hanged is in a distinguished situation. Men crowd to such extent, that Greenacre's is not the only life choked out there. Again. ask of these leathern vehicles, cabriolets, neat-flies, with blue men and women in them, that scour all thoroughfares,

Whither so fast? To see dear Mrs Rigmarole, the distinguished female; great Mr Rigmarole, the distinguished male! Or, consider that crowning phenomenon, and summary of modern civilization, a *soirée* of lions. Glittering are the rooms, well-lighted, thronged; bright flows their undulatory flood of blonde gowns and dress-coats, a soft smile dwelling on all faces; for behold there also flow the lions, hovering distinguished: oracles of the age, of one sort or another. Oracles really pleasant to see; whom it is worth while to go and see: look at them, but inquire not of them, depart rather and be thankful. For your lion-*soirée* admits not of speech; there lies the specialty of it. A meeting together of human creatures; and yet (so high has civilization gone) the primary aim of human meeting, that soul might in some articulate utterance unfold itself to soul, can be dispensed with in it. Utterance there is not; nay, there is a certain grinning play of tongue-fence, and make-believe of utterance, considerably worse than none. For which reason it has been suggested, with an eye to sincerity and silence in such lion-*soirées,* Might not each lion be, for example, ticketed, as wine-decanters are? Let him carry, slung round him, in such ornamental manner as seemed good, his silver label with name engraved; you lift his label, and read it, with what farther ocular survey you find useful, and speech is not needed at all. O Fenimore Cooper, it is most true there is "an instinctive tendency in men to look at any man that has become distinguished;" and, moreover, an instinctive desire in men to become distinguished and be looked at!

For the rest, we will call it a most valuable tendency this; indispensable to mankind. Without it where were star-and-garter, and significance of rank; where were all ambition, money-getting, respectability of gig or no gig; and, in a word, the main impetus by which society moves, the main force by which it hangs together? A tendency, we say, of manifold results; of manifold origin, not ridiculous only, but sublime;—which some incline to deduce from the mere gregarious purblind nature of man, prompting him to run, "as dim-eyed animals do, towards any glittering object, were it but a scoured tankard, and mistake it for a solar luminary," or even, "sheep-like, to run and crowd because many *have* already run!" It is, indeed, curious to consider how men do make the gods that themselves worship. For the most famed man, round whom all the world now rapturously huzzahs and venerates as if his like were not, is the same man whom all the world was wont to jostle into the kennels; not a changed man, but in every fibre of him the same man. Foolish world, what went ye out to see? A tankard scoured bright; and do there not lie, of the self-same pewter, whole barrowfuls of tankards, though by worse fortune all still in the dim state?

And yet, at bottom, it is not merely our gregarious sheep-like quality, but something better, and indeed best: what has been called " the perpetual fact of hero-worship;" our inborn sincere love of great men! Not the gilt farthing, for its own sake, do even fools covet; but the gold guinea which they mistake it for. Veneration of great men is perennial in the nature of man; this, in all times, especially in these, is one of the blessedest facts predicable of him. In all times, even in these seemingly so disobedient times, " it remains a blessed fact, so cunningly has nature ordered it, *that whatsoever man ought to obey he cannot but obey.* Show the dullest clodpole, show the haughtiest featherhead, that a soul higher than himself is actually here; were his knees stiffened into brass, he must down and worship." So it has been written; and may be cited and repeated till known to all. Understand it well, this of " hero-worship" was the primary creed, and has intrinsically been the secondary and ternary and will be the ultimate and final creed of mankind; indestructible, changing in shape, but in essence unchangeable; whereon polities, religions, loyalties, and all highest human interests have been and can be built, as on a rock that will endure while man endures. Such is hero-worship; so much lies in that our inborn sincere love of great men!—In favour of which unspeakable benefits of the reality, what can we do but cheerfully pardon the multiplex ineptitudes of the semblance,—cheerfully wish even lion-*soirées*, with labels for their lions or without that improvement, all manner of prosperity? Let hero-worship flourish, say we; and the more and more assiduous chase after gilt farthings while guineas are not yet forthcoming. Herein, at lowest, is proof that guineas exist; that they are believed to exist, and valued. Find great men if you can; if you cannot, still quit not the search; in defect of great men, let there be noted men, in such number, to such degree of intensity as the public appetite can tolerate.

Whether Sir Walter Scott was a great man, is still a question with some; but there can be no question with any one that he was a most noted and even notable man. In this generation there was no literary man with such a popularity in any country; there have only been a few with such, taking in all generations and all countries. Nay, it is farther to be admitted that Sir Walter Scott's popularity was of a select sort rather; not a popularity of the populace. His admirers were at one time almost all the intelligent of civilized countries; and to the last, included and do still include a great portion of that sort. Such fortune he had, and has continued to maintain for a space of some twenty or thirty years. So long the observed of all observers; a great man, or only a considerable man; here surely, if ever, is a singularly circumstanced, is a "distinguished" man! In regard to whom, therefore, the "instinctive tendency" on other men's part cannot be wanting. Let men look, where the world has already so long looked. And now, while the new, earnestly expected 'Life by his Son-in-law and literary executor' again summons the whole world's attention round him, probably for the last time it will ever be so summoned; and men are in some sort taking leave of a notability, and about to go their way, and commit him to his fortune on the flood of things,—why should not this periodical publication likewise publish its thought about him? Readers of miscellaneous aspect, of unknown quantity and quality, are waiting to hear it done. With small inward vocation, but cheerfully obedient to destiny and necessity, the present reviewer will follow a multitude; to do evil or to do no evil, will depend not on the multitude but on himself. One thing he did decidedly wish; at least to wait till the work were finished: for the six promised volumes, as the world knows, have flowed over into a seventh, which will not for some weeks yet see the light. It will tell us, say they, little new and nothing pleasing to know. But the editorial powers, wearied with waiting, have become peremptory; and declare that, finished or not finished, they will have their hands washed of it at this opening of the year. Perhaps it is best. The physiognomy of Scott will not be much altered for us by the seventh volume; the prior six have altered it but little;—as, indeed, a man who has written some two hundred volumes of his own, and lived for thirty years amid the universal speech of friends, must have already left some likeness of himself. Be it as the peremptory editorial powers require.

First, therefore, a word on the 'Life' itself. Mr Lockhart's known powers justify strict requisition in his case. Our verdict in general would be, that he has accomplished the work he schemed for himself in a creditable workmanlike manner. It is true, his notion of what the work was does not seem to have been very elevated. To picture forth the life of Scott according to any rules of art or composition, so that a reader, on adequately examining it, might say to himself, "There is Scott, there is the physiognomy and meaning of Scott's appearance and transit on this earth; such was he by nature, so did the world act on him, so he on the world, with such result and significance for himself and us:" this was by no manner of means Mr Lockhart's plan. A plan which, it is rashly said, should preside over every biography! It might have been fulfilled with all degrees of perfection from that of the 'Odyssey' down to 'Thomas Ellwood' or lower. For there is no heroic poem in the world but is at bottom a biography, the life of a man; also, it may be said, there is no life of a man, faithfully recorded, but is a heroic poem of its sort, rhymed or unrhymed. It is a plan one would prefer, did it otherwise suit; which it does not, in these days. Seven volumes sell so much dearer than one; are so much easier to write than one. The 'Odyssey,' for instance, what were the value of the 'Odyssey,' sold per sheet? One paper of 'Pickwick;' or say, the inconsiderable fraction of one. This, in commercial algebra, were the equation: 'Odyssey' equal to 'Pickwick' divided by an unknown integer.

There is a great discovery still to be made in literature, that of paying literary men by the quantity they *do not* write. Nay, in sober truth, is not this actually the rule in all writing; and, moreover, in all conduct and acting? Not what stands above ground, but what lies unseen *under* it, as the root and subterrene element it sprang from and emblemed forth, determines the value. Under all speech that is good for anything there lies a silence that is better. Silence is deep as eternity; speech is shallow as time. Paradoxical does it seem? Wo for the age, wo for the man, quack-ridden, bespeeched, bespouted, blown about like barren Sahara, to whom this world-old truth were altogether strange!—Such we say is the rule, acted on or not, recognised or not; and he who departs from it, what can he do but spread himself into breadth and length, into superficiality and saleability; and, except as filigree, become comparatively useless? One thinks, had but the hogshead of thin wash, which sours in a week ready for the kennels, been *distilled*, been concentrated! Our dear Fenimore Cooper, whom we started with, might, in that way, have given us one *Natty Leatherstocking,* one melodious synopsis of man and nature in the West (for it lay in him to do it), almost as a Saint Pierre did for the islands of the East; and the hundred incoherences, cobbled hastily together by order of Colburn and Company, had slumbered in Chaos, as all incoherences ought if possible to do. Verily this same genius of diffuse-writing, of diffuse-acting, is a Moloch; and souls pass through the fire to him more than enough. Surely, if ever discovery was valuable and needful, it were that above indicated, of paying by the work *not* visibly done!—Which needful discovery we will give the whole projecting, railwaying, knowledge-diffusing, march-of-intellect and other-wise promotive and locomotive societies in the Old and New World, any required length of centuries to make. Once made, such discovery once made, we too will fling cap into the air, and shout *Io Pæan,* the Devil *is* conquered; and in the *mean*while study to think it nothing miraculous that seven biographical volumes are given where one had been better; and that several other things happen, very much as they from of old were known to do, and are like to continue doing.

Mr Lockhart's aim, we take it, was not that of producing any such highflown work of art as we hint at; or indeed to do much other than to print, intelligibly bound together by order of time, and by some requisite intercalary exposition, all such letters, documents, and notices about Scott as he found lying suitable, and as it seemed likely the world would undertake to read. His work, accordingly, is not so much a composition, as what we may call a compilation well done. Neither is this a task of no difficulty; this too is a task that may be performed with extremely various degrees of talent: from the 'Life and Correspondence of Hannah More,' for instance, up to this 'Life of Scott,' there is a wide range indeed! Let us take the seven volumes, and be thankful that they are genuine in their kind. Nay, as to that of their being seven and not one, it is right to say that the public so required it. To have done other would have shown little policy in an author. Had Mr Lockhart laboriously compressed himself, and, instead of well-done compilation, brought out the well-done composition in one volume instead of seven, which not many men in England are better qualified to do, there can be no doubt that his readers for the time had been immeasurably fewer. If the praise of magnanimity be denied him, that of prudence must be conceded, which perhaps he values more.

The truth is, the work, done in this manner too, was good to have: Scott's Biography, if uncomposed, lies printed and indestructible here, in the elementary state, and can at any time be composed, if necessary, by whosoever has call to that. As it is, as it was meant to be, we repeat, the work is vigorously done. Sagacity, decision, candour, diligence, good manners, good sense: these qualities are throughout observable. The dates, calculations, statements, we suppose to be all accurate; much laborious inquiry, some of it impossible for another man, has been gone into, the results of which are imparted with due brevity. Scott's letters, not interesting generally, yet never absolutely without interest, are copiously given; copiously, but with selection; the answers to them still more select. Narrative, delineation, and at length personal reminiscences, occasionally of much merit, of a certain rough force, sincerity and picturesqueness, duly intervene. The scattered members of Scott's Life do lie here, and could be disentangled. In a word, this compilation is the work of a manful, clear-seeing, conclusive man, and has been executed with the faculty and combination of faculties the public had a right to expect from the name attached to it.

One thing we hear greatly blamed in Mr Lockhart: that he has been too communicative, indiscreet, and has recorded much that ought to have lain suppressed. Persons are mentioned, and circumstances, not always of an ornamental sort. It would appear there is far less reticence than was looked for! Various persons, name and surname, have "received pain:" nay, the very hero of the biography is rendered unheroic; unornamental facts of him, and of those he had to do with, being set forth in plain English: hence "personality," "indiscretion," or worse, "sanctities of private life," &c. &c. How delicate, decent is English biography, bless its mealy mouth! A Damocles' sword of *Respectability* hangs for ever over the poor English life-writer (as it does over poor English life in general), and reduces him to the verge of paralysis. Thus it has been said, "there are no English lives worth reading except those of Players, who by the nature of the case have bidden Respectability good-day." The English biographer has long felt that if in writing his Man's Biography, he wrote down anything that could by possibility offend any man, he had written wrong. The plain consequence was that, properly speaking, no biography whatever could be produced. The poor biographer, having the fear *not* of God before his eyes, was obliged to retire as it were into vacuum; and write in the most melancholy, straitened manner, with only vacuum for a result. Vain that he wrote, and that we kept reading volume on volume: there was no biography, but some vague ghost of a biography, white, stainless; without feature or substance; *vacuum*, as we say, and wind and shadow,—which indeed the material of it was.

No man lives without jostling and being jostled; in all ways he has to *elbow* himself through the world, giving and receiving offence. His life is a battle, in so far as it is an entity at all. The very oyster, we suppose, comes in collision with oysters: undoubtedly enough it does come in collision with Necessity and Difficulty; and helps itself through, not as a perfect ideal oyster, but as an imperfect real one. Some kind of remorse must be known to the oyster; certain hatreds, certain pusillanimities. ' But as for man, his conflict is continual with the spirit of contradiction, that is without and within; with the evil spirit, (or call it with the weak, most necessitous, pitiable spirit), that is in others and in himself. His walk, like all walking (say the mechanicians), is a series of *falls*. To paint man's life is to represent these things. Let them be represented, fitly, with dignity and measure; but above all, let them be represented. No tragedy of *Hamlet*, with the part of Hamlet omitted by particular desire! No ghost of a Biography, let the Damocles' sword of Respectability (which after all is but a pasteboard one) threaten as it will! One hopes that the public taste is much mended in this matter; that vacuum-biographies, with a good many other vacuities related to them, are withdrawn or withdrawing into vacuum. Probably it was Mr Lockhart's feeling of what the great public would approve that led him, open-eyed, into this offence against the small criticizing public: we joyfully accept the omen.

Perhaps then, of all the praises copiously bestowed on his work, there is none in reality so creditable to him as this same censure, which has also been pretty copious. It is a censure better than a good many praises. He is found guilty of having said this and that, calculated not to be entirely pleasant to this man and that; in other words, calculated to give him and the thing he worked in a living set of features, not leave him vague, in the white beatified ghost-condition. Let it be so. Several men, as we hear, cry out, " See, there is something written not entirely pleasant to me!" Good friend, it is pity; but who can help it? They that will crowd about bonfires may, sometimes very fairly, get their beards singed ; it is the price they pay for such illumination: natural twilight is safe and free to all. For our part, we hope all manner of biographies that are written in England will henceforth be written so. If it is fit that they be written otherwise, then it is still fitter that they be not written at all: to produce not things but ghosts of things can never be the duty of man. The biographer has this problem set before him: to delineate a likeness of the earthly pilgrimage of a man. He will compute well what profit is in it, and what disprofit; under which latter head this of offending any of his fellow-creatures will surely not be forgotten. Nay, this may so swell the disprofit side of his account, that many an enterprise of biography, otherwise promising, shall require to be renounced. But once taken up, the rule before all rules is to do *it*, not to do the ghost of it. In speaking of the man and men he has to deal with, he will of course keep all his charities about him, but also all his eyes open. Far be it from him to set down aught *untrue;* nay, not to abstain from, and leave in oblivion, much that is true. But having found a thing or things essential for his subject, and well computed the for and against, he will in very deed set down such thing or things, nothing doubting,—*having,* we may say, the fear of God before his eyes, and no other fear whatever. Censure the biographer's prudence; dissent from the computation he made, or agree with it; be all malice of his, be all falsehood, nay, be all offensive avoidable inaccuracy, condemned and consumed; but know that by this plan only, executed as was possible, could the biographer hope to make a biography; and blame him not that he did what it had been the worst fault not to do.

As to the accuracy or error of these statements about the Ballantynes and other persons aggrieved, which are questions much mooted at present in some places, we know nothing at all. If they are inaccurate, let them be corrected; if the inaccuracy was avoidable, let the author bear rebuke and punishment for it. We can only say, these things carry no look of inaccuracy on the face of them; neither is anywhere the smallest trace of ill-will or unjust feeling discernible. Decidedly the probabilities are, and till better evidence arise, the fair conclusion is, that this matter stands very much as it ought to do. Let the clatter of censure, therefore, propagate itself as far as it can. For Mr Lockhart it virtually amounts to this very considerable praise, that, standing full in the face of the public, he has set at nought, and been among the first to do it, a public piece of cant; one of the commonest we have, and closely allied to many others of the fellest sort, as smooth as it looks.

The other censure, of Scott being made unheroic, springs from the same stem; and is, perhaps, a still more wonderful flower of it. Your true hero must have no features, but be white, stainless, an impersonal ghost-hero! But connected with this, there is a hypothesis now current, due probably to some man of name, for its own force would not carry it far: That Mr Lockhart at heart has a dislike to Scott, and has done his best in an underhand treacherous manner to dishero him! Such hypothesis is actually current: he that has ears may hear it now and then. On which astonishing hypothesis, if a word must be said, it can only be an apology for silence, "that there are things at which one stands struck silent, as at first sight of the Infinite." For if Mr Lockhart is fairly chargeable with any radical defect, if on any side his insight entirely fails him, it seems even to be in this, that Scott is altogether lovely to him; that Scott's greatness spreads out for him on all hands beyond reach of eye; that his very faults become beautiful, his vulgar worldlinesses are solid prudences, proprieties; and of his worth there is no measure. Does not the patient biographer dwell on his *Abbots, Pirates,* and hasty theatrical scene-paintings; affectionately analyzing them, as if they were Raphael-pictures, time-defying *Hamlets, Othellos?* The novel-manufactory, with its 15,000*l.* a-year, is sacred to him as creation of a genius, which carries the noble victor up to heaven. Scott is to Lockhart the unparalleled of the time; an object spreading out before him like a sea without shore. Of *that* astonishing hypothesis, let expressive silence be the only answer.

And so in sum, with regard to 'Lockhart's Life of Scott,' readers that believe in us shall read it with the feeling that a man of talent, decision, and insight wrote it; wrote it in seven volumes, not in one, because the public would pay for it better in that state; but wrote it with courage, with frankness, sincerity; on the whole, in a very readable, recommendable manner, as things go. Whosoever needs it can purchase it, or the loan of it, with assurance more than usual that he has ware for his money. And now enough of the written life: we will glance a little at the man and his acted life.

Into the question whether Scott was a great man or not, we do not propose to enter deeply. It is, as too usual, a question about words. There can be no doubt but many men have been named and printed *great* who were vastly smaller than he; as little doubt moreover that of the specially *good* a very large portion, according to any genuine standard of man's worth, were worthless in comparison to him. He for whom Scott is great may most innocently name him so; may with advantage admire his great qualities, and ought with sincere heart to emulate them. At the same time, it is good that there be a certain degree of precision in our epithets. It is good to understand, for one thing, that no popularity, and open-mouthed wonder of all the world, continued even for a long series of years, can make a man great. Such popularity is a remarkable fortune; indicates a great adaptation of the man to his element of circumstances; but may or may not indicate anything great in the man. To our imagination, as above hinted, there is a certain apotheosis in it; but in the reality no apotheosis at all. Popularity is as a blaze of illumination, or alas, of conflagration kindled round a man; *showing* what is in him; not putting the smallest item more into him; often abstracting much from him; conflagrating the poor man himself into ashes and *caput mortuum!* And then, by the nature of it, such popularity is transient; your "series of years," quite unexpectedly, sometimes almost on a sudden, terminates! For the stupidity of men, especially of men congregated in masses round any object, is extreme. What illuminations and conflagrations have kindled themselves, as if new heavenly suns had risen, which proved only to be tar-barrels, and terrestrial locks of straw! Profane princesses cried out, 'One God, one Farinelli?'—and whither now have they and Farinelli danced? In literature too, there have been seen popularities greater even than Scott's, and nothing perennial in the interior of them. Lope de Vega, whom all the world swore by, and made a proverb of; who could make an acceptable five-act tragedy in almost as many hours; the greatest of all popularities past or present, and perhaps one of the greatest men that ever ranked among popularities: Lope himself, so radiant, far-shining, has not proved to be a sun or star of the firmament; but is as good as lost and gone out, or plays at best, in the eyes of some few, as a vague aurora-borealis, and brilliant ineffectuality. The great man of Spain sat obscure at the time, all dark and poor, a maimed soldier; writing his Don Quixote in prison. And Lope's fate withal was sad, his popularity perhaps a curse to him; for in this man there was something ethereal too, a divine particle traceable in few other popular men; and such far shining diffusion of himself, though all the world swore by it, would do nothing for the true life of him even while he lived: he had to creep into a convent, into a monk's cowl, and learn, with infinite sorrow, that his blessedness had lain elsewhere; that when a man's life feels itself to be sick and an error, no voting of byestanders can make it well and a truth again. Or coming down to our own times, was not August Kotzebue popular? Kotzebue, not so many years since, saw himself, if rumour and handclapping could be credited, the greatest man going; saw visibly his Thoughts, dressed out in plush and pasteboard, permeating and perambulating civilized Europe; the most iron visages weeping with him, in all theatres from Cadiz to Kamtchatka; his own "astonishing genius," meanwhile producing two tragedies or so per month: he on the whole blazed high enough; he too has gone out into Night and *Orcus*, and already is not.—We will omit this of popularity altogether, and account it as making simply nothing towards Scott's greatness or non-greatness, as an accident, not a quality.

Shorn of this falsifying *nimbus*, and reduced to his own natural dimensions, there remains the reality, Walter Scott, and what we can find in him: to be accounted great, or not great, according to the dialects of men. Friends to precision of epithet will probably deny his title to the name "great." It seems to us there goes other stuff to the making of great men than can be detected here. One knows not what idea worthy of the name of great, what purpose, instinct or tendency that could be called great, Scott ever was inspired with. His life was worldly; his ambitions were worldly. There is nothing spiritual in him; all is economical, material, of the earth earthy. A love of picturesque, of beautiful, vigorous and graceful things; a genuine love, yet not more genuine than has dwelt in hundreds of men named minor poets: this is the highest quality to be discerned in him. His power of representing these things too, his poetic power, like his moral power, was a genius *in extenso*, as we may say, not *in intenso*. In action, in speculation, *broad* as he was, he rose nowhere high; productive without measure as to quantity, in quality he for the most part transcended but a little way the region of commonplace. It has been said, "no man has written as many volumes with so few sentences that can be quoted." Winged words were not his vocation; nothing urged him that way: the great mystery of existence was not great to him; did not drive him into rocky solitudes to wrestle with it for an answer, to be answered or to perish. He had nothing of the martyr; into no " dark region to slay monsters for us," did he, either led or driven, venture down: his conquests were for his own behoof mainly, conquests over common market labour, and reckonable in good metallic coin of the realm. The thing he had faith in, except power, power of what sort soever, and even of the rudest sort, would be difficult to point out. One sees not that he believed in anything: nay, he did not even disbelieve; but quietly acquiesced, and made himself at home in a world of conventionalities: the false, the semi-false, and the true were alike true in this, that they were there, and had power in their hands more or less. It was well to feel so; and yet not well! We find it written, " Wo to them that are at ease in Zion;" but surely it is a double wo to them that are at ease in Babel, in Domdaniel. On the other hand he wrote many volumes, amusing many thousands of men. Shall we call this great? It seems to us there dwells and struggles another sort of spirit in the inward parts of great men!

Brother Ringletub, the missionary, inquired of Ram-Dass, a Hindoo man-god, who had set up for godhood lately, What he meant to do, then, with the sins of mankind? To which Ram-Dass at once answered, he had *fire enough in his belly* to burn up all the sins in the world. Ram-Dass was right so far, and had a spice of sense in him; for surely it is the test of every divine man this same, and without it he is not divine or great,—that he *have* fire in him to burn up somewhat of the sins of the world, of the miseries and errors of the world: why else is he there? Far be it from us to say that a great man must needs, with benevolence prepense, become a "friend of humanity;" nay, that such professional self-conscious friends of humanity are not the fatallest kind of persons to be met with in our day. All greatness is unconscious, or it is little and naught. And yet a great man without *such* fire in him, burning dim or developed as a divine behest in his heart of hearts, never resting till it be fulfilled, were a solecism in nature. A great man is ever, as the Transcendentalists speak, possessed with an *idea*. Napoleon himself, not the superfinest of great men, and ballasted sufficiently with prudences and egoisms, had nevertheless, as is clear enough, an idea to start with: the idea that Democracy was the Cause of Man, the right and infinite Cause. Accordingly he made himself "the armed soldier of Democracy;" and did vindicate it in a rather great manner. Nay, to the very last, he had a kind of idea, that, namely, of "*la carriere ouverte aux talens,* the tools to him that can handle them;" really one of the best ideas yet promulgated on that matter, or rather the one true central idea, towards which all the others, if they tend anywhither, must tend. Unhappily it was in the military province only that Napoleon could realize this idea of his, being forced to fight for himself the while: before he got it tried to any extent in the civil province of things, his head by much victory grew light (no head can stand more than its quantity); and he lost head, as they say, and became a selfish ambitionist and quack, and was hurled out, leaving his idea to be realized, in the civil province of things, by others! Thus was Napoleon; thus are all great men: children of the idea; or, in Ram-Dass's phraseology, furnished with fire to burn up the miseries of men. Conscious or unconscious, latent or unfolded, there is small vestige of any such fire being extant in the inner-man of Scott.

Yet, on the other hand, the surliest critic must allow that Scott was a genuine man, which itself is a great matter. No affectation, fantasticality or distortion, dwelt in him; no shadow of cant. Nay withal, was he not a right brave and strong man, according to his kind? What a load of toil, what a measure of felicity, he quietly bore along with him; with what quiet strength he both worked on this earth, and enjoyed in it; invincible to evil fortune and to good! A most composed invincible man; in difficulty and distress, knowing no discouragement, Samson-like, carrying off on his strong Samson-shoulders the gates that would imprison him; in danger and menace, laughing at the whisper of fear. And then, with such a sunny current of true humour and humanity, a free joyful sympathy with so many things; what of fire he had, all lying so beautifully *latent,* as radical latent heat, as fruitful internal warmth of life; a most robust, healthy man! The truth is, our best definition of Scott were perhaps even this, that he was, if no great man, then something much pleasanter to be, a robust, thoroughly healthy, and withal, very prosperous and victorious man. An eminently well-conditioned man, healthy in body, healthy in soul; we will call him one of the *healthiest* of men. Neither is this a small matter: health is a great matter, both to the possessor of it and to others. On the whole, that humorist in the Moral Essay was not so far out, who determined on honouring health only; and so instead of humbling himself to the highborn, to the rich and well-dressed, insisted on doffing hat to the healthy: coronetted carriages with pale faces in them passed by as failures miserable and lamentable; trucks with ruddy-cheeked strength dragging at them were greeted as successful and venerable. For does not health mean harmony, the synonym of all that is true, justly-ordered, good; is it not, in some sense, the net-total, as shown by experiment, of whatever worth is in us? The healthy man is a most meritorious product of nature, so far as he goes. A healthy body is good; but a soul in right health,—it is the thing beyond all others to be prayed for; the blessedest thing this earth receives of Heaven. Without artificial medicament of philosophy, or tight-lacing of creeds (always very questionable), the healthy soul discerns what is good, and adheres to it, and retains it; discerns what is bad, and spontaneously casts it off. An instinct from nature herself, like that which guides the wild animals of the forest to their food, shows him what he shall do, what he shall abstain from. The false and foreign will not adhere to him; cant and all fantastic, diseased incrustations are impossible—as Walker the *Original*, in such eminence of health was *he* for his part, *could* not, by much abstinence from soap and water, attain to a dirty face! This thing thou canst work with and profit by, this thing is substantial and worthy; that other thing thou canst not work with, it is trivial and inapt: so speaks unerringly the inward monition of the man's whole nature. No need of logic to prove the most argumentative absurdity absurd; as Goethe says of himself, " all this ran down from me like water from a man in wax-cloth dress." Blessed is the healthy nature; it is the coherent, sweetly co-operative, not incoherent, self-distractive, self-destructive one! In the harmonious adjustment and play of all the faculties, the just balance of oneself gives a just feeling towards all men and all things. Glad light from within radiates outwards, and enlightens and embellishes.

Now all this can be predicated of Walter Scott, and of no British literary man that we remember in these days, to any such extent,—if it be not perhaps of one, the most opposite imaginable to Scott, but his equal in this quality and what holds of it: William Cobbett! Nay, there are other similarities, widely different as they two look; nor be the comparison disparaging to Scott: for Cobbett also, as the pattern John Bull of his century, strong as the rhinoceros, and with singular humanities and genialities shining through his thick skin, is a most brave phenomenon. So bounteous was Nature to us; in the sickliest of recorded ages, when British literature lay all puking and sprawling in Werterism, Byronism, and other sentimentalism, tearful or spasmodic (fruit of internal *wind*), Nature was kind enough to send us two healthy Men, of whom she might still say, not without pride, 'These also were made in England; such limbs do I still make there!' It is one of the cheerfullest sights, let the question of its greatness be settled as you will. A healthy nature may or may not be great; but there is no great nature that is not healthy.— Or, on the whole, might we not say, Scott, in the new vesture of the nineteenth century, was intrinsically very much the old fighting Borderer of prior centuries; the kind of man Nature did of old make in that birthland of his? In the saddle, with the foray-spear, he would have acquitted himself as he did at the desk with his pen. One fancies how, in stout *Beardie* of Harden's time, he could have played Beardie's part; and *been* the stalwart buff-belted *terræ filius* he in this late time could only delight to draw. The same stout self-help was in him; the same oak and triple brass round his heart. He too could have fought at Redswire, cracking crowns with the fiercest, if that had been the task; could have harried cattle in Tynedale, repaying injury with compound interest; a right sufficient captain of men. A man without qualms or fantasticalities; a hard-headed, sound-hearted man, of joyous robust temper, looking to the main chance, and fighting direct thitherward: *valde stalwartus homo!*—How much in that case had slumbered in him, and passed away without sign. But indeed, who knows how much slumbers in many men. Perhaps our greatest poets are the *mute* Miltons; the vocal are those whom by happy accident we lay hold of, one here, one there, as it chances, and *make* vocal. It is even a question whether, had not want, discomfort, and distress-warrants been busy at Stratford-on-Avon, Shakspeare himself had not lived killing calves or combing wool! Had the Edial Boarding-school turned out well, we had never heard of Samuel Johnson; Samuel Johnson had been a fat schoolmaster and dogmatic gerundgrinder, and never known that he was more. Nature is rich: those two eggs thou art eating carelessly to breakfast, could they not have been hatched into a pair of fowls, and have covered the whole world with poultry?

But it was not harrying of cattle in Tynedale, or cracking of crowns at Redswire, that this stout Border chief was appointed to perform. Far other work. To be the song-singer and pleasant tale-teller to Britain and Europe, in the beginning of the artificial nineteenth century; here, and not there, lay his business. Beardie of Harden would have found it very amazing. How he shapes himself to this new element; how he helps himself along in it, makes it too do for him, lives sound and victorious in it, and leads over the marches such a spoil as all the cattle-droves the Hardens ever took were poor in comparison to: this is the history of the life and achievements of *our* Sir Walter Scott, Baronet;—whereat we are now to glance for a little! It is a thing remarkable; a thing substantial; of joyful, victorious sort; not unworthy to be glanced at. Withal, however, a glance here and there will suffice. Our limits are narrow; the thing, were it never so victorious, is not of the sublime sort, nor extremely edifying; there is nothing in it to censure vehemently, nor love vehemently: there is more to wonder at than admire; and the whole secret is not an abstruse one.

Till towards the age of thirty, Scott's life has nothing in it decisively pointing towards literature, or indeed towards distinction of any kind; he is wedded, settled, and has gone through all his preliminary steps, without symptom of renown as yet. It is the life of every other Edinburgh youth of his station and time. Fortunate we must name it, in many ways. Parents in easy or wealthy circumstances, yet unincumbered with the cares and perversions of aristocracy: nothing eminent in place, in faculty, or culture, yet nothing deficient; all around is methodic regulation, prudence, prosperity, kind-heartedness; an element of warmth and light, of affection, industry, and burgherly comfort, heightened into elegance; in which the young heart can wholesomely grow. A vigorous health seems to have been given by Nature; yet, as if Nature had said withal, "Let it be a health to express itself by mind, not by body," a lameness is added in childhood; the brave little boy, instead of romping and bickering, must learn to think; or at lowest, what is a great matter, to sit still. No rackets and trundling-hoops for this young Walter; but ballads, history-books, and a world of legendary stuff, which his mother and those near him are copiously able to furnish. Disease, which is but superficial, and issues in outward lameness, does not cloud the young existence; rather forwards it towards the expansion it is fitted for. The miserable disease had been one of the internal nobler parts, marring the general organization; under which no Walter Scott could have been forwarded, or with all his other endowments could have been producible or possible. " Nature gives healthy children much; how much! Wise education is a wise unfolding of this; often it unfolds itself better of its own accord."

Add one other circumstance: the place where; namely, Presbyterian Scotland. The influences of this are felt incessantly, they stream in at every pore. " There is a country accent," says La Rochefoucault, " not in speech only, but in thought, conduct, character, and manner of existing, which never forsakes a man." Scott, we believe, was all his days an Episcopalian Dissenter in Scotland; but that makes little to the matter. Nobody who knows Scotland and Scott can doubt but Presbyterianism, too, had a vast share in the forming of him. A country where the entire people is, or even once has been, laid hold of, filled to the heart with an infinite religious idea, has " made a step from which it cannot retrograde." Thought, conscience, the sense that man is denizen of a universe, creature of an eternity, has penetrated to the remotest cottage, to the simplest heart. Beautiful and awful, the feeling of a heavenly behest, of duty god-commanded, overcanopies all life. There is an inspiration in such a people; one may say in a more special sense, " the inspiration of the Almighty giveth them understanding." Honour to all the brave and true; everlasting honour to brave old Knox, one of the truest of the true! That in the moment while he and his cause, amid civil broils, in convulsion and confusion, were still but struggling for life, he sent the schoolmaster forth to all corners, and said, " Let the people be taught:" this is but one, and indeed an inevitable and comparatively inconsiderable item in his great message to men. His message, in its true compass, was, " Let men know that they are men; created by God, responsible to God; who work in any meanest moment of time what will last through eternity." It is verily a great message. Not ploughing and hammering machines, not patent digesters (never so ornamental) to digest the produce of these; no, in no wise; born slaves neither of their fellow-men, nor of their own appetites; but men! This great message Knox did deliver, with a man's voice and strength; and found a people to believe him.

Of such an achievement, we say, were it to be made once only, the results are immense. Thought, in such a country, may change its form, but cannot go out; the country has attained *majority*: thought, and a certain spiritual manhood, ready for all work that man can do, endures there. It may take many forms: the form of hard-fisted, money-getting industry, as in the vulgar Scotchman, in the vulgar New Englander; but as compact developed force and alertness of faculty, it is still there; it may utter itself, one day, as the colossal scepticism of a Hume (beneficent this too, though painful, wrestling, Titan-like, through doubt and inquiry towards new belief); and again, some better day, it may utter itself as the inspired melody of a Burns: in a word, it is and continues in the voice and the work of a nation of hardy, endeavouring, considering men, with whatever that may bear in it, or unfold from it. The Scotch national character originates in many circumstances; first of all, in the Saxon stuff there was to work on; but next, and beyond all else except that, in the Presbyterian Gospel of John Knox. It seems a good national character; and, on some sides, not so good. Let Scott thank John Knox, for he owed him much, little as he dreamed of debt in that quarter! No Scotchman of his time was more entirely Scotch than Walter Scott; the good and the not so good, which all Scotchmen inherit, ran through every fibre of him.

Scott's childhood, school-days, college-days, are pleasant to read of, though they differ not from those of others in his place and time. The memory of him may probably enough last till this record of them become far more curious than it now is. " So lived an Edinburgh Writer to the Signet's son in the end of the eighteenth century," may some future Scotch novelist say to himself in the end of the twenty-first! The following little fragment of infancy is all we can extract. It is from an autobiography which he had begun, which one cannot but regret he did not finish. Scott's best qualities never shone out more freely than when he went upon anecdote and reminiscence. Such a master of narrative and of himself could have done personal narrative well. Here, if anywhere, his knowledge was complete, and all his humour and good-humour had free scope:

" An odd incident is worth recording. It seems my mother had sent a maid to take charge of me, at this farm of Sandy-Knowe, that I might be no inconvenience to the family. But the damsel sent on that important mission had left her heart behind her, in the keeping of some wild fellow, it is likely, who had done and said more to her than he was like to make good. She became extremely desirous to return to Edinburgh; and, as my mother made a point of her remaining where she was, she contracted a sort of hatred at poor me, as the cause of her being detained at Sandy-Knowe. This rose, I suppose, to a sort of delirious affection, for she confessed to old Alison Wilson, the housekeeper, that she had carried me up to the craigs under a strong temptation of the Devil to cut my throat with her scissors, and bury me in the moss. Alison instantly took possession of my person, and took care that her confidant should not be subject to any further temptation, at least as far as I was concerned. She was dismissed, of course, and I have heard afterwards became a lunatic.

" It is here, at Sandy-Knowe, in the residence of my paternal grandfather, already mentioned, that I have the first consciousness of existence; and I recollect distinctly that my situation and appearance were a little whimsical. Among the odd remedies recurred to to aid my lameness, some one had recommended that so often as a sheep was killed for the use of the family, I should be stripped, and swathed up in the skin warm as it was flayed from the carcass of the animal. In this Tartar-like habiliment I well remember lying upon the floor of the little parlour in the farm-house, while my grandfather, a venerable old man with white hair, used every excitement to make me try to crawl. I also distinctly remember the late Sir George M'Dougal of Mackerstown, father of the present Sir Henry Hay M'Dougal, joining in the attempt. He was, God knows how, a relation of ours; and I still recollect him in his old-fashioned military habit (he had been Colonel of the Greys), with a small cocked-hat deeply laced, an embroidered scarlet waistcoat, and a light-coloured coat, with milk-white locks tied in a military fashion, kneeling on the ground before me, and dragging his watch along the carpet to induce me to follow it. The benevolent old soldier and the infant wrapped in his sheep-skin, would have afforded an odd group to uninterested spectators. This must have happened about my third year (1774), for Sir George M'Dougal and my grandfather both died shortly after that period."—Vol. i, pp. 15—17.

We will glance next into the "*Liddesdale raids.*" Scott has grown up to be a brisk-hearted jovial young man and advocate: in vacation time he makes excursions to the Highlands, to the Border Cheviots and Northumberland; rides free and far, on his stout galloway, through bog and brake, over the dim moory debateable land,—over Flodden and other fields and places, where, though he yet knew it not, his work lay. No land, however dim and moory, but either has had or will have its poet, and so become not unknown in song. Liddesdale, which was once as prosaic as most dales, having now attained illustration, let us glance thitherward: Liddesdale too is on this ancient Earth of ours under this eternal Sky; and gives and takes, in the most incalculable manner, with the Universe at large! Scott's experiences there are rather of the rustic Arcadian sort; the element of whisky not wanting. We should premise that here and there a feature has perhaps been aggravated for effect's sake:

" During seven successive years," writes Mr Lockhart (for the autobiography has long since left us), " Scott made a *raid,* as he called it, into Liddesdale with Mr Shortreed, sheriff-substitute of Roxburgh, for his guide; exploring every rivulet to its source, and every ruined *peel* from foundation to battlement. At this time no wheeled carriage had ever been seen in the district;—the first indeed was a gig, driven by Scott himself for a part of his way, when on the last of these seven excursions. There was no inn nor public-house of any kind in the whole valley; the travellers passed from the shepherd's hut to the minister's manse, and again from the cheerful hospitality of the manse to the rough and jolly welcome of the homestead; gathering, wherever they went, songs and tunes, and occasionally more tangible relics of antiquity;—even such a 'routh of auld nicknackets' as Burns ascribes to Captain Grose. To these rambles Scott owed much of the materials of his 'Minstrelsy of the Scottish Border;' and not less of that intimate acquaintance with the living manners of these unsophisticated regions, which constitutes the chief charm of one of the most charming of his prose works. But how soon he had any definite object before him in his researches seems very doubtful. ' He was *makin' himsell* a' the time,' said Mr Shortreed; 'but he didna ken may be what he was about till years had passed; at first he thought o' little I daresay but the queerness and the fun.'

" ' In those days,' says the memorandum before me, ' advocates were not so plenty, at least about Liddesdale;' and the worthy sheriff-substitute goes on to describe the sort of bustle, not unmixed with alarm, produced at the first farm-house they visited (Willie Elliott's, of Millburnholm), when the honest man was informed of the quality of one of his guests. When they dismounted, accordingly, he received Mr Scott with great ceremony, and insisted upon himself leading his horse to the stable. Shortreed accompanied Willie however, and the latter, after taking a deliberate peep at Scott, ' out by the edge of the door-cheek,' whispered, ' weel Robin, deil hae me if I'se be a bit feared for him now; he's just a chield like oursels, I think.' Half a dozen dogs of all degrees had already gathered round the advocate, and his way of returning their compliments had set Willie Elliott at once at his ease.

" According to Mr Shortreed, this good man of Millburnholm was the great original of Dandie Dinmont." * * * "They dined at Millburnholm; and, after having lingered over Willie Elliott's punch-bowl until, in Mr Shortreed's phrase, they were 'half-glowring,' mounted their steeds again, and proceeded to Dr Elliott's at Cloughhead, where the two travellers ('for,' says my memorandum, ' folk were not very nice in those days,') slept in one and the same bed,—as indeed seems to have been the case with them throughout most of their excursions in this primitive district. Dr Elliott, a clergyman, had already a large MS. collection of the ballads Scott was in quest of." * * * " Next morning they seem to have ridden a long way for the express purpose of visiting one ' auld Thomas of Tuzzilhope,' another Elliott, I suppose, who was celebrated for his skill on the Border pipe, and in particular for being in possession of the real *lilt** of *Dick o' the Cove*. Before starting, that is, at six o'clock, the ballad hunters had taken, 'just to lay the stomach, a devilled duck or two, and some London porter.' Auld Thomas found them, nevertheless, well disposed for ' breakfast' on their arrival at Tuzzilhope; and this being over, he delighted them with one of the most hideous and unearthly of all the specimens of 'riding-music;' and moreover with considerable libations of whisky-punch, manufactured in a certain wooden vessel,

---

* Loud tune: German, *lallen.*

resembling a very small milk-pail, which he called 'wisdom,' because it 'made' only a few spoonfuls of liquor,—though he had the art of replenishing it so adroitly, that it had been celebrated for fifty years as more fatal to sobriety than any bowl in the parish. Having done due honour to wisdom, they again mounted, and proceeded over moss and moor to some other equally hospitable master of the pipe. 'Ah me,' says Shortreed, 'sic an endless fund o' humour and drollery as he then had wi' him! Never ten yards but we were either laughing or roaring and singing. Wherever we stopped, how brawly he suited himsell to everybody! He aye did as the rest did; never made himsell the great man or took any airs in company. I've seen him in a' moods in these jaunts, grave and gay, daft and serious, sober and drunk (this however, even in our wildest rambles, was rare); but, drunk or sober, he was aye the gentleman. He lookit excessively heavy and stupid when he was *fou*, but he was never out o' gude humour."

These are questionable doings, questionably narrated; but what shall we say of the following, wherein the element of whisky plays an extremely prominent part? We will say that it *is* questionable, and not exemplary, whisky mounting clearly beyond its level; that indeed charity hopes and conjectures, here may be some aggravating of features for effect's sake!

" On reaching, one evening, some *Charlieshope* or other (I forget the name) among those wildernesses, they found a kindly reception as usual; but, to their agreeable surprise, after some days of hard living, a measured and orderly hospitality as respected liquor. Soon after supper, at which a bottle of elderberry wine alone had been produced, a young student of divinity, who happened to be in the house, was called upon to take the 'big ha' Bible,' in the good old fashion of ' Burns's Saturday Night;' and some progress had been already made in the service, when the good man of the farm, whose 'tendency,' as Mr Mitchell says, 'was soporific,' scandalized his wife and the dominie by starting suddenly from his knees, and, rubbing his eyes, with a stentorian exclamation of ' By ——, here's the keg at last!' and in tumbled, as he spoke the word, a couple of sturdy herdsmen, whom, on hearing a day before of the advocate's approaching visit, he had despatched to a certain smuggler's haunt, at some considerable distance, in quest of a supply of *run* brandy from the Solway Frith. The pious exercise of the household was hopelessly interrupted. With a thousand apologies for his hitherto shabby entertainment, this jolly Elliott or Armstrong had the welcome *keg* mounted on the table without a moment's delay, and gentle and simple, not forgetting the dominie, continued carousing about it until daylight streamed in upon the party. Sir Walter Scott seldom failed, when I saw him in company with his Liddesdale companion, to mimic, with infinite humour, the sudden outburst of his old host on hearing the clatter of horses' feet, which he knew to indicate the arrival of the keg; the consternation of the dame; and the rueful despair with which the young clergyman closed the book."—Vol. i, pp. 195—9.

From which Liddesdale *raids*, which we here, like the young clergyman, close not without a certain rueful despair, let the reader draw what nourishment he can. They evince satisfactorily, though in a rude manner, that in those days young advocates, and Scott, like the rest of them, were *alive* and alert,—whisky sometimes preponderating. But let us now fancy that the jovial young advocate has pleaded his first cause; has served in yeomanry drills; been wedded, been promoted sheriff, without romance in either case; dabbling a little the while, under guidance of Monk Lewis, in translations from the German, in translation of 'Goethe's Götz with the Iron Hand;'—and we have arrived at the threshold of the 'Minstrelsy of the Scottish Border,' and the opening of a new century.

Hitherto, therefore, there has been made out, by nature and circumstance working together, nothing unusually remarkable, yet still something very valuable: a stout effectual man of thirty, full of broad sagacity and good humour, with faculties in him fit for any burden of business, hospitality, and duty, legal or civic;—with what other faculties in him no one could yet say. As indeed who, after lifelong inspection, can say what is in any man? The uttered part of a man's life, let us always repeat, bears to the unuttered, unconscious part a small unknown proportion; he himself never knows it, much less do others. Give him room, give him *impulse*: he reaches down to the infinite with that so straitly-imprisoned soul of his; and *can* do miracles if need be! It is one of the comfortablest truths that great men abound, though in the unknown state. Nay, as above hinted, our greatest, being also by nature our *quietest*, are perhaps those that remain unknown! Philosopher Fichte took comfort in this belief, when from all pulpits and editorial desks, and publications, periodical and stationary, he could hear nothing but the infinite chattering and twittering of common-place become ambitious; and in the infinite stir of motion nowhither, and of din which should have been silence, all seemed churned into one tempestuous yeasty froth, and the stern Fichte almost desired "taxes on knowledge" to allay it a little;—he comforted himself, we say, by the unshaken belief that Thought did still exist in Germany; that thinking men, each in his own corner, were verily doing their work, though in a silent latent manner.*
Walter Scott, as a latent Walter, had never amused all men for

---

* Fichte: *Ueber das Wesen des Gelehrten.*

a score of years in the course of centuries and eternities, or gained and lost, say a hundred thousand pounds sterling by literature; but he might have been a happy, and by no means a useless,—nay, who knows at bottom whether not a still usefuller Walter! However, that was not his fortune. The Genius of a rather singular age,—an age at once destitute of faith and terrified at scepticism, with little knowledge of its whereabout, with many sorrows to bear or front, and on the whole with a life to lead in these new circumstances,—had said to himself: What man shall be the temporary comforter, or were it but ,the spiritual comfit-maker, of this my poor singular age, to solace its dead tedium and manifold sorrows a little? So had the Genius said, looking over all the world, what man? and found him walking the dusty outer parliament-house of Edinburgh, with his advocate-gown on his back; and exclaimed, That is he!

The 'Minstrelsy of the Scottish Border' proved to be a well, from which flowed one of the broadest rivers. Metrical romances (which in due time pass into prose romances); the old life of men resuscitated for us: it is a mighty word! Not as dead tradition, but as a palpable presence, the past stood before us. There they were, the rugged old fighting men; in their doughty simplicity and strength, with their heartiness, their healthiness, their stout self-help, in their iron basnets, leather jerkins, jack-boots, in their quaintness of manner and costume; there as they looked and lived! It was like a new-discovered continent in literature; for the new century, a bright El Dorado,—or else some fat beatific land of Cockaigne, and paradise of Donothings. To the opening nineteenth century, in its languor and paralysis, nothing could have been welcomer. Most unexpected, most refreshing, and exhilarating: behold our new El Dorado; our fat beatific Lubberland, where one can enjoy and do nothing! It was the time for such a new literature; and this Walter Scott was the man for it. The *Lays*, the *Marmions*, the *Ladyes* and *Lords* of Lake and Isles, followed in thick succession, with ever-widening profit and praise. How many thousands of guineas were paid down for each new Lay; how many thousands of copies (fifty, and more sometimes) were printed off then and subsequently; what complimenting, reviewing, renown and apotheosis there was: all is recorded in these seven volumes, which will be valuable in literary statistics. It is a history, brilliant, remarkable; the outlines of which are known to all. The reader shall recal it, or conceive it. No blaze in his fancy is like to mount higher than the reality did.

At this middle period of his life, therefore, Scott, enriched with copyrights, with new official incomes and promotions, rich in money, rich in repute, presents himself as a man in the full career of success. "Health, wealth, and wit to guide them" (as his vernacular proverb says), all these three are his. The field is open for him, and victory there; his own faculty, his own self, unshackled, victoriously unfolds itself,—the highest blessedness that can befall a man. Wide circle of friends, personal loving admirers; warmth of domestic joys, vouchsafed to all that can trueheartedly nestle down among them; light of radiance and renown given only to a few: who would not call Scott happy? But the happiest circumstance of all is, as we said above, that Scott had in himself a right healthy soul, rendering him little dependent on outward circumstances. Things showed themselves to him not in distortion or borrowed light or gloom, but as they were. Endeavour lay in him and endurance, in due measure; and clear vision of what was to be endeavoured after. Were one to preach a Sermon on Health, as really were worth doing, Scott ought to be the text. Theories are demonstrably true in the way of logic; and then in the way of practice, they prove true or else not true: but here is the grand experiment, Do they turn out well? What boots it that a man's creed is the wisest, that his system of principles is the superfinest, if, when set to work, the life of him does nothing but jar, and fret itself into *holes?* They are untrue in that, were it in nothing else, these principles of his; openly convicted of untruth;—fit only, shall we say, to be rejected as counterfeits, and flung to the dogs? We say not that; but we do say that ill-health, of body or of mind, is *defeat*, is battle (in a good or in a bad cause) with bad success; that health alone is victory. Let all men, if they can manage it, contrive to be healthy! He who in what cause soever sinks into pain and disease, let him take thought of it; let him know well that it is not good *he* has arrived at yet, but surely evil,—may, or may not be, on the way towards good.

Scott's healthiness showed itself decisively in all things, and nowhere more decisively than in this: the way in which he took his fame; the estimate he from the first formed of fame. Money will buy money's worth; but the thing men call fame, what is it? A gaudy emblazonry, not good for much,—except indeed as it too may turn to money. To Scott it was a profitable pleasing superfluity, no necessary of life. Not necessary, now or ever! Seemingly without much effort, but taught by nature, and the instinct which instructs the sound heart what is good for it and what is not, he felt that he could always do without this same emblazonry of reputation; that he ought to put no trust in it; but be ready at any time to see it pass away from him, and to hold on his way as before. It is incalculable, as we conjecture, what evil he escaped in this manner; what perversions, irritations, mean agonies without a name, he lived wholly apart from, knew nothing of. Happily before fame arrived, he had reached the mature age at which all this was easier for him. What a strange Nemesis lurks in the felicities of men! In thy mouth it shall be sweet as honey, in thy belly it shall be bitter as gall! Some weakly-organized individual, we will say at the age of five-and-twenty, whose main or whole talent rests on some prurient susceptivity, and nothing under it but shallowness and vacuum, is clutched hold of by the general imagination, is whirled aloft to the giddy height; and taught to believe the divine-seeming message that he is a great man: such individual seems the luckiest of men; and *is* he not the unluckiest? Swallow not the Circe-draught, O weakly-organized individual; it is fell poison; it will dry up the fountains of thy whole existence, and all will grow withered and parched; thou shalt be wretched under the sun! Is there, for example, a sadder book than that 'Life of Byron,' by Moore? To omit mere prurient susceptivities that rest on vacuum, look at poor Byron, who really had much substance in him. Sitting there in his self-exile, with a proud heart striving to persuade itself that it despises the entire created universe; and far off, in foggy Babylon, let any pittifullest whipster draw pen on him, your proud Byron writhes in torture,—as if the pitiful whipster were a magician, or his pen a galvanic wire stuck into the Byron's spinal marrow! Lamentable, despicable,—one had rather be a kitten and cry mew! O, son of Adam, great or little, according as thou art loveable those thou livest with will love thee. Those thou livest *not* with, is it of moment that they have the alphabetic letters of thy name engraved on their memory with some signpost likeness of thee (as like as I to Hercules) appended to them? It is not of moment; in sober truth, not of any moment at all! And yet, behold, there is no soul now whom thou canst love freely,—from *one* soul only art thou always sure of reverence enough; in presence of no soul is it rightly well with thee! How is thy world become desert; and thou, for the sake of a little babblement of tongues, art poor, bankrupt, insolvent not in purse, but in heart and mind. "The golden calf of self-love," says Jean Paul, "has grown into a burning Phalaris' bull, to consume its owner and worshipper." Ambition, the desire of shining and outshining, was the beginning of sin in this world. The man of letters who founds upon his fame, does he not thereby alone declare himself a follower of Lucifer (named *Satan*, the Enemy), and member of the Satanic school?— —

It was in this poetic period that Scott formed his connexion with the Ballantynes; and embarked, though under cover, largely in trade. To those who regard him in the heroic light, and will have *vates* to signify prophet as well as poet, this portion of his biography seems somewhat incoherent. Viewed as it stood in the reality, as he was and as it was, the enterprise, since it proved so unfortunate, may be called lamentable, but cannot be called unnatural. The practical Scott, looking towards practical issues in all things, could not but find hard cash one of the most practical. If, by any means, cash could be honestly produced, were it by writing poems, were it by printing them, why not? Great things might be done ultimately; great difficulties were at once got rid of,—manifold higgling of booksellers, and contradiction of sinners hereby fell away. A printing and bookselling speculation was not so alien for a maker of books. Voltaire, who indeed got no copyrights, made much money by the war-commissariat, in his time; we believe, by the victualling branch of it. Saint George himself, they say, was a dealer in bacon in Cappadocia. A thrifty man will help himself towards his object by such steps as lead to it. Station in society, solid power over the good things of this world, was Scott's avowed object; towards which the precept of precepts is that of Iago: Put money in thy purse.

Here indeed it is to be remarked, that, perhaps, no literary man of any generation has less value than Scott for the immaterial part of his mission in any sense: not only for the fantasy called fame, with the fantastic miseries attendant thereon; but also for the spiritual purport of his work, whether it tended hitherward or thitherward, or had any tendency whatever; and indeed for all purports and results of his working, except such, we may say, as offered themselves to the eye, and could in one sense or the other be handled, looked at, and buttoned into the breeches-pocket. Somewhat too little of a fantast, this *vates* of ours! But so it was: in this nineteenth century, our highest literary man, who immeasurably beyond all others commanded the world's ear, had, as it were, no message whatever to deliver to the world; wished not the world to elevate itself, to amend itself, to do this or to do that, except simply pay him for the books he kept writing. Very remarkable; fittest, perhaps, for an age fallen languid, destitute of faith, and terrified at scepticism? Or, perhaps, for quite another sort of age, an age all in peaceable triumphant motion? But, indeed, since Shakspeare's time there has been no great speaker so unconscious of an aim in speaking. Equally unconscious these two utterances; equally the sincere complete product of the minds they came from: and now if they were equally *deep?* Or, if the one was living fire, and the other was futile phosphorescence and mere resinous firework? It will depend on the relative worth of the minds; for both were equally spontaneous, both equally expressed themselves unincumbered by an ulterior aim. Beyond drawing audiences to the Globe Theatre, Shakspeare contemplated no result in those plays of his. Yet they have had results! Utter with free heart what thy own *daemon* gives thee: if fire from heaven, it shall be well; if resinous firework, it shall be—as well as *it* could be, or better than otherwise!—The candid judge will, in general, require that a speaker, in so extremely serious a universe as this of ours, have something to speak about. In the heart of the speaker there ought to be some kind of gospel-tidings burning till it be uttered; otherwise it were better for him that he altogether held his peace. A gospel somewhat more decisive than this of Scott's,—except to an age altogether languid, without either scepticism or faith! These things the candid judge will demand of literary men; yet withal will recognize the great worth there is in Scott's honesty if in nothing more, in his being the thing he was with such entire good faith. Here is a something not a nothing. If no skyborn messenger, heaven looking through his eyes; then neither is it a chimera with its systems, crotchets, cants, fanaticisms, and "last infirmity of noble minds,"—full of misery, unrest, and ill-will; but a substantial, peaceable, terrestrial man. Far as the Earth is under the Heaven does Scott stand below the former sort of character; but high as the cheerful flowery Earth is above waste Tartarus does he stand above the latter. Let him live in his own fashion, and do honour to him in that.

It were late in the day to write criticisms on those Metrical Romances: at the same time, the great popularity they had seems natural enough. In the first place, there was the indisputable impress of worth, of genuine human force, in them. This which lies in some degree, or is thought to lie, at the bottom of all popularity, did, to an unusual degree, disclose itself in these rhymed romances of Scott's. Pictures were actually painted and presented; human emotions conceived and sympathized with. Considering what wretched Della-Cruscan and other vamping-up of old worn-out tatters was the staple article then, it may be granted that Scott's excellence was superior and supreme. When a Hayley was the main singer, a Scott might well be hailed with warm welcome. Consider whether the *Loves of the Plants,* and even the *Loves of the Triangles,* could be worth the loves and hates of men and women! Scott was as preferable to what he displaced, as the substance is to the wearisomely repeated shadow of a substance. But, in the second place, we may say that the *kind* of worth which Scott manifested was fitted especially for the then temper of men. We have called it an age fallen into spiritual langour, destitute of belief, yet terrified at scepticism; reduced to live a stinted half-life, under strange new circumstances. Now vigorous whole-life, this was what of all things these delineations offered. The reader was carried back to rough strong times, wherein those maladies of ours had not yet arisen. Brawny fighters, all cased in buff and iron, their hearts too sheathed in oak and triple brass, caprioled their huge war-horses, shook their death-doing spears; and went forth in the most determined manner, nothing doubting. The reader sighed, yet not without a reflex solacement: " O, that I too had lived in those times, had never known these logic-cobwebs, this doubt, this sickliness; and been and felt myself alive among men alive !" Add lastly, that, in this new-found poetic world there was no call for effort on the reader's part; what excellence they had, exhibited itself at a glance. It was for the reader, not an El Dorado only, but a beatific land of Cockaigne and Paradise of Donothings! The reader, what the vast majority of readers so long to do, was allowed to lie down at his ease, and be ministered to. What the Turkish bath-keeper is said to aim at with his frictions, and shampooings, and fomentings, more or less effectually, that the patient in total idleness may have the delights of activity,—was here to a considerable extent realized. The languid imagination fell back into its rest; an artist was there who could supply it with high-painted scenes, with sequences of stirring action, and whisper to it, Be at ease, and let thy tepid element be comfortable to thee. " The rude man," says a critic, " requires only to see something going on. The man of more refinement must be made to feel. The man of complete refinement must be made to reflect."

We named the ' Minstrelsy of the Scottish Border' the fountain from which flowed this great river of Metrical Romances; but according to some they can be traced to a still higher obscurer spring: to Goethe's ' Götz von Berlichingen with the Iron Hand;' of which, as we have seen, Scott in his earlier days executed a translation. Dated a good many years ago, the following words in a criticism on Goethe are found written; which probably are still new to most readers of this Review:

" The works just mentioned, ' Götz' and ' Werter,' though noble specimens of youthful talent, are still not so much distinguished by their intrinsic merits as by their splendid fortune. It would be difficult to name two books which have exercised a deeper influence on the subsequent literature of Europe than these two performances of a young author; his first fruits, the produce of his twenty-fourth year. *Werter* appeared to seize the hearts of men in all quarters of the world, and to utter for them the word which they had long been waiting to hear. As usually happens too, this same word once uttered was soon abundantly repeated; spoken in all dialects, and chaunted through all the notes of the gamut, till the sound of it had grown a weariness rather than a pleasure. Sceptical sentimentality, view-hunting, love, friendship, suicide, and desperation, became the staple literary ware: and though the epidemic, after a long course of years, subsided in Germany, it re-appeared with various modifications in other countries; and everywhere abundant traces of its good and its bad effects are still to be discerned. The fortune of ' Berlichingen with the Iron Hand,' though less sudden, was by no means less exalted. In his own country, *Götz*, though he now stands solitary and childless, became the parent of an innumerable progeny of chivalry plays, feudal delineations, and poetico-antiquarian performances; which, though long ago deceased, made noise enough in their day and generation: and with ourselves his influence has been perhaps still more remarkable. Sir Walter Scott's first literary enterprise was a translation of 'Götz von Berlichingen:' and if genius could be communicated like instruction, we might call this work of Goethe's the prime cause of ' Marmion' and the ' Lady of the Lake,' with all that has since followed from the same creative hand. Truly a grain of seed that has lighted in the right soil! For, if not firmer and fairer, it has grown to be taller and broader than any other tree; and all the nations of the earth are still yearly gathering of its fruit."

How far ' Götz von Berlichingen' actually affected Scott's literary destination, and whether without it the rhymed romances, and then the prose romances of the Author of Waverley, would not have followed as they did, must remain a very obscure question; obscure, and not important. Of the fact, however, there is no doubt but these two tendencies, which may be named *Götzism* and *Werterism*, of the former of which Scott was representative with us, have made, and are still in some quarters making, the tour of all Europe. In Germany too there was this affectionate half-regretful looking back into the past; Germany had its buff-belted watch-tower period in literature, and had even got done with it, before Scott began. Then as to *Werterism*, had not we English our Byron and his genus? No form of Werterism in any other country had half the potency: as our Scott carried chivalry literature to the ends of the world, so did our Byron Werterism. France, busy with its Revolution and its Napoleon, had little leisure at the moment for Götzism or Werterism; but it has had them both since, in a shape of its own: witness the whole " Literature of Desperation" in our own days, the beggarliest form of Werterism yet seen, probably its expiring final form: witness also, at the other extremity of the scale, a nobly-gifted Chateaubriand, Götz and Werter, both in one.—Curious: how all Europe is but like a set of parishes of the same country; participant of the self-same influences, ever since the Crusades, and earlier;—and these glorious wars of ours are but like parish-brawls, which begin in mutual ignorance, intoxication and boastful speech; which end in broken windows, damage, waste, and bloody noses; and which one hopes the general good sense is now in the way towards putting down, in some measure!

But, however, leaving this to be as it can, what it concerned us here to remark, was that British Werterism, in the shape of those Byron Poems, so potent and poignant, produced on the languid appetite of men a mighty effect. This too was a "class of feelings deeply important to modern minds; feelings which arise from *passion incapable of being converted into action*, which belong to an age as indolent, cultivated, and unbelieving as our own!" The "languid age without either faith or scepticism" turned towards Byronism with an interest altogether peculiar: here, if no cure for its miserable paralysis and languor, was at least an indignant statement of the misery; an indignant Ernulphus' curse read over it,—which all men felt to be something. Half-regretful lookings into the Past gave place, in many quarters, to Ernulphus' cursings of the Present. Scott was among the first to perceive that the day of Metrical Chivalry Romances was declining. He had held the sovereignty for some half-score of years, a comparatively long lease of it; and now the time seemed come for dethronement, for abdication; an unpleasant business; which however he held himself ready, as a brave man will, to transact with composure and in silence. After all, Poetry was not his staff of life; Poetry had already yielded him much money; *this* at least it would not take back from him. Busy always with editing, with compiling, with multiplex official, commercial business, and solid interests, he beheld the coming change with unmoved eye.

Resignation he was prepared to exhibit in this matter;—and now behold there proved to be no need of resignation. Let the Metrical Romance become a Prose one; shake off its rhyme-fetters, and try a wider sweep! In the spring of 1814 appeared 'Waverley;' an event memorable in the annals of British literature; in the annals of British bookselling thrice and four times memorable. Byron sang, but Scott narrated; and when the song had sung itself out through all variations onwards to the 'Don-Juan' one, Scott was still found narrating, and carrying the whole world along with him. All bygone popularity of chivalry lays was swallowed up in a far greater. What "series" followed out of 'Waverley,' and how and with what result, is known to all men; was witnessed and watched with a kind of rapt astonishment by all. Hardly any literary reputation ever rose so high in our Island; no reputation at all ever spread so wide. Walter Scott became Sir Walter Scott, Baronet, of Abbotsford; on whom fortune seemed to pour her whole cornucopia of wealth, honour, and worldly good; the favourite of Princes and of Peasants, and all intermediate men. His "Waverley series," swift-following one on the other apparently without end, was the universal reading, looked for like an annual harvest, by all ranks in all European countries. A curious circumstance superadded itself, that the author though known was unknown. From the first, most people suspected, and soon after the first, few intelligent persons much doubted, that the Author of 'Waverley' was Walter Scott. Yet a certain mystery was still kept up; rather piquant to the public; doubtless very pleasant to the author, who saw it all; who probably had not to listen, as other hapless individuals often had, to this or the other long-drawn "clear proof at last," that the author was not Walter Scott, but a certain astonishing Mr So-and-so;—one of the standing miseries of human life in that time. But for the privileged author, it was like a king travelling incognito. All men know that he is a high king, chivalrous Gustaf or Kaiser Joseph; but he mingles in their meetings without cumber of etiquette or lonesome ceremony, as Chevalier du Nord, or Count of Lorraine: he has none of the weariness of royalty, and yet all the praise, and the satisfaction of hearing it with his own ears. In a word, the Waverley Novels circulated and reigned triumphant; to the general imagination the " Author of ' Waverley' " was like some living mythological personage, and ranked among the chief wonders of the world.

How a man lived and demeaned himself in such unwonted circumstances is worth seeing. We would gladly quote from Scott's correspondence of this period; but that does not much illustrate the matter. His letters, as above stated, are never without interest, yet also seldom or never very interesting. They are full of cheerfulness, of wit, and ingenuity; but they do not treat of aught intimate; without impeaching their sincerity, what is called sincerity, one may say they do not, in any case whatever, proceed from the innermost parts of the mind. Conventional forms, due considerations of your own and your correspondent's pretensions and vanities, are at no moment left out of view. The epistolary stream runs on, lucid, free, glad-flowing; but always, as it were, *parallel* to the real substance of the matter, never coincident with it. One feels it hollowish under foot. Letters they are of a most humane man of the world, even exemplary in that kind; but with the man of the world always visible in them;—as indeed it was little in Scott's way to speak perhaps even with himself in any other fashion. We select rather some glimpses of him from Mr Lockhart's record. The first is of dining with Royalty or Prince-Regentship itself; an almost official matter:

" On hearing from Mr Croker, then Secretary to the Admiralty, that Scott was to be in town by the middle of March (1815), the Prince said, ' Let me know when he comes, and I'll get up a snug little dinner that will suit him;' and after he had been presented and graciously received at the levee, he was invited to dinner accordingly, through his excellent friend Mr Adam (now Lord Chief Commissioner of the Jury Court in Scotland), who at that time held a confidential office in the royal household. The Regent had consulted with Mr Adam also as to the composition of the party. ' Let us have,' said he, ' just a few friends of his own, and the more Scotch the better;' and both the Commissioner and Mr Croker assure me that the party was the most interesting and agreeable one in their recollection. It comprised, I believe, the Duke of York, the Duke of Gordon (then Marquis of Huntly), the Marquis of Hertford (then Lord Yarmouth), the Earl of Fife, and Scott's early friend, Lord Melville. ' The Prince and Scott,' says Mr Croker, ' were the two most brilliant story-tellers, in their several ways, that I have ever happened to meet; they were both aware of their *forte*, and both exerted themselves that evening with remarkable effect. On going home, I really could not decide which of them had shone the most (!) The Regent was enchanted with Scott, as Scott with him; and on all subsequent visits to London, he was a frequent guest at the royal table.' The Lord Chief Commissioner remembers that the Prince was particularly delighted with the poet's anecdotes of the old Scotch judges and lawyers, which his Royal Highness sometimes *capped* by ludicrous traits of certain ermined sages of his own acquaintance. Scott told, among others, a story which he was fond of telling, of his old friend the Lord Justice-Clerk Braxfield; and the commentary of his Royal Highness on hearing it amused Scott, who often mentioned it afterwards. The anecdote is this:—Braxfield, whenever he went on a particular circuit, was in the habit of visiting a gentleman of good fortune in the neighbourhood of one of the assize towns, and staying at least one night, which, being both of them ardent chess-players, they usually concluded with their favourite game. One Spring circuit the battle was not decided at day-break; so the Justice-Clerk said, ' Weel, Donald, I must e'en come back this gate, and let the game lie over for the present;' and back he came in October, but not to his old friend's hospitable house; for that gentleman had in the interim been apprehended on a capital charge (of forgery), and his name stood on the *Porteous Roll*, or list of those who were about to be tried under his former guest's auspices. The laird was indicted and tried accordingly, and the jury returned a verdict of *guilty*. Braxfield forthwith put on his cocked hat (which answers to the black cap in England), and pronounced the sentence of the law in the usual terms: ' To be hanged by the neck until you be dead; and may the Lord have mercy upon your unhappy soul!' Having concluded this awful formula in his most sonorous cadence, Braxfield, dismounting his formidable beaver, gave a familiar nod to his unfortunate acquaintance, and said to him in a sort of chuckling whisper, ' And now Donald, my man, I think I've checkmated you for ance.' The Regent laughed heartily at this specimen of Macqueen's brutal humour; and 'i'faith, Walter,' said he, ' this old big-wig seems to have taken things as coolly as my tyrannical self. Don't you remember Tom Moore's description of me at breakfast,

> ' The table spread with tea and toast,
> Death-warrants and the Morning Post?'

" Towards midnight the Prince called for ' a bumper with all the honours to the Author of Waverley;' and looked significantly, as he was charging his own glass, to Scott. Scott seemed somewhat puzzled for a moment; but instantly recovering himself, and filling his glass to the brim, said, ' Your Royal Highness looks as if you thought I had some claim to the honours of this toast. I have no such pretensions, but shall take good care that the real Simon Pure hears of the high compliment that has now been paid him.' He then drank off his claret; and joined with a stentorian voice in the cheering, which the Prince himself timed. But before the company could resume their seats his Royal Highness exclaimed, ' Another of the same, if you please, to the Author of Marmion, —and now, Walter, my man, I have checkmated you for *ance*.' The second bumper was followed by cheers still more prolonged: and Scott then rose, and returned thanks in a short address, which struck the Lord Chief Commissioner as ' alike grave and graceful.' This story has been circulated in a very perverted shape." * * *
" Before he left town he again dined at Carlton House, when the party was a still smaller one than before, and the merriment if possible still more free. That nothing might be wanting, the Prince sang several capital songs."—Vol. iii, pp. 340—3.

Or take, at a very great interval in many senses, this glimpse of another dinner, altogether *unofficially* and much better described. It is James Ballantyne the printer and publisher's dinner, in Saint John street, Canongate, Edinburgh, on the birth-eve of a Waverley Novel:

" The feast was, to use one of James's own favourite phrases, *gorgeous;* an aldermanic display of turtle and venison, with suitable accompaniments of iced punch, potent ale, and generous Madeira. When the cloth was drawn, the burly preses arose, with all he could muster of the port of John Kemble, and spouted with a sonorous voice the formula of *Macbeth*—

'Fill full!
I drink to the general joy of the whole table!'

This was followed by 'the King, God bless him!' and second came, 'Gentlemen, there is another toast which never has been nor shall be omitted in this house of mine: I give you the health of Mr Walter Scott, with three times three!' All honour having been done to this health, and Scott having briefly thanked the company, with some expressions of warm affection for their host, Mrs Ballantyne retired;—the bottles passed round twice or thrice in their usual way; and then James rose once more, every vein on his brow distended: his eyes solemnly fixed on vacancy, to propose, not as before in his stentorian key, but 'with 'bated breath,' in the sort of whisper by which a stage conspirator thrills the gallery, '*Gentlemen, a bumper to the immortal Author of Waverley!*' The uproar of cheering, in which Scott made a fashion of joining, was succeeded by deep silence; and then Ballantyne proceeded,

'In his Lord Burleigh look, serene and serious,
A something of imposing and mysterious'—

to lament the obscurity in which his illustrious but too modest correspondent still chose to conceal himself from the plaudits of the world; to thank the company for the manner in which the *nominis umbra* had been received; and to assure them that the Author of 'Waverley' would, when informed of the circumstance, feel highly gratified, 'the proudest hour of his life,' &c. &c. The cool, demure fun of Scott's features during all this mummery was perfect; and Erskine's attempts at a gay *nonchalance* was still more ludicrously meritorious. Aldiborontiphoscophornio, however, bursting as he was, knew too well to allow the new Novel to be made the subject of discussion. Its name was announced, and success to it crowned another cup; but after that, no more of Jedediah. To cut the thread, he rolled out unbidden some one of his many theatrical songs, in a style that would have done no dishonour to almost any orchestra, 'The Maid of Lodi,' or perhaps 'The Bay of Biscay, O,' or 'The sweet little cherub that sits up aloft.' Other toasts followed, interspersed with ditties from other performers; old George Thompson, the friend of Burns, was ready, for one, with 'The Moorland Wedding,' or 'Willie brew'd a peck o' maut;'—and so it went on, until Scott and Erskine, with any clerical or very staid personage that had chanced to be admitted, saw fit to withdraw. Then the scene was changed. The claret and olives made way for broiled bones and a mighty bowl of punch; and when a few glasses of the hot beverage had restored his powers, James opened ore *rotundo* on the merits of the forthcoming romance. ' One chapter,— one chapter only!' was the cry. After ' Nay, by'r lady, nay !' and a few more coy shifts, the proof-sheets were at length produced, and James, with many a prefatory hem, read aloud what he considered as the most striking dialogue they contained.

" The first I heard so read was the interview between Jeanie Deans, the Duke of Argyle, and Queen Caroline, in Richmond Park; and, notwithstanding some spice of the pompous tricks to which he was addicted, I must say he did the inimitable scene great justice. At all events, the effect it produced was deep and memorable; and no wonder that the exulting typographer's ' *One bumper more to Jedediah Cleishbotham*' preceded his parting stave, which was uniformly ' The Last Words of Marmion,' executed certainly with no contemptible rivalry of Braham."—Vol. iv, p. 166—8.

Over at Abbotsford, things wear a still more prosperous aspect. Scott is building there, by the pleasant banks of the Tweed; he has bought and is buying land there; fast as the new gold comes in for a new Waverley Novel, or even faster, it changes itself into moory acres, into stone and hewn or planted wood :

" About the middle of February (1820)," says Mr Lockhart, " it having been ere that time arranged that I should marry his eldest daughter in the course of the spring, I accompanied him and part of his family on one of those flying visits to Abbotsford, with which he ofter indulged himself on a Saturday during term. Upon such occasions, Scott appeared at the usual hour in Court ; but wearing, instead of the official suit of black, his country morning-dress, green jacket, and so forth, under his clerk's gown."—" At noon, when the Court broke up, Peter Mathieson was sure to be in attendance in the Parliament Close ; and, five minutes after, the gown had been tossed off; and Scott, rubbing his hands for glee, was under way for Tweedside. As we proceeded," &c.

" Next morning there appeared at breakfast John Ballantyne, who had at this time a shooting or hunting box a few miles off, in the vale of the Leader, and with him Mr Constable his guest; and it being a fine clear day, as soon as Scott had read the church service and one of Jeremy Taylor's sermons, we all sallied out before noon on a perambulation of his upland territories; Maida (the hound) and the rest of the favourites accompanying our march. At starting we were joined by the constant henchman, Tom Purdie,— and I may save myself the trouble of any attempt to describe his appearance, for his master has given us an inimitably true one in introducing a certain personage of his ' Redgauntlet :'—' He was perhaps sixty years old; yet his brow was not much furrowed, and his jet-black hair was only grizzled, not whitened, by the advance of age. All his motions spoke strength unabated ; and, though rather under-sized, he had very broad shoulders, was square made, thin-flanked, and apparently combined in his frame muscular strength and activity; the last somewhat impaired perhaps by years, but the first remaining in full vigour. A hard and harsh countenance; eyes far sunk under projecting eyebrows, which were grizzled like his hair; a wide mouth, furnished from ear to ear with a range of unimpaired teeth of uncommon whiteness, and a size and breadth which might have become the jaws of an ogre, completed this delightful portrait.' Equip this figure in Scott's cast-off green jacket, white hat, and drab trousers; and imagine that years of kind treatment, comfort, and the honest consequence of a confidential *grieve*,* had softened away much of the hardness and harshness orginally impressed on the visage by anxious penury, and the sinister habits of a *black-fisher*;—and the Tom Purdie of 1820 stands before us.

" We were all delighted to see how completely Scott had recovered his bodily vigour; and none more so than Constable, who, as he puffed and panted after him, up one ravine and down another, often stopped to wipe his forehead, and remarked, that ' it was not every author who should lead him such a dance.' But Purdie's face shone with rapture as he observed how severely the swag-bellied bookseller's activity was tasked. Scott exclaimed exultingly, though, perhaps, for the tenth time, ' This will be a glorious spring for our trees, Tom!'—' You may say that, Sheriff,' quoth Tom,—and then lingering a moment for Constable,—' My certy,' he added, ' scratching his head, ' and I think it will be a grand season for *our buiks*, too.' But indeed Tom always talked of *our buiks* as if they had been as regular products of the soil as *our aits* and *our birks*. Having threaded first the Hexilcleugh and then the Rhymer's Glen, we arrived at Huntly Burn, where the hospitality of the kind *Weird Sisters*, as Scott called the Miss Fergusons, reanimated our exhausted bibliopoles, and gave them courage to extend their walk a little farther down the same famous brook. Here there was a small cottage in a very sequestered situation" (named Chiefswood), " by making some little additions to which Scott thought it might be converted into a suitable summer residence for his daughter and future son-in-law." * * " As we walked homeward, Scott being a little fatigued, laid his left hand on Tom's shoulder, and leaned heavily for support, chatting to his *Sunday pony*, as he called the affectionate fellow, just as freely as he did with the rest of the party; and Tom put in his word shrewdly and manfully, and grinned and grunted whenever the joke chanced to be within his apprehension. It was easy to see that his heart swelled within him from the moment the Sheriff got his collar in his gripe."—Vol. iv, p. 349—53.

That Abbotsford became infested to a great degree with tourists, wonder-hunters, and all that fatal species of people, may be supposed. Solitary Ettrick saw itself populous; all paths were beaten with the feet and hoofs of an endless miscellany of pilgrims. As many as "sixteen parties" have arrived

---

* Overseer: German, *graf*.

at Abbotsford in one day; male and female; peers, Socinian preachers, whatsoever was distinguished, whatsoever had love of distinction in it! Mr Lockhart thinks there was no literary shrine ever so bepilgrimed, except Ferney in Voltaire's time, who, however, was not half so accessible. A fatal species! These are what Schiller calls "the flesh-flies;" buzzing swarms of blue-bottles, who never fail where any taint of human glory or other corruptibility is in the wind. So has Nature decreed. Scott's *healthiness*, bodily and mental, his massive solidity of character, nowhere showed itself more decisively than in his manner of encountering this part of his fate. That his blue-bottles were blue, and of the usual tone and quality, may be judged. Hear Captain Basil Hall (in a very compressed state):

"We arrived in good time, and found several other guests at dinner. The public rooms are lighted with oil gas, in a style of extraordinary splendour. The," &c.—" Had I a hundred pens, each of which at the same time should separately write down an anecdote, I could not hope to record one-half of those which our host, to use Spenser's expression, ' welled out alway.' "—" Entertained us all the way with an endless string of anecdotes;"—" came like a strain of poetry from his lips;"—" path muddy and scarcely passable, yet I do not remember ever to have seen any place so interesting as the skill of this mighty magician had rendered this narrow ravine."—" Impossible to touch on any theme but straightway he has an anecdote to fit it."—" Thus we strolled along, borne, as it were, on the stream of song and story."—" In the evening we had a great feast indeed. Sir Walter asked us if we had ever read ' Christabel.' "—" Interspersed with these various readings, were some hundreds of stories, some quaint, some pathetical."—" At breakfast to-day we had, as usual, some 150 stories: God knows how they came in."—" In any man so gifted; so qualified to take the loftiest, proudest line at the head of the literature, the taste, the imagination of the whole world!"—" For instance, he never sits at any particular place at table, but takes,"&c. &c.—Vol. v, p. 375—402.

Among such worshippers, arriving in "sixteen parties a-day," an ordinary man might have grown buoyant; have felt the god, begun to nod, and seemed to shake the spheres. A slightly splenetic man, possessed of Scott's sense, would have swept his premises clear of them: Let no blue-bottle approach here, to disturb a man in his work,—under pain of sugared *squash* (called quassia) and king's-yellow! The good Sir Walter, like a quiet brave man, did neither. He let the matter take its course; enjoyed what was enjoyable in it; endured what could not well be helped; persisted meanwhile in writing his daily portion of romance-*copy*, in preserving his composure of heart;—in a word, accommodated himself to this loud-buzzing environment, and made it serve him, as he would have done (perhaps with more ease) to a silent, poor, and solitary one. No doubt it affected him too, and in the lamentablest way fevered his internal life,—though he kept it well down; but it affected him *less* than it would have done almost any other man. For his guests were not all of the blue-bottle sort; far from that. Mr Lockhart shall furnish us with the brightest aspect a British Ferney ever yielded, or is like to yield: and therewith we will quit Abbotsford and the dominant and culminant period of Scott's life:

" It was a clear, bright September morning, with a sharpness in the air that doubled the animating influence of the sunshine; and all was in readiness for a grand coursing match on Newark hill. The only guest who had chalked out other sport for himself was the stanchest of anglers, Mr Rose; but he too was there on his *shelty*, armed with his salmon-rod and landing-net, and attended by his Hinves, and Charlie Purdie, a brother of Tom, in those days the most celebrated fisherman of the district. This little group of Waltonians, bound for Lord Somerville's preserve, remained lounging about, to witness the start of the main cavalcade. Sir Walter, mounted on Sibyl, was marshalling the order of procession with a huge hunting-whip; and among a dozen frolicsome youths and maidens, who seemed disposed to laugh at all discipline, appeared, each on horseback, each as eager as the youngest sportsman in the troop, Sir Humphry Davy, Dr Wollaston, and the patriarch of Scottish *belles-lettres*, Henry Mackenzie. The Man of Feeling, however, was persuaded with some difficulty to resign his steed for the present to his faithful negro follower, and to join Lady Scott in the sociable, until we should reach the ground of our *battue*. Laidlaw, on a long-tailed wiry Highlander yclept *Hoddin Gray*, which carried him nimbly and stoutly, although his feet almost touched the ground as he sat, was adjutant. But the most picturesque figure was the illustrious inventor of the safety-lamp. He had come for his favourite sport of angling, and had been practising it successfully with Rose, his travelling companion, for two or three days preceding this; but he had not prepared for coursing fields, or had left Charlie Purdie's troop for Sir Walter's on a sudden thought; and his fisherman's costume, a brown hat with flexible brim, surrounded with line upon line of catgut, and innumerable fly-hooks; jackboots worthy of a Dutch smuggler, and a fustian surtout dabbled with the blood of salmon, made a fine contrast with the smart jackets, white-cord breeches, and well-polished jockey-boots of the less distinguished cavaliers about him. Dr Wollaston was in black, and with his noble serene dignity of countenance might have passed for a sporting archbishop. Mr Mackenzie, at this time in the seventy-sixth year of his age, with a white hat turned up with green, green spectacles, green jacket, and long brown leathern gaiters buttoned on his nether anatomy, wore a dog-whistle round his neck, and had, all over, the air of as resolute a devotee as the gay captain of Huntly Burn. Tom Purdie and his subalterns had preceded us by a few hours, with all the greyhounds that could be collected at Abbotsford, Darnick, and Melrose; but the giant Maida had remained as his master's orderly, and now gambolled about Sibyl Gray, barking for mere joy like a spaniel puppy.

"The order of march had been all settled, and the sociable was just getting under way, when *the Lady Anne* broke from the line, screaming with laughter, and exclaimed, ' Papa, papa, I knew you could never think of going without your pet.' Scott looked round, and I rather think there was a blush as well as a smile upon his face, when he perceived a little black pig frisking about his pony, and evidently a self-elected addition to the party of the day. He tried to look stern, and cracked his whip at the creature, but was in a moment obliged to join in the general cheers. Poor piggy soon found a strap round its neck, and was dragged into the background: Scott watching the retreat, repeated with mock pathos the first verse of an old pastoral song :—

' What will I do gin my hoggie die?
My joy, my pride, my hoggie!
My only beast, I had nae mae,
And wow but I was vogie!'

—the cheers were redoubled, and the squadron moved on.

"This pig had taken, nobody could tell how, a most sentimental attachment to Scott, and was constantly urging its pretensions to be admitted a regular member of his *tail* along with the greyhounds and terriers; but indeed I remember him suffering another summer under the same sort of pertinacity on the part of an affectionate hen. I leave the explanation for philosophers; but such were the facts. I have too much respect for the vulgarly calumniated donkey to name him in the same category of pets with the pig and the hen; but a year or two after this time, my wife used to drive a couple of these animals in a little garden-chair, and whenever her father appeared at the door of our cottage, we were sure to see Hannah More and Lady Morgan (as Anne Scott had wickedly christened them) trotting from their pasture, to lay their noses over the paling, and, as Washington Irving says of the old white-haired hedger with the Parisian snuff-box, ' to have a pleasant crack wi' the laird.'"—Vol. v, pp. 7—10.*

---

* On this subject let us report an anecdote furnished by a correspondent of our own, whose accuracy we can depend on :—" I myself was acquainted with a little Blenheim cocker, one of the smallest, beautifullest, and wisest of lap-dogs, or dogs, which, though Sir Walter knew it not, was very singular in its behaviour towards him. *Shandy,* so hight this remarkable cocker, was extremely shy of strangers: promenading on Princes street, which in fine weather used to be crowded in those days, he seemed to live in perpetual fear of being stolen; if any one but looked at him admiringly, he would draw back with angry timidity, and crouch towards his own lady-mistress. One

"There (at Chiefswood) my wife and I spent this summer and autumn of 1821,—the first of several seasons which will ever dwell on my memory as the happiest of my life. We were near enough Abbotsford to partake as often as we liked of its brilliant and constantly-varying society; yet could do so without being exposed to the worry and exhaustion of spirit which the daily reception of new comers entailed upon all the family except Sir Walter himself. But, in truth, even he was not always proof against the annoyances connected with such a style of open house-keeping. Even his temper sank sometimes under the solemn applauses of learned dulness, the vapid raptures of painted and perriwigged dowagers, the horse-leech avidity with which underbred foreigners urged their questions, and the pompous simpers of condescending magnates. When sore beset at home in this way, he would every now and then discover that he had some very particular business to attend to on an outlying part of his estate; and, craving the indulgence of his guests overnight, appear at the cabin in the glen before its inhabitants were astir in the morning. The clatter of Sibyl Gray's hoofs, the yelping of Mustard and Spice, and his own joyous shout of *reveillé* under our windows, were the signal that he had burst his toils, and meant for that day to "take his ease at his inn." On descending, he was to be found seated with all his dogs and curs about him, under a spreading ash that overshadowed half the bank between the

---

day a tall, irregular, busy-looking man came halting by; the little dog ran towards him, began fawning, frisking, licking at his feet: it was Sir Walter Scott! Had Shandy been the most extensive reader of Reviews, he could not have done better. Every time he saw Sir Walter afterwards, which was some three or four times in the course of visiting Edinburgh, he repeated his demonstrations, ran leaping, frisking, licking the Author of 'Waverley's' feet. The good Sir Walter endured it with good humour; looked down at the little wise face, at the silky shag-coat of snow-white and chesnut-brown; smiled, and avoided hitting him as they went on,— till a new division of streets or some other obstacle put an end to the interview. In fact, he was a strange little fellow this Shandy. He has been known to sit for hours looking out at the summer moon, with the saddest wistfullest expression of countenance; altogether like a Werterean Poet. He would have been a Poet, I dare say, if he could have found a *publisher*. But his moral tact was the most amazing. Without reason shown, without word spoken or act done, he took his likings and dislikings; unalterable; really almost unerring. His chief aversion, I should say, was to the genus *quack*, above all to the genus *acrid-quack*; these, though never so clear-starched, bland-smiling and beneficent, he absolutely would have no trade with. Their very sugar-cake was unavailing. He said with emphasis, as clearly as barking could say it: 'Acrid-quack, avaunt!' Would to Heaven many a prime minister and high person in authority had such an invaluable talent! On the whole, there is more in this universe than our philosophy has dreamt of. A dog's instinct is a voice of Nature too; and farther, *it* has never babbled itself away in idle jargon and hypothesis, but always adhered to the practical, and grown in silence by continual communion with fact. We do the animals injustice. Their body resembles our body, Buffon says; with its four limbs, with its spinal marrow, main organs in the head, and so forth: but have they not a kind of soul, equally the rude draught and imperfect imitation of ours? It is a strange, an almost solemn and pathetic thing to see an intelligence imprisoned in that dumb rude form; struggling to express itself out of that;—even as we do out of our imprisonment; and succeed very imperfectly!"

cottage and the brook, pointing the edge of his woodman's-axe, and listening to Tom Purdie's lecture touching the plantation that most needed thinning. After breakfast he would take possession of a dressing-room up stairs, and write a chapter of the 'Pirate;' and then, having made up and despatched his packet for Mr Ballantyne, away to join Purdie wherever the foresters were at work, and sometimes to labour among them as strenuously as John Swanston,— until it was time either to rejoin his own party at Abbotsford, or the quiet circle of the cottage. When his guests were few and friendly, he often made them come over and meet him at Chiefswood in a body towards evening; and surely he never appeared to more amiable ade vantage than when helping his young people with their littl- arrangements on such occasions. He was ready with all sorts of devices to supply the wants of a narrow establishment; he used to delight particularly in sinking the wine in a well under the *brae* ere he went out, and hauling up the basket just before dinner was announced; this primitive device being, he said, what he had always practised when a young housekeeper, and in his opinion far superior in its results to any application of ice: and in the same spirit, whenever the weather was sufficiently genial, he voted for dining out of doors altogether, which at once got rid of the inconvenience of very small rooms, and made it natural and easy for the gentlemen to help the ladies, so that the paucity of servants went for nothing."—Vol. v, pp. 123-4.

Surely all this is very beautiful; like a picture of Boccaccio: the ideal of a country life in our time. Why could it not last? Income was not wanting: Scott's official permanent income was amply adequate to meet the expense of all that was valuable in it; nay, of all that was not harassing, senseless, and despicable. Scott had some 2,000*l.* a year without writing books at all. Why should he manufacture and not create, to make more money; and rear mass on mass for a dwelling to himself, till the pile toppled, sank crashing, and buried him in its ruins, when he had a safe pleasant dwelling ready of its own accord? Alas, Scott, with all his health, was *infected;* sick of the fearfullest malady, that of Ambition! To such length had the King's baronetcy, the world's favour, and "sixteen parties a day," brought it with him. So the inane racket must be kept up, and rise ever higher. So masons labour, ditchers delve; and there is endless, altogether deplorable correspondence about marble-slabs for tables, wainscotting of rooms, curtains with the trimmings of curtains, orange-coloured or fawn-coloured: Walter Scott, one of the gifted of the world, whom his admirers called the most gifted, must kill himself that he may be a country gentleman, the founder of a race of Scotch lairds. It is one of the strangest, most tragical histories ever enacted under this sun. So poor a passion can lead so strong a man into such mad extremes. Surely, were not man a fool always, one might say there was something eminently distracted in this, *end* as it would, of a Walter Scott writing daily with the ardour of a steam-engine, that he might make 15,000*l.* a year, and buy upholstery with it. To cover the walls of a stone house in Selkirkshire with nicknacks, ancient armour, and genealogical shields, what can we name it but a being bit with delirium of a kind? That tract after tract of moorland in the shire of Selkirk should be joined together on parchment and by ring-fence, and named after one's name,—why, it is a shabby small-type edition of your vulgar Napoleons, Alexanders, and conquering heroes, not counted venerable by any teacher of men!—

"The whole world was not half so wide
To Alexander when he cried
Because he had but one to subdue,
As was a narrow paltry tub to
Diogenes; who ne'er was said,
For aught that ever I could read,
To whine, put finger i' the eye and sob,
Because he had ne'er another tub!"

Not he! And if, "looked at from the Moon, which itself is far from Infinitude," Napoleon's dominions were as small as mine, *what*, by any chance of possibility, could Abbotsford landed-property ever have become? As the Arabs say, there is a black speck, were it no bigger than a bean's eye, in every soul; which, once set it a-working, will overcloud the whole man into darkness and quasi-madness, and hurry him balefully into Night!

With respect to the literary character of these 'Waverley Novels,' so extraordinary in their commercial character, there remains, after so much reviewing, good and bad, little that it were profitable at present to say. The great fact about them is, that they were faster written and better paid for than any other books in the world. It must be granted, moreover, that they have a worth far surpassing what is usual in such cases; nay, that if literature had no task but that of harmlessly amusing indolent, languid men, here was the very perfection of literature; that a man, here more emphatically than ever elsewhere, might fling himself back, exclaiming, "Be mine to lie on this sofa, and read everlasting Novels of Walter Scott!" The composition, slight as it often is, usually hangs together in some measure, and *is* a composition. There is a free flow of narrative, of incident and sentiment; an easy master-like coherence throughout, as if it were the free dash of a master's hand, "round as the O of

Giotto."* It is the perfection of extemporaneous writing. Farthermore, surely he were a blind critic who did not recognise here a certain genial sunshiny freshness and picturesqueness; paintings both of scenery and figures, very graceful, brilliant, occasionally full of grace and glowing brightness blended in the softest composure; in fact, a deep sincere love of the beautiful in nature and man, and the readiest faculty of expressing this by imagination and by word. No fresher paintings of nature can be found than Scott's; hardly anywhere a wider sympathy with man. From Davie Deans up to Richard Cœur-de-Lion; from Meg Merrilies to Die Vernon and Queen Elizabeth! It is the utterance of a man of open soul; of a brave, large, free-seeing man, who has a true brotherhood with all men. In joyous picturesqueness and fellow-feeling, freedom of eye and heart; or to say it in a word, in general *healthiness* of mind, these novels prove Scott to have been amongst the foremost writers.

Neither in the higher and highest excellence, of drawing character, is he at any time altogether deficient; though at no time can we call him, in the best sense, successful. His Bailie Jarvies, Dinmonts, Dalgettys (for their name is legion) do look and talk like what they give themselves out for; they are, if not *created* and made poetically alive, yet deceptively *enacted* as a good player might do them. What more is wanted then? For the reader lying on a sofa, nothing more; yet for another sort of reader, much. It were a long chapter to unfold the difference in drawing a character between a Scott and a Shakspeare, a Goethe! Yet it is a difference literally immense; they are of different species; the value of the one is not to be counted in the coin of the other. We might say in a short word, which means a long matter, that your Shakspeare fashions his characters from the heart outwards; your Scott fashions them from the skin inwards, never getting near the heart of them! The one set became living men and women; the other amount to little more than mechanical cases, deceptively painted automatons. Compare Fenella with Goethe's Mignon, which it was once said, Scott had "done Goethe the honour" to borrow. He has borrowed what he

---

* " Venne a Firenze (il cortigiano del Papa), e andato una mattina in bottega di Giotto, che lavorava, gli chiese un poco di disegno per mandarlo a sua Santità. Giotto, che garbatissimo era, prese un foglio, ed in quello con un pennello tinto di rosso, fermato il braccio al fianco per farne compasso, e girato la mano fece un tondo sì pari di sesto e di profilo, che fu a vederlo una marairglia. Ciò fatto ghignando disse al cortigiano, Eccovi il disegno." . . . . " Onde il Papa, e molti cortigiani intendenti conobbero per ciò, quanto Giotto avanzasse d'eccelenza tutti gli altri pittori del suo tempo. Divolgatasi poi questa cosa, ne nacque il proverbio, che ancora è in uso dirsi a gli uomini di grossa pasta: *Tu sei più rondo, che l' O di Giotto.*"— Vasari, *Vite* (Roma, 1759), i. 46.

could of Mignon. The small stature, the climbing talent, the trickiness, the *mechanical case*, as we say, he has borrowed; but the soul of Mignon is left behind. Fenella is an unfavourable specimen for Scott; but it illustrates, in the aggravated state, what is traceable in all the characters he drew. To the same purport indeed we are to say that these famed books are altogether addressed to the every-day mind; that for any other mind, there is next to no nourishment in them. Opinions, emotions, principles, doubts, beliefs, beyond what the intelligent country gentleman can carry along with him, are not to be found. It is orderly, customary, it is prudent, decent; nothing more. One would say, it lay not in Scott to give much more : getting out of the ordinary range, and attempting the heroic, which is but seldom the case, he falls almost at once into the rose-pink sentimental,—descries the Minerva Press from afar, and hastily quits that course ; for none better than he knew it to lead nowhither. On the whole, contrasting Waverley, which was carefully written, with most of its followers, which were written extempore, one may regret the extempore method. Something very perfect in its kind might have come from Scott; nor was it a low kind: nay, who knows how high, with studious self-concentration, he might have gone; what wealth nature had implanted in him, which his circumstances, most unkind while seeming to be kindest, had never impelled him to unfold?

But after all, in the loudest blaring and trumpetting of popularity, it is ever to be held in mind, as a truth, remaining true for ever, that literature *has* other aims than that of harmlessly amusing indolent, languid men : or if literature have them not, then literature is a very poor affair; and something else must have them, and must accomplish them, with thanks or without thanks; the thankful or thankless world were not long a world otherwise ! Under this head, there is little to be sought or found in the ' Waverley Novels.' Not profitable for doctrine, for reproof, for edification, for building up or elevating, in any shape ! The sick heart will find no healing here, the darkly struggling heart no guidance : the Heroic that is in all men no divine awakening voice. We say, therefore, that they do not found themselves on deep interests, but on comparatively trivial ones, not on the perennial, perhaps not even on the lasting. In fact, much of the interest of these novels results from what may be called contrasts of costume. The phraseology, fashion of arms, of dress and life, belonging to one age, is brought suddenly, with singular vividness, before the eyes of another. A great effect this; yet by the very nature of it, an altogether temporary one. Consider, brethren, shall not we too one day be antiques, and grow to have as quaint a costume as the rest? The stuffed dandy, only give him *time*, will become one of the wonderfullest mummies. In antiquarian museums, only two centuries hence, the steeple-hat will hang on the next peg to Franks and Company's patent, antiquaries deciding which is uglier; and the Stulz swallow-tail, one may hope, will seem as incredible as any garment that ever made ridiculous the respectable back of man. Not by slashed breeches, steeple-hats, buff-belts, or antiquated speech, can romance heroes continue to interest us; but simply and solely, in the long run, by being men. Buff-belts and all manner of jerkins and costumes are transitory; man alone is perennial. He that has gone deeper into this than other men, will be remembred longer than they; he that has not, not. Tried under this category, Scott with his clear practical insight, joyous temper, and other sound faculties, is not to be accounted little,—among the ordinary circulating library heroes he might well pass for a demigod. Not little; yet neither is he great; there were greater, more than one or two, in his own age: among the great of all ages, one sees no likelihood of a place for him.

What then is the result of these Waverley romances? Are they to amuse one generation only? One or more. As many generations as they can, but not all generations: ah no, when our swallow-tail has become fantastic as trunk-hose, they will cease to amuse!—Meanwhile, as we can discern, their results have been several-fold. First of all, and certainly not least of all, have they not perhaps had this result: that a considerable portion of mankind has hereby been sated with mere amusement, and set on seeking something better? Amusement in the way of reading can go no farther, can do nothing better, by the power of man; and men ask, Is this what it can do? Scott, we reckon, carried several things to their ultimatum and crisis, so that change became inevitable: a great service, though an indirect one. Secondly, however, we may say, these historical novels have taught all men this truth, which looks like a truism, and yet was as good as unknown to writers of history and others, till so taught: that the bygone ages of the world were actually filled by living men, not by protocols, state-papers, controversies, and abstractions of men. Not abstractions were they, not diagrams and theorems; but men, in buff or other coats and breeches, with colour in their cheeks, with passions in their stomach, and the idioms, features, and vitalities of very men. It is a little word this; inclusive of great meaning! History will henceforth have to take thought of it. Her faint hearsays of "philosophy teaching by experience" will have to exchange themselves everywhere for direct inspection and imbodiment: this, and this only, will be counted experience; and till once experience have got in, philosophy will reconcile herself to wait at the door. It is a great service, fertile in consequences, this that Scott has done; a great truth laid open by him;—correspondent indeed to the substantial nature of the man; to his solidity and veracity even of imagination, which, with all his lively discursiveness, was the characteristic of him.

A word here as to the extempore style of writing, which is getting much celebrated in these days. Scott seems to have been a high proficient in it. His rapidity was extreme, and the matter produced was excellent considering that: the circumstances under which some of his novels, when he could not himself write, were dictated, are justly considered wonderful. It is a valuable faculty this of ready writing; nay farther, for Scott's purpose it was clearly the only good mode. By much labour he could not have added one guinea to his copyright; nor would the reader on the sofa have lain a whit more at ease. It was in all ways necessary that these works should be produced rapidly; and, round or not, be thrown off like Giotto's O. But indeed, in all things, writing or other, which a man engages in, there is the indispensablest beauty in knowing *how to get done.* A man frets himself to no purpose; he has not the sleight of the trade; he is not a craftsman, but an unfortunate borer and bungler, if he know not when to have done. Perfection is unattainable: no carpenter ever made a mathematically accurate right-angle in the world; yet all carpenters know when it is right enough, and do not botch it, and lose their wages by making it too right. Too much pains-taking speaks disease in one's mind, as well as too little. The adroit sound-minded man will endeavour to spend on each business approximately what of pains it deserves; and with a conscience void of remorse will dismiss it then. All this in favour of easy writing shall be granted, and, if need were, enforced and inculcated. And yet, on the other hand, it shall not less but more strenuously be inculcated, that in the way of writing no great thing was ever, or will ever be done with ease, but with difficulty! Let ready writers with any faculty in them, lay this to heart. Is it with ease, or not with ease, that a man shall *do his best*, in any shape; above all, in this shape, justly named of "soul's travail," working in the deep places of thought, embodying the true out of the obscure and possible, environed on all sides with the uncreated false? Not so, now or at any time. The experience of all men belies it; the nature of things contradicts it. Virgil and Tacitus, were they ready writers? The whole *Prophecies of Isaiah* are not equal in extent to this cobweb of a review article. Shakspeare we may fancy, wrote with rapidity; but not till he had thought with intensity: long and sore had this man thought, as the seeing eye may discern well, and had dwelt and wrestled amid dark pains and throes,—though his great soul is silent about all that. It was for him to write rapidly at fit intervals, being ready to do it. And herein truly lies the secret of the matter: such swiftness of mere writing, after due energy of preparation, is doubtless the right method; the hot furnace having long worked and simmered, let the pure gold flow out at one gush. It was Shakspeare's plan; no easy writer he, or he had never been a Shakspeare. Neither was Milton one of the mob of gentlemen that write with ease; he did not attain Shakspeare's faculty, one perceives, of even writing fast *after* long preparation, but struggled while he wrote. Goethe also tells us he " had nothing sent him in his sleep;" no page of his but he knew well how it came there. It is reckoned to be the best prose, accordingly, that has been written by any modern. Schiller, as an unfortunate unhealthy man, "*könnte nie fertig werden*, never could get done;" the noble genius of him struggled not wisely but too well, and wore his life itself heroically out. Or did Petrarch write easily? Dante sees himself "growing grey" over his *Divine Comedy;* in stern solitary death-wrestle with it, to prevail over it, and do it, if his uttermost faculty may: hence, too, it is done and prevailed over, and the fiery life of it endures for evermore among men. No: creation, one would think, cannot be easy; your Jove has severe pains and fire-flames in the head out of which an armed Pallas is struggling! As for manufacture, that is a different matter, and may become easy or not easy, according as it is taken up. Yet of manufacture too the general truth is that, given the manufacturer, it will be worthy in direct proportion to the pains bestowed on it; and worthless always, or nearly so, with no pains. Cease, therefore, O ready-writer, to brag openly of thy rapidity and facility; to thee (if thou be in the manufacturing line) it is a benefit, and increase of wages; but to me it is sheer loss, worsening of my pennyworth: why wilt thou brag of it to me? Write easily, by steam if thou canst contrive it, and canst sell it; but hide it like virtue! "Easy writing," said Sheridan, " is sometimes d——d hard reading." Sometimes; and always it is sure to be rather useless reading, which indeed (to a creature of few years and much work) may be reckoned the hardest of all.

Scott's productive facility amazed everybody; and set Captain Hall, for one, upon a very strange method of accounting for it without miracle;—for which see his 'Journal,' above quoted from. The Captain, on counting line for line, found that he himself had written in that journal of his almost as much as Scott, at odd hours in a given number of days; " and as for the invention," says he, " it is known that this costs Scott nothing, but comes to him of its own accord." Convenient indeed!—But for us too Scott's rapidity is great, is a proof and consequence of the solid health of the man, bodily and spiritual; great, but unmiraculous; not greater than that of many others besides Captain Hall. Admire it, yet with measure. For observe always, there are two conditions in work: let me fix the quality, and *you* shall fix the quantity! Any man may get through work rapidly who easily satisfies himself about it. Print the *talk* of any man, there will be a thick octavo volume daily; make his writing three times as good as his talk, there will be the third part of a volume daily, which still is good work. To write with never such rapidity in a passable manner is indicative not of a man's genius, but of his habits; it will prove his soundness of nervous system, his practicality of mind, and in fine, that he has the knack of his trade. In the most flattering view, rapidity will betoken health of mind; much also, perhaps most of all, will depend on health of body. Doubt it not, a faculty of easy writing is attainable by man! The human genius, once fairly set in this direction, will carry it far. William Cobbett, one of the healthiest of men, was a greater improviser even than Walter Scott: his writing, considered as to quality and quantity, of Rural Rides, Registers, Grammars, Sermons, Peter Porcupines, Histories of Reformation, ever-fresh denouncements of Potatoes and Paper-money,—seems to us still more wonderful. Pierre Bayle wrote enormous folios, one sees not on what motive-principle; he flowed on for ever, a mighty tide of ditch-water; and even died flowing, with the pen in his hand. But indeed the most unaccountable ready-writer of all is, probably, the common editor of a Daily Newspaper. Consider his leading-articles; what they treat of, how passably they are done. Straw that has been thrashed a hundred times without wheat; ephemeral sound of a sound; such portent of the hour as all men have seen a hundred times turn out inane: how a man, with merely human faculty, buckles himself nightly with new vigour and interest to this thrashed straw, nightly thrashes it anew, nightly gets up new thunder about it; and so goes on thrashing and thundering for a considerable series of years; this is a fact remaining still to be accounted for, in human physiology. The vitality of man is great.

Or shall we say, Scott, among the many things he carried towards their ultimatum and crisis, carried this of ready-writing too, that so all men might better see what was in it? It is a valuable consummation. Not without results;—results, at some of which Scott as a Tory politician would have greatly shuddered. For if once Printing have grown to be as Talk, then DEMOCRACY (if we will look into the roots of things) is not a bugbear and probability, but a certainty, and event as good as come! " Inevitable seems it me."—But leaving this, sure enough the triumph of ready-writing appears to be even now; everywhere the ready-writer is found bragging strangely of his readiness. In a lately translated ' Don Carlos,' one of the most indifferent translations ever done with any sign of ability, a hitherto unknown individual is found assuring his reader, " The reader will possibly think it an excuse when I assure him that the whole piece was completed within the space of ten weeks, that is to say, between the 6th of January and the 18th of March of this year (inclusive of a fortnight's interruption from over-exertion); that I often translated twenty pages a-day, and that the fifth act was the work of five days." * O hitherto unknown individual, what is it to me what time it was the work of, whether five days or five decades of years? The only question is, How hast thou done it?—So, however, it stands; the genius of Extempore irresistibly lording it, advancing on us like ocean-tides, like Noah's deluges—of ditch-water! The prospect seems one of the lamentablest. To have all Literature swum away from us in watery Extempore, and a spiritual time of Noah supervene? That surely is an awful reflection, worthy of dyspeptic Matthew Bramble in a London fog! Be of comfort, O splenetic Matthew; it is not Literature they are swimming away; it is only Book-publishing and Book-selling. Was there not a Literature *before* Printing or Faust of Mentz, and yet men wrote extempore? Nay, before Writing or Cadmus of Thebes, and yet men spoke extempore? Literature is the Thought of thinking Souls; this, by the blessing of God, can in no generation be swum away, but remains with us to the end.

Scott's career, of writing impromptu novels to buy farms with, was not of a kind to terminate voluntarily, but to accelerate itself more and more; and one sees not to what wise goal it could, in any case, have led him. Bookseller Constable's bankruptcy was not the ruin of Scott; his ruin was that ambition, and even false ambition, had laid hold of him; that his way of life was not wise. Whither could it lead? Where could it stop? New farms there remained ever to be bought, while new novels could pay for them. More and more success but gave more and more appetite, more and more audacity. The impromptu writing must have waxed ever thinner; declined faster and faster

---

* ' Don Carlos,' a Dramatic Poem, from the German of Schiller. Mannheim and London, 1837.

into the questionable category, into the condemnable, into the generally condemned. Already there existed, in secret, everywhere a considerable opposition party; witnesses of the Waverley miracles, but unable to believe in them, forced silently to protest against them. Such opposition party was in the sure case to grow; and even, with the impromptu process ever going on, ever waxing thinner, to draw the world over to it. Silent protest must at length have come to words; harsh truths, backed by harsher facts of a world-popularity overwrought and worn out, behoved to have been spoken;—such as can be spoken now without reluctance when they can pain the brave man's heart no more. Who knows? Perhaps it was better ordered to be all *otherwise.* Otherwise, at any rate, it was. One day the Constable mountain, which seemed to stand strong like the other rock-mountains, gave suddenly, as the icebergs do, a loud-sounding crack; suddenly, with huge clangour, shivered itself into ice-dust; and sank, carrying much along with it. In one day, Scott's high-heaped money-wages became fairy-money and nonentity; in one day the rich man and lord of land saw himself penniless, landless, a bankrupt among creditors.

It was a hard trial. He met it proudly, bravely,—like a brave proud man of the world. Perhaps there had been a prouder way still: to have owned honestly that he *was* unsuccessful then, all bankrupt, broken, in the world's goods and repute; and to have turned elsewhither for some refuge. Refuge did lie elsewhere; but it was not Scott's course, or fashion of mind, to seek it there. To say, Hitherto I have been all in the wrong, and this my fame and pride, now broken, was an empty delusion and spell of accursed witchcraft! It was difficult for flesh and blood! He said, I will retrieve myself, and make my point good yet, or die for it. Silently, like a proud strong man, he girt himself to the Hercules' task, of removing rubbish-mountains, since that was it; of paying large ransoms by what he could still write and sell. In his declining years too; misfortune is doubly and trebly unfortunate that befalls us then. Scott fell to his Hercules' task like a very man, and went on with it unweariedly; with a noble cheerfulness, while his life-strings were cracking, he grappled with it, and wrestled with it, years long, in death-grips, strength to strength;—and *it* proved the stronger; and his life and heart did crack and break: the cordage of a most strong heart! Over these last writings of Scott, his *Napoleons, Demonologies, Scotch Histories,* and the rest, criticism, finding still much to wonder at, much to commend, will utter no word of blame; this one word only, Woe is me! The noble warhorse that once laughed at the shaking of the spear, how is he doomed to toil himself dead, dragging ignoble wheels! Scott's descent was like that of a spent projectile; rapid, straight down;—perhaps mercifully so. It is a tragedy, as all life is; one proof more that Fortune stands on a restless *globe;* that Ambition, literary, warlike, politic, pecuniary, never yet profited any man.

Our last extract shall be from Volume Sixth; a very tragical one. Tragical, yet still beautiful; waste Ruin's havoc borrowing a kind of sacredness from a yet sterner visitation, that of Death! Scott has withdrawn into a solitary lodging-house in Edinburgh, to do daily the day's work there; and had to leave his wife at Abbotsford in the last stage of disease. He went away silently; looked silently at the sleeping face he scarcely hoped ever to see again. We quote from a Diary he had begun to keep in those months, a hint from Byron's *Ravenna Journal:* copious sections of it render this sixth volume more interesting than any of the former ones :—

"*May* 11 (1826).— * * It withers my heart to think of it, and to recollect that I can hardly hope again to seek confidence and counsel from that ear, to which all might be safely confided. But in her present lethargic state, what would my attendance have availed,—and Anne has promised close and constant intelligence. I must dine with James Ballantyne to-day *en famille.* I cannot help it; but would rather be at home and alone. However, I can go out too. I will not yield to the barren sense of hopelessness that struggles to invade me.

"*Edinburgh, Mrs Brown's lodgings, North St David street, May* 12.—I passed a pleasant day with kind J. B., which was a great relief from the black dog, which would have worried me at home. He was quite alone.

"Well, here I am in Arden. And I may saw with *Touchstone,* 'when I was at home I was in a better place.' I must, when there is occasion, draw to my own Bailie Nicol Jarvie's consolation, 'One cannot carry the comforts of the Saut-Market about with one.' Were I at ease in mind, I think the body is very well cared for. Only one other lodger in the house, a Mr Shandy,—a clergyman; and despite his name, said to be a quiet one.

"*May* 14.—A fair good-morrow to you, Mr Sun, who are shining so brightly on these dull walls. Methinks you look as if you were looking as bright on the banks of the Tweed; but look where you will. Sir Sun, you look upon sorrow and suffering. Hogg was here yesterday; in danger, from having obtained an accommodation of 100*l.* from James Ballantyne, which he is now obliged to repay. I am unable to help the poor fellow; being obliged to borrow myself.

"*May* 15.—Received the melancholy intelligence that all is over at Abbotsford.

"*Abbotsford, May* 16.—She died at nine in the morning, after being very ill for two days; easy at last. I arrived here late last night. Anne is worn out, and has had hysterics, which returned on my arrival. Her broken accents were like those of a child, the language as well as the tones broken, but in the most gentle voice of submission. 'Poor mamma—never return again—gone for ever—a better place.' Then, when she came to herself, she spoke with sense, freedom, and strength of mind, till her weakness returned. It would have been inexpressibly moving to me as a stranger: what was it then to the father and the husband? For myself I scarce know how I feel; sometimes as firm as the Bass Rock, sometimes as weak as the water that breaks on it. I am as alert at thinking and deciding as I ever was in my life. Yet, when I contrast what this place now is with what it has been not long since, I think my heart will break. Lonely, aged, deprived of my family, all but poor Anne; an impoverished, an embarrassed man, deprived of the sharer of my thoughts and counsels, who could always talk down my sense of the calamitous apprehensions which break the heart that must bear them alone. Even her foibles were of service to me, by giving me things to think of beyond my own weary self-reflections.

"I have seen her. The figure I beheld is, and is not my Charlotte, my thirty-years' companion. There is the same symmetry of form, though those limbs are rigid which were once so gracefully elastic;— but that yellow mask, with pinched features, which seems to mock life rather than emulate it, can it be the face that was once so full of lively expression? I will not look on it again. Anne thinks her little changed; because the latest idea she had formed of her mother is as she appeared under circumstances of extreme pain. Mine go back to a period of comparative ease. If I write long in this way, I shall write down my resolution, which I should rather write up if I could."

"*May* 18.— * * Cerements of lead and of wood already hold her; cold earth must have her soon. But it is not my Charlotte, it is not the bride of my youth, the mother of my children, that will be laid in the ruins of Dryburgh, which we have so often visited in gaiety and pastime. No, no."

"*May* 22.— * * Well, I am not apt to shrink from that which is my duty, merely because it is painful; but I wish this funeral-day over. A kind of cloud of stupidity hangs about me, as if all were unreal that men seem to be doing and talking."

"*May* 26.— * * Were an enemy coming upon my house, would I not do my best to fight, although oppressed in spirits; and shall a similar despondency prevent me from mental exertion? It shall not, by heaven!"

"*Edinburgh, May* 30.—Returned to town last night with Charles. This morning resume ordinary habits of rising early, working in the morning, and attending the Court. * * I finished correcting the proofs for the 'Quarterly;' it is but a flimsy article, but then the circumstances were most untoward.—This has been a melancholy day, most melancholy. I am afraid poor Charles found me weeping. I do not know what other folks feel, but with me the hysterical passion that impels tears is a terrible violence; a sort of throttling sensation; then succeeded by a state of dreaming stupidity, in which I ask if my poor Charlotte can actually be dead."—Vol. vi, pp. 297—307.

This is beautiful as well as tragical. Other scenes, in that Seventh Volume, must come, which will have no beauty, but be tragical only. It is better that we are to end here.

And so the curtain falls; and the strong Walter Scott is with us no more. A possession from him does remain; widely scattered; yet attainable; not inconsiderable. It can be said of him, "when he departed he took a Man's life along with him." No sounder piece of British manhood was put together in that eighteenth century of time. Alas, his fine Scotch face, with its shaggy honesty, sagacity and goodness, when we saw it latterly on the Edinburgh streets, was all worn with care, the joy all fled from it;—ploughed deep with labour and sorrow. We shall never forget it; we shall never see it again. Adieu, Sir Walter, pride of all Scotchmen, take our proud and sad farewell.

Carlyle.

ART. III.—*On Warming and Ventilating: with Directions for making and using the Thermometer Stove, or Self-Regulating Fire, and other new Apparatus.* By Neil Arnott, M.D., Physician Extraordinary to the Queen, Author of 'Elements of Physics.' Longman, 1838.

TO be ignorant is to be helpless. The man who knows, is able to free himself from natural physical miseries in proportion as he knows; while he who knows not, must (unless his neighbours help him) endure them in proportion to the amount of his ignorance. And this is a most hopeful condition of human existence, for it teaches us that the time may come when physical misery shall cease to exist. In the present condition of society, the greatest benefactors of the human race are those who labour most effectively at the extinction of physical misery, for until then we can scarcely hope for much further moral progress.

Food, clothes, lodging, and fuel—in other words, food and warmth, are our strongest necessities; and, in climates like that we dwell in, artificial warmth is nearly as essential as food—nay,

HINTS FOR BIOGRAPHERS.

POPE—SCOTT AND ABBOTSFORD—DR. JOHNSON—JAMES MACPHERSON—BYRON—BURNS—CANNING—SIR JAMES MACKINTOSH—SIR FRANCIS CHANTREY—THE WITCHES OF MACBETH—NICHOLAS FERRAR.

> " So holy and so perfect is my love,
> That I shall think it a most plenteous crop
> To glean the broken ears after the man
> That the main harvest reaps—loose now and then
> A scattered smile."—SHAKSPEARE.

POPE.

IN the library of the late Earl of Carysfort, a nobleman of literary taste and acquirements, there was a full-length portrait of Pope, by Jervas, which had been presented by the poet to his friend Mr. Cleland, an ancestor of Lord Carysfort. At the time we saw the portrait, the earl mentioned that he was in possession of a curious and characteristic letter which Pope had written to Cleland, accompanying the present of the portrait. We mention this, as a hint to future biographers and commentators. The present Earl of Carysfort is, unfortunately, in a state of mind which precludes any application to him; but such a document is too precious to be suffered to fall into what Jeremy Taylor calls " the portion of weeds and outworn things." In the noble lord's library at this time (1828), there was a fine copy of the quarto edition of Pope's *Homer,* inscribed, in the neat and classically distinct handwriting of the poet, on a blank leaf, in the following terms:—

" Mr. Cleland, who reads all other books, will please read this, from his affectionate friend,   A. POPE."

In this brief private inscription we may trace " the fine Roman hand," the terse expression, and elegant flattery of Pope. The world has seen no such courtly and accomplished poet since Augustus received the praises of Horace and Virgil. Whether coquetting with ministers of state, peers, or ladies,—with Swift, or Gay, or Arbuthnot,—with plain Martha Blount or the charming Lady Mary Wortley, Pope is always the same easy, delicate, self-possessed, and delightful man of genius. We leave the critics to adjudicate on his pretensions as a poet of the first order. Be ours to read his strains spring, summer, and winter, as a chart of life, with its streams and wanderings, " its fluctuations and its vast concerns."

" I would give many a sugar-cane
Monk Lewis were alive again."

So said Byron; and Scott added, " I would pay my share." Neither of them had sugar-canes to give; they were planters of a different order. With equal liberality, therefore, we would give the half of *Don Juan,* and the whole of *Marino Faliero,* to have sat with Pope at one of his oyster-suppers, or to have heard him read aloud his *Eloisa, currente calamo,* on a summer noon, in his garden at Twickenham!

SCOTT AND ABBOTSFORD.

In a late publication, it is calculated that the present estate of Abbotsford, which scarcely brings in 700*l.* a-year, must have cost Sir Walter Scott 50,000*l.* If we are to believe the shrewd people about Melrose, the cost was, indeed, enormous. Here are the separate purchases:—

	£.
Abbotsford, or Cartley-hole....	4,000
Kaeside	4,100
Outfield of Toftfield	6,000
Toftfield and Parks	10,000
Abbotslee	5,000
Field at Langside	500
Shearing Flat................	3,500
Broomielees	4,200
Short Acres and Scrabtree Park	700
Planting, draining, &c.........	5,000
House and garden	30,000
	71,000

The two last-mentioned items must, of course, be partly conjectural; but we believe they are founded on correct and minute calculations. And what a gigantic scheme of personal ambition, rashness, heedless profusion, and *literary* resources, does the whole unfold! "Was ever poet so trusted before?" exclaimed Johnson, when poor Goldsmith died 200*l.* in debt. Goldsmith lived in costermonger times compared with the present. Even Shenstone, building, and planting, and forming his vistas and alcoves, at Leasowes, was nothing to Scott. The latter was, indeed, the great magician. He was in his nature an humble and happy man;

"The lowliest duties on himself did lay."

This foible of being a rural squire, or baron, with a castle for his residence, and scores of workmen and dependents about him,— saying to one, Do this, and he doeth it, and to another, Come, and he cometh, was his only weakness. "Behold," said he one morning, as the sun shone on his lands and plantations, " I crossed the Tweed with my staff in my hand, and now I am become a great nation."

Mr. Lockhart is at fault respecting the original of Dandie Dinmont. Mr. James Davidson, a tenant of Lord Douglas, is said to be the prototype of honest Dandie, because he was a strong, blunt yeoman, and the owner of a family of terriers named Pepper and Mustard. Sir Walter Scott said he had never met Davidson when he *formed the character; and that if he had any south-country farmer in his eye more than another, it was Mr. Robert Elliott, of Whitehouse.* The first hill fox-hunt that Sir Walter ever witnessed was at Blackhouse (occupied by Mr. William Laidlaw's father), in company with Mr. Skene, of Rubislaw, in the year 1806.

Sir Walter Scott states, that an English lady of high rank and fashion, being desirous to possess a brace of the celebrated Mustard and Pepper terriers, expressed her wishes in a letter, which was literally addressed, "Mr. Dandie Dinmont;" under which very general direction it reached Mr. Davidson, who was justly proud of the application, and failed not to comply with a request which did him and his favourite attendants so much honour. This lady was the late Lady Castlereagh, afterwards Marchioness of Londonderry.

DR. JOHNSON.

The prejudice which Johnson suffered himself to entertain against Scotsmen was sufficiently illiberal and unjust; it was a canker that clung to his noble mind, not a poison that penetrated to the core, and corrupted the stream of his affections. With all his errors and infirmities, the great lexicographer had a warm and generous heart, even towards Scotsmen; and the following anecdote, which we give on the authority of a highly respectable clergyman, now "passing rich" in an humble living in Argyleshire, tends to prove the truth of Goldsmith's remark, that there was nothing of the bear about Johnson but the skin. A young man, a native of the Isle of Skye, and tutor in a family there, shortly after the period of Dr. Johnson's visit, conceived the ambitious project of proceeding to London, to try his fortune in the world of letters. He applied to his employer, Mr. Macdonald, for an introduction to the English moralist, whose temporary sojourn in the Hebrides had caused a sensation that is even yet vividly remembered by a few of the aged inhabitants. The laird was not a little surprised at the request of the dominie, and assured him, that if even he himself were to think of visiting Dr. Johnson, he would consider it necessary first to apply for an introduction: the doctor had only spent a day or two with him, and this is a measure of hospitality and friendship which a Highlander thinks himself bound to bestow upon every stranger. Nothing daunted, however, the youth proceeded to London, and waited upon Johnson in his well-known residence, Bolt Court, Fleet Street. He was received with great kindness; and, after numerous inquiries about his Highland friends, including the chivalrous Flora Macdonald, the doctor promised to do something for the adventurer. The latter wished to obtain employment as classical teacher in some academy; but a slight examination convinced his patron that he was unfit for such an office. In a few days, however, he procured for him a situation as clerk in the extensive brewery of Mr. Thrale, with a salary of 100*l*. per annum. The doctor had the young man frequently at his lodgings, and employed him to read to his blind old friend, Mrs. Williams. In this situation our Skye friend continued some years; but at length ambition, or a love of novelty, revived the vagrant propensity in his mind, and he expressed a wish to leave the service of Mr. Thrale, in order to repair to India. Dr. Johnson dissuaded him from the wild project, and obtained an addition of 50*l*. per annum to his salary. This reconciled the Highlander for a time; but on the lamented death of Dr. Johnson, his desire of visiting the East returned upon him so strongly, that he enlisted in the East India Company's service as a private soldier. He went abroad, fought with the characteristic bravery of his countrymen, and at length returned to his native isle comparatively rich. But such, alas! is the uncertain tenure of human happiness, in a few years he became insane, and expired in a madhouse!

The latest of Dr. Johnson's friends in the Highlands, who had shared the familiar converse of the English moralist during his memorable journey, in 1773, was the Rev. Mr. Grant, minister of Calder, who died in June 1828. Mr. Grant was formerly incumbent of the neighbouring parish of Daviot; and on Johnson's staying for a night at the manse, or parsonage, of Calder, " the intelligent and well-bred minister of Daviot," as Boswell designates Mr. Grant, attended, and assisted with his conversation. On the Sunday following, Johnson was in Inverness; and Mr. Grant, accompanied by the collector of excise, supped with him at the inn. Johnson was in high spirits. They had roasted kid for supper; the cookery was excellent; the landlord attentive; Boswell, as usual, obsequious as a courtier; and all was " nods, and becks, and wreathed smiles" with the philosopher and his friends. In the course of conversation, Johnson happened to mention that Mr. (afterwards Sir Joseph) Banks had, in his travels, discovered an extraordinary animal, called the kangaroo. He described its motions and appearance; he stood erect, put out his hands like feelers, and gathering up the tails of his huge brown coat so as to resemble the pouch of the animal, made two or three vigorous bounds across the room. The company stared; and Mr. Grant used to say, that nothing could be more ludicrous than the appearance of a tall, heavy, grave-looking man like Dr. Johnson standing up to mimic the shape and motions of a kangaroo. " Sir," said he to the minister, in high glee, and in his lofty *bow-wow* manner, " it is a wonderful animal!" " Wonderful, indeed!" rejoined the minister of Daviot, casting a sly glance at the uncouth imitator; while Boswell and the collector were vainly trying to preserve their gravity. The whole scene would form an admirable subject for Cruikshank.

The following is a good specimen of pompous inanity. When Johnson visited the seat of Sir Alexander Macdonald (afterwards Lord Macdonald), at Armadale, in Skye, the chief, though a cold Highlander, greeted his distinguished visitor with a copy of Latin verses,—" little better than the nonsense verses of a schoolboy," as Mr. Croker justly designates them, which may be found in Boswell. Sir Alexander sent a copy of the stanzas to Macpherson, the translator of Ossian, with the following amusing epistle. Little did the vainglorious head of the Macdonalds conceive how deadly was the hatred that was then brewing betwixt his correspondent and the object of his eulogium!

"*London, June 5, 1774.*

" Sir,—The annexed congratulatory ode was written and presented by me to Mr. Samuel Johnson, the day of his arriving at my house. I had assembled some of my friends to welcome him when he landed. From my windows he viewed the ocean. He trembled for the distress of the small boats which were fishing, and likely to be overwhelmed in the gulf,—a sight unusual to him, a station frequently experienced by them. I wish my time and my abilities had been such as to have permitted and enabled me to have conducted and placed you on the right hand of Fingal, when we trod the hallowed mansions of the hero. A sketch drawn by me is unworthy of your acceptance (whose genius is above my capacity), and unnecessary, as your pencil has already made our every sense of feeling to catch the fire, and glow with the warmth of perfection!

"I am, with the greatest pride in ranking myself amid your admirers, dear sir, your most humble servant,
"ALEXANDER MACDONALD.
"To James Macpherson, Esq., London."

JAMES MACPHERSON.
Translator of Ossian.

Having cited the name of Macpherson, we may state a few particulars, gleaned in the course of a day — one of the *dies notandi* on which we delight to look back — spent on the banks of the Spey with Sir David Brewster, the distinguished son-in-law of Macpherson. The poet left a mass of manuscripts and correspondence behind him. Part of these his executors lent to Sir Nathaniel Wraxall, who made use of them in his *Historical Memoirs;* and in this way, through negligence, many valuable papers were lost. There is not a line existing among the manuscripts to throw any light on the Ossianic controversy. Macpherson left a sum of 1000*l.* for the purpose of completing a translation of Ossian into Gaelic; and this subject appears to have engaged his attention in the latter years of his life. Various notes passed between him and his friend Mr. Mackenzie, of the Temple, appointing meetings in London and its vicinity, to enjoy what they termed "a dish of Gaelic." The turmoil of politics and party warfare, added to the labour of historical compilation, would seem to have withdrawn the translator of Ossian in a great degree from service to the Muses. It is not known that Macpherson was the *Scævola* of Junius, whom he also attacked under a dozen of other signatures, in defence of the ministry of the day. He wrote an answer to Junius's celebrated letter to the king, which, from its high-sounding, ornate, and polished periods, was ascribed to Gibbon. The acrimonious controversy with Johnson irritated him extremely; and there are many coarse epigrams, lampoons, and parodies among his unpublished papers, in which the great moralist is treated very unceremoniously. Macpherson's genius was at all times an overmatch for his taste, and his principles were liable to be overpowered by the impulse of the moment. His returning good sense, or right feeling, however, prevented the publication of such effusions, which appear to have been thrown aside when the fit was off. The following lines are worthy of preservation. Macpherson was mediocre enough when he had not the groundwork of Ossian to build upon; yet this stanza has a portion of classic elegance, as well as warmth, with a touch of the polished diction of Gray. It is indorsed on the back, "First Stanza of an Address to Venus—1785."

" Thrice blest, and more than thrice, the morn
Whose genial gale and purple light
Awaked, then chased the night
On which the Queen of Love was born!
Yet hence the sun's unhallow'd ray—
With native beams let beauty glow;
What need is there of other day
Than the twin-stars that light those hills of snow?"

James Macpherson was a remarkable man; in some respects not of "most blessed conditions," yet full of lofty aspirings, true genius, and certainly of marvellous success. The publication of *Ossian* formed an era in the history of British literature. We ridicule it now as a sort of spurious coin, a copper-gilt *rifaccimento* of the antique. The poems were not so thought of in their day. Read what Gray says of the "Celtic fragments," which so powerfully caught his imagination. David Hume, too, pored over them as a precious bequest to these later days. But David, who wrote his history on a sofa (not much of a "task" to him), could never rise to the region of poetical imagination; he thought Shakspeare somewhat of a barbarian, and therefore we do not place much faith in his critical judgments. But James Macpherson's *Ossian* was the Scott or Byron of his day — a new day to the blind, old, Celtic bard, when he was chanted in hall and boudoir, and in the sunny regions of the south, so different from his stern mountain solitude in Glen-Almond, where

" He sang of battles, and the breath
Of stormy war and violent death."

Thus sings Wordsworth, a confirmed worshipper; and who will gainsay the great Pan of the wild woodlands, rocks, and lakes? Napoleon, too, carried *Ossian* about with him even in the camp. It is true he wrote the bard's name *Ocean*, but Sheridan could not spell, the Duke of Marlborough was not over correct (as, for example, " pictars" for pictures); and the man who is imbued with a taste for *orthoepy*, may afford occasionally to despise *orthography*. The poetical schoolmaster of Badenoch became a Napoleon among authors, overturning old dynasties, and erecting in their stead the rude produce of moor and mountain, glen and stream. Fragments of Celtic song, which had cheered the firesides of cottars in their lonely huts, when winter nights were long and dark, were suddenly elevated into a rivalship with Homer and Shakspeare. A thousand pens were at work inditing dissertations and criticisms; even Johnson was moved to leave Bolt Court, and forego the Mitre Tavern and the club, to travel to the Hebrides — in quest of *Ossian*, and in search of trees! Abroad, the poems were translated into various languages, and found admirers among all classes. James Macpherson's fortune was made: he rose like an aeronaut. He got public appointments, sat in parliament, served the Nabob of Arcot; and, in so doing, served himself. Finally, after attaining honour and riches, he retired to his native mountains, built a splendid mansion (designed by the Adelphi Adams) among the scenes where, in lowly life, he first felt the aspirations of genius, and laboured to improve the condition of his countrymen, the broken and dispersed Gael. We were once ferried over the Spey by an old gray-headed Celt—a capital head for Caravaggio—who had, forty years before, done the same duty for Macpherson on his return to Scotland. The poet was a great man from London and the court, bedizened with rings, gold seals, and furs; but he looked with a moistened eye on the turf school-house in which he had once taught Gaelic, and on the hills on which he had run barefoot: they were then his own property, purchased with his own proper monies; and he told the ferryman, with strong emotion, and no doubt with Highland pride, that he would make every poor Highlander on his estate a comfortable and a happy man! We have always thought more of Macpherson since.

BYRON.

The following instance of spontaneous and flattering homage to genius is worth noting. In 1815, Byron visited Cambridge at the time when the university confers its degrees; and, attracted by a kindred feeling, as well perhaps as by a love of display, the poet, accompanied by the late Dr. Clarke, went to the senate-house to be a spectator of the interesting scene. After remaining a few minutes under the gallery, Lord Byron proceeded to the other end of the room (the senate-house is a noble hall, lofty and spacious, but externally its Grecian architecture harmonises ill with the colleges) in order to address the vice-chancellor. He had only gone a few paces on the marble floor, when he was recognised by the sons of Alma Mater in the gallery, and immediately a chorus of voices repeated aloud simultaneously, the two well-known opening lines of the *Bride of Abydos*:

" Know ye the land where the cypress
and myrtle
Are emblems of deeds that are done in
their clime ?"

Lord Byron stopped and smiled, but the vice-chancellor rebuked the breach of collegiate discipline and decorum. " I know not what possessed us," said a man of Trinity, whom we heard relate the circumstance; " but it was a sort of free-masonry feeling — we could not restrain ourselves."

BURNS.

Little traits of character and feeling are worth preserving, even of humbler men than Burns. We were much gratified, on visiting Ellisland, in Dumfrieshire, where the poet lived, to find on one of the windows of his house, written with a diamond, in his bold, upright hand, his own name and that of his wife, and their initials, traced in various shapes; the " R. B.'s" and

"J. B.'s" interlacing and circling each other. He has also inscribed on one pane of glass, with a playful alteration, the line of Pope:—

"*An honest woman's the noblest work of God.*"

The coming events in the poet's life had not then cast their dark shadow before. Fortune seemed to smile on him, by the rocky banks and hermit groves of the Nith. His ambition was satisfied; his marriage had gratified his feelings of love and honour; his heart and affections were at rest, throned, as it were, in a centre of light. His "fancies and good-nights" were then all innocent and happy, the overflowings of a buoyant and delighted spirit. It was the Sabbath of his days, soon to be clouded and overcast, and never to be restored.

When Cromek was in Scotland, collecting the fragments of prose and verse left by Burns, and which he afterwards published, he applied to Mr. Allan Cunningham to assist him in procuring some visible and tangible relic of the poet, which he might preserve among the *lares* and *penates* of his London home. "Honest Allan," as fond of a joke as of a song or a bust, took him to the bed of the river Nith, by Ellisland; and, pointing to a large stone, "a boulder," as the geologists would say, observed, "There is the stone with which Burns used to press his cheese!" The relic-hunting Southron gravely proposed to convey it to London.

When Burns visited Atholl in 1787, he was hospitably entertained by the late duke, at his princely castle. One of the party who met the poet on this occasion was Dr. Baird, the venerable Principal of the University of Edinburgh, lately deceased. Burns was accompanied by William Nicol of the High School; his wild and witty, but, we fear, worthless friend. While Burns was partaking of the refined hospitalities of the ducal mansion, Nicol was sitting sulkily at the inn (he had previously refused to go to the castle), and he at length addressed a note to the poet, stating he would proceed on his journey without him. "No," said his grace, as he glanced over the billet handed to him by Burns, "you shall wait with us to-morrow, and have another bowl of Atholl brose." The duke then sent one of his coachmen to the inn *to cut the chaise-harness of the travellers* with as little mercy as he chose to exercise. Nicol again wrote, and Burns answered, "None ought to visit the Highlands, but disciples of the Man of Uz." Nicol had no such patience, and, in a few minutes, he was at the door of the inn with his portmanteau in his hand, swearing and looking unutterable things. But he could not proceed; the harness was in shreds and patches, and a saddler had to be sent for. At this juncture the duke and Burns arrived, and the enraged dominie was persuaded to go with them to the castle. Here the good wine and the affable manners of his Grace of Atholl, joined to the sorcery of Burns's conversation, banished for a time the demon of discord.

CANNING.

We once heard Mr. Charles Grant, the present Lord Glenelg, say that when he took leave of Canning, previous to the intended departure of the latter as Governor-General of India, Canning remarked, in his quiet, emphatic manner, "When I come back to England, seven years hence, I shall find Parliamentary Reform carried." How does this square with the conjectures of Wilberforce and Brougham as to the course Canning was likely to have pursued, had he lived into the days of William IV.?

SIR JAMES MACKINTOSH.

In the biographies of Mackintosh, there is nothing said of his occasional fits of absence, which used to amuse his friends excessively. One of his Highland relations, a lady, once told us that, at a family dinner one day, Lady Mackintosh put two knives beside his plate, instead of a knife and fork, being sure that he would not, for some time, discover the difference. The bait took: after soup, Sir James commenced upon his beef, and had proceeded a few minutes before he observed that he was using a knife, instead of a fork. He laughed heartily at this practical joke. The same lady informed us, that on Mackintosh's arrival in London, his friends in the north being all loyalists or Jacobites, were so disgusted with his democratical opinions and writings, that they ceased to interest themselves in his fortunes. They lost sight of him for several years, she said, being ashamed of him! Of course, they afterwards abated of this Highland pride and jealousy, but they never forgave him for selling his small patrimonial inheritance. As Mackintosh drew to the grave, the Highlander revived within him, and he expressed a strong anxiety about his family pedigree, and the history of his clan. We have seen some letters from him on these points, curiously minute and expressive. There is a theory sported by the late Sir John Sinclair, and unmercifully quizzed by Jeffrey in the high and palmy days of the Blue and Yellow, that a man generally takes his talents and dispositions from his mother. Sir James Mackintosh's mother was a clever woman of American origin! This would have been a good stone for the old baronet to have pelted at the Reviewers. The *Vindiciæ Gallicæ* would at once have stood explained, if not justified.

SIR FRANCIS CHANTREY.

Chantrey's first bust was one of Horne Tooke, a warm friend to the sculptor in his early days. His second was Sir Francis Burdett; and his third, Major Cartwright. "If you do not get *six* Tories to sit to you," said Tooke, "as a set-off to the *three* Reformers, you will be ruined as a professional man!" The sculptor, whose sympathies are all for art and nature, not for politics, immediately set about realising the idea of his mentor. With what success have his labours been crowned? And his manners still as unassuming, his Derbyshire heart and tongue still as unsophisticated, as when his ambition reached no higher than that of a country farmer. A finer picture of genius, united to simplicity and overflowing kindness of heart and affections, never emanated from the great mould of Nature. His appearance corresponds with his character. His full, round figure, his cheerful, ruddy complexion, fine eye and forehead (he is bald, which, as in the case of Lawrence, heightens the effect), all speak of the happy-tempered, easy-minded, benevolent man. We are not sure that he is not quite as fond of angling by the side of a good fly-fishing river, as of labouring in Pimlico at clay or marble —*rudis indigestaque moles*, which he transforms into such breathing life and beauty. Moore was travelling with Chantrey in Italy when he visited Byron, and obtained from the noble poet his celebrated autobiography, which he afterwards destroyed. They conned over the stray leaves in their carriage as they returned homewards, but there was not much in them. In truth, Byron had very little to tell that was not previously known; and the world lost little, though Moore lost much, by his holocaust at the shrine of public decency and virtue.

The Sheffield Radical poet, Ebenezer Elliot, has some vigorous and picturesque lines, descriptive of Chantrey's early obscurity and native genius:—

" The worm came up to drink the welcome shower;
The red-breast quaff'd the rain-drop in the bower;
The flaskering duck through freshen'd lilies swam;
The bright roach took the fly below the dam;
Ramp'd the glad colt, and cropp'd the pensile spray;
No more in dust uprose the sultry way;
The lark was in the cloud; the woodbine hung
More sweetly o'er the chaffinch while he sung;
And the wild rose, from every dripping bush,
Beheld on silvery Sheaf the mirror'd blush;
When calmly seated on his pannier'd ass,
Where travellers hear the steel hiss as they pass,
A milkboy, sheltering from the transient storm,
Chalked on the grinder's wall an infant's form:
Young Chantrey smiled; no critic praised or blamed;
And golden promise smiled, and thus exclaimed:
' Go child of genius! rich be thine increase;
Go — be the Phidias of the second Greece.'"

THE WITCHES OF MACBETH.

" *How far is't called to Forres?* So solemnly repeated Johnson, when, with his *fidus Achates*, the Laird of Auchinleck, he drove over the heath where Macbeth did *not* meet the witches. They had mistaken the spot, and expended their enthusiasm some dozen leagues away.* " *How far is't called*

---

* See a note in Croker's excellent edition of Boswell.

to *Forres?*" we repeated yesterday on the self-same spot where, if tradition may be in aught believed, the memorable rencounter took place. The sun shone brightly over the level moor, and the little clump of pines, and not another " inhabitant o' the earth " was in sight. It is a dreary place, and looks, as Robert Hall said of the vicinity of Cambridge, like nature *laid out.* The heath is situated a little to the west of the town of Forres, and is still the same sterile moor that it was in the days of the gracious Duncan — undistinguished by aught save its wide, black expanse of moss and heather; and undisturbed, except by the sportsman's gun, or the rattling of the stagecoach that winds along the road, now intersecting its monotonous surface. A small knoll is pointed out under the name of " Macbeth's hillock," as the place where the Thane was accosted by the Weird Sisters. The latter have not faded away altogether into thin air. They have not buried their book, like Prospero, or disappeared like Michael Scott, after he had cloven the Eildon Hills in twain. Circumstances have occurred which induce a suspicion that they still " round about the caldron go," and evince their predilection for the blasted heath, in contempt of Picturesque Price, and Sir Henry Steuart of Allanton. Far back in the abyss of time, two of the hags are said to have been tried and convicted at Forres, and condemned to be rolled in barrels, provided with sharp iron spikes, from the top of Cluny, a high hill in the immediate vicinity of the town. The sentence was duly executed, and the lacerated bodies of the witches were interred on the road-side east of Forres, where two gigantic stones, called " The Witch Stones," mark the unhallowed spot. Anathemas were fulminated against the hill of Cluny, dooming it to perpetual barrenness, and against all who should dare to disturb the stones. Ages rolled on; many forgot, and more contemned, the malediction; at length the people resolved to plant and adorn the hill of Cluny. The spot is indeed a beautiful one, commanding one of the most extensive prospects in Britain, in which the mighty waters of the sea are interposed betwixt a range of magnificent hills and a fine expanse of plain, rich with woods, streams, and cottages. On the summit of the hill is a monument to the memory of Nelson. For some time the plantation prospered, and was like to form a lasting ornament to the place. One day, however, nobody could ascertain how or wherefore, a fire broke out, and, in a few hours, almost every shoot and sapling was consumed or blasted; and instead of the green shady boughs and leaves which graced the scene, nothing was seen but gloomy charcoal spar and other marks of desolation. This was the first prank of the witches, but it was not the last. The hill was again planted, again the shoots and stems put forth their gay and glorious garniture, and again the same calamity occurred. Rewards were offered, and punishment threatened to malicious boys and needy stick-gatherers, but no incendiary could be discovered. Other attempts at cultivation were made, but invariably with the same result. The young people still had hope, but the sage and considerate shook their heads and thought of Macbeth's witches, and the unrepealed curse of barrenness! Notwithstanding these startling occurrences, a gentleman lately attempted to break one of the Witch stones, to furnish materials for building; but the inhabitants rose *en masse,* and insisted on the stone being replaced in its ancient site, where it remains at present, bound together with iron bars. To crown this supernatural machinery, a fire broke out *spontaneously* a short time since in the moss of Inshoch (which forms part of the celebrated heath), which we were assured " looked for a' the world like the caldron itsel';" and a strange serpent was seen flying about in the air! Still, the lairds are resolved to cultivate the blasted heath; and the people of Forres have begun to plant once more their favourite hill of Cluny—trusting rather to close observation and a better police, than dreading the " skyey influences " of superstition. We hope the witches will at last, like Cybele, take the pine-tree under their protection.

NICHOLAS FERRAR, FOUNDER OF THE " PROTESTANT NUNNERY."

A Protestant nunnery sounds like something not dreamt of by our philosophers; yet under this name flourished a singular and interesting institution in the reign of Charles I., and in the county of Huntingdon. The readers of good old Izaak Walton, of the poet Crashaw, and of the less poetical *Ecclesiastical Biography* of Dr. Dodsworth, must be familiar with the name of Nicholas Ferrar. He was a gentleman of fortune and education. He travelled with the Lady Elizabeth, daughter of James I., on her marriage with the Elector Palatine, afterwards King of Bohemia; and, on his return, he associated himself with a company formed by Raleigh, Hawkins, and Drake, for the promotion of the colonisation and improvement of Virginia. He was a man of splendid talents and varied accomplishments. Yet, at the age of thirty-four, he fled from the court and from public life, took orders in the church, and, removing with his mother, his sister, and her family, to a small, depopulated, and obscure place, named Little Gidding, lived and died in a state of pious and almost monastic seclusion. The little chapel which he founded, and wherein he officiated with saintlike zeal, still stands, a memento of the recluse.

Having established his conventual system—adopting in his religious exercises the liturgy and collects of the Church of England—Ferrar did not close his door on the world. He was ever ready to welcome the stray wanderer into the wilderness, which he had beautified till literally it blossomed like the rose; and he set up in the great parlour of the establishment a large tablet, thus inscribed:—

I. H. S.

"He that, by reproof of our errors, and remonstrance of that which is more perfect, seeks to make us better, is welcome as an angel of God; he that, by a cheerful participation of that which is good, confirms us in the same, is welcome as a Christian friend. But he that any way goes about to disturb us in that which is, and ought to be, among Christians, though it be not usual in the world, is a burden while he stays, and shall bear his judgment wherever he be. He that censures us in absence, for that which in presence he made a shew to approve of, both by a double guilt of flattery and slander, violates the bond of friendship and Christianity."

The nunnery was all in motion by four o'clock each summer morning, and by five in winter. The whole Psalter was duly and devoutly said over by them, verse by verse, interchangeably, within the twenty-four hours;* music lent its aid to devotion; and with a ceaseless round of duties of charity, piety, innocent labour, and cheerful benevolence, "the day flew by on angel wings." There is something very marvellous in all this. We are such creatures of habit and of sense—or rather of the *senses*—that a life so completely spiritualised seems something like a sustained miracle. Many a bright spirit has mouldered in monastic retirement, yet comparatively few have descended from the glittering heights of power, and popularity, and opulence, to take up the crown of thorns, and wear it so resigned and meekly as the recluse of Little Gidding. The pulses of ambition have often beat under the garb of affected austerity; and retirement from the world does not always imply insensibility to its praise or its censure. But Charles V., in the monastery of St. Justus, chanting the hymns of the missal, or cultivating the plants in his garden with his own hands, was not more surely weaned from the world than Nicholas Ferrar; while the enthusiasm of the latter was more generous, active, and diffusive. Like Charles, too, this remarkable man hastened his death by his austerities. He slept on a bear's skin upon the boards of his chamber, and sat up *watching* three nights a-week. Hence, before he had passed twelve years in his retreat, he sunk under the burden, and died in December 1637. So great had been the popularity of the Protestant nunnery, that both Charles I. and Henrietta Maria visited the spot. It is painful to relate that the army of the parliament, in the subsequent civil war, plundered the church and mansion of the Ferrars. They broke the organ into pieces, with which they made a

---

* Even this was inferior to the perseverance of St. Neot, in the reign of Alfred, who, during his residence in Cornwall as an anchoret, is said to have been accustomed to repeat the whole Psalter once each day, *standing in the fountain of clear water near his hermitage.* It appears from Gorham's *Antiquities of St. Neot's*, that the celebrity of this spring has been perpetuated by tradition: it is yet to be seen at the foot of a hill not far from the church; and a venerable oak, bending forward from the bank above, spreads it branches, like a fan, over the sainted well.

fire, and roasted some sheep that they had killed in the grounds. This was what Johnson would have called a good mob-trick. The remaining branches of the Ferrar family were driven from Huntingdonshire: no trace of their buildings is now left. But the church at Gidding is maintained from lands appropriated by them for that purpose; and the sacred edifice itself, as we have already mentioned, survived the storms of the Great Rebellion, and still exists —

"A chapel lurking among trees,
Where a few villagers, on bended knees,
Find solace which a busy world disdains."

The numerous writings and manuscripts of Nicholas Ferrar are reported to have perished in the devastation of the civil war. We happened, however, to have accidentally one day fallen in with some of these *in a grocer's shop in Huntingdon*. They are wholly devotional — written out in a neat, distinct hand; and each page marked at the top with the sacred letters, " I. H. S." They are dated September 9, 1631. The subject is a strain of pious admonitions, addressed to the younger members of the establishment, on their daily duties and intercourse with the world. The style is clear and simple, with less intricacy and involvement in the construction of the sentences than is common with the religious writers of that period. For example:

" The night is a time of rest, but not of security; and sleep is a freedom from labour, but not from danger. ' Thou makest darkness that it may be night, wherein all the beasts of the forest do move,' is in the mystical sense as true, but much more considerable. Dangers multiply with the departure of the light; even the very air which we breathe every moment turns prejudicial to our health, when the sun is turned from us. The enemies of our bodies, of our estates, and of our souls, enforce their strength, but ours abates. They double their assaults, and we draw back from the defence. And how shall they not prevail, except we seek for better help than we can find in ourselves?

" But our houses serve for keeping of our goods, and we have many provisions of apparel, and otherwise, for preservation of our health. Be it so. But how shall we escape those invisible, those unassailable enemies, which never sleep or cease to plot our ruin? That's a danger, in every man's judgment, utterly beyond the ability of our own prevention. Our largest forecast is too short, our deepest contrivances too shallow, and our best repairs too weak, against these many and inevitable dangers that encompasseth us on every side, touching our estate and body. How many, by their wariness in shutting out thieves, have shut out the succour that they afterwards needed? Bolts and bars may keep out strangers; but what security have we against the household? what assurance against the falling of the roof or sinking of the floor? what restraint of the breaking out of the fire, or of the waters breaking in upon us? How many have had their joints dissolved by an unexpected palsy, their hearts stifled by qualms, or their breath stopped by sudden catarrhs, which had been all perhaps easily remedied in the light, and by the helps that the day affords? Nay, truly, my sons, if we duly examine the number and weight of dangers on both sides, we must needs resolve, that if we cannot pass our lives without fear when we are waking, we cannot lie down to sleep without trembling, nor look upon our beds but as on our graves, into which we cannot enter without manifest hazard of our estates, our lives, and our souls, for any help, repair, or defence, we can find in ourselves against the innumerable perils that every way hang over our heads. Our hope, therefore, lieth altogether in the name of the Lord. We are bound to do what we may, by the use of right means, for prevention of danger of every kind, but our confidence must be in nothing but in God's mercy."

The following is a good description of ingratitude; a vice which, as Johnson remarks, no man is willing to plead guilty to: —

" What you shall constantly observe in generous-minded men, is much more infallible in the proceedings of the Divine bounty,— that a grateful acknowledgment of the first always brings in a second favour; and oftentimes makes that favour excessive in the progress that was but little in the intendment. On the contrary, a light esteem or negligent requital of former hath often undoubtedly turned away many after benefits; and therefore St. Austin resembles ingratitude to a cover upon a springhead, whereby the flowing of the waters is restrained, saying that it stops the infinite and eternal fountain of the Divine mercy itself from breaking out to our good. That which all the powers of darkness are not able to do — for they are not able to divert the least of God's favours — this root and mother of all evil, unthankfulness, doth in an instant effect;

so stopping up the current of God's mercy and comforts, as even blessings turn to punishment, and content to bitterness."

We are tempted to transcribe another sentence, very finely written, though somewhat obscure. Does Mr. Ferrar allude to the general decay of piety, or to the abolition of the monastic institutions, the system of which was partly " recalled " by himself at Gidding?

" Though opportunities may not always serve for a solemn invocation of God in every particular business, yet shall you not enter upon any thing without an inward recommendation of it to God, however with brevity of words, yet with earnestness and abundance of affection. ' O God, make speed to save us! O Lord, make haste to help us!' was the prayer with which the holy fathers in old time laid hand to any work they undertook; and truly at this day, although the devotion be withered, yet the body of this godly practice remains, and walks about, though like a lifeless corpse. And so in all formal deeds and actions the name of God is premised — either by wishing His presence, ' God be here,' or the acknowledgment of His benefits, ' God be thanked,' which the Italians use. Men make entrance into others' houses, merchants write over their letters and books, some ' Emmanuel ;' and others, the saving name of ' Jesus.' And to speak truly, but where atheism and irreligion, under colour of discretion, hath banished it, there is neither place, nor person, nor action, but you shall evidently perceive, by the remaining footsteps, the greatness and beauty of the ancient body of this holy and virtuous institution, the recalling whereof was most profitable, so most necessary."

This reflection of the recluse on the "remaining footsteps," and the " greatness and beauty " of the ancient glories he lamented, reminds us of a very striking passage in one of South's sermons on the fall of man :—

" We may collect the excellency of the understanding before the fall by the glorious remainders of it now, and guess at the stateliness of the building by the magnificence of its ruins. All those arts, rarities, and inventions, which vulgar minds gaze at, the ingenious pursue, and all admire, are but the relics of an intellect defaced with sin and time. We admire it now only as antiquaries do a piece of old coin, for the stamp it once bore, and not for those vanishing lineaments and disappearing drafts that remain upon it at present. And, certainly, that must needs have been very glorious, the decays of which are so admirable. He that is comely when old and decrepit, surely was very beautiful when he was young. An Aristotle was but the rubbish of an Adam, and Athens but the rudiments of Paradise."

Rather of the *heart* than of the *understanding*, good bishop! The imagination dwells upon the inhabitants of Paradise as excelling in purity and loveliness, not in what is termed knowledge or philosophy. Their richest dower was " simplicity and spotless innocence."

With the devotional writings of Hooker, Jeremy Taylor, and Barrow, before us, we feel that it is not necessary to quote further from the manuscripts of Nicholas Ferrar. His history, however, is a very remarkable one; and we have often wished to see it form the subject of Southey's prose or Wordsworth's poetry. The recluse of Little Gidding might well be added to the " worthies " so beautifully commemorated in the sonnet on Walton's *Book of Lives* :—

" There are no colours in the fairest sky
So fair as these. The feather whence the
 pen
Was shaped, that traced the lives of these
 good men,
Dropped from an angel's wing. With
 moisten'd eye,
We read of faith and purest charity
In statesman, priest, and humble citizen :
Oh, could we copy their mild virtues, then
What joy to live, what blessedness to die !
Methinks their very names shine still and
 bright ;
Apart like glow-worms on a summer
 night ;
Or lonely tapers, when from far they fling
A guiding ray ; or seen, like stars on
 high,
Satellites burning in a lucid ring
Around meek Walton's heavenly memory."

MODERN BIOGRAPHY.

BEATTIE'S LIFE OF CAMPBELL.

THE ancients, who lived beyond the reach of the fangs and feelers of the printing press, had, in one respect, a decided advantage over us unlucky moderns. They were not beset by the terrors of biography. No hideous suspicion that, after he was dead and gone—after the wine had been poured upon the hissing embers of the pyre, and the ashes consigned, by the hands of weeping friends, to the oblivion of the funereal urn—some industrious gossip of his acquaintance would incontinently sit down to the task of laborious compilation and collection of his literary scraps, ever crossed, like a sullen shadow, the imagination of the Greek or the Latin poet. Homer, though Arctinus was his near relative, could unbosom himself without the fear of having his frailties posthumously exposed, or his amours blazoned to the world. Lucius Varius and Plotius Tucca, the literary executors of Virgil, never dreamed of applying to Pollio for the I O Us which he doubtless held in the handwriting of the Mantuan bard, or to Horace for the confidential notes suggestive of Falernian inspiration. Socrates, indeed, has found a liberal reporter in Plato; but this is a pardonable exception. The son of Sophroniscus did not write; and therefore it was incumbent on his pupil to preserve for posterity the fragments of his oral wisdom. The ancient authors rested their reputation upon their published works alone. They knew, what we seem to forget, that the poet, apart from his genius, is but an ordinary man, and, in many cases, has received, along with that gift, a larger share of propensities and weaknesses than his fellow-mortals. Therefore it was that they insisted upon that right of domestic privacy which is common to us all. The poet, in his public capacity as an author, held himself responsible for what he wrote; but he had no idea of allowing the whole world to walk into his house, open his desk, read his love-letters, and criticise the state of his finances. Had Varius and Tucca acted on the modern system, the ghost of Virgil would have haunted them on their death-beds. Only think what a legacy might have been ours if these respectable gentlemen had written to Cremona for anecdotes of the poet while at school! No doubt, in some private nook of the old farm-house at Andes, there were treasured up, through the infinite love of the mother, tablets scratched over with verses, composed by young Master Maro at the precocious age of ten. We may, to a certainty, calculate—for maternal fondness always has been the same, and Virgil was an only child—that, in that emporium, themes upon such topics as "Virtus est sola nobilitas" were religiously treasured, along with other memorials of the dear, dear boy who had gone to college at Naples. Modern Varius would remorselessly have printed these: ancient Tucca was more discreet. Then what say you to the college career? Would it not be a nice thing to have all the squibs and feuds, the rows and rackettings of the jovial student preserved to us precisely as they were penned, projected, and perpetrated? Have we not lost a great deal in being defrauded of an account of the manner in which he singed the wig of his drunken old tutor, Parthenius Nicenus, or the scandalously late hours which he kept in company with his especial chums? Then comes the period, darkly hinted at by Donatus, during which he was, somehow or other, connected with the imperial stable; that is, we presume, upon the turf. What would we not give for a sight of Virgil's betting-book! Did he back the field, or did he take the odds on the Emperor's bay mare, Alma Venus Genetrix? How stood he with the legs? What sort of reputation did he maintain in the ring of the Roman Tattersall?

Life and Letters of Thomas Campbell. Edited by WILLIAM BEATTIE, M.D., one of his Executors. 3 vols. London: Moxon, 1849.

Was he ever posted as a defaulter? Tucca! you should have told us this. Then, when sobered down, and in high favour with the court, where is the private correspondence between him and Mæcenas, the President of the Roman Agricultural Society, touching the compilation of the Georgics? The excellent Equestrian, we know, wanted Virgil to construct a poem, such as Thomas Tusser afterwards wrote, under the title of a "*Hondreth Good Points of Husbandrie,*" and, doubtless, waxed warm in his letters about draining, manure, and mangel-wurzel. What sacrifice would we not make to place that correspondence in the hands of Henry Stephens! How the author of the *Book of the Farm* would revel in his exposure of the crude theories of the Minister of the Interior! What a formidable phalanx of facts would he oppose to Mæcenas' misconceptions of guano! Through the sensitive delicacy of his executors, we have lost the record of Virgil's repeated larks with Horace: the pleasant little supper-parties celebrated at the villa of that dissipated rogue Tibullus, have passed from the memory of mankind. We know nothing of the state of his finances, for they have not thought fit to publish his banking-account with the firm of Lollius, Spuræna, and Company. Their duty, as they fondly believed, was fulfilled, when they gave to the world the glorious but unfinished Æneid.

Under the modern system, we constantly ask ourselves whether it is wise to wish for greatness, and whether total oblivion is not preferable to fame, with the penalty of exposure annexed. We shudder at the thoughts of putting out a book, not from fear of anything that the critics can do, but lest it should take with the public, and expose us to the danger of a posthumous biography. Were we to awake some fine morning, and find ourselves famous, our peace of mind would be gone for ever. Mercy on us! what a quantity of foolish letters have we not written during the days of our youth, under the confident impression that, when read, they would be immediately committed to the flames. Madrigals innumerable recur to our memory; and, if these were published, there would be no rest for us in the grave! If any misguided critic should say of us, "The works of this author are destined to descend to posterity," our response would be a hollow groan. If convinced that our biography would be attempted, from that hour the friend of our bosom would appear in the light of a base and ignominious spy. How durst we ever unbosom ourselves to him, when, for aught we know, the wretch may be treasuring up our casual remarks over the fifth tumbler, for immediate registration at home? Constitutionally we are not hard-hearted; but, were we so situated, we own that the intimation of the decease of each early acquaintance would be rather a relief than otherwise. Tom, our intimate fellow-student at college, dies. We may be sorry for the family of Thomas, but we soon wipe away the natural drops, discovering that there is balm in Gilead. We used to write him letters, detailing minutely our inward emotions at the time we were distractedly in love with Jemima Higginbotham; and Tom, who was always a methodical dog, has no doubt docqueted them as received. Tom's heirs will doubtless be too keen upon the scent of valuables, to care one farthing for rhapsodising: therefore, unless they are sent to the snuff-merchant, or disseminated as autographs, our epistles run a fair chance of perishing by the flames, and one evidence of our weakness is removed. A member of the club meets us in George Street, and, with a rueful longitude of countenance, asks us if we have heard of the death of poor Harry? To the eternal disgrace of human nature, be it recorded, that our heart leaps up within us like a foot-ball, as we hypocritically have recourse to our cambric. Harry knew a great deal too much about our private history just before we joined the Yeomanry, and could have told some stories, little flattering to our posthumous renown.

Are we not right, then, in holding that, under the present system, celebrity is a thing to be eschewed? Why is it that we are so chary of receiving certain Down-Easters, so different from the real American gentlemen whom it is our good fortune to know? Simply because Silas

Fixings will take down your whole conversation in black and white, deliberately alter it to suit his private purposes, and Transatlantically retail it as a specimen of your life and opinions. And is it not a still more horrible idea that a Silas may be perpetually watching you in the shape of a pretended friend? If the man would at once declare his intention, you might be comparatively at ease. Even in that case you never could love him more, for the confession implies a disgusting determination of outliving you, or rather a hint that your health is not remarkably robust, which would irritate the meekest of mankind. But you might be enabled, through a strong effort, to repress the outward exhibition of your wrath; and, if high religious principle should deter you from mixing strychnia or prussic acid with the wine of your volunteering executor, you may at least contrive to blind him by cautiously maintaining your guard. Were we placed in such a trying position, we should utter, before our intending Boswell, nothing save sentiments which might have flowed from the lips of the Venerable Bede. What letters, full of morality and high feeling, would we not indite! Not an invitation to dinner—not an acceptance of a tea and turn-out, but should be flavoured with some wholesome apothegm. Thus we should strive, through our later correspondence, to efface the memory of the earlier, which it is impossible to recall,—not without a hope that we might throw upon it, if posthumously produced, a tolerable imputation of forgery.

In these times, we repeat, no man of the least mark or likelihood is safe. The waiter with the bandy-legs, who hands round the negus-tray at a blue-stocking coterie, is in all probability a leading contributor to a fifth-rate periodical; and, in a few days after you have been rash enough to accept the insidious beverage, M'Tavish will be correcting the proof of an article in which your appearance and conversation are described. Distrust the gentleman in the plush terminations; he, too, is a penny-a-liner, and keeps a commonplace-book in the pantry. Better give up writing at once than live in such a perpetual state of bondage. What amount of present fame can recompense you for being shown up as a noodle, or worse, to your children's children? Nay, recollect this, that you are implicating your personal, and, perhaps, most innocent friends. Bob accompanies you home from an insurance society dinner, where the champagne has been rather superabundant, and, next morning, you, as a bit of fun, write to the President that the watchman had picked up Bob in a state of helpless inebriety from the kennel. The President, after the manner of the Fogies, duly docquets your note with name and date, and puts it up with a parcel of others, secured by red tape. You die. Your literary executor writes to the President, stating his biographical intentions, and requesting all documents that may tend to throw light upon your personal history. Preses, in deep ecstasy at the idea of seeing his name in print as the recipient of your epistolary favours, immediately transmits the packet; and the consequence is, that Robert is most unjustly handed down to posterity in the character of a habitual drunkard, although it is a fact that a more abstinent creature never went home to his wife at ten. If you are an author, and your spouse is ailing, don't give the details to your intimate friend, if you would not wish to publish them to the world. Drop all correspondence, if you are wise, and have any ambition to stand well in the eyes of the coming generation. Let your conversation be as curt as a Quaker's, and select no one for a friend, unless you have the meanest possible opinion of his capacity. Even in that case you are hardly secure. Perhaps the best mode of combining philanthropy, society, and safety, is to have nobody in the house, save an old woman who is so utterly deaf that you must order your dinner by pantomime.

One mode of escape suggests itself, and we do not hesitate to recommend it. Let every man who underlies the terror of the *peine forte et dure*, compile his own autobiography at the ripe age of forty-five. Few people, in this country, begin to establish a permanent reputation before thirty; and we allow them fifteen years to complete it. Now, supposing your existence should be protracted to seventy, here are clear five-and-twenty years remaining, which may be profitably employed in autobiography, by which means you secure three vast advantages. In the first place, you can deal with your own earlier history as you please, and provide against the subsequent production of inconvenient documents. In the second place, you defeat the intentions of your excellent friend and gossip, who will hardly venture to start his volumes in competition with your own. In the third place, you leave an additional copyright as a legacy to your children, and are not haunted in your last moments by the agonising thought that a stranger in name and blood is preparing to make money by your decease. It is, of course, unnecessary to say one word regarding the general tone of your memoirs. If you cannot contrive to block out such a fancy portrait of your intellectual self as shall throw all others into the shade, you may walk on fearlessly through life, for your biography never will be attempted. Goethe, the most accomplished literary fox of our age, perfectly understood the value of these maxims, and forestalled his friends, by telling his own story in time. The consequence is, that his memory has escaped unharmed. Little Eckermann, his amanuensis in extreme old age, did indeed contrive to deliver himself of a small Boswellian volume; but this publication, bearing reference merely to the dicta of Goethe at a safe period of life, could not injure the departed poet. The repetition of the early history, and the publication of the early documents, are the points to be especially guarded.

We beg that these remarks may be considered, not as strictures upon any individual example, but as bearing upon the general style of modern biography. This is a gossiping world, in which great men are the exceptions; and when one of these ceases to exist, the public becomes clamorous to learn the whole minutiæ of his private life. That is a depraved taste, and one which ought not to be gratified. The author is to be judged by the works which he voluntarily surrenders to the public, not by the tenor of his private history, which ought not to be irreverently exposed. Thus, in compiling the life of a poet, we maintain that a literary executor has purely a literary function to perform. Out of the mass of materials which he may fortuitously collect, his duty is to select such portions as may illustrate the public doings of the man: he may, without transgressing the boundaries of propriety, inform us of the circumstances which suggested the idea of any particular work, the difficulties which were overcome by the author in the course of its composition, and even exhibit the correspondence relative thereto. These are matters of literary history which we may ask for, and obtain, without any breach of the conventional rules of society. Whatever refers to public life is public, and may be printed: whatever refers solely to domestic existence is private, and ought to be held sacred. A very little reflection, we think, will demonstrate the propriety of this distinction. If we have a dear and valued friend, to whom, in the hours of adversity or of joy, we are wont to communicate the thoughts which lie at the bottom of our soul, we write to him in the full conviction that he will regard these letters as addressed to himself alone. We do not insult him, nor wrong the holy attributes of friendship so much, as to warn him against communicating our thoughts to any one else in the world. We never dream that he will do so, else assuredly those letters never would have been written. If we were to discover that we had so grievously erred as to repose confidence in a person who, the moment he received a letter penned in a paroxysm of emotion and revealing a secret of our existence, was capable of exhibiting it to the circle of his acquaintance, of a surety he should never more be troubled with any of our correspondence. Would any man dare to print such documents during the life of the writer? We need not pause for a reply: there can be but one. And *why* is this? Because these communications bear on their face the stamp of the strictest privacy —because they were addressed to, and meant for the eye of but one human being in the universe—because they betray the emotions of a soul which asks sympathy from a friend, with only less reverence than it implores comfort from its God! Does death, then, free the friend and the confidant from all restraint? If the knowledge that his secret had been divulged, his agonies exposed, his weaknesses surrendered to the vulgar gaze, could have pained the living man—is nothing due to his memory, now that he is laid beneath the turf, now that his voice can never more be raised to upbraid a violated confidence? Many modern biographers, we regret to say, do not appear to be influenced by any such consideration. They never seem to have asked themselves the question—Would my friend, if he had been compiling his own memoirs, have inserted such a letter for publication—does it not refer to a matter eminently private and personal, and never to be communicated to the world? Instead of applying this test, they print everything, and rather plume themselves on their impartiality in suppressing nothing. They thus exhibit the life not only of the author but of the man. Literary and personal history are blended together. The senator is not only exhibited in the House of Commons, but we are courteously invited to attend at the *accouchement* of his wife.

What title has any of us, in the abstract, to write the private history of his next-door neighbour? Be he poet, lawyer, physician, or divine, his private sayings and doings are his property, not that of a gaping and curious public. No man dares to say to another, " Come, my good fellow! it is full time that the world should know a little about your domestic concerns. I have been keeping a sort of notebook of your proceedings ever since we were at school together, and I intend to make a few pounds by exhibiting you in your true colours. You recollect when you were in love with old Tomnoddy's daughter? I have written a capital account of your interview with her that fine forenoon in the Botanical Gardens! True, she jilted you, and went off with young Heavystern of the Dragoons, but the public won't relish the scene a bit the less on that account. Then I have got some letters of yours from our mutual friend Fitzjaw. How very hard-up you must have been at the time when you supplicated him for twenty pounds to keep you out of jail! You were rather severe, the other day when I met you at dinner, upon your professional brother Jenkinson; but I daresay that what you said was all very true, so I shall publish that likewise. By the way—how is your wife? She had a lot of money, had she not? At all events people say so, and it is shrewdly surmised that you did not marry her for her beauty. I don't mean to say that *I* think so, but such is the *on dit*, and I have set it down accordingly in my journal. Do, pray, tell me about that quarrel between you and your mother-in-law! Is it true that she threw a joint-stool at your head? How our friends will roar when they see the details in print!" Is the case less flagrant if the manuscript is not sent to press, until our neighbour is deposited in his coffin? We cannot perceive the difference. If the feelings of living people are to be taken as the criterion, only one of the domestic actors is removed from the stage of existence. Old Tomnoddy still lives, and may not be abundantly gratified at the fact of his daughter's infidelity and elopement being proclaimed. The intimation of the garden scene, hitherto unknown to Heavystern, may fill his warlike bosom with jealousy, and ultimately occasion a separation. Fitzjaw can hardly complain, but he will be very furious at finding his refusal to accommodate a friend appended to the supplicating letter. Jenkinson is only sorry that the libeller is dead, otherwise he would have treated him to an action in the Jury Court. The widow believes that she was made a bride solely for the sake of her Californian attractions, and reviles the memory of her spouse. As for the mother-in-law, now gradually dwindling into dotage, her feelings are perhaps of no great consequence to any human being. Nevertheless, when the obnoxious paragraph in the Memoirs is read to her by a shrill female companion, nature makes a temporary rally, her withered frame shakes with agitation, and she finally falls backward in a fit of hopeless paralysis.

Such is a feeble picture of the results that might ensue from private biography, were we all permitted, without reservation, to parade the lives and domestic circumstances of our neighbours to a greedy and gloating world. Not but that, if our neighbour has been a man of sufficient distinction to deserve commemoration, we may gracefully and skilfully narrate all of him that is worth the knowing. We may point to his public actions, expatiate on his achievements, and recount the manner in which he gained his intellectual renown; but further we ought not to go. The confidences of the dead should be as sacred as those of the living. And here we may observe, that there are other parties quite as much to blame as the biographers in question. We allude to the friends of the deceased, who have unscrupulously furnished them with materials. Is it not the fact that in very many cases they have divulged letters which, during the writer's lifetime, they would have withheld from the nearest and dearest of their kindred? In many such letters there occur observations and reflections upon living characters, not written in malice, but still such as were never intended to meet the eyes of the parties criticised; and these are forthwith published, as racy passages, likely to gratify the appetite of a coarse, vulgar, and inordinate curiosity. Even this is not the worst. Survivors may grieve to learn that the friend whom they loved was capable of ridiculing or misrepresenting them in secret, and his memory may suffer in their estimation; but, put the case of detailed private conversations, which are constantly foisted into modern biographies, and we shall immediately discover that the inevitable tendency is to engender dislikes among living parties. Let us suppose that three men, all of them professional authors, meet at a dinner party. The conversation is very lively, takes a literary turn, and the three gentlemen, with that sportive freedom which is very common in a society where no treachery is apprehended, pass some rather poignant strictures upon the writings or habits of their contemporaries. One of them either keeps a journal, or is in the habit of writing, for the amusement of a confidential friend at a distance, any literary gossip which may be current, and he commits to paper the heads of the recent dialogue. He dies, and his literary executor immediately pounces upon the document, and, to the confusion of the two living critics, prints it. Every literary brother whom they have noticed is of course their enemy for life.

If, in private society, a snob is discovered retailing conversations, he is forthwith cut without compunction. He reads his detection in the calm, cold scorn of your eye; and, referring to the mirror of his own dim and dirty conscience, beholds the reflection of a hound. The biographer seems to consider himself exempt from such social secrecy. He shelters himself under the plea that the public are so deeply interested, that they must not be deprived of any memorandum, anecdote, or jotting, told, written, or detailed by the gifted subject of their memoirs. Therefore it is not a prudent thing to be familiar with a man of genius. He may not betray your confidence, but you can hardly trust to the tender mercies of his chronicler.

Such are our deliberate views upon the subject of biography, and we state them altogether independent of the three bulky volumes which are now lying before us for review.

We cordially admit that it was right and proper that a life of Campbell should be written. Although he did not occupy the same commanding position as others of his renowned contemporaries — although his writings have not, like those of Scott, Byron, and Southey, contributed powerfully to give a tone and idiosyncrasy to the general literature of the age—Campbell was nevertheless a man of rich genius, and a poet of remarkable accomplishment. It would not be easy to select, from the works of any other writer of our time, so many brilliant and polished gems, without flaw or imperfection, as are to be found amongst his minor poems. Criticism, in dealing with these exquisite lyrics, is at fault. If sometimes the suspicion of a certain effeminacy haunts us, we have but to turn the page, and we arrive at some magnificent, bold, and trumpet-toned ditty, appealing directly from the heart of the poet to the imagination of his audience, and proving, beyond all contest, that power was his glorious attribute. True, he was unequal; and towards the latter part of his career, exhibited a marked failing in the qualities which originally secured his renown. It is almost impossible to believe that the *Pilgrim of Glencoe*, or even *Theodric*, was composed by the author of the *Pleasures of Hope* or *Gertrude;* and if you place the *Ritter Bann* beside *Hohenlinden* or the *Battle of the Baltic*, you cannot fail to be struck with the singular diminution of power. Campbell started from a high point—walked for some time along level or undulating ground —and then began rapidly to descend. This is not, as some idle critics have maintained, the common course of genius. Chaucer, Spenser, Shakspeare, Milton, Dryden, Scott, Byron, and Wordsworth, are remarkable instances to the contrary. Whatever may have been the promise of their youth, their matured performances, eclipsing their earlier efforts, show us that genius is capable of almost boundless cultivation, and that the fire of the poet does not cease to burn less brightly within him, because the sable of his hair is streaked with gray, or the furrows deepening on his brow. Sir Walter Scott was upwards of thirty before he began to compose in earnest: after thirty, Campbell wrote scarcely anything which has added permanently to his reputation. Extreme sensitiveness, an over-strained and fastidious desire of polishing, and sometimes the pressure of outward circumstances, may have combined to damp his early ardour. He evidently was deficient in that resolute pertinacity of labour, through which alone great results can be achieved. He allowed the best years of his life to be frittered away, in pursuits which could not secure to him either additional fame, or the more substantial rewards of fortune: and, though far from being actually idle, he was only indolently active. Campbell wanted an object in life. Thus, though gifted with powers which, directed towards one point, were capable of the highest concentration, we find him scattering these in the most desultory and careless manner; and surrendering scheme after scheme, without making the vigorous effort which was necessary to secure their completion. This is a fault by no means uncommon in literature, but one which is highly dangerous. No work requiring great mental exertion should be undertaken rashly, for the enthusiasm which has prompted it rapidly subsides, the labour becomes distasteful to the writer, and unless he can bend himself to his task with the most dogged perseverance, and a determination to vanquish all obstacles, the result will be a fragment or a failure. Of this we find two notable instances recorded in the book before us. Twice in his life had Campbell meditated the construction of a great poem, and twice did he relinquish the task. Of the *Queen of the North* but a few lines remain: of his favourite projected epic on the subject of Wallace, nothing. Elegant trifles, sportive verses, and playful epigrams were, for many years, the last fruits of that genius which had dictated the *Pleasures of Hope*, and rejoiced the mariners of England with a ballad worthy of the theme. And yet, so powerful is early association—so universal was the recognition of the transcendant genius of the boy, that when Campbell sank into the grave, there was lamentation as though a great poet had been stricken down in his prime, and all men felt that a brilliant light had gone out among the luminaries of the age. Therefore it was seemly that his memory should receive that homage which has been rendered to others less deserving of it, and that his public career, at least, should be traced and given to the world.

It was Campbell's own wish that Dr Beattie should undertake his biography. Few perhaps knew the motives which led to this selection; for the assiduity, care, and filial attachment, bestowed for years by the warm-hearted physician upon the poet, was as unostentatious as it was honourable and devoted. Not from the pages of this biography can the reader form an adequate idea of the extent and value of such disinterested friendship: indeed it is not too much to say, that the rare and exemplary kindness of Dr Beattie was the chief consolation of Campbell during the later period of his existence. It was therefore natural that the dying poet should have confided this trust to one of whose affection he was assured by so many rare and signal proofs; and it is with a kindly feeling to the author that we now approach the consideration of the literary merits of the book.

The admiration of Dr Beattie for the genius of Campbell has in some respects led him astray. It is easy to see at a glance that his measure of admiration is not of an ordinary kind, but so excessive as to lead him beyond all limit. He seems to have regarded Campbell not merely as a great poet, but as the great poet of the age; and he is unwilling, æsthetically, to admit any material diminution of his powers. He still clings with a certain faith to *Theodric;* and declines to perceive any palpable failure even in the *Pilgrim of Glencoe.* Verses and fragments which, to the casual reader, convey anything but the impression of excellence, are liberally distributed throughout the pages of the third volume, and commented on with evident rapture. He seems to think that, in the case of his author, it may be said, " *Nihil tetigit quod non ornavit;*" and accordingly he is slow to suppress, even where suppression would have been of positive advantage. In short, he is too full of his subject to do it justice. In the hands of a skilful and less biassed artisan, the materials which occupy these three volumes, extending to nearly fourteen hundred pages of print, might have been condensed into one highly interesting and popular volume. We should not then, it is true, have been favoured with specimens of Campbell's college exercises, with the voluminous chronicles of his family, with verses written at the age of eleven, or with correspondence purely domestic; but we firmly believe that the reading public would have been grateful to Dr Beattie, had he omitted a great deal of matter connected with the poet's earlier career, which is of no interest whatever. The Campbells of Kirnan were, we doubt not, a highly respectable sept, and performed their duty as kirk-elders for many generations blamelessly in the parish of Glassary. But it was not necessary on that account to trace their descent from the Black Knight of Lochawe, or to give the particular history of the family for more than a century and a half. Gillespic-le-Camile may have been a fine fellow in his day; but we utterly deny, in the teeth of all the Campbells and Kembles in the world, that he had a drop of Norman blood in his veins. It is curious to find the poet, at a subsequent period, engaged in a correspondence, as to the common ancestor of these names, with one of the Kembles, who, as Mrs Butler somewhere triumphantly avers, were descended from the lords of Campo-bello. Where that favoured region may be, we know not; but this we know, that in Gaelic *Cambeul* signifies *wry - mouth*, and hence, as is the custom with primitive nations, the origin of the name. And let not the sons of Diarmid be offended at this, or esteem their glories less, since the gallant Camerons owe their name to a similar conformation of the nose, and the Douglases to their dark complexion. Having put this little matter of family etymology right, let us return to Dr Beattie.

The first volume, we maintain, is terribly overloaded by trivial details, and specimens of the kind to which we have alluded. We need not enter into these, except in so far as to state that Thomas Campbell was the youngest child of most respectable parents: that his father, having been unfortunate in business, was so reduced in circumstances, that, whilst attending Glasgow College, the young student was compelled to have recourse to teaching; that he acquitted himself admirably, and to the satisfaction of all his professors in the literary classes; and that, for one vacation at least, he resided as private tutor to a family in the island of Mull. He was then about eighteen, and had already exhibited symptoms of a rare poetical talent, particularly in translations from the Greek. Dr Beattie's zeal as a biographer may be gathered from the following statement:—

" I applied last year to the Rev. Dr M'Arthur, of Kilninian in Mull, requesting him to favour me with such traditional particulars regarding the poet as might still be current among the old inhabitants; but I regret to say that nothing of interest has resulted. 'In the course of my inquiries,' he says, 'I have met with only two individuals who had seen Mr Campbell while he was in Mull, and the amount of their information is merely that he was *a very pretty young man*. Those who must have been personally acquainted with him in this country, have, like himself, descended into the tomb; so that no authentic anecdotes of him can now be procured in this quarter.'"

There is a simplicity in this which has amused us greatly. Campbell, in those days, was conspicuous for nothing—at least, for no accomplishment which could be appreciated in that distant island. In all probability two-thirds of the inhabitants of the parish were Campbells, who expired in utter ignorance of the art of writing their names; so that to ask for literary anecdotes, at the distance of half a century, was rather a work of supererogation.

For two years more, Campbell led a life of great uncertainty. He was naturally averse to the drudgery of teaching,—an employment which never can be congenial to a poetical and creative nature. He had no decided predilection for any of the learned professions; for though he alternately betook himself to the study of law, physic, and divinity, it was hardly with a serious purpose. He visited Edinburgh in search of literary employment, was for some time a clerk in a writer's office, and, through the kindness of the late Dr Anderson, editor of a collection of the British poets,—a man who was ever eager to acknowledge and encourage genius,—he received his first introduction to a bookselling firm. From them he received some little employment, but not of a nature suited to his taste; and we soon afterwards find him in Glasgow, meditating the establishment of a magazine—a scheme which proved utterly abortive.

In the mean time, however, he had not been idle. At the age of twenty the poetical instinct is active, and, even though no audience can be found, the muse will force its way. Campbell had already translated two plays of Æschylus and Euripides—an exercise which no doubt developed largely his powers of versification—and, further, had begun to compose original lyric verses. In the foreign edition of his works, there is inserted a poem called the Dirge of Wallace, written about this period, which, with a very little concentration, might have been rendered as perfect as any of his later compositions. In spirit and energy it is assuredly inferior to none of them. "But," says Dr Beattie, "the fastidious author, who thought it too rhapsodical, never bestowed a careful revision upon it, and persisted in excluding it from all the London editions." We hope to see it restored to its proper place in the next: in the mean time we select the following noble stanzas:—

"They lighted the tapers at dead of night,
 And chaunted their holiest hymn:
But her brow and her bosom were damp with affright,
 Her eye was all sleepless and dim!
And the Lady of Ellerslie wept for her lord,
 When a death-watch beat in her lonely room,
When her curtain had shook of its own accord,
And the raven had flapped at her window board,
 To tell of her warrior's doom.

"'Now sing ye the death-song, and loudly pray
 For the soul of my knight so dear!
And call me a widow this wretched day,
 Since the warning of GOD is here.
For a nightmare rests on my strangled sleep;
 The lord of my bosom is doomed to die!
His valorous heart they have wounded deep,
And the blood-red tears shall his country weep
 For Wallace of Ellerslie!'

"Yet knew not his country, that ominous hour—
 Ere the loud matin-bell was rung—
That the trumpet of death, from an English tower,
 Had the dirge of her champion sung.
When his dungeon-light looked dim and red
 On the highborn blood of a martyr slain,
No anthem was sung at his lowly death-bed—
No weeping was there when *his* bosom bled,
 And his heart was rent in twain.

"Oh! it was not thus when his ashen spear
 Was true to that knight forlorn,
And hosts of a thousand were scattered like deer
 At the blast of a hunter's horn;
*When he strode o'er the wreck of each well-fought field,
 With the yellow-haired chiefs of his native land;*

> *For his lance was not shivered on helmet or shield,*
> *And the sword that was fit for archangel to wield*
> *Was light in his terrible hand!*
> "Yet, bleeding and bound, though the Wallace wight
> For his long-loved country die,
> The bugle ne'er sung to a braver knight
> Than William of Ellerslie!
> *But the day of his triumphs shall never depart;*
> *His head, uncntombed, shall with glory be palmed—*
> *From its blood-streaming altar his spirit shall start;*
> *Though the raven has fed on his mouldering heart,*
> *A nobler was never embalmed!*"

Nothing can be finer than the lines we have quoted in Italics, nor perhaps did Campbell himself ever match them. Local reputations are dearly cherished in the west of Scotland, and even at this early period our poet was denominated "the Pope of Glasgow."

Again Campbell migrated to Edinburgh, but still with no fixed determination as to the choice of a profession: his intention was to attend the public lectures at the University, and also to push his connexion with the booksellers, so as to obtain the means of livelihood. Failing this last resource, he contemplated removing to America, in which country his eldest brother was permanently settled. Fortunately for himself, he now made the acquaintance of several young men who were destined afterwards to attract the public observation, and to win great names in different branches of literature. Among these were Scott, Brougham, Leyden, Jeffrey, Dr Thomas Brown, and Grahame, the author of *The Sabbath*. Mr John Richardson, who had the good fortune to remain through life the intimate friend both of Scott and Campbell, was also, at this early period, the chosen companion of the latter, and contributed much, by his judicious counsels and criticisms, to nerve the poet for that successful effort which, shortly afterwards, took the world of letters by storm. Dr Anderson also continued his literary superintendence, and anxiously watched over the progress of the new poem upon which Campbell was now engaged. At length, in 1799, the *Pleasures of Hope* appeared.

Rarely has any volume of poetry met with such rapid success. Campbell had few living rivals of established reputation to contend with; and the freshness of his thought, the extreme sweetness of his numbers, and the fine taste which pervaded the whole composition, fell like magic on the ear of the public, and won their immediate approbation. It is true that, as a speculation, this volume did not prove remarkably lucrative to the author: he had disposed of the copyright before publication for a sum of sixty pounds, but, through the liberality of the publishers, he received for some years a further sum on the issue of each edition. The book was certainly worth a great deal more; but many an author would be glad to surrender all claim for profit on his first adventure, could he be assured of such valuable popularity as Campbell now acquired. He presently became a lion in Edinburgh society; and, what was far better, he secured the countenance and friendship of such men as Dugald Stewart, Henry Mackenzie, Dr Gregory, the Rev. Archibald Alison, and Telford, the celebrated engineer. It is pleasant to know that the friendships so formed were interrupted only by death.

Campbell had now, to use a common but familiar phrase, the ball at his foot, but never did there live a man less capable of appreciating opportunity. At an age when most young men are students, he had won fame—fame, too, in such measure and of such a kind as secured him against reaction, or the possibility of a speedy neglect following upon so rapid a success. Had he deliberately followed up his advantage with anything like ordinary diligence, fortune as well as fame would have been his immediate reward. Like Aladdin, he was in possession of a talisman which could open to him the cavern in which a still greater treasure was contained; but he shrunk from the labour which was indispensable for the effort. He either could not or would not summon up sufficient resolution to betake himself to a new task; but, under the pretext of improving his mind by travel, gave way to his erratic propensities, and departed for the Continent with a slender purse, and, as usual, no fixity of purpose.

We confess that the portion of his correspondence which relates to this expedition does not appear to us remarkably interesting. He resided chiefly at Ratisbon, where his time appears to have been tolerably equally divided between writing lyrics for the *Morning Chronicle*, then under the superintendence of Mr Perry, and squabbling with the monks of the Scottish Convent of Saint James. Some of his best minor poems were composed at this period; but it will be easily comprehended that, from the style of their publication in a fugitive form, they could add but little at the time to his reputation, and certainly they did not materially improve his finances. With a contemplated poem of some magnitude—the *Queen of the North*—he made little progress; and, upon the whole, this year was spent uncomfortably. After his return to Britain, he resided for some time in Edinburgh and London, mixing in the best and most cultivated society, but sorely straitened in circumstances, which, nevertheless, he had not the courage or the patience to improve.

A quarto edition of the *Pleasures*, printed by subscription for his own benefit, at length put him in funds, and probably tempted him to marry. Then came the real cares of life,—an increased establishment, an increasing family: new mouths to provide for, and no settled mode of livelihood. Of all literary men, Campbell was least calculated, both by habit and inclination, to pursue a profession which, with many temptations, was then, and is still, precarious. He was not, like Scott, a man of business habits and unflagging industry. His impulses to write were short, and his fastidiousness interfered with his impulse. Booksellers were slow in offering him employment, for they could not depend on his punctuality. Those who have frequent dealings with the trade know how much depends upon the observance of this excellent virtue; but Campbell never could be brought to appreciate its full value. The printing-press had difficulty in keeping pace with the pen of Scott: to wait for that of Campbell was equivalent to a cessation of labour. Therefore it is not surprising that, about this period, most of his negotiations failed. Proposals for an edition of the British Poets, a large and expensive work, to be executed jointly by Scott and Campbell, fell to the ground: and the bard of Hope gave vent to his feelings by execrating the phalanx of the Row.

At the very moment when his prospects appeared to be shrouded in the deepest gloom, Campbell received intimation that he had been placed on the pension-list as an annuitant of £200. Never was the royal bounty more seasonably extended; and this high recognition of his genius seems for a time to have inspired him with new energy. He commenced the compilation of the *Specimens of British Poets:* but his indolent habits overcame him, and the work was not given to the public until *thirteen years* after it was undertaken. No wonder that the booksellers were chary of staking their capital on the faith of his promised performances!

Ten years after the publication of the *Pleasures of Hope*, *Gertrude of Wyoming* appeared. That exquisite little poem demonstrated, in the most conclusive manner, that the author's poetical powers were not exhausted by his earlier effort, and the same volume contained the noblest of his immortal lyrics. Campbell was now at the highest point of his renown. Critics may compare together the longer poems, and, according as their taste leans towards the didactic or the descriptive form of composition, may differ in awarding the palm of excellence, but there can be but one opinion as to the lyrical poetry. In this respect Campbell stands alone among his contemporaries, and since then he has never been surpassed. *Lochiel's Warning* and the *Battle of the Baltic* were among the pieces then published; and it would be difficult, out of the whole mass of British poetry, to select two specimens, by the same author, which may fairly rank with these.

A new literary field was shortly after this opened to Campbell. He was engaged to deliver a course of lectures on poetry at the Royal Institution of London, and the scheme proved not only successful but lucrative. In after years he lectured repeatedly on the belles lettres at Liverpool, Birmingham, and other places, and the celebrity of his name always commanded a crowd of listeners. We learn from Dr Beattie, that at two periods of his life it was proposed to bring him forward as a candidate, either for the chair of Rhetoric or that of History in the University of Edinburgh; but he seems to have recoiled from the idea of the labour necessary for the preparation of a thorough academical course, a task which his extreme natural fastidiousness would doubtless have rendered doubly irksome. Several more years, a portion of which time was spent on the Continent, passed over without any remarkable result, until, at the age of forty-three, Campbell entered upon the duties of the editorship of the *New Monthly Magazine*.

He held this situation for ten years, and resigned it, according to his own account, "because it was utterly impossible to continue the editor without interminable scrapes, together with a law-suit now and then." In the interim, however, certain important events had taken place. In the first place, he had published *Theodric*—a poem which, in spite of a most laudatory critique in the *Edinburgh Review*, left a painful impression on the public mind, and was generally considered as a symptom either that the rich mine of poesy was worked out, or that the genius of the author had been employed in a wrong direction. In the second place, he took an active share in the foundation of the London University. He appears, indeed, to have been the originator of the scheme, and to have managed the preliminary details with more than common skill and prudence. It was mainly through his exertions that it did not assume the aspect of a mere sectarian institution, bigoted in its principles and circumscribed in its sphere of utility. Shortly after this academical experiment, he was elected Lord Rector of the Glasgow University. Whatever abstract value may be attached to such an honour—and we are aware that very conflicting opinions have been expressed upon the point—this distinction was one of the most gratifying of all the tributes which were ever rendered to Campbell. He found himself preferred, by the students of that university where his first aspirations after fame had been roused, to one of the first orators and statesmen of the age; and his warm heart overflowed with delight at the kindly compliment. He resolved not to accept the office as a mere sinecure, but strictly to perform those duties which were prescribed by ancient statute, but which had fallen into abeyance by the carelessness of nominal Rectors. He entered as warmly into the feelings, and as cordially supported the interests of the students, as if the academical red gown of Glasgow had been still fresh upon his shoulders; and such being the case, it is not surprising that he was almost adored by his youthful constituents. This portion of the memoirs is very interesting: it displays the character of Campbell in a most amiable light; and the coldest reader cannot fail to peruse with pleasure the records of an ovation so truly gratifying to the sensibilities of the kind and affectionate poet. For three years, during which unusual period he held the office, his correspondence with the students never flagged; and it may be doubted whether the university ever possessed a better Rector.

In 1831 he took up the Polish cause, and founded an association in London, which for many years was the main support of the unfortunate exiles who sought refuge in Britain. The public sympathy was at that time largely excited in their favour, not only by the gallant struggle which they had made for regaining their ancient independence, but from the subsequent severities perpetrated by the Russian government. Campbell, from his earliest years, had denounced the unprincipled partition of Poland; he watched the progress of the revolution with an anxiety almost amounting to fanaticism; and when the outbreak was at last put down by the strong hand of power, his passion exceeded all bounds. Day and night his thoughts were of Poland only: in his correspondence he hardly touched upon any other theme; and, carried away by his zeal to serve the exiles, he neglected his usual avocations. The mind of Campbell was naturally of an impulsive cast: but the fits were rather violent than enduring. This psychological tendency was, perhaps, his most serious misfortune, since it invariably prevented him from maturing the most important projects he conceived. Unless the scheme was such as could be executed with rapidity, he was apt to halt in the progress.

He next became engaged in a new magazine speculation—*The Metropolitan*—which, instead of turning out, as he anticipated, a mine of wealth, very nearly involved him in serious pecuniary responsibility. After this, his public career gradually became less marked. The last poem which he published, *The Pilgrim of Glencoe*, exhibited few symptoms of the fire and energy conspicuous in his early efforts. "This work," says Dr Beattie, "in one or two instances was very favourably reviewed—in others, the tone of criticism was cold and austere; but neither praise nor censure could induce the public to judge for themselves; and silence, more fatal in such cases than censure, took the poem for a time under her wing. The poet himself expressed little surprise at the apathy with which his new volume had been received; but whatever indifference he felt for the influence it might have upon his reputation, he could not feel indifferent to the more immediate effect which a tardy or greatly diminished sale must have upon his prospects as a householder. 'A new poem from the pen of Campbell,' he was told, 'was as good as a bill at sight;' but, from some error in the drawing, as it turned out, it was not negotiable; and the expenses into which he had been led, by trusting too much to popular favour, were now to be defrayed from other sources." It ought, however, to be remarked, that he had now arrived at his great climacteric. He was sixty-four years of age, and his constitution, never very robust, began to exhibit symptoms of decay. Dr Beattie, who had long watched him with affectionate solicitude, in the double character of physician and friend, thus notes his observation of the change. "At the breakfast or dinner table—particularly when surrounded by old friends—he was generally animated, full of anecdote, and always projecting new schemes of benevolence. But still there was a visible change in his conversation: it seemed to flow less freely; it required an effort to support it; and on topics in which he once felt a keen interest, he now said but little, or remained silent and thoughtful. The change in his outward appearance was still more observable; he walked with a feeble step, complained of constant chilliness; while his countenance, unless when he entered into conversation, was strongly marked with an expression of languor and anxiety. The sparkling intelligence that once animated his features was greatly obscured; he quoted his favourite authors with hesitation—because, he told me, he often could not recollect their names."

The remainder of his life was spent in comparative seclusion. Long before this period he was left a solitary man. His wife, whom he loved with deep and enduring affection, was taken away—one of his sons died in childhood, and the other was stricken with a malady which proved incurable. But the kind offices of a nephew and niece, and the attentions of many friends, amongst whom Dr Beattie will always be remembered as the chief, soothed the last days of the poet, and supplied those duties which could not be rendered by dearer hands. He expired at Boulogne, on 15th June 1844, his age being sixty-seven, and his body was worthily interred in Westminster Abbey, with the honours of a public funeral.

"Never," says Beattie, "since the death of Addison, it was remarked, had the obsequies of any literary man been attended by circumstances more honourable to the national feeling, and more expressive of cordial respect and homage, than those of Thomas Campbell.

"Soon after noon, the procession began to move from the Jerusalem Chamber to Poet's Corner, and in a few minutes passed slowly down the long lofty aisle—

'Through breathing statues, then unheeded
    things;
Through rows of warriors, and through walks
    of kings.'

On each side the pillared avenues were lined with spectators, all watching the solemn pageant in reverential silence, and mostly in deep mourning. The Rev. Henry Milman, himself an eminent poet, headed the procession; while the service for the dead, answered by the deep-toned organ, in sounds like distant thunder, produced an effect of indescribable solemnity. One only feeling seemed to pervade the assembled spectators, and was visible on every face—a desire to express their sympathy in a manner suitable to the occasion. He who had celebrated the glory and enjoyed the favour of his country for more than forty years, had come at last to take his appointed chamber in the Hall of Death—to mingle ashes with those illustrious predecessors, who, by steep and difficult paths, had attained a lofty eminence in her literature, and made a lasting impression on the national heart."

We observe that Dr Beattie has, very properly, passed over with little notice certain statements, emanating from persons who styled themselves the friends of Campbell, regarding his habits of life during the latter portion of his years. It is a misfortune incidental to almost all men of genius, that they are surrounded by a fry of small literary adulators, who, in order to magnify themselves, make a practice of reporting every circumstance, however trivial, which falls under their observation, and who are not always very scrupulous in adhering to the truth. Campbell, who had the full poetical share of vanity in his composition, was peculiarly liable to the attacks of such insidious worshippers, and was not sufficiently careful in the selection of his associates. Hence imputations, not involving any question of honour or morality, but implying frailty to a considerable degree, have been openly hazarded by some who, in their own persons, are no patterns of the cardinal virtues. Such statements do no honour either to the heart or the judgment of those who devised them: nor would we have even touched upon the subject, save to reprobate, in the strongest manner, these breaches of domestic privacy, and of ill-judged and unmerited confidence.

A good deal of the correspondence printed in these volumes is of a trifling nature, and interferes materially with the conciseness of the biography. We do not mean to say that anything objectionable has been included, but there are too many notes and epistles upon familiar topics, which neither illustrate the peculiar tone of Campbell's mind, nor throw any light whatever upon his poetical history. But the correspondence with his own family is highly interesting. Nowhere does Campbell appear in a higher and more estimable point of view, than in the character of son and brother. Even in the hours of his darkest adversity, we find him sharing his small and precarious gains with his mother and sisters; and they were in an equal degree the participators of his better fortunes. His fondness and consideration for his wife and children are most conspicuous; and many of his letters regarding his boy, when "the dark shadow" had passed across his mind, are extremely affecting. Those who have a taste for the modern style of maundering about children, and the perverted pictures of infancy so common in our social literature, may not, perhaps, see much to admire in the following extract from a letter by Campbell, announcing the birth of his eldest child: to us it appears a pure and exquisite picture:—

"This little gentleman all this while looked to be so proud of his new station in society, that he held up his blue eyes and placid little face with perfect indifference to what people about him felt or thought. Our first interview was when he lay in his little crib, in the midst of white muslin and dainty lace, prepared by Matilda's hands, long before the stranger's arrival. I verily believe, in spite of my partiality, that lovelier babe was never smiled upon by the light of heaven. He was breathing sweetly in his first sleep. I durst not waken him, but ventured to give him one kiss. He gave a faint murmur, and opened his little azure lights. Since that time he has continued to grow in grace and stature. I can take him in my arms; but still his good nature and his beauty are but provocatives to the affection which one must not indulge: he cannot bear to be hugged, he cannot yet stand a worrying. Oh! that I were sure he would live to the days when I could take him on my knee, and feel the strong plumpness of childhood waxing into vigorous youth. My poor boy! shall I have the ecstasy to teach him thoughts and knowledge, and reciprocity of love to me? It is bold to venture into futurity so far L at present his lovely little face is a comfort to me; his lips breathe that fragrance which it is one of the loveliest kindnesses of Nature that she has given to infants—a sweetness of smell more delightful than all the treasures of Arabia. What adorable beauties of God and Nature's bounty we live in without knowing! How few have ever seemed to think an infant beautiful! But to me there seems to be a beauty in the earliest dawn of infancy which is not inferior to the attractions of childhood, especially when they sleep. Their looks excite a more tender train of emotions. It is like the tremulous anxiety which we feel for a candle new lighted, which we dread going out."

The sensibility, too, which he uniformly exhibited towards those who had shown him kindness, especially his older and earlier friends, is exceedingly pleasing. In writing to or speaking of the Rev. Archibald Alison and Dugald Stewart, his tone is one of heartfelt, and almost filial, affection and reverence; and amongst all the benevolent actions performed by those great and good men, there were few to which they could revert with more pleasure than to their seasonable patronage of the young and sanguine poet. With his literary contemporaries, also, he lived upon good terms,— a circumstance rather remarkable, for Campbell, notwithstanding his good-nature, was sufficiently touchy, and keenly alive to satire or hostile criticism. Excepting an early quarrel with John Leyden, on the score of some reported misrepresentation, a temporary feud with Moore, which was speedily reconciled, and a short and unacrimonious disruption from Bowles, we are not aware that he ever differed with any of his gifted brethren. He was upon the best terms with Scott; and Dr Beattie has given us several valuable specimens of their mutual correspondence. With Rogers he was intimate to the last; and even the sarcastic and dangerous Byron always mentioned him with expressions of regard. Let us add, moreover, that, whenever he had the power, he was ready, even in instances where his own interest might have counselled otherwise, to lend a helping hand to others who were struggling for literary reputation. This generous impulse was sometimes carried so far as to injure him in his editorial capacity; for, although fastidious to a degree as to the quality of his own writings, it was always with a sore heart that he shut the door in the face of a needy contributor.

The querulousness with which Campbell complains throughout, of the cruel treatment which he met with at the hands of the publishers, would be amusing, if it were not at the same time most unjust. He acknowledges, in a letter written to Mr Richardson, so late as 1842, that the sale of his poems, for a series of years before, had yielded him, on an average, £500 per annum: not a bad annuity, we think, as the proceeds of a couple of volumes! We happen to know, moreover, that by the first publication of *Gertrude* Campbell made upwards of a thousand pounds; and, unless we are grievously misinformed, he received from Mr Murray, for the copyright of the *Specimens*, a similar sum, being double the amount contracted for. We have already mentioned the publication of a subscription edition of the *Pleasures of Hope*, "which," says Dr Beattie, "with great liberality on the part of the publishers, was to be brought out for his own exclusive benefit." We should not have alluded to these matters, which, however, we believe, are no secrets, but for the publication by Dr Beattie of some very absurd expressions used and reiterated by Campbell. Such phrases as the following constantly occur: "They are the greatest ravens on earth with whom we have to deal—liberal enough as booksellers go —but still, you know, ravens, croakers, suckers of innocent blood, and living men's brains." Nor, in the opinion of Campbell, were these outrages confined merely to the living subjects, for he says, in reference to the older tenants of Parnassus, "Poor Bards! you are all ill used, even after death, by those who have lived upon your brains. And now, having scooped out those brains, they drink out of them, like Vandals out of the skulls of the severed and slain, served up by a Gothic Ganymede!" Further, in speaking of Napoleon, he says, "Perhaps in my feelings towards the Gallic usurper there may be some personal bias; for I must confess that, ever since he shot the bookseller in Germany, I have had a warm side to him. It was sacrificing an offering, by the hand of genius, to the manes of the victims immolated by the trade; and I only wish we had Nap here for a short time, to cut out a few of our own cormorants." The fact is, that so far from Campbell being ill-used by the trade, they behaved towards him with uncommon liberality. It is true that, in several instances, they hesitated in making high terms for work not yet commenced, with a man who was notoriously deficient in punctuality and perseverance; nor are they to be blamed, when we consider the number of his schemes, and the very few instances in which these were brought to maturity.

On the whole, then, though we cannot bestow unqualified praise upon Dr Beattie, for the manner in which he has compiled these volumes, we shall state that we have passed no unprofitable hours in their perusal. We rise from them with full appreciation of the many excellent points in the poet's character, with an augmented regard for his memory on account of the virtues so eminently displayed, and with no lessened reverence for the man in consequence of the admitted foibles from which none of the human family are exempt. The book may be practically useful to those who aspire to literary eminence, and who are apt to rely too confidently and implicitly on the powers with which they are naturally gifted. So long as Campbell was under restraint—so long as he was subjected to the wholesome discipline of the University, and forced into the race of emulation, we find that his genius was largely and rapidly developed. He was not a mere philological scholar, though his attainments in Greek might have put many a pedant to the blush; but he improved his sense of beauty and his taste by the contemplation of the Attic flowers; and, without injuring his style by any affectation of antiquity unsuited to the tone of his age, he adorned it by many of the graces which are presented by the ancient models. At Glasgow he worked hard and won merited honours. But afterwards, by abandoning himself to a desultory course of study and of composition, by never acting upon the wise and sure plan of keeping one object only steadily in view, and persevering in spite of all difficulties until that point was attained,— he failed in realising the high expectations which were justified by his early promise. As it is, Campbell's name is ranked high in the roll of the British poets; but assuredly he would have occupied a still more exalted place, and also have avoided much of that anxiety which at times clouded his existence, if he had used his fine natural gifts with but a portion of the energy and determination of his great compatriot, Scott.

In conclusion let us remark, that however Dr Beattie may have erred on the side of prolixity, by including in the compass of the memoirs some trifling and irrelevant matter, he is more than concise whenever it is necessary to allude to his own relationship with Campbell. He has made no parade whatever of his intimacy with the poet; and no stranger, in perusing these volumes, could discover that to Beattie Campbell was substantially indebted for many disinterested acts of friendship, which contributed largely to the comfort of his declining years. This modesty is a rare feature in modern biography; and, when it does occur so remarkably as here, we are bound to mention it with special honour.

BIOGRAPHIA DRAMATICA.

If you have the happiness to possess a garrulous and clear-headed old friend of seventy or eighty years of age, you will see what a hold the stage and its professors had on the generation at the commencement of this century. "John Kemble, sir, always wore knee-breeches of grey cloth when he was in the country. Mrs Siddons, sir, once tumbled over a stile near Coventry, and bore the mark of the accident on the instep of her right foot to her dying day. She died on a Friday, sir, and I have heard she was married on a Thursday." The newspapers of 1809 are filled with more columns of discussion on the late quarrel between Y. Z. of the T. R. D. L. and X. Y. of the T. R. C. G. than of information about the armies in Spain. Who would trouble his head now if all the actors of Drury Lane libelled all the actresses of Covent Garden once a-week? Nay, put your hand to your heart, reader, and answer this, Do you know the name, the quality, the character, or appearance of any performer, male or female, at either of the above-named theatres? Would it give you any pain to be informed that the second murderer of the one had long been privately married to the singing chambermaid of the other? or that the youthful lover of either had thrashed the heavy father within an inch of his life? The marvel to us of this later generation is, how anybody could have had any greater interest in the private proceedings and previous history of the man who acted Friar Lawrence than in the parentage and education of the man who made his boots. If Crispin makes the Wellingtons easy yet close-fitting, with a flexible yet impermeable sole and glossy upper-leather, who cares whether his mother was at all times in possession of her marriage certificate or not?—who cares whether his father sent him very early to a school, or neglected his education till he grew up as ignorant as a young "honourable" of the Whig and evangelical persuasion? But nobody had so much reason to complain of this indecent prying into all their affairs—matrimonial, pecuniary, moral, and religious—as the unhappy actors themselves. Poor mimes for three or four hours a-day, making their bread in the contortion of their faces and inflation of their lungs, it was too bad that they should be followed from their uneasy position before the foot-lights, and traced, with the minuteness and accuracy of a detective, to the cider-cellar, to the finish, to the police-office, to the van, to the bridewell; or, following

Biographia Dramatica. Four vols. London.

the sunny path of success, and changing the sex of the performers,—from the smothering pillow of Desdemona to the drawing-room, to the park, to the church, to the coronets of dukes and earls. It seemed as if the moment an unlucky person, whether an ambitious Hamlet or an aspiring Ophelia, set foot upon the boards, they were forced in all future time to dance a torch-dance down the great hall of life, like a set of princes and potentates at a Prussian wedding, and found repose and shadow never more. To exist for ever within the glare of lamps and the smell of orange-peel was a heavy price to pay for the chance of making a palpable hit as Laertes, or captivating a marquess in the white robes of Miranda. But this suffering actors were willing to endure and the public to inflict. Once encircled with the tinfoil crown—once robed in imitation ermine—once grasping the wooden sceptre—private existence was from thenceforth impossible to the vexed majesty of Sicily or the ill-favoured king of Denmark. His ways were marked in Wardour Street—his appearance was greeted in Martin's Lane. The first seat of the gallery recognised him as he dived into a ham and beef shop to cheapen a sausage; the waiter at the Tavistock door pointed him out to the rural clergyman who was waiting for a coach. "That's Mr Brown, sir, of Covent Garden; he is going to appear to-night as the crabbed old gent in the *Winter's Tale;*" or, "That's Mr Jones, sir, of Drury; he is to act Hamlet's uncle; a big man, and very strong. He began with gymnastics, but when he grew too heavy for the rope, he took to kings, sir; he has almost always a crown on his head. I've heard say, what with four hours' rehearsal and three hours' play, his reign would be nearly as long as George IV.'s, if they were all added together, without counting the time they're both asleep."

This morbid curiosity about the denizens of the stage has completely died out. Sufficient interest, no doubt, is still felt about the gentlemen and scholars who were really lords of the scene, and whose tones and looks are remembered as, with the magic of eye and voice, they summoned a meaning from some hidden phrase which had hitherto escaped us, or gave bodily presence to the great thoughts which Shakespeare had condensed into the name of Lear. We may still inquire with interest about men of this mark and likelihood, and hear with pleasure that Charles Young led a life of honoured ease and social enjoyment till his many parts were played out—the Christian's the happiest part of all; that Charles Kemble showed the liveliness of Benedict and the grace of Anthony beneath the weight of years and the infirmity of deafness. But for the mass of the *dramatis personæ* —for the strong Gyas and the strong Cloanthus—there is no room in people's memories. They are now reduced to the rank-and-file of the great histrionic army, and are buried *in cumulo*, like the unknown yet useful heroes of Inkermann and Lucknow. The race, alas, of tittle-tattle critics and dramatic gossip-mongers, who would have made Havelocks and Nicholsons of the whole force—drummer-boys, pioneers and all—has passed away.

But the passion for dragging every one connected with the theatre before the public was not restricted, in that earlier day, to the mere wearers of the sock and buskin. Woe befall the aspirant for dramatic reputation in any shape or form! If poverty, and beer, and vanity, and a cousin promoted to be prompter, induced a youthful Shakespeare to write a farce, he was a public character till the earth was shovelled over him, at the parish expense, in the pauper's grave. Chields were among the audience, or in the orchestra among the fiddlers, or behind the scenes among the paint-pots, taking notes; and whether the poor effort succeeded or not—whether triumphant shouts brought forward the author to the front of his private box, or indignant hisses drove him distracted from the house—the notes were printed; they were sent to a yearly volume of theatrical intelligence; they were incorporated with a thousand other records equally important; and he flourished for ever in a dictionary, with all his previous life, and vaticinations of his future destiny, inscribed at full length; and, to bar all chance of immunity from the world's research, this history of him was to be found in the index, either under the initial of his name or of the title of his work. A man might write an Epic, and be laughed at for a fortnight—or a History, and be forgotten in a shorter time; but if he tried a melodrama, or a tragedy, or a pantomime, or soared into opera and comedy, it was all the same—he was pilloried in the biography of dramatic authors; and the hiss of that furious pit, the groans of that frantic gallery, never left his ears; anybody that heard his name could turn to the book; and the misfortune was, that if his cognomen happened to be a common one, or if the biographer was deceived by the identity of patronymic, the wretched subject of commemoration was credited with the doings of his double, and had follies and iniquities of every kind to blush for, as well as the failure of his literary attempt. "Robinson, William, author of a farce called *Phantoms in Love*—hissed off in the middle of the first act; drove the Bristol mail, died of *delirium tremens*, August 1834." What a perpetual source of irritation to our friend Mr Robinson, who is churchwarden in our town, and president of the Teetotal Society, to have had his simple story so confounded by means of a literary escapade in his youth, when he was serving his time in a fleecy hosiery house in London, with the life and demise of another gentleman of the same appellation! His descendants will never be able to separate the amiable and unsuccessful writer of the amorous phantoms from the charioteering skill and tipsy propensities of the other Dromio who drove the Bristol coach, and finally expired of gin-and-water.

People of unsympathetic minds feel a sort of scorn at the sufferings of those unwillingly-commemorated candidates for theatrical fame. "The fellow failed in writing a play, but who heeds the foolish books where his failure is announced? I wouldn't care sixpence to be called a rascal every day of the week in the *Chinese Times* at Pekin. Let the blockhead hold his tongue, and nobody is a bit the wiser." But forty or even thirty years ago everybody was a great deal the wiser. The *Chinese Times* was written in good English, and published in London. Everybody read it. A man's sons at school turned to a passage like this: Ephraim Blunt—educated at Oxford; expelled for thrashing the proctor; came to London; was refused admission to the bar; wrote for the stage. The following are the pieces for which we are indebted to this gentleman: *Go it, Cripples*—a comedy of no merit, condemned the first night. *Hoky Poky Winky Wan*—a burlesque, so filled with insolent allusions to the king and ministers, that a justly-indignant audience desired the author to be delivered into their hands; and when they had discovered him in one of the private boxes, he was taken to a coach-stand in the neighbourhood, and soused with the waterman's buckets till his life was in danger. *Love Conquers the World*—a tragedy, hissed and laughed at. This gentleman, finding himself out to be the noodle his wisest friends had long pronounced him, retired from further intercourse with the muses; and on the death of his father succeeded to a good estate in Suffolk. He married Maria, eldest daughter of Joseph Muck, Esquire, the agricultural improver. He is chairman of the quarter-sessions, and stood unsuccessfully for the county at the last election." Can young Reginald Blunt believe his eyes?

Can it be his father, the steady, turnip-loving, vagrant-quelling, dozy, prosy old squire and magistrate, who led such a terrible life in his youth, and left the university under a cloud, and wrote such dull, wicked, idiotic plays, that he was hissed, and sneered at, and ducked? Will his daughters see this hideous biography? If they do, will they have such respect and affection for the jolly, old, kind-hearted governor, or will they not hear perpetual sibilations when they look at his benevolent countenance, and tremble when they see a horse-bucket at the stable door, remembering what a tremendous part it played in the reception of Hoky Poky? For you will observe that the biographer of the stage differs from almost all other biographers in the relation he bears to the subject of his labours. In ordinary cases, a life-writer is a life-embellisher. He sees no spots on the character of his hero, and presents him at the end of his work as a model for the imitation of mankind, though he began his inquiries in a very different spirit. Judge Jeffreys emerges from the beautifying hands of his recorder a firm and incorruptible magistrate, executing justice with a severity founded on the highest principles of loyalty and honour. As to Henry VIII. and Bloody Mary, let us be thankful we have such specimens of heavenly virtue surmounted by an earthly crown, for they compensate for all the crimes and monstrosities of all other rulers. But the dramatic biographer proceeds generally on a very different principle. If he can fling an orange or whistle a cat-call, he does it. Mossop is not genteel; Garrick is not more than five feet three; such an author was eaten up with jealousy; such an actor cheated his landlady; Desdemona drank; Ophelia deserted her children; Joseph Surface kept a spirit-shop in Drury Lane; and Dr Dodd was hanged for forgery.

The reader will ask, what has Dr Dodd to do with a theatrical biography? Didn't we tell you, that if at any period of a man's life he appeared either as actor or author, or in the remotest way connected with the drama, he became the property of this gatherer up of all the scandals and failures of his whole life? Accordingly, we find not only the name of Dr Dodd, who published selections from Shakespeare, but an incredible number of the clergy—rectors, deans, and bishops—who sighed for dramatic fame; for it seems that in ancient days a perfect mania of play-writing seized the thoughtful student in the dangerous two years between his degree and his orders. Æschylus, Sophocles, Terence, Aristophanes— all fermenting in those learned heads, foamed off into comedy or farce; and sticking up for ever in front of the gates of Bishopsthorpe or Lambeth, or the Deanery of St Paul's, there was a glaring ticket with the name of some adolescent drama, or scholar-like play, or elegant and pathetic tragedy, of which the residents in those spacious mansions, though by no means ashamed of their performances, did not wish a perpetual memorial held up in the eyes of their rustic vicars or minor canons — not to mention their churchwardens and choir.

The particular work that has given rise to these learned and indignant remarks is called *Biographia Dramatica; or, a Companion to the Playhouse.* It was commenced by Mr Baker, and brought down by him to the year 1764. Mr Reed carried on the fatal record to the year 1782; and flowers and brickbats are distributed with impartial hand on all the sons and daughters of Momus who flourished or failed between that date and 1811 by Mr Stephen Jones. Who may have been the continuators of this dramatic Newgate Calendar to the present time, we do not know. Perhaps the disregard for stage affairs of which we spoke a page or two ago had already set in, and the grinning, jumping, howling, and roaring histrions, and adapters from the French and Elizabethan of our own day, may be allowed to rest in the shade. Baker, indeed, sets a very good example in this respect, in cases where he is obliged by his plan to immortalise an author or performer who won't stand the process of embalming. For instance, his first subject under the letter A is this—" A. R., gent. These initials we find prefixed to a dramatic piece, entitled the *Valiant Welchman,* tragi-comedy." Oh everlasting Muses, who sit for ever carving the names of the great and wonderful on the rock of immortality, is this all that can be said about the author of the *Valiant Welchman?* A vain guess is made, indeed, by the sagacious editor, that the initials represent a Mr Robert Armin who wrote a comedy called *The History of the Two Maids of More Clacke*— " because," he says, " the dates of the two performances are within six years of each other, and the styles are similar." Bad jokes, ungrammatical expressions, dull situations, doubtless, were in both, as there were salmon, look you, in two rivers, one of which the Valiant Welchman knew from his boyish years. It is far clearer to us that the initials represent Ap Ryce, or, better perhaps, Rice Ap Tudor, who claimed the great dignity of gent. on the title-page, on the strength not only of his dramatic genius, but of his royal descent from Cadwallader the First.

Next to him comes "Adams, George, M.A., Fellow of St John's, Cambridge, in 1735." If the incumbent of Drizzle-cum-Fogy, which is still in the patronage of St John's and the county of Suffolk, died in 1746, when the too poetic Fellow published the drama which has procured him his niche in the *Biographia,* we may feel sure that George gave up his fellowship, and married not later than 1747. If George's son was born in 1748, he has probably a grandson at this moment, with the corners of his mouth very much bent down, and his eyes very much turned up, in expectation of an ultra-evangelical mitre, as the greatest theologian of modern times is again prime minister; and how will that worthy and theatre-hating divine like to have it blown on trumpets all round the episcopal palace, that his ancestor, the Reverend George, was author of a profane stage-play called *The Death of Socrates,* which, with a sarcastic humour of which he was probably unconscious, Mr Baker has described, by the abbreviations he uses for its nature or kind, as " A Hist. Trag." We have little doubt that it was a trag. which was very powerfully hist. Triumphant over George Adams, Mr Baker goes back again to the Robert Armin whom he thought he perceived hiding himself in the gossamer disguise of A. R. He catches the author of *The Two Maids of More Clacke* by the throat, after the instructions of Dogberry, and asks whether he is a true man or a thief; and when Robert Armin contumaciously declines to answer, the biographer adds a paragraph, which throws a very groundless imputation on the honour and respectability of Mr Armin's matrimonial connections. He says: "There was published in the year 1604 a pamphlet entitled *A Discourse of Elizabeth Armin,* who, with some other complices, attempted to poison her husband;" and in a manner, and with an evident animus, which would have procured a handsome sum in damages to the outraged feelings of A. R., he adds this frightful insinuation — " Whether this anecdote has any reference to our author, we cannot pretend to affirm, but think it by no means improbable, from the correspondence of the date with the time in which he flourished." It is a kind of relief to turn from these accusations of capital crimes to the milder punishments he administers to the follies and vanities of mankind. Poor Samuel Brandon, of whom nothing whatever is known but his name, and the title of his one play, called the *Virtuous Octavia,* affixed to his published work a motto from the Italian, which, by a good-humoured construction of the words, may be made to appear a modest confession of his undeservings, "L' acqua non temo dell' eterno oblio"—"I have no fear of the waters of eternal oblivion," which, however, I know very well I have no chance of escaping. This, in the absence of all knowledge of who or what Samuel Brandon was, we maintain to have been the meaning of the quotation; but Mr Baker, *more suo*, is down upon the unknown Samuel and the virtuous lady he celebrated with the acerbity of an inquisitor condemning a contumacious heretic to the stake. "What profession he was of," says the biographical Dominic, "or what rank he held in life, we have not been able to procure any information. He appears, however, to have been possessed of no small share of vanity and self-sufficiency, from the Italian verse he has subjoined to the only dramatic piece he wrote, and which, notwithstanding the high opinion he, and perhaps some of his partial friends, might entertain of it, is now entirely forgotten."

The war carried on against the forgotten and unknown is as bitter as if it arose from the refusal of the loan of half-a-crown, or any personal discourtesy of the same unpardonable kind. From the deepest stratum of clay at the bottom of the lowest depth of Lethe, an unhappy Anthony Brewer is hauled up, to be stripped of feathers which nobody except a few bookworms from the same layer of mud ever knew he wore, and to be reduced to the small amount of fame he was entitled to, of which nobody, with the above exception, has had a conception for two hundred and fifty years. Anthony is the undoubted author, the reader will be pleased henceforth to remember, of *The Country Girl*, a comedy, and of *The Love-Sick King*, a trag. hist.; but if he hears, as is very probable, violent discussions going on at his club, in his family, at dinner-parties, and on excursions to see a volunteer shooting-match, as to whether the said Anthony was also author of the trag. com. of *Landgartha*, of the past. of *Love's Dominion*, and of the com. of *Love's Loadstone*, let him indignantly deny it on the authority of Baker; and explain, as that ingenious Œdipus does, the cause of the mistake. He points out that the plays attributed to this peerless Anthony all begin with the same letter—*Landgartha, Love's Dominion,* and *Love's Loadstone*—all commence with L; "and so," cries the triumphant biographer, "does Brewer's acknowledged historical tragedy of the *Love-Sick King*. Now, in the catalogue of plays printed by Kirkman in 1661, the author's name is set opposite his work, and where the writer of a piece was unknown, a blank was left. But Philips and Winstanley"—two wretches who ought to have been put to death for stupidity on a subject of such importance—"were not aware of this; and, seeing a blank following the name of Brewer, which was attached to the *Love-sick King*, they mistook the alphabetical arrangement for a repetition of the same author, and ascribed these three L's in succession to the writer of that one play." Was ever such a confusion? Will the world go on much longer—will it last even to 1867—if this is not rectified, for the universal enlightenment of the ultimate generation of men? But the Chief Baker is like some husbands and Scotsmen of our acquaintance, who will allow nobody to abuse their wives or country but themselves, and breaks out in indignant denial when anybody else attempts to diminish the glory of Anthony Brewer. "Langbaine," he says, "absolutely denies that the comedy of *Lingua*—(mark the identity of initial)—is the work of this gentleman, yet assigns no other reason for so doing but his own bare *ipse dixit*." Winstanley, on the same classical authority, attributes it to him; so does Theophilus Cibber, on Winstanley's word; so does Dodsley on Cibber's; and so does Mr Baker on those three excellent men's asseveration, with the additional argument in favour of the name of Brewer, that it was published without any name at all, which, says the acute logician, "makes his authorship more probable, it being much earlier in date than his other works, and therefore likely to have appeared anonymously." Capital news this for any obscure aspirant after notoriety, if the prodigious density of some future Baker endows some future Liggnis with the fame of some popular work on the strength of its being anonymous, and his never having published anything with his name.

After this disquisition about Anthony, let us turn to Cæsar. Baker affirms that a passage in this comedy of *Lingua* struck the first spark of ambition in the heart of Oliver Cromwell. He tells us the play was acted at Cambridge, and that the future Protector took the part of Tactus, or the Touch, in a discussion between the senses, among whom Lingua was admitted as chief and ornament of them all. Mr Foster, the eloquent and enthusiastic biographer of Old Noll, alludes to the fact, transferring the scene of it, out of deference to chronology, to Huntingdon Free School, but without indorsing the assertion of Mr Baker, that the civil war and the death of Charles were caused by half-a-dozen lines of Anthony Brewer. Tactus, in coming on the scene, stumbles over a crown, and Oliver exclaims—

" Was ever man so fortunate as I,
To break his shins at such a stumbling-block?
Roses and bays, pack hence!—this crown and robe
My brows and body circles and invests.
How gallantly it fits me! sure the slave
Measured my head that wrought this coronet!
They lie that say complexions cannot change:
My blood's ennobled, and I am transformed
Into the sacred temper of a king."

Whereupon, in the opinion of the worthy *Biographia* critic, the grasping soul of the little boy of fourteen (who was certainly flogged by Dr Beard for the false syntax of the crown *and* robe with the singular verbs) never forgot the glories of that hour, but mused on them at Worcester and Dunbar, and finally saw them nearly reproduced in soldier form when the sceptre of England was almost within his grasp. We maintain that, within one fortnight after the aforesaid flogging, Master O. Cromwell as completely forgot *Lingua* and Mr Anthony Brewer as all the rest of the world, except the late Charles Lamb. The late Charles Lamb! with his Elias, and his quiddities—he also has found a place in this congress of immortals, in right of his unnameable and unnamed comedy. Let us see. "Lamb, Charles. Of this gentleman we only know that he is the author of *John Woodvill*, T., and *Mr H.*, farce. But we suppose he is the same writer who, in 1808, gave to the public a very agreeable selection, entitled *Specimens of English Dramatic Poets who lived about the Time of Shakespeare;* and had previously published *Tales from Shakespeare*, a work of very considerable merit."

It is a pity for Mr Baker and Co.'s gossiping propensities, that Charles Lamb had no brother with any peculiarity of adventure—no cousin who had made a fortune by the slave-trade, or been prosecuted for a libel. The touching and really romantic history of poor Mary Lamb, the sister, was yet to come; but wherever, in other instances, a collateral anecdote can be introduced, an ancestral indiscretion exposed, or a youthful dramatic failure recorded, of the most distant relation, or even a namesake, the curtain is infallibly drawn up, and we read—" We are sorry to say, a near relative of this gentleman, a granduncle by the mother's side, was hanged for uttering base coin in the reign of George II." Turning to the name next in alphabetical order to Charles's, we are pleased to see, "Lamb, the Honourable George. This gentleman, whom we suppose to be one of the sons of Lord Viscount Melbourne, is author of *Whistle for it*, Op. piece." And this is all! No intimation of how *Whistle for it* was received, or whether it was praised or—not; no anecdote of the author, and no allusion to his brother, who afterwards achieved greatness, if indeed he had not greatness thrust upon him against his will. When *Whistle for it* was published, William, afterwards Lord Melbourne, was thirty years of age. Had all the inquisitive powers of the biographer failed to discover any remarkable incident in his past career, or to foresee any distinction in the future? No great blame can be atttached to him if this was really the case, for "this gentleman," as he would say, reversed the ordinary course of human reputation, and only became illustrious after his demise. In 1837, five-and-twenty years after the publication of his book, surrounded with power and patronage, Lord Melbourne had credit, indeed, for being a cleverer man than he appeared—a Sardanapalus in a humble way, with his loftier qualities obscured by the carelessness of his manner and his hatred of intellectual display. But nobody thought of him as of a great ruler of men—a politician, philosopher, and scholar, of whom hereafter the land would be proud. He was an amiable, pleasant, unaffected, well-read country gentleman, of which noble race every county in England possesses "five hundred as good as he." So thought the public, the press, and both Houses of Parliament. Melbourne was delightful in private, and not more mischievous in affairs than he could possibly help. But upward from the very mouth of the river on which a man and his fortunes are generally floated off to oblivion, comes a backwater so strong that it reaches the scene of his exploits while alive, and shows him triumphant on the summit of that unexpected tide, "and blest with all the virtues under heaven." Sir Bulwer Lytton, than whom no man is more fitted to pass judgment on intellect and acquirement, has pronounced his panegyric in terms which could only apply to a man of the highest order in genius and sagacity; and Sir Lawrence Peel, in his interesting sketch of the life and character of his great relative, Sir Robert, has corroborated the decision of the distinguished orator and novelist, in the same graceful and unbiassed spirit in which his whole volume is composed. Is this a reaction against unjust disparagement? or is it in both the Colonial Secretary and the Chief Justice—*jam rude donati*—a good-natured protest against the hustings brawlers and pot-house politicians of the present time, and a reminder to Birmingham and Sheffield, and even the city of London, that the gay and graceful William Lamb, the gentleman and scholar, was a far cleverer fellow and wiser man, in the midst of his apparent idleness and fashionable nonchalance, than the fussiest and most perspiring advocate of the paper-duty repeal, six-pound enfranchised pauperdom, and down with the House of Lords? But the fascinating Viscount Melbourne escaped the vengeful steel of the truculent life-writer by his obscurity in 1807. He would at most only have been consigned to fame as the relative of the author of *Whistle for it*.

We think we perceive a mellowing of tone as the dates approach the present time. Mr Baker in 1764, or Isaac Reed in 1782, can say things which Stephen Jones, the continuator, would not venture on in 1812. Later editions may be softer still, and perhaps, to save the feelings of Mr Froude, the notice of a certain Edward Lewis may be entirely missed out. A paradox is nothing if not new, and it will be seen from the following extract how very second-hand are all the virtues with which that eloquent and romantic historian has bedizened the husband of Anne Boleyn: "Lewis, Edward, M.A. Of this gentleman we know no more than that he is author of *The Ita-*

lian Husband; or, the Violated Bed Avenged. A Moral Dram., 1754." The Moral Dram. has had a tremendous effect on the easily intoxicated biographer; and, having confessed how little he knows, he proceeds to display what a quantity he can guess. "We suspect him, however, to be the same Edward Louis, M.A., who, in the year 1769, published a work, entitled 'The Patriot King Displayed in the Life and Reign of Henry the Eighth, King of England, from the Time of his Quarrel with the Pope to his Death. Printed for Charles Dilly in the Poultry.' In the title-page to this performance he styles himself Rector of Waterstock and Emington, in Oxfordshire. We would, if possible, avoid leading our readers into mistakes, and yet it is natural for us to suppose the author of the two most ridiculous of all dramatic performances might likewise have written the absurdest of all historical productions, especially when there occurs such a coincidence between dates and names. The tendency of the latter piece is to represent our lewd and sanguinary tyrant Henry VIII. as an exemplar of chastity and mercy."

This has the bite of Reed, who seems never so rabid as when he can tear up the reputation of some ludicrous old parson who has been long in his grave. Even Baker the Bitter is more pitiful, and tries to cast a veil over some of the foibles of his subjects, and to evoke romance from what to ordinary eyes seems very like profligacy and degradation. Turn to Mrs De la Rivière Manley. This eighteenth century Aspasia had the remarkable fortune (according to her biographer, whose strong point was not geography) of being born in the county of Southampton and the island of Jersey, during the governorship of her father, Sir Roger Manley. Sir Roger was more romantic than wise in his politics and conduct, for he followed the standard of King Charles I., and trusted for recompense to King Charles II. The Merry Monarch, perhaps, had only a laugh the more at the want and weakness of the decayed old royalist, and gave no help to the gallant soldier who converted his sword into a pen, and recorded in choice Latin the victories and reverses of the civil war. If it be true that he was also the author of the first volume of *The Turkish Spy*, "which was continued after his death by his relative Dr Midgeley, who never had the honesty to mention his name," the neglected Soldado was a man of as much talent as courage. We may therefore give him credit for educating his daughter, who lost her mother at an early age, with skill and success; but the mother's care was wanting. A childhood passed under the care of a disappointed cavalier — cherishing high notions of loyalty, and finding solace from penury and neglect in turning the fortunes of the Great Rebellion into Patavinian prose — was succeeded by her dawn of womanhood, under the guardianship of an aunt who has figured more than once in the pages of romance — a stiff, rigid, aristocratic, old spinster, contemptuous of the everyday world which neglected her charms, and living in a world of her own, in which cold lovers and butcher's bills are unknown,—casting a beautiful maiden of fifteen in her own formal and unnatural mould, and persuading her that there is a state of society somewhere—name of the country undiscovered — where all the men are heroes and all the women divine. This was the position and character of a sister of Sir Roger, who read the books of chivalry as models of sentiment and manners, and believed in them as sincerely as in her Bible. And to this spectacled and furbelowed Quixote, the cleverest, the loveliest, and most independent of young ladies was intrusted, when she had mastered the Roman and French classics, with which her father was familiar. She was now an orphan, beautiful as the day, full of spirit and accomplishments, her head stuffed with learning, and her heart with dreams, when the old lady took off her spectacles, laid down *Amadis de Gaul*, and was buried. La Rivière and her sister found themselves poor and unfriended; and now, as might be expected, the villain of the story made his appearance. The fairy realm in which the maiden had hitherto lived was knocked to pieces, and the rude world came upon her in a storm of misery and shame. Her cousin, a son of Sir Roger's brother—a fellow evidently beyond the bounds of Baker's Christian forgiveness, for he had joined the Parliament, and borne arms against the King—revealed his hereditary disloyalty, and, as he had been false to Church and Crown, was now false to beauty and honour. Under what base pleas, and by what intolerable arts, he obtained his object, we need not inquire; but La Rivière found herself, with blighted reputation and broken heart, thrown entirely on her own resources. Shut out by the society in which she would otherwise have been received, she betook herself to the companionship of that half-and-half sort of world, where the restraints of propriety are thrown away, but the charms of manner and intelligence retained. There she shone beyond all rivals by the grace of her behaviour and brilliancy of her wit, and in a short time was admitted to the "inner ring" of that life of frivolity and excitement of which the King himself was the bright central star. She became a favourite with the Duchess of Cleveland, at that time the sovereign mistress of Whitehall, and perhaps excited her wonder as much by the correctness of her behaviour as by the quickness of her repartee. But the Duchess was as capricious in her female friendships as in love, and ere six months elapsed became jealous of the talents and beauty of La Rivière, and led a crusade against her—a happy circumstance for the object of her hate, for it threw her into wiser counsels, and rescued her from the dangerous associations she had formed. Excluded from both the hemispheres into which the habitable globe of society was at that time divided, she betook herself to the point where both were united, and sent a tragedy to the theatre. It was received with universal acclamation, and her name became a household word in the assemblies of wit and fashion. The authoress of the *Royal Mischief* achieved an entrance into another and higher circle, where everything was forgiven to the possessor of genius, but where, probably, the only difference between the poetess and the purest of her admirers was, that she had been discovered and they had not. It was in the later days of our Merry Monarch, when the forced Puritanism of the Commonwealth had burst forth into universal licence. The salons of Versailles were imitated in their life and talent. Conversation was studied as an art, and everybody paid homage to what they called the charms of mind. But even here it was soon found out how amazingly the charms of mind are enhanced by a graceful figure and lovely face. All the great and rich and gay attended the levees of the new muse; and as she had hitherto shown great circumspection in her conduct, though sufficiently free in manner and conversation, fears were entertained that she would forfeit the world's good opinion, which it had cost her such trouble to regain. And in this the history takes a more ingenious turn than would have suggested itself to an ordinary concocter of a three-volume novel. Proof against the allurements of wealth and rank, rejecting the advances of any dangerous wooer, she gave herself up entirely to the delights of listening to the flatterers of her intellectual pre-eminence; and glozing old knights and superannuated courtiers mumbled her praises from morn to night, and " who peppered the highest was surest to please." General Tidcombe laid his poor, rusty old sword at her feet, and warned her against the designs of another aged swain, who was the silliest old noodle and basest liar of his time. This respectable character was a certain Sir Thomas Shepwith, who made up for his senility and unsuccess by boasting away the reputation of any beauty who allowed him to visit at her house. What youth and elegance had failed in, the false tongue of this dotard attained. He spread reports and imagined victories, and the world, with a shrug and a laugh, believed in the fall of the wittiest and most celebrated of her sex. From that time no steadiness of life, no pertinacity of denial, availed. La Rivière was the victim of a sexagenarian Lothario's unfounded calumnies, and fell upon evil tongues and evil days. New triumphs at the theatre only led to a wider diffusion of her fame and her fancied guilt. Losing at last the reality of virtue, as well as its reputation, she justified the fears of her friends and prognostications of her enemies by the irregularity of her course; but not without gleams of a nobler disposition. Borrowing a romantic sentiment from her dramatic experience, she persuaded the best beloved of her admirers to repair the fortune he had wasted in her service by marrying a rich widow, and retired for a while to lament over her separation, and triumph in her generosity. How long this lasted we are not told; but she came out in a new character when the curtain drew up again. Disappointed in love, and soured perhaps by the docility with which her self-sacrificing advice had been followed, she became a politician of the most rabid kind, and wrote libels on the ministry, for which she was brought up in custody before the Secretary of State. Her book was called *A New Atalantis*, and contained the most ferocious assaults on her political opponents, under false names. "Her defence," says Baker, "was made with much humility and sorrow, at the same time denying that any persons were concerned with her, or that she had a further design than writing for her own amusement and diversion in the country, without intending particular reflections on characters." When this was not believed, and the contrary urged against her, by several circumstances, she said, "Then it must be by inspiration, because, knowing her own innocence, she could account for it no other way." Lord Sunderland replied, " that inspiration used to be upon a good account, and her writings were stark naught." She, with an air of penitence, acknowledged "that his Lordship's observation might be true, but that there were evil angels as well as good; so that, nevertheless, what she had wrote might still be by inspiration." This—said, we have no doubt, with a pretty laugh and a coquettish toss of the head—seems to have silenced the eloquence of Lord Sunderland. He took his revenge, however, in sending her off in custody of a messenger, and did not relax his hold till her *habeas corpus* was sued out, and she was set at liberty by law. Poor shaky, quaky, old General Tidcombe had been in agonies on her account. He had begged her to fly to France to avoid her examination, and had offered, says Baker, his purse for that purpose; but as we feel certain, judging from the persevering gallantry of that military Methuselah, that he offered himself at the same time "for that purpose," we need not feel surprised that the heroine refused the offer, and faced the Secretary of State, in hopes of an easy martyrdom and eventual triumph.

As beauty decayed, the pamphlets grew. They were a sort of eruption, betraying a gradual corruption of the blood and decay of teeth and blushes. Her enemies were now turned out of office, and the day of retribution had come. Every month saw an assault upon her ancient foes, and she became invaluable to Downing Street (if such was the haunt of the triumphant party at that time). Bitterness, falsehood, hatred, and unscrupulous assertion, were so characteristic of these lucubrations, that they moved the sympathetic feelings of the great satirist and traducer of the day, and Dean Swift extended the hand of fellowship to the equally fierce but less malicious Mrs Manley. We confess it is a relief to get her into connection with a personage of flesh and blood; the Tidcombes, the Shepwiths, the Tillys, and even her villanous cousin and foolish old aunt, are like the well-imagined but rather feebly sustained characters in a romance; but the touch of Swift's most unromantic finger dissipates the suspicion, and we are informed that, "after he relinquished the *Examiner*, she continued it with great spirit for a considerable time, and frequently finished pieces begun by that excellent writer, who also used often to furnish her with hints for those of her own composition." It is a pity the biographer gives us no specimens of these Siamese productions, where the rage and venom of a neglected woman and disappointed priest must have been as inextricably mingled as the poetry and passion of Beaumont and Fletcher. But here ends the tale of the beauty and adventuress. Her beauty and adventures probably came to a close together; and passing some years of age and idleness in the house of Alderman Barber, she saw the curtain fall without any demonstration of applause, and "was buried," says the chronicler of her life, "in the middle aisle of the church of St Bennet, Paul's Wharf, where a marble gravestone was erected to her memory."

We have dwelt on this account of Mrs Manley because it reproduces a state of manners of which we have no specimen at the present day. But even in the interval between the flaring patronage of the Duchess of Cleveland and the decent dulness and pious hypocrisy of Queen Anne, she must have outlived her period, as if a flying serpent had survived to be contemporary with the dodo. The nearest approach to the wit and profligacy which had formed the atmosphere of her youth was supplied by the Dean of St Patrick's; and audiences had turned so absurdly respectable, and language and literature had grown so polished and gentlemanly, that Swift must have endeared himself to the congenial La Rivière by the contrast he offered to the improved spirit of the time. In him she recognised the coarseness, the immorality, and debasing tendencies which had won her earlier admiration in Wycherley and Congreve, and she must have clung to that impure concentration of humour and ferocity as her protection against the humanities of the *Tattler* and the frigidity of Cato. The list of her plays is as follows: 1. *The Royal Mischief* (Trag.); 2. *The Lost Lover; or, the Jealous Husband* (Com.); 3. *Almyna; or, the Arabian Vow* (T.); and 4. *Lucius, the First Christian King of Britain* (T.). What we have said may give an interest to the works of this "ingenious gentlewoman," if perchance they present themselves on a bookstall at a price not exceeding half-a-crown.

But the list of dramatic authoresses of this period would be incomplete without the name of Mrs Aphra Behn. Like her contemporary, La Rivière Manley, "she devoted herself," as Mr Baker observes, "to love and the muses;" but Aphra was of a nobler spirit of self-dedication than the other, and made no attempt to conceal the objects of her worship. No halfway resting-place between the temples of Venus and Diana would have been satisfactory to this priestess of obscenity and vice; and with a redeeming touch of self-knowledge, the society which had looked coldly on the slightly-veiled improprieties of the writer of *The Royal Mischief* was ten times more indulgent to the unconcealed iniquities of the authoress of *The Lucky Chance*. The nude was thought less offensive than the inadequately draped. Plays, romances, and novels, rushed down from that polluted pen like the contents of a sewer after rain, and for a quarter of a century after her death formed the favourite reading of respectable English homes. It is of this amazing perversion of literary taste, and the rapid steps by which it was finally improved, that Sir Walter Scott speaks in his letter to Lady Louisa Stuart : " A grandaunt of my own, Mrs Keith of Ravelstone, who was a person of some condition, being a daughter of Sir John Swinton, of Swinton, lived with unabated vigour of intellect to a very advanced age. She was very fond of reading, and enjoyed it to the last of her long life. One day she asked me, when we happened to be alone together, whether I had ever seen Mrs Behn's novels ? I confessed the charge. Whether I could get her a sight of them ? I said, with some hesitation, I believed I could; but that I did not think she would like either the manners or the language, which approached too near that of Charles II.'s time to be quite proper reading. ' Nevertheless,' said the good old lady, ' I remember her being so much admired, and being so interested in them myself, that I wish to look at them again.' To hear was to obey. So I sent Mrs Aphra Behn, curiously sealed up, with ' private and confidential' on the packet, to my gay old aunt. The next time I saw her afterwards, she gave me back Aphra, properly wrapped up, with nearly these words : ' Take back your bonny Mrs Behn ; and if you will take my advice, put her in the fire, for I found it impossible to get through the very first novel. But is it not,' she said, ' a very odd thing that I, an old woman of eighty and upwards, sitting alone, feel ashamed to read a book which, sixty years ago, I have heard read aloud for the amusement of large circles, consisting of the first and most creditable society in London.' "

An old woman of eighty and upwards, when Walter Scott was a very young man, was probably born at the end of the previous century. If she listened to these delectable scenes when she was sixteen years of age, it will take us into the decorous period preceding the first George. We must take the fact, therefore, of the continuance of Aphra's novels as favourite reading at that time as a proof of the survival of some old and highly-respectable noodles of both sexes who were yet unaware of the change of taste, and had not perceived the clearing of the air. The theatres became comparatively purified before " the first and most creditable society in London" when confidentially gathered round its tea-table. For public taste and morality have always a higher standard in England than private conduct; and who knows but in some quiet libraries and prettily furnished drawing - rooms the novels of Mrs Behn or plays of Mrs Manley may not have continued their course till they were succeeded by the French literature of the present time ? But Aphra was a heroine as well as an authoress, and met with as strange adventures as she invented. Born in the reign of Charles I., she came to the maturity of her vice and beauty in the palmy days of the Restoration. Her father, a Mr Johnson, had died at sea, on his way to take possession of the governorship of " Surinam, and six-and-thirty islands" (of which one, we think, must have been Barataria); and the family had persisted in their voyage, and landed in the unknown land. There she made acquaintance with Oroonoko and Imoïnda, who furnished Southerne with a subject for his tragedy ; and, narrowly escaping the breath of scandal for her regard for the heroic prince, she returned to her native country with her way to make—and wit, beauty, and fascination to make it. In a sort of parenthesis, the biographer informs us that at this time she became the wife of one Mr Behn, a merchant residing in the city, but of Dutch extraction. What became of this convenient Hollander nobody knows, and nobody cares; but Aphra, availing herself of the amphibious qualities of her mate, made herself equally at home in both countries, and was employed by the congenial Charles to act as his confidential agent at Amsterdam during the Dutch war. None of the many-trousered ministry had a chance with the new ambassador. She ogled, and whispered, and beguiled them out of all their state secrets, and no small amount of their solid florins, and communicated the former results of her political courtships to the dastardly buffoons at Whitehall. If she had sent them the florins, they would have been better pleased; but, despising the information which had been won by the wheedling endearments of this irresistible representative, the King made many excellent jokes on the news she gave him of the intended attack on Chatham and London, and only was convinced of her value when he saw the flames of the English dockyards and heard the booming of De Ruyter's guns. Disgusted with the disregard shown to her despatches, her Excellency resigned her post, and coquetted with admirals and swindled burgomasters on her own account. Alas, alas! for the ephemeral nature of the qualities which conquer admirals and set burgomasters on fire! Mr Baker, forgetting that his hurried narrative, though consisting of only three pages, contains the experience of forty years, becomes pathetic at the end of his account. "Nor does she appear," he says, with tears in his eyes, "to have been any stranger to the delicate sensations of the passion of love, as appears from some of her letters to a gentleman with whom she corresponded under the name of Lycidas, and who seems not to have returned her flame with equal ardour, or received it with that rapture her charms might well have been expected to command." We come, shortly after this, to her epitaph, for she died in 1689 :—

"Here lies a proof that wit can never be
Defence enough against mortality.'

We shut up our account of the Behns and Manleys, and the other revolting reactions against the lawless period of the Rebellion, and the hypocritical pretences of the Republic, well pleased to accept a little less brilliancy, in consideration of a great deal more modesty, and trace the upward course of the modern drama, past the quiet dulnesses of Rowe and Thomson, till, passing through Murphy and Goldsmith, we come at last to wit and propriety such as the Stuart theatre never knew, combined in the plays of Sheridan. From that period the motto was still "Excelsior," if not in dramatic merit, at least in purity of tone, till a vulgarising spirit of parody and burlesque banished sobriety and literature from the stage, and supplied the attraction originally found in gross situation and coarse expression by glittering and meretricious display. The eyes are now offended where the ears are spared; but it needs the accuracy and fury of some future Baker to apportion just degrees of punishment among the syllable-catching punsters who conceal the poverty of their invention behind the scanty dresses and exposed limbs of a line of fascinating *figurantes*. We doubt whether the spoken ribaldry of Aphra Behn was more objectionable than the short-robed indecency of the actual boards.

Back, as into a purer atmosphere, we go to the days of intellectual effort, where the actor did not depend on the upholsterer or the petticoat-maker, but produced his effects by the passionate utterance of the great sentiments he had to display in act. People have accounted for the paucity of great actors by telling off upon their fingers the numerous qualities required—voice, eye, figure, height, and motion; knowledge of the heart, susceptibility to strong emotion, appreciation of poetry, and dramatic perception of the shades of character: these, and many more, are the indispensables sententiously annexed to the aspirant for Othello's jealousy and Shylock's revenge. As to the personal requisites, we think very little of their absence, unless it is so very observable as never to be lost sight of by the attentive pit. A Coriolanus five feet high would never do—a humpbacked Hamlet would philosophise in vain; but a moderate amount of personal advantages is quite enough. Macbeth need not be like a hero of romance in beauty of feature and form. He can slay King Duncan even though slightly bandy-legged, and woo and win the Lady Anne though a little husky in his speech. Let him have the one great and indispensable qualification of being able to feel his part, and show his feeling in judicious action, and he may laugh at the blockheads who say his nose is scarcely Roman enough and his limbs are a trifle too strong. Now we will dip into the earlier pages of Baker, and under the letter B we come to Betterton.

This was the greatest actor the English stage ever possessed, with the exception, perhaps, of the more versatile Garrick. Almost incredible accounts remain to us of the effects produced by his performance. The magnetic influence of tone and expression seemed to mesmerise an audience, and make them the followers of his slightest intonation. Almost without speaking, he could let them into the workings of his mind, and anticipate his next motion, as if it arose from their own volition. And yet, cheer up, our dumpy friend with the passionate will to tread the boards! If you have only the tremendous energy which likes to surmount difficulties rather than glide along without an obstacle, never mind your inelegant figure and utterly ungracious face —your scrambling walk and clodhopping calves. If you feel the divine fury in your heart, and know it to be no exhalation from the stagnant marshes of your self-conceit, but the genuine fire that warmed the stuttering Demosthenes till he became an orator, and the skeleton Luxembourg till he rivalled the Caesars and Alexanders of ancient story, be not afraid of external deficiencies. We don't see them when our eyes are filled with tears. We don't believe in them when the pulse is stopped in terror and surprise. Read the following description of Betterton, and take courage. It is quoted from a pamphlet by Anthony Aston, called "A Brief Supplement to Colley Cibber, Esquire, his Lives of the Famous Actors and Actresses."

"Mr Betterton, although a superlative good actor, laboured under an ill figure, being clumsily made, having a great head, short thick neck, stooped in the shoulders, and had fat short arms, which he rarely lifted higher than his stomach. His left hand frequently lodged in his breast, between his coat and waistcoat, while with his right he prepared his speech. His actions were few but just. He had little eyes, and a broad face, a little pockpitten, a corpulent body, and thick legs, with large feet. He was better to meet than to follow, for his aspect was serious, venerable, and majestic —in his latter time a little paralytic. His voice was low and grumbling; yet he could time it by an artful climax, which enforced universal attention even from the fops and orange-girls. He was incapable of dancing, even in a country-dance, as was Mrs Barry, but their good qualities were more than equal to their deficiencies."

Surely this is the picture of a chawbacon, qualifying, by a long course of awkward stolidity of look and attitude, to grin successfully through a horse-collar at a fair! Yet this quintessence of the sublime and beautiful threw the brazen Duchess of Cleveland into hysterics, and moved the talkative Nell Gwynne to silence. Of him also Addison wrote a criticism distinguished by his usual refinement :—

"Such an actor as Mr Betterton ought to be recorded with the same respect as Roscius among the Romans. I have hardly a notion that any performer of antiquity could surpass the action of Mr Betterton in any of the occasions in which he has appeared upon our stage. The wonderful agony which he appeared in when he examined the circumstance of the handkerchief in the part of Othello, the mixture of love that intruded upon his mind upon the innocent answers Desdemona makes, betrayed in his gesture such a variety and vicissitude of passions as would admonish a man to be afraid of his own heart, and perfectly convince him that it is to stab it to admit that worst of daggers—jealousy. Whoever reads in his closet this admirable scene will find that he cannot (except he has as warm an imagination as Shakespeare himself) find any but dry, incoherent, and broken sentences. But a reader that has seen Betterton act it observes there could not be a word added—that longer speeches had been unnatural, nay impossible, in Othello's circumstances. This is such a triumph over difficulties, that we feel almost persuaded that the deficiencies themselves contributed to the success." We can now understand how our cripple and grimy friend Vulcan cut out the well-made Mars. We can understand, in short, how a real dramatic genius will carry a man to the top of his profession, though his defects of expression and articulation might seem to condemn him to continue a candle-snuffer to the end of his life. This, perhaps, is better expressed in the words of Voltaire, when he accused Mademoiselle Dumesnil of not having rage enough in one of her speeches. "It would require, sir, to have the *diable au corps* to do as you wish me." "Exactly, mademoiselle," said the great man; "one must have the *diable au corps* to excel in anything!"

In all the pages of Baker we can find nothing to guide us to a judgment of the style of the actors of the various periods. There seems, indeed, to have been a regular ebb and flow of the natural and the artificial, the declamatory and colloquial, in the personations of the stage. If Burbadge was easy and lifelike, his successor got on stilts, and taught the myrmidons of the pit that a stage hero was not a sort of fellow you could see any day of the week, but a portentous apparition, embodying all lofty thoughts and glorious passions, and therefore not to be criticised by ordinary standards, nor expected to have the modes of expression, or even the style of walking, of common men. If it were not for the admiration we are all bound to profess for the Greek drama, we should say that this supernatural and imaginative representation was the offspring of a semi-barbarous age; but as we remember the two feet thick buskin heels and the enormous mask for the countenance with which Œdipus or Ajax was lifted out of the category of everyday people, and elevated into a region proper only for demigods and mythical kings, we accept the impassive face of the vizard, the stilted increase of the stature, and the ear-splitting thunder of the speaking-trumpet (with which the actors electrified the farthest denizens of the theatre), as something sublimely intellectual, and carefully designed to draw an impassable distinction between the looks, manners, and sentiments of the stage and those of the street or forum. On the French boards, also, as long as the personages of a play were taken entirely from the accomplished cavaliers who fought before Troy, or distracted Greece with their crimes and dissensions after their return, it was all right and proper that a severe dignity of language and statue-like attitudes should characterise Monseigneur Achilles or his Majesty Agamemnon, because those gentlemen could not be judged by any code of sentiment or behaviour recognised by the citizens of Paris. The shopkeepers, therefore, who would have been quick in discovering any departure from probability in a farce of Molière, accepted with entire submission the grandiloquent orations and pompous action of Rodogune or Pompey. That either the sister of Phraates the Parthian, or the great rival of Cæsar, should call a spade a spade, or express the slightest longing for a glass of beer, never entered into the expectation of the enraptured auditor, who felt no slight increase of self-respect from the ennobling fact that he had been called on to listen to a conversation carried on in the tone and manner peculiar to conquerors and queens. Talma was the first man on the modern French stage who made the discovery that kings, after all, were only men, and was bold enough to explain his novel method of representing monarchs, by stating his belief that the most overbearing of potentates, with his crown on and his courtiers round him in the reception hall, was a very different personage in the privacy of his own room; that probably Semiramis herself answered her friend in a mild tone of voice when they were *tête-à-tête;* and Orestes was not always on the high ropes when having a confidential conversation with Pylades. He therefore moderated his roar and softened his look till people changed their sentiments about the individuals he represented, and saw the distinctive peculiarities of his tragedy kings and murderers as clearly as we see the differences between Hamlet and Macbeth. His object was to give the fictitious personages of Corneille and Racine back to nature—in short, to Shakespeareanise the stage; and he offended the classicists accordingly. For we are not to take for granted the undeniableness of our superiority to the laboured and declamatory school, because we have had Edmund Kean and Macready to give passionate motion to the stately castings which awed and charmed our forefathers.

Some people prefer Madame Tussaud to the *poses plastiques*. The stage, they say, is the home of the artificial; you can't attempt to deceive us into a belief of the reality of the men or events you show us. Let us have it all, therefore, artificial — voice, attitude, expression. Show us you are acting, only act " excellent well;" declaim your speeches, exaggerate your movements, aggravate your voice. Don't try to pretend you are a Danish prince or a Scottish thane. Show us what Shakespeare meant to be the spirit of the scene, but don't pretend that you are deceived by the witch's caldron or the old gentleman's ghost. Start in a heroic manner, avoiding the natural expressions of fear, as unworthy the rank of the personages whose words you repeat. Above all things, be neither below nature, nor exactly *like* nature—be above it. Lekain was the ornament and exemplar of this school; and see what such a judge of men and things as Frederick of Prussia said of him, his criticism exhausting all that can be advanced in favour of presentation as opposed to personation: " Here is what I thought when I saw Lekain. The first time I saw him I compared him only with the nature we are in the habit of seeing. I found he was not the least like it, and I considered his acting false and exaggerated. The second time I saw him, I thought he was practising an art, and that his art had rules which he had carefully studied and followed out with great intelligence. I still thought, however, that he made too much of his art, and that he should have stuck closer to nature. But now I think I have got to the point of view from which an actor should be judged. High tragic poetry should only copy a particular nature; therefore the actor cannot copy ordinary nature, such as encounters us every day, without producing an unfaithful likeness. Besides, the scene which the poet puts on the stage is not a scene in an ordinary circle of society, or in the bosom of a family. It is transported to the boards of a great theatre, and appears to the eyes of nations. What an immensity of preparation this requires! And can the actor forget this great consideration? Is he, indeed, on the same ground with us? By no means. We only see him in the distance, indefinite and diminished according to the rules of perspective. Must he not proportionally aggrandise all he says and does? Everything in Lekain is gigantic, or rather heroic and colossal. He is on a pedestal, and he could not appear otherwise without being awkward and false." The result of all these conflicting judgments is, that stateliness is good, and impulsiveness is good, when each is the best of its kind, but which is best in itself nobody can tell.

Caustic and bitter as Baker and his continuators show themselves too often, they are not without the faculty of perceiving the soul of good in things evil, and bring forward the better qualities of their victims at the very time when they are plying their heaviest cudgel. Less tiresome is this mixture of praise and blame than the unvaried song of glorification to which more modern biographers of the stage have descended. With these we will not meddle. The subjects and writers are excellently matched. Yet an exception must be made in favour of the *Memoirs of Charles Matthews*, in which the merits of a first-rate actor and excellent man are lovingly commemorated by the hand of true affection, but not of undistinguishing panegyric. Charles was perhaps the last survivor of the period we spoke of, when the dramatic world was separate from our own, and examined with more curiosity than we now bestow on ministers and kings. The attention paid to the proceedings of the green-room was an indemnification for the social disabilities to which custom (and at one time law) had condemned the whole profession. It was, in a certain degree, like the interest we took in the lives of the pirates or highwaymen; and we shut up this laborious compilation of dramatic lives with the comfortable assurance that it will be the last of its kind, for the social bar is withdrawn. Actors live in the full view of the everyday world; they are no more separated from the rest of us than curates or attorneys; and furnish no more inviting subjects for biography than the law-list or a catalogue of the unbeneficed clergy.

A SUGGESTION FOR A NEW KIND OF BIOGRAPHY.

WE must begin by admitting that until within the last hundred years there has been no idea of biography at all. It is a modern attainment, and Goethe and Rousseau have opened the double valves through which the world has arrived at it. These two great autobiographers had to come first, before men could learn how to look at their fellow-man with an interest that terminates simply in himself. The one, with his fiery self-analysis, his shamelessness of candour, his baring of passion to the fascinated eye; the other, with his solid-set and statuesque calmness, his slow and passive and mighty growth, and his enlargement of a many-sided nature through the acquisition of all experiences, and the sacrifice of every man and every woman around him—both lives, differing in so many things, agreed in one point. In each case the man was unmistakeably his own first object; and the book, whatever other things it might treat of, and however interestingly, was before all things a biography. In Rousseau's narrative, the first person, and the second person, and the third person, is Jean Jacques. In Goethe's wonderful book there is no pretence that any other divides the interest; his own life and his own nature are unaffectedly set forth as the central objects, for the illustration of which everything in the century is used. But now that these two great hands have opened the kingdom of biography, every one presses into it; and though all do not finish their work with the same skill, yet the fundamental lesson has at least been learned. What in an autobiography looks egotistical, in a biography is of course mere portraiture; only the biographer now has learned to pourtray with that single attention to his subject, with that admiration of it in itself and for itself, which was at first secured only in a few exceptional cases by the strong grasp of self-love. But is this not a new thing on the earth—a strictly modern attainment? I think it is. Plutarch's Lives are not biography in the modern sense. Those stately forms stalk across the arena in the interest of virtue and nobleness, as the later Greek mind understood the τὸ καλόν. They are magnificent men—in buckram; grand actors upon a sounding stage. Yet the interest they excite, even when they most take captive the imagination, is not that passionate interest in the individual which we have come to demand as the first and necessary quality. Plutarch's readers study each hero, not for his own sake, but as an illustration of history, or an illustration of virtue. The case of Socrates comes a little nearer to what we want; for the folds of those dialogues have in all ages revealed the outlines and the features of him who stands behind them. Yet even here, and at least as remarkably in the fragmentary records of some other Greek thinkers, the seeker after truth comes out somewhat more than the man. Socrates after all was a teacher of wisdom, and notwithstanding those delicious touches of portraiture which meet us here and there, the great object which his pupils attempt is to render the influence which he exerted upon them, not deliberately and at full length to pourtray the man. And when we come into Christian times the thing is still more striking. Down to the date of the French Revolution, no one wrote biography at all. It seems to have been considered a sin so to do. Augustine was tempted to do it, having his own marvellous history, and his glowing, crystalline, many-angled soul for a subject: but he did not dare. And so what in our days would have been his autobiography, became merely his confessions; a series of pious and passionate apologies to his God for delaying at all over so worthless a subject as his own history is in itself, though God's dealings with him in it may perhaps by the Christian and charitable reader be counted worthy of the record which he scarce brings himself to bestow. The stories of the martyrs were not biographies; each of them rushed *praeceps in ruinam*, and like one of the meteors that lately entered our atmosphere from remotest space, became visible only in the sudden flame that told of its extinction. The *Acta Sanctorum* were lower still. The chroniclers of the Middle Age, like Plutarch (himself one of their objects of admiration), pourtrayed their knights only in so far as they did great deeds, or were mirrors of chivalry. When the Reformation came, it made no change in this respect. Both that movement, and the Puritanism that succeeded it, were fertile in great men; but the great men had none to whom they were heroes. The doctrine of Luther, Calvin, and Baxter did not produce valets. The intense individualism of conscious relation to God which each man felt, almost incapacitated him from studying the nature and life of another; and the solemn weight, partly of doctrine and partly of devotion, which lay upon himself, prevented him equally from unfolding his own inner life by way of autobiography. Besides, this was the age of doctrine, just as a somewhat earlier time was the age of the feudal king and of the Church, and as the classic time was the age of the State. In the days behind us, the individual was subordinated, first to the commonweal, and afterwards to the civil or spiritual superior. His value as a unit was little or nothing. Puritanism, in the hands of Knox and Latimer, and their continental brethren, rescued man from insignificance; but this was counterbalanced by the supreme position which they (or their immediate successors) gave to doctrine. Henceforth biography of religious men became what in some hands it still continues to be, a mere illustration of dogmas, one or more, and was valuable only in so far as it had a purpose. And down to the Revolution all these lines of influence, converging and mingling as they no doubt did, yet failed among them all to produce what we recognise as biography. The *humani nihil a me alienum* of an old poet was a word spoken long before its time, and we are its legitimate inheritors. The ages past sometimes gave a man's life if he was a great king, or a great philosopher, or a great theologian, or a great saint; but never simply because he was a man.

But what they failed to do we have learned; and what prophets and wise men of old were unable to attain to is now the most easily acquired virtue of every *littérateur*. It is a great question whether this age believes in God; but it is certain that at least it believes in man. "And because we believe in man; because we reason, if not always aright, of truth, of beauty, of perfection, and are full of reverence, full of pity, for the nature in which we find ourselves so fearfully and wonderfully fashioned; because our age, with all its wants and errors, is still a loving, a believing, an essentially human age," therefore, as the rich-thoughted writer whom we quote argues, there is hope for us. Now into the general battle between humanitarianism and dogma we do not enter. It is, as most people come to find, a necessarily endless conflict, extending over the whole fields of history, of thought, of politics, of literature, and of social life; and whatever men's individual leanings may be, in most of the regions we are forced to admit a practical equipoise between the subjective and objective way of looking at things. But is there not one exception? Is there not one department of literature which in the nature of it is essentially and only humanitarian, and whose excellence is measured by the degree in which it succeeds in being so? Is this not the very meaning of *Biography*? We rather think this is the accepted idea at present—one too in which all the different schools find it possible to unite, and from which it is difficult on any grounds to escape. This is not so wonderful with regard to those (now the great mass of mankind, we should say, were it not that the utterance might draw forth a platoon fire from the Positive camp) who have no delight in the study of either nature or history as mere external fact, and cannot bear to look on them as valuable in themselves apart from the subjective human interest. These outside regions are to most people vast figured curtains, in which they trace remote adumbrations of something like biography.

"Literature and art, even Nature herself, these, which for freer spirits once had a charm of their own, and needed not any other, now breathe and burn in the fulness of a parasitical life; the fever of man's conflict has passed across them; their bloom and fragrance feeds, and is fed, by fire kindled far down in the central heart. The shadow of Humanity falls wide, darkening the world's play-ground; and games, be they those of man and demi-god, can no more enthral us. What is science itself but a gigantic toy, which may delight, but can never satisfy the heart, which, even through its sadness and perplexity, has learnt that it is greater than all that surrounds it?"*

Femininely surcharged with sentiment as this is, it reflects, we are inclined to think, the mood of the manlier manhood of our time, quite as much as the pure thinkers of the school opposed do; and in the great debateable land of general literature, we look for an equal war of most ambiguous event. But even those who think that the purity of science, of thought, and of literature is compromised by any thing but disinterested study, and is smirched by human interests consciously or unconsciously mingling with it—even this school does not seem, on its own principles, to take a different view of biography from that which we have described as the modern one. On the contrary, that modern view is perhaps in special accordance with their doctrine. For in biography the object of study is the man himself; and the same rules which forbid any intrusion of subjectivity into all other pursuits, demand that here nothing else shall have place, but mere delineation and portraiture. All the religious, metaphysical, and even social relations which were at one time supposed to be the chief thing about a man, all here exploded; *if* we are to have an account of him, the one thing to be desired is that he

* The "Patience of Hope."

be given us not only in form and manner as he lived openly, but exactly and simply as he was inwardly. Any pretence of preference of one part of his development to another; any impertinence of criticising what the biographer is only asked to pourtray; any distortion of the nature delineated in order to make it grow more to what its chronicler is pleased to call the light, is of course in the eyes of this school a sin of the first magnitude.

But indeed this seems to be accepted generally, and apart from literary sectarianisms. *A biography with a purpose* is held an abomination. And the only variation permitted on the modern idea of the thing is this—you may make the man of whom you write your hero, and be very enthusiastic about him. That is not necessary, but it is permissible. There is, *e. g.*, no better biography, none more characteristic of the modern type to which it belongs, than that of Edward Irving. It is written with enthusiasm, but the enthusiasm is all for the man. Irving had abundance of that sort of thing during his life, but it was unconfessed. His friends and followers loudly protested that the spring of their exertions was not their love and admiration for him, but that they and he lived for the common objects, which, as preacher or as prophet, he passionately set forth. But in his biography all that is dismissed almost contemptuously: and so Irving, who in his lifetime received only disguised incense and diverted offerings, from men who refused to admit that they were his worshippers, stands forth at last an unveiled idol. For he has fallen upon an age when, whatever happens to a man while living, there is nothing permissible to his biographer, but praise of the dead—enthusiasm for the personality which is pourtrayed. And if the life of Xavier or Marat had to be written, the rule is the same and the result would be similar. You must make him your sole subject, and if possible your hero. It is allowable to abstain from moral judgment altogether; but if you do otherwise all the praise must be accumulated on him whom you draw : and in any event he is to be kept the centre of the canvas, and subordinated to nothing and to no one.

Now I am wearied of this way of writing people's lives—wearied, in the first place, of its monotony and falseness. There are innumerable people whose personal histories are intensely interesting, and yet they are not perfect. And I object to treating them in either of the two ways now in vogue—either on the one hand standing up for them as if they were perfect, and attacking all around who do not bow to them ; or on the other, making a nice little study of their lives, and abstaining from looking at them in any of the higher elations to the perfection plainly not attained. Is there no more excellent way, no way accordant with that mingled tenderness and truth which is due to our poor humanity? I think there is; and that without falling back on the old plan of dogmatic biography.

In the first place, is it not certain that for each human life there is a separate and peculiar and absolutely individual ideal? I do not mean the ideal which the man had before his own eyes while living it; but the ideal which he ought to have had, or might have had, or (for we must not exclude the possibility that no man can see his own supreme good) the ideal which was visible all along to " greater, other eyes" than his and ours? And this is not the same thing with the ancient plan of comparing the man with some great common standard of truth or moral beauty. For we do not here speak of an ideal common to all, and to which it is possible for others to approximate—but of the solitary and separate ideal *for him* —the ideal, or rather idea, on which and for which the subject of our biography was originally framed, and by his approximation to which he is to be judged. It seems to be the favourite doctrine at present that, whatever may be the case with the moralist, it is an impertinence for the mere biographer to take to do with this. On the contrary, we hold that this idea of the man's life, unfulfilled or partially fulfilled or broken all away, is the one thing which it is essential for a true biographer to have got some hold of. For it is not something outside of the man—some mere pattern of things in the heavens to which he was destined by an external power to become conformed to—of which we speak. It may be that, but it is also, and it is much more, the inmost thread of the man's whole being: that which runs through all his development so far as it has gone, and which projects itself unseen into an endless future even where that development has been cut short. Of course it is a hard and a high thing to get possession of this—hard for the man himself during his militant life (and impossible unless his habitual attitude be one of dependence), and hard, too, for others outside, even after his fragmentary course on earth is finished. But it is not impossible for either, and what we maintain is that without this it is impracticable to have any biography of the highest and truest kind. And why should biography of the kind proposed be thought inconsistent with any of the best qualities sought after in the modern art? Is our statement of the facts of the man's life likely to be less true, because we have, in the first place, secured some hold of the essential scope of the unequal history and the individual goal to which it streams? Are we likely to be less candid in our narration of incidents, less accurate in our judgment of details? Does not this plan, on the contrary, set us at once free from the continual temptation which otherwise oppresses us, to prolong the development of the history a little more towards perfection than the facts warrant, and to round off the broken and baffling and disappointing angles which occur in every real life? These broken angles and flaws have their own intense interest, in relation to an unseen ideal which accompanies the man in his progress through them, and which we also, as biographers, may believe in : while, if we refuse to do so, and deal only with the facts themselves, the temptation is practically overpowering to smooth them away, and so make the actual life supply the place of that poem-life which our heart rightly tells us was hidden far beyond it. And if the plan of treating every life as only an approximation to an ideal life is rather favourable to historical truth, is it not equally conducive to that other great biographical quality of tenderness? The biographer is no longer a partisan—no longer a mere admirer—on the contrary, the first thing obvious in his work is that he holds his hero, however loved and reverenced, to be imperfect. And how can he be other thereafter than infinitely tender? He deals with a man of like passions, compassed with the same infirmities, baffled by the same imperfection ; and this being once broadly acknowledged in the whole conception of the life, there must be a ripple of continual tenderness in the treatment of all details. We have, in fact, only thus got back to truth, and we now deal with the printed life we read as we always deal with an actual life which we remember—with the same mingled admiration and sadness, the same loving acknowledgment of imperfection on earth, and the same transfer of unshaken faith to the ideal which completes itself nowhere but in heaven.

But take the suggestion in another form. Instead of saying anything about ideals, let us say that each human life has all through an individual and separate and personal relation to God, and that its whole course (whether it be according to an ideal plan or not) is a dealing with him in the way of guidance or at least of dependence. The modern idea of biography is essentially opposed to this. The *totus teres atque rotundus* view of life; that which treats each history as fed by its proper springs, and dependent on nothing outside, and which, if it approves of piety and devotion at all, treats them with much admiration as a beautiful efflorescence of life rather than its fundamental and central condition—this whole view of life tends, as it seems to us, rather to hero-worship than to either tenderness or truth. At all events, it might be possible to have the tenderness and truth while transferring the loyalty to some other use than the worship of the hero. And is this not an experiment worth trying? The result would be almost a new thing in literature. We long to see a biography with a passionate love and an enthusiastic admiration of the subject of it, in which, nevertheless, there should be an equally strong feeling not only of failure in the close, but of imperfection and dependence at every point—in which, in fact, there should be a double interest, one in the man whose life is narrated, and one in the Supreme Biographer who, as we hold, is mixed up in the plan and in the details of every life of all His children here.

Now, this is not a biography with a purpose, nor is it mere illustration of doctrine under a biographical disguise. We claim—and we are fairly bound to meet the question—that for pure biography, for biography in the strictest sense of it, this suggested view of a man's life as essentially dependent and imperfect, is the best thing. Is it not the view most likely to give a *true* account of what the life actually was? Do you not put yourself on a vantage-ground for understanding your friend by thus viewing him from above? Of course it is an excessively difficult thing to do, even after it is acceded to in theory; you will be continually liable to lapse into the ordinary lazy form of religious biography, and to compare the facts of a real life with the dogmas of a system more or less venerable in idea and more or less practical in application. Or in seeking to avoid this, you will be likely to invent a fictitious theory of the highest and supreme relations of your friend, and to compare the real life once more with an imaginary ideal of it. It is difficult—intensely difficult. But who denies that a first-rate biography is one of the highest and most difficult things that can be attained? Only, in order to even conceiving or planning it, we urge, as a pre-requisite, that we should look at it in connection with its unfulfilled ideal, and not shirk its dependence and imperfection.—But let us concede as much as we can, and instead of demanding that our future biographer shall see the ideal and shall trace the personal connection with the higher leading, let us say merely this: he must *acknowledge* all through that there is such an ideal, that there is such a higher leading, and that the life is an imperfect approximation. Without this much, we honestly do not see how the life is to escape a charge of central falsehood and misrepresentation. On the other hand, if this is heartily done, the man escapes being made a hero, and falls into that true relation to all above him and around him in which our brotherly sympathy for one imperfect as ourselves is most heartily roused. And at the same time all the facts of his life fall into their proper places; each assumes a true and real meaning; and the whole, which was before a fragment of meaningless natural history, or at the best of graceful egotism, suddenly becomes instinct with a divine lesson, a lesson taught by the success and by the failure alike. But indeed, from this point of view, what do we call failure? On the self-centred plan of life and biography, failure meets us almost inevitably. The man is struck down amid the works of his hands, or he totters along that shadier slope of life which, at its best, is such an anti-climax to the morning's hope. And then in so many of the most precious lives, failure does not wait for the close, but some blow intervenes which throws all into anguish and confusion. It is impossible to escape from it so long as we make the life itself our object and our end; as impossible for the biographer as it is for the man himself. Our hope for *him*, no more our hero, but our brother, is that, at that close, if not before, he may have finally risen to the position in which there is no failure; in which the life seen from end to end is known by vision of faith to have been a successful work of God, and as such to be rejoiced in even amid the wreck and imperfection which on the human side have most accumulated upon it. Now why should not the biographer view his work from the beginning in that light which the subject of it at last sees to have been the only true one—the only one in which he could have truly moved through it while it lasted, and in which others can truly understand it now that it has passed? And if in aught he has failed in a wise humility, while yet that life unrolled itself under human eyes, what nobler task remains for the pen of love than to reproduce the history as he now rejoices to view it, and wishes that he had viewed it ere yet the golden bowl slipped from his failing hands? *Sero vixi, Domine Deus meus.*

ROBERT GOODBRAND.

CONTEMPORARY LITERATURE.

V. BIOGRAPHY, TRAVEL, AND SPORT.

NOTHING is more fascinating than good biography, and assuredly it is the more precious for its rarity. The books we really love, the books that make the illustrious dead our friends and companions, and which may be carried about with one like the Bible or Shakespeare, may almost be counted on the fingers. That is at first blush the more surprising, since it seems there should be no very insuperable difficulty in writing an excellent life. Fidelity of portraiture, sympathy, and tact, with a discriminating use of ample materials, ought surely to be sufficient to assure success. As a matter of fact, it evidently is not so. Clever and congenial biographers take up the pen to turn out the volumes which are read or merely glanced through and laid aside. Perhaps, when we say "volumes," we have gone some way towards the explanation. For there can be no question that the most common defects of biography are useless repetition and provoking redundancy. The more earnestly the biographer throws himself into his task, the more indispensable does each trivial detail appear to him. In working out the features and the figure of his subject, he is slow to reject anything as inconsequent or insignificant. Then he is in even a worse position than the editor of a daily newspaper. He should make up his mind to seem ungracious and ungrateful. He must say "No" civilly to people who have been doing him a kindness, when he declines to make use of the valued matter they have placed at his disposal as the greatest of favours. He has been indefatigably collecting a mass of voluminous correspondence from a great variety of quarters; yet many of the letters, when they come to be read, are either unimportant or really reproductions of each other. He gets into the way of going about his labours like the watchmaker, who works with a powerful magnifying-glass in his eye. In the assiduous attention he bestows on each step in the career, he is apt to lose all sense of proportion; while in the unconscious exercise of their natural critical powers, his readers become unpleasantly alive to the results.

We need hardly say that our complaints of the average quality of biography do not extend to the quantity of these publications. There is no lack of the "Lives," bad, fair, and indifferent, of big and little men. Not a few of these we may owe to selfish motives; but for the most of them we are undoubtedly indebted to love, gratitude, or friendship. Now and then the office of elegist or literary executor may well excite an eager rivalry among those who can put forward any reasonable pretensions to it. There are splendid examples of reputations made vicariously by laying hold of the mantle of some illustrious man. Boswell's 'Johnson' is an instance which must of course occur to everybody. His is a book that stands alone and unapproached. We subscribe to what Macaulay wrote in his essay, that "Eclipse is first, and the rest nowhere;" although we can by no means agree with the brilliant essayist in his contemptuously depreciatory estimate of the biographer.

That Boswell's fortunate weaknesses went far to insure him his astonishing triumph is not to be denied for a moment. It is seldom, indeed, that one finds in an educated man of the world, who was indisputably possessed of ordinary intelligence, so ludicrous a mixture of shrewdness and simplicity; such a *naïve* indifference to mortifying rebuffs, and so complacent a superiority to humiliating self-exposure. It is rarer still to find an appreciative enthusiast, who, rather than not show the powers of his idol at their best, will set himself up to be shot at with poisoned arrows. But those who, going on the estimate of Macaulay, should try to rival the achievement of Boswell by simply putting self-respect and self-esteem in their pocket, and letting one form of vanity swallow all the rest, may find themselves far astray in their expectations. Boswell can have been by no means the nonentity it has pleased Macaulay to represent him. Far better judges have differed entirely from the brilliant Whig partisan when he declares that no one of Boswell's personal remarks would bear repetition for its own sake. Independently of the culture and various information they show, many of them strike us as extremely incisive — for in thought as well as in style he had borrowed much from his model. Not unfrequently the remarks are epigrammatic, and almost invariably they are ingeniously suggestive. If Boswell was no great lawyer, he had a genius for one important branch of the profession. He was a master of insidious examination and cross-examination. He made it his business and study to "draw" the sparkling and bitter conversationalist, till he had acquired an intuitive perception of how to set about it, ready as he was to risk the hug of the bear. The direct evidences of his talents must be matter of opinion, and each reader can form an independent judgment on them. But there is no gainsaying the indirect testimony to his merits in the illustrious company he habitually kept. It is unfair, and opposed to all probability, to suppose that the most refined intellectual society of the day merely tolerated the shadow of Johnson as their butt. Men like Burke and Reynolds, who, as Johnson would have said, had no great "gust" for humour, do not drag a "sot and idiot" about with them to quiet little dinners, with the simple notion of amusing themselves by his follies. We never hear that Foote formed one at their parties, though he was courted by such *spirituel roués* as the Delavals. But the most conclusive testimony to Boswell's powers is the pleasure Johnson took in his company. Johnson no doubt loved flattery; but he was ruffled by praise indiscreetly administered, and was the last man in the world to tolerate the intimacy of a bore. He was certainly no hypocrite; and, setting aside innumerable passages in his letters, he gave the most unmistakable proof of his consideration for Boswell, when he chose him for his companion in the tour to the Hebrides, and encouraged him in the intention of writing his life. If Boswell's 'Johnson' be the life of lives, we may be sure that no ordinary literary skill, disguised under great apparent simplicity, must have gone to the composition, with much of the talent for biography that can only be a natural gift. But when all has been said in the author's favour that can be said, aspirants should remember that he has been living in literature as the object of a fortunate accident and a still more happy conjunction. He suited

Johnson, dissimilar as they were, and the mind and qualities of the one man became the complements of those of the other. While if Johnson had followed up the famous snub at Cave's; if he had not taken a capricious fancy to the raw importation from the country he professed to detest, the Scotch advocate might have travelled to Corsica, strutted at the carnival at Stratford-on-Avon, and dined and drunk port with the wits, but he would never have emerged from obscurity in the remarkable book which claims more than a passing notice in any article on biography.

But if vanity and ambition have inspired many indifferent biographies, the partiality of love or friendship has to answer for many more. We are all familiar with the emotional mourners who will obtrude the heartfelt expressions of their grief and affection into the brief obituary notice in the newspaper, which is paid at so many shillings the line. So there are sorrowing widows and admiring intimates who seem to consider an elaborate memoir of the departed as much *de rigueur* as the tombstone that is to commemorate his gifts and his virtues. Very possibly he may have done something considerable for himself. Probably he was a most respectable member of society, and benefited his fellow-creatures in some shape or other. He has died in the fulness of years and regard; or a promising career has been prematurely cut short before it had well begun, or just as it seemed approaching fruition. In the latter case especially, the biographical tribute becomes a sacred duty. The literary legatee feels himself bound to turn architect, completing and embellishing in the realms of fancy the edifice that in actual fact had barely risen above the foundations. He has accepted the duties that are pressed upon him with reluctance, real or feigned; though in his innermost heart he has hardly a doubt that he will discharge them something more than satisfactorily. Writing a life seems so exceedingly easy; indeed, undertaking it involves a certain self-sacrifice, seeing that it scarcely gives sufficient scope for the play of original genius. If regard or ambition did not sweeten the labour, and if the biographer did not show himself so confident in that genius of his, we should be inclined to feel sincere sympathy for him. For working out the most brilliant memoir must involve an inordinate amount of wearisome drudgery, while it lays the writer under an infinity of trifling obligations to people who are ready enough to remind him of them. Even if you employ a staff of secretaries and amanuenses, your own gifts of selection must be sorely taxed. If the object of your hero-worship was a busy man, the chances are that he wrote a villanous hand. As he should have had time to make a certain reputation, the odds are that he died in ripe maturity. So you have masses of crabbed manuscript consigned to you, in boxes and packets, and by single communications; and the earlier of these letters have been penned on old-fashioned paper, in ink that has been fading with time and damp. These date, moreover, from the days of prohibitory postage, and are written in the most minute of hands, and crossed and recrossed to the edge of the seal. If the talent of the departed lay in sentimental verse, or if he were a reforming or philosophical genius in embryo, of course they are magniloquently diffuse; and though you hardly dare reprint his rhapsodies in replica, you are loath to waste any of the flowers of his eloquence. Most of us have been committed to some unpleasant piece of business where we have had to rake among the melancholy ashes of the past, undoing the moth-eaten tape that ties up the mildewed packets. Imagine having to pursue such a task indefinitely, with no particular point to aim at, but vaguely searching for appropriate matter. As it seems to us, only the most plodding and patient-minded of men would be content to persevere with unabated application; and it is comparatively seldom that acute and imperturbable patience is united to real literary ability. Should you happen to be blessed with a retentive memory, perhaps it may prove wisest in the end to trust to it in great measure; though in that case, undoubtedly, the probabilities are that you do very partial justice to the subject. Otherwise, with a view to comprehensive reference, you must make a careful *précis* of your researches as you go along, and that infers some deficiency in those faculties of memory and concentration which are essential to really superior work. Or else you must decide to print wholesale, making very perfunctory attempts at selection. The relatives who see your manuscript or revise your book in the proof, are sure to look leniently on that latter fault. Nothing, they think, is too insignificant to be recorded of a man so essentially superior and remarkable. And the result is a mass of ill-arranged matter, where the currants and spice bear no proportion to ingredients that are unpalatable and unpleasantly indigestible.

Turning to Mrs Glass's cookery-book for another metaphor, you must catch your hare before you cook him. The first condition of a good book is a suitable subject. It by no means follows that, because a man has made his way to prominent places — because he has played a conspicuous part in public affairs — because he has been a shining light in the churches, and the most soul-stirring of pulpit orators—because he has held high commands in wars that have remodelled the map of the world— that his life must necessarily be worth the writing. A man may have high talents of a certain order, though he is no more than a fair representative of a class, and has never gone far beyond the commonplace. The test of a successful biography is the pleasure one takes in reading it; and to give it point and piquancy, the eminent subject must have shown some originality of genius or character. No doubt, a distinguished statesman or general must have been concerned in much that deserves to be recorded. But there the personal may be merged in the abstract, as biography drifts into history, which is a different department altogether: and not a few of those biographies which have become standard authorities, are in reality history in a flimsy disguise. We miss those little personal traits which reflect the distinctive lights of a marked individuality; and although the biographer turned historian may possibly have overlooked these, the presumption is that they had scarcely an existence. On the other hand, the life of some very obscure individual may supply admirable matter for the reality of romance. Thus, in singling out those self-reliant individuals who have raised themselves to distinction by self-help, Dr Smiles has hit on a most happy vein. Who can fail to follow with the closest interest the achievements of those adventurous engineering knight-errants, who vanquished by the vigorous efforts of their brains the material obstacles which had been baffling our progress? Nor is it merely in the story of their most celebrated feats that the Stephensons or Arkwrights or Brunels impress us. Their whole experiences from their parish school-days, were a battle that ended in the triumph of faith. In the face of discouragements and difficulties, they are carried along by the natural bent that is absolutely irresistible; and often, fortunately for society, beyond either reason or control. Edward, the Banffshire naturalist —Dick, the Caithness-shire geologist, could hardly have imagined in their wildest dreams that Mr Mudie would have been circulating their memoirs by thousands. Yet for once the readers of the fashionable world have been just as well as generous in appreciation; for the lives of the humble shoemaker and baker are pregnant with lessons and their practical illustrations.

We assume that the biographer has some power of the pen, though the rule that we take for granted has many exceptions. But undoubtedly the first of his qualifications should be tact, for without that all the rest must be comparatively worthless. He should show his tact, in the first place, in deciding whether the life be worth writing or not. He must next exhibit it in the method of his scheme, and in his notions of literary perspective and proportion. Many a life that has proved intolerably dull, might well have repaid perusal had it taken the shape of slightly-linked fragments; each fragment embracing some episode of the career. First impressions in making acquaintance with a man go for a great deal. Many a life has been hastily thrown aside because we were bored by the hero in his school and college days. It may be true that the child is the father of the man; yet we do not care to be personally introduced to the parent of each new acquaintance who promises to interest us. When the man has developed into an illustrious character, the child has often been an insufferable prig, who must have made itself a nuisance to the friends of the family. We may pity those unfortunates who could scarcely help themselves; but it is hard upon us half a century later to have more than some faint indication of the little student's precocious tastes. Macaulay sneers at Warren Hastings' habit of appearing morning after morning at the breakfast-table at Daylesford with the sonnet that was served with the eggs and rolls. But on the whole, we should rather have put up with the sonnets of the ex-Governor-General of Hindostan than with the sermons, essays, and political disquisitions in which the juvenile Macaulay showed such appalling fertility in the heavy dissenting atmosphere of his Clapham forcing-house. We admit that the interesting life by his nephew would have been altogether incomplete without a reference to these; and we merely take the book as an illustration of disproportion because it is in many respects admirable, and was universally read. Yet, though Mr Trevelyan, in the opinion of some people, may not have been unduly prolix, for ourselves we might possibly have stopped short on the threshold of his volumes, had we not been assured of the interest that must await us farther on.

Then tact is essential in collecting as well as in selecting. If the importance of your undertaking be sufficient to justify it, possibly the most comfortable way of collecting is by public advertisement. You intimate a desire that any correspondents of the deceased may forward communications or letters—to be returned — to the care of the publishers. In the case of those who respond, you are only laid under a general obligation, and need make as little use as you please of the communication intrusted to your care. The objection to this plan appears to be, that it can but partially answer the purpose. Busy men may neither see nor heed the advertisement. And then there is the numerous class of *dilettante littérateurs*, who will only do a favour of the kind on urgent personal entreaty; and possibly, like the modest Mr Jonathan Oldbuck, in the expectation that it will be publicly acknowledged in some shape. When your store is amassed, as we have remarked already, your literary discretion is merely beginning to be tried. You have to face the invidious task of rejection, unless you mean consciously to mar your work and do injustice to the reputation you are responsible for. You find that your correspondent, the fussy *dilettante*, has been cackling over illusory treasures. You can make nothing of the packet of brief dinner invitations; or the note paying a civil compliment to the poem in manuscript that was promptly sent back. You give offence in other quarters with better reason. You cannot reproduce indefinitely very similar ideas; and there are passages and personalities in really suggestive letters which you are bound in common prudence to suppress. All that, however, is matter of personal feeling and sacrifice. You must make up your mind to make a certain number of enemies, and to brazen out a good deal of obloquy and abuse. After all, your rejected correspondents cannot cherish their malice for ever; nor are you likely to trouble them soon

again for another *magnum opus*. But when your materials have been sifted, and when what is worthless has been refused, you enter on the more delicate and critical stage of dealing with them as between yourself and your public. You must keep the fear of being wearisome perpetually before your eyes, and resign yourself to retrenching mercilessly on what at first sight seemed worthy of preservation. No matter how full of interest a life may have been, the public will not tolerate more than a reasonable amount of it; and it should be your study to bring out in striking relief those features which gave your subject his special claims to notoriety. It may have been lucky perhaps for Boswell, though of course he deplored it, that he should have made the acquaintance of his hero so late in life. Otherwise, though it is difficult indeed to believe, those delightful volumes of his might have been multiplied disagreeably.

Judicious glimpses at the domestic interior are indispensable; but unless, perhaps, in the case of a woman who has been throwing lustre on her times, without having recognised any "special mission" that way, it seems to us that those glimpses should be indulged in with extreme discretion. Much of course depends upon the man. We should never have loved either Scott or Southey half so much, had we not seen them sitting among their books or breaking loose upon their afternoon rambles, surrounded by the children they encouraged to be their playmates. The children who had the run of the inner book-room at Abbotsford, and kept possession of the little tenement at Keswick, became a part of the professional life of their parents. But that kind of domestic revelation may be very easily overdone; as when a widow or daughter writes the life of the husband or father whose loss has left a grievous chasm in her existence. Then we have her—and very naturally, should she once have decided to make the public her confidants—always twining herself round the memory of the lost one, and recalling the thousand unsuggestive trifles which have a living and touching interest for herself; while an enthusiastic friend, though with less excuse, is apt to fall into a similar error.

That leads one naturally to the cardinal virtue of self-suppression, which, after all, is only another form of tact. If you are bent on killing two birds with one stone—if you hope to immortalise yourself in commemorating your friend—there is no more to be said save that doubtless you will go far towards defeating your own purpose; for a book can hardly fail to be poor when half the contents are either indifferent to the reader or objectionable. But a man's unconscious vanity may innocently enough cast a heavy shadow over his hero; or the writer may honestly multiply useful details, which as matter of self-regard he had better have restricted. If he be a Boswell or choose to play the Boswell, there is no great harm in that; but Boswells, as we have observed, are almost as rare as phœnixes. More often we have something in the style of Foster's 'Life of Dickens,' though the author will almost necessarily have been less fortunate in a subject. Mr Foster, in writing a most entertaining narrative, said nothing, of course, that was not strictly true, nor perhaps did he exaggerate either his intimacy or the influence he exercised on his friend. But though the delicate flatteries he published, and the details he gave, may have added life and colour to the story he was writing, they threw Dickens himself into the background; and at all events, so far as its author was concerned, the impression of the book was decidedly unpleasing.

There is one kind of memoir in which the writer must come to the front, and that is autobiography. If undertaken in a spirit of absolute candour and simplicity, nothing may be made more instructive and entertaining. Nor does it follow by any means that the autobiographer need be one of those men whose name has been much in the mouth of the world. On the contrary, in our opinion, the best of our autobiographies are those that have chiefly a domestic or personal interest. They should be the honest confessions of a nature that has the power of self-analysis; and nobody but the individual himself can make the disclosures which give such a history completeness. No incident can then be too insignificant, provided it have some distinct bearing on the end in view. The author must necessarily have a retentive memory, and he should have a natural instinct of self-observation. For in telling his plain unvarnished tale, he reveals himself more or less consciously; and if he have the knack of picturesque narrative, it is so much the better; while literary experience may be a positive snare. It may tempt him into the laying himself out for effect, which will almost inevitably defeat its purpose—into giving an air of artifice and sentiment to the confessions that should be unmistakably genuine. Some of the most satisfactory autobiographies we are acquainted with, have been written by women. Women, and especially French women, are more emotional and impressionable than the rougher sex. When they are warmed to their work, they have less hesitation in unbosoming themselves unreservedly in the public confessional: nor are they embarrassed by false shame or overstrained sensitiveness, when they are impelled to lay bare their innermost feelings. But if a public man becomes his own historiographer, it is an incessant effort to be either straightforward or dispassionate. He places himself involuntarily on his defence, and is vindicating his reputation with his contemporaries and posterity. Naturally he cannot be over scrupulous in putting his conduct in the most favourable light: he launches cross indictments against the opponents who have impeached it; and even if in his own judgment he be punctiliously conscientious, his conscience may have been warped by the habit of self-deception.

What comes very near to actual autobiography, and may be even more strikingly indicative of character, is the publication of copious correspondence, either by itself or slightly connected by a commentary. The Duke of Wellington was a man of few words, and the Wellington despatches are models of terse narrative and pointed English. The writer, though he only alludes to himself incidentally, necessarily fills a great space in them, since he was making the war history he describes so lucidly. Yet with hardly a single directly personal touch, how forcibly and graphically we have the hero presented to us! Or take a genius of a very different order, who wrote with a different purpose, and in very different style. We have lately had a voluminous collection of the letters of Honoré de Balzac. The most important of these were addressed to two ladies—to the sister whom he had always made his *confidante*, and to the Russian baroness whom he afterwards married. We do not know if he had any idea that they might ultimately be published. Nor if he had, do we imagine that it would have made any great difference; for a Frenchman whose soul is steeped in romance is likely to be transcendently feminine in his emotional candour. At all events, that lifelong series of letters makes up the most vividly descriptive of autobiographies. We know the novel-writer, with his bursts of sustained industry, when the fancy was working at high-pressure pace; with his trials, his triumphs, his eccentricities, and his extravagances, as if we had lived in his intimacy all his days. It is not only that we hear the duns knocking at his door, and see them assembled to lay siege to his ante-room, while he was feverishly toiling against time, filliping himself by perpetual doses of coffee in the sumptuous apartments they had furnished on credit. But he reveals all the caprices of his changing moods; he shows himself in his alternations of excitement and depression; he has no conception of drawing a veil over the failings and sensibility he is inclined to take pride in; he returns time after time to his literary feuds and resentments, as he is inexhaustible in his abuse of the pettifogging lawyers who strewed thorns among the rose-leaves on which he would have loved to repose. He cannot be said to exhibit himself to advantage, and yet somehow we like him. Not certainly on account of his genius, for that was decidedly of the cynical cast that repels affection though it compels admiration. We believe we take to him chiefly because he is so entirely without reserve for us. In ordinary biographies you feel that much may be kept back, and suspicion suggests or exaggerates the concealments; while, if a man be entirely outspoken, and seems to take your sympathy with him as a matter of course, we give him more than due credit for his amiable qualities. Unhappily, it is seldom we have such elaborate self-portraiture nowadays, seeing that painstaking letter-writing is become a fashion of the past, and it is only one of the indefatigable French romance-writers like Balzac, Sand, or Dumas, who can spare time and thought for it from their multifarious avocations.

We are disposed to wonder at the courage or rashness of those who write the biographies of living men. The work can be but an unsatisfactory instalment at the best; and it is impossible to overrate its delicacy or difficulty. It must tend to be either a libel or unmitigated eulogy, though much more often it is the latter. When an enemy undertakes it—and we have seen an instance of that lately in memoirs of the Premier—he must judge his subject solely by public appearances. He can have no access to those materials for the *vie intime* which can alone give truthful colour to the portrait. Besides, he holds a brief for the prosecution; he has to vindicate the prejudices which warp his judgment, and he lays himself out to invent misconstruction of motives, if not for actual misrepresentations. While the partial friend or enthusiastic devotee can scarcely steer clear of indiscriminate puffing. Whatever he may do for the reputation of his subject, he can hardly fail to injure his own. As his readers are disposed to set him down as either a dupe or a shameless panegyrist, he pays the penalty of having thrust himself into a false position. If he has really much that is new and original to tell, it will be assumed that he has had direct encouragement to undertake the task. Few men are cast in such a mould, or occupy a position so unmistakably independent, that they can dare in such embarrassing circumstances to show the serene impartiality of the judge. If they have gone for their information to the fountainhead, they have, in fact, committed themselves to a tacit arrangement by which they undertake to be nothing but laudatory. Should they insinuate blame, it is in such softened terms that they almost turn condemnation into compliments. And even when the writer can honestly be lavish of his praise, he must feel that his praises sound unbecoming. In short, as it seems to us, it is work that can scarcely be undertaken by any man of sensitive feeling.

Yet in more ways than one the production of a good biography is a most praiseworthy ambition, for no one is a greater benefactor alike to literature and posterity than the man who has achieved it. In spite of his amiable superstition and his tedious digressions, Plutarch is still a standard classic. Nor is there anything on which the popularity of ancient and modern historians like Tacitus or Clarendon, is more solidly established than their striking contemporary portraits. The sketch of Catiline is perhaps the most impressive part of Sallust's history of the famous conspiracy. What would we give now for the most meagre memoir of Shakespeare, were it only authoritative? and had he found his Boswell or Lockhart, we might have had a book that would have gone down to posterity with his poems. So much is that the case, that one of the most favourite modern forms of biography consists in ransacking the authorities of the remote past, and piecing together such disjointed materials as they can supply. That must be more or less like reconstructing the mastodon from the traces he has left on the primeval rocks. Learned Germans, distinguished members of the French Academy, deeply-read professors in the English universities, have betaken themselves to rewriting the lives of illustrious Greeks and Romans. They have done most creditable work, we confess; and yet, however acutely logical the treatment may be, we have the impression that we are being beguiled into historical romance where the actual has been ingeniously merged in the ideal. In lives that came nearer to our own times, that impression naturally diminishes; and we grant that there is more satisfactory reason for writing them. The discoveries of gossipy State-papers all the world over—notably those in the archives of Simancas, and the official correspondence of accomplished Venetian emissaries—have thrown floods of unexpected light on some of the most remarkable personages of the middle ages. There is an odd fashion too in those subjects, and certain picturesque people and periods seem to have an irresistible fascination for literary men. Paradoxical conclusions, that are due in a great degree to the author's ingenuity, have of course their charm; and we can understand the taste that finds delight in whitewashing the most doubtful or disreputable figures in history. But the fact of some impressive character having already been repeatedly appropriated, appears to be a challenge to other artists to take him in hand; and thus, for example, we see a religious reformer like Savonarola, or such a subtle thinker as his contemporary Machiavelli, receiving, noteworthy as they undoubtedly were, more than their fair share of attention.

Next to Boswell's Johnson, to our mind the most enjoyable life in the language, is Lockhart's Scott. And a model biography it is for the practical purpose of example, since no one who can avail himself of somewhat similar advantages need despair of producing a creditable imitation. As we have remarked already, the secret of Boswell's success in some degree defies and eludes detection; while some of the conditions to which it is most obviously due are such as few men would care to accept. They would object to discarding delicacy and reserve, and to pursuing their purpose with a sublime indifference as to whether or not they made themselves the laughing-stock of their readers. But Lockhart produced his fascinating work simply by writing a straightforward narrative. He was entirely outspoken as to the private life of his illustrious subject, except in so far as disclosures of family secrets were necessarily limited by good taste and good feeling. As we are taught to admire Sir Walter's genius in the critical appreciation of his works, we learn to love the man in his domestic intercourse. What can be pleasanter, for instance, than the picture of the lion taking refuge from the houseful of guests his hospitality had gathered into Abbotsford, at his favourite daughter's quiet breakfast-table under the trees in the little garden at Huntly Burn. We learn to love him in his friendship for his pets, for it was friendship at least as much as fondness; and they and their master thoroughly understood each other. Lockhart, with the true feeling of an artist, has painted Scott among his dogs as Raeburn did. We know them all, from Camp, whose death made him excuse himself from a dinner-party on account of the loss of a much-loved friend—from Maida sitting solemnly at his elbow in his study, or stalking gravely by his master's side, while the rest of the pack were gambolling ahead of them—down to "the shamefaced little terrier," who would hide himself at a word of reproof, and who could only be lured out of his seclusion by the irresistible sound of the meat-chopper at the dinner-hour. To be sure no biographer could have been more fortunate in a subject. The life of Scott from first to last was overcharged with diversified elements of romance. His lines were cast in the land of the Border, where every hamlet and peel-tower had its legend, and each stream and dale their ballads. There was an extraordinary blending of the picturesque with the practical as the lawyer turned into the poet and novelist; and the pen of the wizard in an evil hour took to backing the bills that landed him in insolvency. Seldom has there been a more strangely checkered career, or a losing campaign more gallantly fought out after the flush of an unexampled series of triumphs. Almost unprecedented prosperity had ended in what might have been the blackest eclipse, but for the manly nature that shone brightest at the last through the clouds that would have depressed any ordinary fortitude. Never was there stronger temptation to indiscriminate hero-worship, for Lockhart was the friend and confidant of his father-in-law, and had watched him with ever-growing admiration through his changing fortunes. No man was better fitted to appreciate that rare versatility of literary genius than one who had himself been a successful romance-writer, and who was a critic by temperament as well as habit. Perhaps it was partly owing to that critical temperament, with the practice of self-control which it inferred, that the biographer proved equal to his splendid opportunities. Partly because, setting the obligations of honesty aside, he felt that all he could tell of his father-in-law would only redound to Scott's honour in the end. But the result has been that we have a Life in many volumes which for once we would very willingly have longer, and for once in a way, if there be a fault in the book, it is the excessive self-effacement of the accomplished author. Had he told all, which of course he could not do, we believe it would appear that his counsels to Scott had been invaluable.

Since Scott wrote the 'Napoleon,' which hardly did justice either to the emperor or to the author, good lives of soldiers have been scarce—although by the way, in that connection, we may refer to the Count de Sèjur's admirable memoir of his master which came out a few years ago. Wellington and the heroes of the Peninsula had been disposed of; and there were few opportunities for soldiers distinguishing themselves in the comparatively peaceful times that followed. In India and the Crimea, though we do not forget dashing leaders like the Napiers, and many distinguished generals of division, no really great commander can be said to have come to the front; and the lives of officers in subordinate positions usually supply incidents that are too episodical. Besides, the memoir of a distinguished soldier must have mainly a strategical interest, and the most accomplished literary artist will find his talent taxed to the utmost if his book is to be made attractive to the general public. No doubt the authoritative life of Von Moltke will be a most valuable work, yet we may surmise that it will be heavy reading. Moreover, the present fashion of war correspondence unpleasantly anticipates the military memoir writer. He must go for his most exciting materials to republications that are universally accessible, though, after having been read, they may have been half forgotten in the newer interest of fresher sensations; while most men will be inclined to renounce in despair the hope of improving on the picturesqueness of the best of these narratives.

It must be much the same in the case of statesmen. Formerly, when there were meagre Parliamentary reports,—when the Premier was a despot like Walpole or Chatham, and the administration arbitrary so long as he held office,—there was much that was interesting to be told, much that was mysterious to be explained, when a biographer found himself in a position to make confidences. Now it is comparatively rarely that we have to wait for the demise of the principal actors in them to learn the exact truth as to important transactions. Each successive step is submitted to the most searching scrutiny. Energetic or fussy members ask questions and raise debates. Ministers are forced to stand on their defence against attacks and insidious suggestions that cannot well be left unanswered. The debates are thrashed out in exhaustive leaders, while correspondents and consuls abroad are contributing to the literature of foreign questions. There is a serial publication of blue-books which are systematically condensed for the information of the public. No Minister dare refuse the publication of a State-paper: at the most, he can only take the responsibility of deferring it. Now and then a man's lips may be sealed by a punctilious sense of honour, or by circumstances which he can hardly command, as to some Cabinet decision or piece of diplomacy in which he played a conspicuous part. But with the lapse of time, people have ceased to feel concerned in that; and even when attention has been subsequently called to it in some keen political critique, it only awakens a languid interest. We are far from saying that the average talent of our statesmen has declined, though the glare of publicity that exposes their shortcomings seems to give greater point every day to the famous dictum of Oxenstiern. But there can be no question that writing their lives in detail is coming more and more to have much in common with the philosophical revision of ancient history.

Even with the lawyers, things have changed for the worse. There used to be fine scope for forcible writing in a brilliant forensic career, when beginning with some unlooked-for exhibition of eloquence; with the lucky hit of a junior stepping into the place of an absent leader, it led him through professional and political intrigues and many a hotly contested election, to land him in the Chief Justiceship or on the woolsack. At present the course of the profession is more prosaic. The young barrister's best chance at his start is a paying family connection, or marriage with a lady who brings clients as her dowry. He climbs the ladder by slow degrees, and it is seldom he clears the first rounds at a spring. The ballot and the new election laws have done away with the romance of the hustings; and even the humours of the circuits seem to have been dying out with the old habits of sociable conviviality. We fear we shall never again have such a book as Twiss's 'Life of Lord Eldon;' nor need future Lord Chancellors fear a new series of a Lord Campbell's 'Lives,' which shall "add a fresh horror to death."

Perhaps in the general decadence of the art, the lives of divines are the sole exception; and that is chiefly because they are so seldom liberally catholic either in their spirit or their interest. A man who has made a name as a pulpit-orator, or who has played a leading part in the affairs of some Church or sect, has his personal following of devoted worshippers. In nine cases out of ten the life has been written by some faithful follower who has clung to him like Elisha to Elijah. The biography becomes the faithful reflection of its subject's views and convictions. We can hardly say that his prejudices are treated with tenderness; for they are adopted, defended, and developed. The people who make a rush on the first edition know exactly what they have to expect, and there is little chance of their being disgusted or disappointed, since the name and familiar opinions of the author guarantee the tone. The bitterness of conflicting creeds is proverbial; and it is too seldom that a writer seizes on the grand opportunity of soaring superior to the narrow prepossessions of sectarianism, into the untroubled atmosphere of the Christian religion. Yet though a sectarian memoir must be one-sided and narrow-minded, it need by no means of necessity be a literary blunder. On the contrary, earnest partisanship may be an antidote to dulness; bitterness of feeling gives it a certain piquancy; and the invective that is inspired by honest self-satisfaction may lend animation and vigour to the style. The pious men who are most likely to be treated catholically, and to be made beacons for the devout of future generations, are those whose influence has extended beyond their communions, and whose intellect has been expanded by circumstances or in the turmoil of religious convictions. As in the case of Chalmers, for example, when he won the respect of the world for the breadth of his labours and the liberality of his opinions, until he broke down in the melancholy struggle which led to the disruption of Christian unity and kindly feeling in the Scotch Church; or of Dr Newman, when, in the height of his reputation as logician and controversialist, he passed over from Oxford to Rome; or, above all, of the self-denying pioneers of missionary enterprise like Xavier or Martyn, Livingstone or Wilson.

We may dismiss the subject of contemporary biography with the briefest notice of some of the works that happen to have appeared very recently, though any attempt at a comprehensive survey is far beyond the compass of our article. And we may go back to the published volumes of the Prince Consort's life, as the work is still uncompleted. By the consent of the critics, Mr Theodore Martin has fully justified the confidence which intrusted to him a task in which her Majesty is so nearly and dearly interested. The Prince's peculiarly difficult position had made him enemies; and excited jealousies which generated prejudices and misrepresentations. The "fierce light that beats upon a throne" is a very deceptive figure of speech; for the fitful flashes that come quicker in times of political excitement are apt to give false ideas of facts; while the shining qualities of the occupant are lost in the dazzle, and unobtrusive family virtues may escape notice altogether. In doing justice to the memory of her husband, by publishing his memoirs with almost absolute unreserve, her Majesty exercised a wise discretion. In unbosoming herself as to the loss she had sustained, she made the nation doubly sympathetic in her sorrow; and in these times, when thrones are shaking abroad, and experience is demonstrating the instability of republican institutions, it is almost impossible to overrate the value of such a book. The Life is full of those high lessons which it should be the chief purpose of biography to convey. There are no symptoms in it of fulsome praise, and yet we may add that there is nothing which does not redound to the honour of its subject. The family details that are given so frankly and naturally, have of course a very exceptional interest. And it presents a remarkable example of versatile energy and keen political insight united to most extraordinary self-restraint. For once the political chapters of a biography have a double interest. For, emanating from the most unexceptionable information, they clear up much that had been hitherto obscure in the most momentous events of recent history; while they show all her Majesty owed to her husband, and with what indefatigable intelligence he had laboured in the interests of the adopted country, that too often repaid him with perverse misrepresentation.

Among the latest publications on our table, we find a miscellany of subjects and styles—the Life of Bismarck, by Busch; of Machiavelli, by Villari; of Madame de Bunsen, by Mr Augustus Hare; of George Moore, by Smiles; of Dr Hook, by his son-in-law; of Sydney Dobell. We may say that we have already passed them indirectly in review. Herr Busch illustrates all the indiscretions of the life of a very great man, written by an obsequious dependant. There are many amusing personal touches, no doubt; but as biography, it is valueless, because it is entirely in rose-colour. The writer's ideas are the reflection of those of his idol, as lizards take their tints from the rocks they crawl on. Besides, the Prince's biography runs into history, and the history is too evidently "inspired." Machiavelli, so far as the subject has yet been carried, is handled with highly creditable impartiality; but the book is in great measure a historical essay, where facts are supplemented by ingenious theories, which, though plausible, are seldom solidly established. Madame de Bunsen's Memoirs are excellent in their way, and we fancy it will prove to be one of the books that you may care to dip into again and again. A charming and highly accomplished woman, who lived in the highest society in Europe, and whose places of residence made her as familiar with the associations of the past as with the intellectual activity of this age of progress, gives the exhaustive diary of an eventful life in a series of delightful letters. But here, too, we are bound to add, that the book would have been the better for judicious retrenchment; and in particular, our remarks as to hesitating on the threshold, will apply to the minute analysis of the lady's pedigree. The same apparently inevitable criticism will apply to George Moore and Sydney Dobell, though both are well worth reading, and the former especially. We hardly know how we came to overlook it in our observations on Dr Smiles. For it shows the author at his best in his nervous though somewhat homely style; and in his intuitive perception of the striking traits that may best serve to illustrate the man he is describing. Not that George Moore is made by any means ideally attractive. There can hardly be a greater contrast between the active career of the pushing commercial traveller and tradesman, who, turning into the generous and religious philanthropist, made friends as fast as he made a fortune, and whose power of activity seemed to be multiplied with the number of objects he took in hand; and the life of the dreamy poet and thinker, whose best efforts were baffled by misfortunes, and by the maladies to which he prematurely succumbed. Yet though comparison must be unfair when the objects of it are so opposed, we do not know that Dobell's memoir is not the more instructive of the two. For it is harder to keep up heart and faith against ever renewed disappointment and bodily anguish; harder to keep the freshness of your kindly sympathies unimpaired, than to carry the full cup with a steady hand when prosperity and the world are conspiring to spoil you.

Johnson on one occasion remarked that no writers were more defective than writers of travels. As we have the highest respect for his critical judgment, we conclude that things have greatly changed since his time. If there has been a decline in biography lately, and if its prospects can hardly be said to be encouraging, works of travels are becoming more valuable. No doubt they are not always so exciting as they once were, and there is less of the sensational in them than there used to be, when the daring adventurer could throw the reins to his imagination, and revel in the wonders he professed to relate, being well assured that nobody could contradict him. These were happy days when the narrator had no fear of the critics; when there were no learned geographical societies to sift his statements and dispute his conclusions; and when the public were willing to swallow everything, from magnetic mountains and ape-headed anthropophagi down to phœnixes and fiery flying-serpents. It is hard to measure the splendid possibilities of the boundless fields of untravelled mystery, when grave men made pilgrimages to empires and potentates that had never existed save in the realms of fable. Even when the world had grown more enlightened, travellers still had magnificent opportunities. Go where they would beyond the frontiers of civilisation, and out of the frequented tracts of commerce, they could never fall on what was flat and unprofitable. Fresh discoveries rewarded each feat of enterprise; for each step they made in advance lay through unknown or forgotten countries. If the risks they ran were great, the rewards were proportionate. No one but the hardiest of enthusiasts would dream of hazarding himself in such work; and we can fancy the thrill of delight that made him forget his sufferings, when he saw the giant columns of Baalbec or Palmyra crimsoned by the gorgeous desert sunset; when he stumbled into such a secluded valley as Petra, where the rock-hewn tombs and temples rose, tier over tier, in the pristine freshness of the rose-tinted granite; or when he identified the site of some seat of world-renowned empire, marked by its shapeless masses of crumbled mud-brick and its mounds of shivered and sun-bleached pottery. And there were incidents enough in all conscience to enliven the narrative. When these travellers observed the manners and customs of sullen fanatics and savage tribes, they had everywhere to run the gauntlet of aggressive suspicion. As our village boys or roughs of the cities would mob a Chinaman in calico and pigtail, they were hooted and hounded through the villages where they sought a supper and a couch. Explorers in Africa nowadays have their troubles and dangers, as we know. But they generally go attended by the formidable escort that enables them to fight a battle on occasion; and they carry ample means of buying provisions, or bartering for them, though the natives must sometimes be forced to deal. Those famous Scotch pioneers, Bruce and Mungo Park, were beggars to all intents and purposes. They had to pray for the daily dole that was to keep body and soul together; they humbly acknowledged such hospitality as was offered them; and were grateful for the cup of cold water that was bestowed by feminine charity. Necessarily their surveying work was roughly done; they had to make their hurried observations by stealth, and put their questions at the peril of their lives. In that respect they much resembled those daring Indian pundits, who have been sent by Montgomery and other of our frontier officials on scientific tours through Thibet and the Himalaya. Making any regular notes was generally out of the question; and when we consider the manner of men they were, and the circumstances under which they had to rely on the memory, we may give them no little credit for their literary workmanship.

Now all that is changed. There are barbarous districts, and even independent semi-civilised states, of which our knowledge is still of the vaguest; and till the other day there were thick clouds of uncertainty hanging over the sources of such rivers as the Nile and the Congo. But on the whole the progress that has been made is marvellous; nor are there many corners of the habitable globe into which civilisation has not pushed its researches. Thus, Russia and England, respectively advancing from the shores of the Caspian and the mouths of the Ganges, have met among the robber races of Central Asia. The American farmers and miners, pushing across through the wilderness on their march to the California coast, have reclaimed the magnificent hunting-grounds of the West, nearly extirpating the Red Indian in the process. Railway companies are projecting Grand Trunk lines through the pampas and forests of Southern America; and we have either formed colonies or established consuls in Australasia and the island groups of the South Seas; while Central Africa is no longer marked "unexplored" in the atlases, and believed to be an inhospitable waste of sand, like the Kali-hari desert or the Great Sahara.

There can be few grand sensations in store for us, since the comprehensive course of a general survey has dashed off the great contours of the globe, and all that is left for us now is to map out the world in detail. But after all, the blanks in the details are innumerable; they excite an increasing and more intelligent interest, and there are abundance of capable men who are eagerly volunteering to gratify that. There are men of wealth and culture and leisure to whom travel is an indispensable distraction. There are merchants whose enterprise carries them along little-trodden trade routes into remote and hitherto inaccessible localities; there are consular and mercantile agents who interest themselves professionally in the people among whom their lot has been cast. They kill the leisure that would otherwise hang heavy on their hands by a course of intelligent study and observation: and they strive to occupy their holidays profitably in expeditions that may do them credit by extending discoveries. The "grand tour" round Europe is long ago gone out of date. One can easily knock it off by instalments in the Easter recess, or in some part of the summer season that comes in between the intervals of shooting. Men think nothing of putting a girdle round the world, though they may not quite accomplish it in forty days, like the hero of the piece at the Porte St Martin; and even ladies like Mrs Brassey, in well-appointed yachts, perform feats of circumnavigation that, in point of time and distance, throw the life-labours of Cook and Wallis into the shade.

While, of course, more serious enterprise with definite objects is being developed in proportion. Those inquisitive geographical bodies, though they may put a curb on the exuberance of the explorer's fancy, serve a very useful purpose after all. International emulation is stimulated, and scientific exploration is systematically organised and generously rewarded with fame and medals. Intelligent curiosity, even more than philanthropy, has been opening up new destinies for Africa, while it promises to rescue the miserable African tribes from the consequences of their own blood-feuds and avarice. Though we must not, in referring to African discovery, overlook the invaluable services of the missionaries, with men like Moffat and Livingstone at their head. Nor have Germany and France been behindhand in the work; although the favourite fields of operations of their emissaries have rather lain in the north and north-west. But it is bare justice to say that it is to a brilliant group of English travellers that Africa and geography are most largely indebted. It would be difficult to exaggerate the qualities of the men who have repeatedly penetrated to the heart of the dark continent, or forced their way through its dangers in various directions. They were greatly helped, no doubt, by the funds and appliances which awakened interest placed at their disposal. But each one of them might have rivalled the most scantily equipped of their predecessors in fertility of resource as in resolute endurance. In some respects, indeed, the modern African traveller has more formidable difficulties to contend with, though they are difficulties of a different kind. Bruce or Park, Denham or Clapperton, had to carry his life in his hand, having made up his mind that he might probably lose it. Having deliberately counted the cost before, they had only themselves to be answerable for; and, next to their courage and presence of mind, they had to trust in great measure to the chapter of accidents. Submission in one shape or another was their sole resource, and they had to do their best to slip through the fingers of the savages. But the modern adventurer should be a general and a diplomat. He conducts an expedition of enterprise that resembles on a small scale the dashing invasion of a Cortes or Pizarro; the difference being that, in place of being at the head of an iron soldiery who will follow his lead in the last extremity, he has to make his way with troops and a bodyguard who are but semi-barbarous volunteers. He has to keep them from flight or mutiny, in the face of threats, terrors, and intrigues; and must buy and negotiate the right of passage through the territories of the grasping petty despots, with whom he may not improbably come to blows.

Hence the story of his perils and adventures must have a many-sided interest, and its incidents may often really resolve themselves into the higher order of biography. We see a rare combination of extraordinary qualities in habitual exercise: we follow the workings of a quick and far-reaching intellect, suggesting to itself those solutions of standing geographical problems which are to guide the future course of the expedition: giving careful thought to political considerations: coming to prompt decisions in critical emergencies: and showing itself, through months of incessant strain, ready to respond to an urgent call at any moment. Though health may relax in an enervating climate, or be broken by prolonged anxiety and want, the spirit is still resolute and vigorous ; and, whatever may be his reasonable apprehensions of the future, the leader must still show a smiling face to his disheartened party. While all the time he is writing up the diary, which not only notes each incident of the march and camp, but is exhaustive in the special information he came in search of. The memory cannot be relied upon for the work of months and years, and his object is precision, so far as it is attainable. The chapters that form a condensed encyclopedia in geography and hydrography, soil, climate, politics, and ethnological characteristics, are illustrated by sketches and skeleton-maps. These invaluable literary treasures run even more risks than their owner. They may sink in the swamping of a canoe, when he may swim and save himself ; or they may be burned in a fire in the camp, for he cannot carry them about on his person ; or they may be captured in a sudden attack, or abandoned by a runaway porter in the jungle. Should they survive to be delivered to an English publisher, they generally well repay the trouble that has been bestowed on them, though our careless ingratitude seldom appreciates that. Considering the qualities that have recommended the writer for his work, we expect to find them full of valuable information. Yet taking into account the circumstances under which they were originally compiled, and the drudgery that necessarily goes to recasting them, we should not be surprised to find them rather heavy reading. The life that was stirring enough to those who led it might easily be made very dull in the narration : one night-alarm, or ambush, or skirmish with savages, very much resembles another. Our sensibility is blunted, after a time, to the record of dreary periods of starvation, broken by an occasional feast ; and scientific observations and speculations are apt, at the best, to be dry. As a matter of fact, and it strikes us as a somewhat extraordinary phenomenon, the literary workmanship of these volumes of African travel has almost invariably left little or nothing to desire. The thrilling vicissitudes of most dangerous adventures are recounted with equal modesty and spirit ; a succession of episodes of thrilling romance are agreeably varied by their distinctive features ; and if there must unavoidably be a considerable amount of repetition, the inevitable *ennui* of it is reduced to a minimum. Not unfrequently the excitement is " piled so high " that were not its truth confirmed by the results of the achievement, we should find it very hard to believe. Occasionally even the scientific chapters have the charm of fairy tales. Incidentally we have vivid descriptions of scenery, which give as clear an idea of the landscapes and their vegetation as the photographs or sketches by which they are illustrated. To beguile the tedium of the monotonous march, we have now and then some exciting narrative of sport : though, except in Baker's books on the Nile tributaries, the sport, for the most part, takes the character of " pot-hunting." While, if the proper study of mankind be man, the writers have industriously availed themselves of their ample opportunities in that department. In those long tedious marches, in the still more heartbreaking halts, they must be always studying the peculiar idiosyncrasies of their followers. The " wily savage " is always willing to shirk ; lying is the virtue that is held in highest esteem by him; and an air of dull or brutal stolidity may conceal the art of an accomplished actor. Many of those pictures of the native, by "one who knows him," are admirably suggestive or extremely humorous. At one time it used to be held as an axiom, that the man of action was seldom likely to be much of a proficient in literary composition. Latterly we have seen occasion to believe that the rule is precisely the reverse. It would appear that the capacity for sustained mental and physical activity implies corresponding literary power; that decision of character and fertility of resource translate themselves into versatile freshness of thought and vigorous treatment in spirited diction. We have listened to eminent travellers who have spent long years away from civilisation, who sometimes, for example, like Gifford Palgrave among the Arabs, have almost had the opportunity of forgetting their native tongue, and who have come home to address a critical assemblage at the Geographical Society in well-chosen language with perfect self-composure. What is more remarkable, perhaps, some of the men who stammer through the formal acknowledgment of their health at a public dinner, become eloquent in an entire absence of self-consciousness when they speak at length on the labours they have delighted in. And so it would appear, that when they sit down to write in their studies they still answer to the spur of the peculiar temperament that animated and sustained them in their hazardous adventures.

Had the books they have written been dull, they would scarcely have been read except by *savants*. As it is, the libraries order them by thousands; the first editions are exhausted before they are well issued, and the ingenious writers of romance may envy the more popular actors of it. Who is not become familiar with African customs and scenery, from the Cataracts on the Nile to the Falls on the Zambesi, from the white-washed frontages of Zanzibar to the palms of S. Paul de Loanda? We are acquainted with the whole trying process of bargaining and recruiting; of collecting the bales of cloth, the coils of wire, and the packages of beads. We know only too well the Arab slave-traders, with caravans where the groans of the victims make chorus to the crack of the lash and clink of the manacles; where the camp-followers are the jackals and the flights of vultures, and where the tracks are marked by bleaching skeletons. We are made to enter into the feelings of Burton and Speke and Grant, where they came unexpectedly upon magnificent highland scenery on what had been supposed to be barren sands; or launched their craft upon inland seas calmly reposing under feathering woods when they are not lashed into turmoil by storms from the mountains. We learn to draw shrewd deductions from the slopes of the watersheds; and in anxious suspense as to possible disappointment, we identify the outflows of infant streams with those sources that have been the standing problem of men of science. Or we commit ourselves with Cameron and Stanley to the tranquil bosom of some "abounding river," that will tumble later down the sides of the tableland in cataracts and swirling whirlpools; and speculation slowly changes to conviction as we mark the affluence of mighty tributaries, since that growing volume of water can only carry us to our foregone conclusion. Without discussing the nicer questions of humanity or necessity, nothing can be more dramatic than the accounts of the hotly contested advance, when the parties are dwindling with death and disease, as day after day they drew nearer to their goal, only to force their way through fresh arrays of combatants. But the tales of bloodshed, sickness, and suffering are varied with lighter and livelier episodes, which show that the most anxious life has its contrasts. As when they find hospitality and temporary repose with some gentler savage who welcomes the strangers, and only fleeces them moderately. When Baker finds himself on the banks of the Blue Nile, camping in a delicious climate, in the happy hunting-grounds that might have gladdened the soul of a Harris or Gordon Cumming. When sitting in his tent-door, like the patriarchs, of a summer evening, he sees the herds of stately elephants and camelopards cropping the drooping foliage in the forest glades. Where the rhinoceros stands scratching his horny hide against the stem of some venerable thorn; and the herds of antelopes are sporting under the mimosa groves or coming down in herds to drink at the water.

Since Vambéry wrote the wonderful account of his travels in disguise, there have been many excellent books on Central Asia; though, as we have already remarked, it is being opened up to Europeans by the steady advance of Russian annexation. But there are still highland states to the north of our Indian mountain boundary which offer all the temptation of being practically inaccessible; while even those of them that indirectly acknowledge our influence have inducements enough in dangers as in sport to invite the enterprise of travelling knight-errants. Though we have already noticed at some length in our pages Mr Andrew Wilson's 'Abode of Snow,' it is well worth recalling, for we have rarely read anything more exciting. It was a novelty in mountaineering for a sick man to be carried in litters and local *chaises-à-porteurs* over the passes that are the drain-pipes of the "Roof of the World." To cross those fragile swinging bridges shockingly out of repair, might test the nerve of a Leotard; or to ride the unwieldly yak along the dizzy ledges that slope over crumbling slate downwards towards bottomless abysses. Shaw and Forsyth and Gordon have depicted the dangers of the storm-beaten trade routes that lead through snow-covered summits to the back-of-the-world dominions of the late Atalik Ghazi, whose death is likely to be lamented by commerce. And to come back under the guns of our English garrisons, into quieter and more settled districts, among the many works that are always appearing, we may call attention to 'Sport and Work on the Nepaul Frontier.' Although unpretending, it is singularly exhaustive and very pleasantly diversified. The writer tells us all about the indigo-planting in Behar, in which he was professionally employed for many years; and while instructing his readers, he interests them in a pursuit which demands extraordinary and unremitting attention. At the same time, he sagely takes it for granted that they are as ignorant as most people of Indian life; and merely communicating his information incidentally, he contrives to throw an infinity of light on it. While he shows, at the same time, what diversified enjoyment may be found by a healthy and active man who depends on exercise, and delights in sport, in a life that would otherwise be intensely depressing.

But it would be difficult indeed to name a country that has not been lately "done" more or less satisfactorily. Not excepting even the daring exploits of the first hardy Arctic explorers, in the wooden craft of a score or two of tons, that would have cracked like walnut shells to the squeeze of the ice-floes, we have no more thrilling narratives of hair-breadth escapes than those by Sir George Nares and Captain Markham. While the science of which our early navigators knew no more than sufficed to read the signs of the weather, plays an important part in these, as in the various "logs" of the Challenger, which Sir George Nares formerly commanded. And to go back from the frozen latitudes to the tropics, we have had 'Burmah' by General Fytche, who was long our Resident there. We have had books on Siam and Cochin China, by consuls and shrewd merchants, who have told us all about the once jealous courts of the White Elephant, and who have visited those wonderful temples in the jungles that have failed to commemorate long-forgotten dynasties. Naturalists, like Wallace in the Spice Islands and Malay Peninsula, or like Bates on the Amazon, have investigated the fauna of tropical forests, undeterred by malaria and those insect pests which indeed were among the agreeable pains of their wanderings. It must be some satisfaction to revenge one's self for a bite by transfixing the fly for the edification of entomologists. We have had more than one fascinating volume on the South Seas, and notably on the Hawaian Archipelago, which seems the nearest approach to a sensual paradise, in spite of its volcanoes and its colonies of lepers. There has been nothing more thrilling than the narratives of the survivors of those forlorn hopes in the interior of Australia, who groped their way through the desolation of the waterless waste, turning back again and again to some scanty spring, and barely sustaining life by the slaughter of the starving camels. All the states of South America, with their earthquakes and revolutions, have been repeatedly described in the minutest detail; and if Peruvian and Venezuelan bondholders, shareholders in Brazilian railways and mines; intending emigrants to the cattle-rearing pampas; and gentlemen who, like the Frenchman lately deceased, dream of cutting out a kingdom in Patagonia, do not have the requisite information at their finger-ends, it is no fault of the great corporation of travellers. Independently of any intrinsic interest, there are few of these books that are not more than readable; and in many of them the mere literary style would do credit to any man who had made a business of authorship. And one new and agreeable feature to be remarked in them is the profusion and excellence of the illustrations. Cities and their modern architecture, ruins and scenery, are reproduced from photographs or capital sketches. While almost invariably the authors show their good sense by putting themselves in the hands of some very capable map-maker. And *apropos* to careful description and exact map-making, Conder's 'Tent-Life in Palestine' deserves a special notice. The scientific survey of the Holy Land was an undertaking worthy of the English nation, and Captain Conder's volumes will be read with the warmest interest by the many who sympathise in the new crusade. He has cleared up many a doubtful point; conclusively settled many a contested site; confirmed, or logically refuted, many an ingenious suggestion; while he has given us what will be indispensable as a work of reference to the critical student of biblical history.

We could run through a long catalogue of entertaining travels—

not forgetting Mr Aylward's book on the Transvaal, full of practical hints and valuable information for the soldiers who are campaigning in Zululand—which might equally overtax our memory and space. But we cannot dismiss the subject without some allusion to the travellers who are rather tourists. Among them we suppose we must include, though they may take it as an insult, the gentlemen who hurry round the globe in a single protracted holiday expedition. Baron Hübner, the Austrian minister, and author of the 'Life of Pope Sixtus V.,' the French Count Roger de Beauvoir, who made his voyages as companion of one of the Orleans princes, are among the most cultivated and intelligent representatives of the class. When we say that they made the tour of the world, we mean of course that they did it by leaps and bounds, yet they have missed few of the chief objects of interest. The rapidity of their panoramic survey is favourable to hitting off its salient features. They contrast the jealously exclusive civilisation of China with revolutionary societies like that of Japan and the go-ahead democracy of our American cousins. Steaming along the grand waterways of commerce, they break the journey at the chief commercial centres. Generally, with their rank or recognised position, they carry their own introductions along with them, and mix as men of another world with the people who are best fitted to enlighten them. The modern tourist of any pretensions has opportunities that were seldom within the reach of his precursors. Either he is socially a personage, or he has an engagement with some great organ of the press. In any case it is known that he goes about taking notes, and the probabilities are that he thinks of publishing. And as all communities wish to be well spoken of nowadays; as every State must contemplate borrowing, and is jealous of consideration in proportion to its shortcomings,—they are desirous of exhibiting themselves to the best advantage. So all doors fly open before the traveller; carriages and special trains are placed at his disposal; high officials insist on acting as cicerones; and debates in representative chambers are got up for his special edification. Possibly all that sweeping and garnishing may throw some dust in the sharpest eyes; but keen observers like Mr Trollope or Mr Brassey, for example, are not very easily blinded, and, on the whole, the world decidedly gains by the new system of dispassionate supervision and publicity.

From travels we may naturally pass to sport, since so many of our travellers are enthusiastic sportsmen. And sport generally includes natural history, for most of the gentlemen who penetrate into the wilds with waggons or a flying camp-train, come back with the trophies they know how to classify. Never are they happier than on the rare occasions when they have added a new variety to the species in our museums or zoological gardens. Sporting books are become more pleasant reading, thanks to the recent improvements in arms and ammunition. A certain amount of suffering there must be; and as pheasants fly away with pellets in their bodies, so the greater game must often go off with the deadly ball festering in their vitals or dragging a shattered limb behind. But we never hear now of the crack shot, galloping behind the shoulder of the camelopard, loading and firing again till the agony of the animal is ended; nor of elephants turning to bay and charging again, till they drop at last to the slow bombardment. A rifle nearly as ponderous as a small field-piece sends the explosive bullet straight to the mark, and concussion with the shivered bone explodes the projectile on the instant. While as mere sportsmen have to go further afield, they are bound to become more and more of geographers. Officers and civilians, when lucky enough to obtain leave from departments morbidly apprehensive of international difficulties, explore the glaciers and snow-heaped valleys in the wildest recesses of the Himalaya and the Hindoo Koosh. The elephant hunter, who used to find magnificent shooting on the Limpopo, has to penetrate to the Zambesi, and even beyond it. While in the great West of America, the buffalo —or bison—has been wellnigh exterminated; and you must seek him to the south on the New Mexican frontier, or to the northward in his circumscribed range on the Yellowstone, or in scattered herds in the valley of the Saskatchewan. Owing to that indiscriminate slaughter, and to the rapid extinction of the Red men, who used to feed their squaws and papooses by the chase, we fear we have seen nearly the last of that library of prairie and Rocky Mountain adventure to which Catlin and Washington Irving and Ruxton contributed. Yet within the last few years we have had two books at least which are by no means unworthy of their more famous predecessors. Colonel Dodge's 'Hunting-Grounds of the Great West' and Major Campion's 'On the Frontier' may probably be among the latest of the standard authorities on American hunting as it used to be, and on the habits of "the skulking savage." Major Campion, by-the-by, published a second book the other day, which for decided originality deserves some notice under the head of travels. So far as we know, he was the first foreigner who undertook a regular walking tour in Spain, everybody else having acted on the dogma of Ford, that the *caballero* must take his horse as a guarantee of respectability, even if he preferred to have the animal led behind him.

As hazards have diminished with improvements in firearms, shooting in the forest and jungle is less risky than formerly, and consequently sporting narratives are less exciting. Moreover, narrow "shaves" and "squeaks" and ventures at close quarters, merging on the foolhardy, have been so often described, that they have naturally been losing much of their zest. Time after time, in the fancy if not in the flesh, we have dodged the charge of the infuriated elephant, or caught the twinkling bloodshot eye of the wounded rhinoceros. We have learned by too manifold experience how hard it is to double through thorny scrub when your pursuer is crashing behind you by sheer weight; and when you are saved by Providence or some lucky accident as you are almost within reach of the tusks or the horn. Time after time we have crouched along the tangled jungle-path in quest of the lurking tiger, looking for the sinister gleam of his eyeballs in the noonday shadows; or have sat watching for a night-shot at the terrible man-eater, with the mangled corpse of his victim for a lure. There is novelty, and consequently more excitement, in the newfangled breakneck mountaineering, when we go scrambling along the precipices or scaling the heights, whence we can drop down on the "bighorn" of the Rocky Mountains, or his cousin the wild goat of Kashmir and Thibet. Nor need one travel to the other side of the world to indulge in that kind of sport; and in the way of European adventure, Mr

Baillie Grohman's book on the 'Tyrol and the Tyrolese' will be found almost as pleasant reading as Boner's more famous 'Chamois-hunting in Bavaria.' The story of the stiff mountain expeditions where he carried a rifle in place of an alpenstock, is told with great spirit and vivacity; and he does justice to the foresters or *freischütze* who shared his bivouacs in the alpine huts or the cover of the pine-woods, without losing sight of those inconsistencies in their character that are more picturesque than engaging. For in the hills that look down upon railways and hotels that are patronised by the troops of peaceful tourists, men still stalk and shoot each other without the smallest hesitation; while their contests of strength and pluck at convivial meetings in the village *wirthhaüsen* are habitually marked by brutal ferocity.

Books of sport and natural history in the British Islands have never been so numerous as we might have expected. Perhaps because the few that are most popular are so excellent that they hold their own against competition, and reduce ordinary writers to despair. Half the world nowadays are keen shots, and a fair sprinkling of sportsmen may be said to be scientific observers. So everything is in the manner of telling the thrice-told story, and of describing those incidents that are familiar to everybody. You can hardly say where the happy knack lies. Yet you acknowledge it in the language which, though natural and unstudied, conveys the most pleasing and vivid impressions. Natural history has made considerable progress since White observed the feathered inhabitants of Selborne Hanger, and Waterton turned his gardens into a sanctuary; yet new editions of their works are perpetually appearing, and each issue has as hearty a welcome as its predecessors. It would seem as if men like these, if once they are induced to take pen in hand, must communicate in their original freshness their own heartfelt impressions. We know that the author of 'The Wild Sports of the Highlands,' and the 'Notes of a Naturalist in Morayshire,' was only reluctantly persuaded to publish by the persuasions of his friend Mr Cosmo Innes; and how many of us have good reason to be grateful for the success of his trial article in the 'Quarterly.' As, not very long ago, we noticed at length the latest edition of 'The Moor and the Loch,' we need not do more than refer to it now as a fascinating encyclopedia of that wide range of Highland and Lowland sports which have been the lifelong delight of its veteran author. And in these days when the rents of forests and moors have been running to figures almost prohibitory to any but millionaires, it is something to "get a wrinkle" about inexpensive shooting. The gentleman who writes under the *noms de plume* of "Snapshot" and "Wild Fowler," has collected a variety of scattered articles into six volumes in three successive series, which supply an infinity of useful and practical information. They are pleasantly written, if occasionally monotonous. He tells how, by simply crossing the Channel, the sportsman, at a very moderate outlay, may find himself comparatively in clover. It appears that in Belgium, notwithstanding the predominance of the class of small peasant-proprietors, there is good varied shooting to be rented very cheaply by a man who knows how to set about it. The writer has found enjoyable quarters in the beautiful woodlands of Alsace and Lorraine; while if you can only spare time for a short excursion, there are *communes* in the French departments of the north and west which will repay a flying visit. The bags of duck that may be made by ambush-shooting in Holland sound almost fabulous. But if you can make yourself happy among wild-fowl and divers, and do not object to some exposure and "roughing it," there is a great deal to be done in the free shooting-grounds that extend along our English shores, between the sea-line and the cultivated country. Near our tidal harbours, and the termini of the great coast railways, you may shoot away a heavy bag of cartridges in the course of a good day's walk. The tidal estuaries of the little rivers, and the swamps overflowed by the spring-tides, are all frequented in the season by great flights of birds. Stepping softly over shingle and sea-weed; carefully approaching the winding creeks and their tributaries; slipping alone under cover of the embankments and sea-walls,—you may shoot successively at herons and curlews, plover, duck, snipe, sandpiper, and swarms of oxbirds, greenshanks, and redshanks.

But by far the most accomplished rural enthusiast who has written of late years, is the anonymous author of 'The Gamekeeper at Home,' and 'Wild Life in a Southern County,' which appeared originally in the 'Pall Mall Gazette.' He is one of the men you cannot help liking, just as he loves the wild creatures of all kinds, among whom he has evidently lived from his childhood. Like our old friend the incumbent of Selborne, nothing has escaped his notice. He has the eye of an artist for the beauties of nature, for the shifting sky-effects of our variable climate, and the venerable churches, manor-houses, and farms. He has been a familiar and welcome guest in the homesteads and cottages, where his quick observation catches each detail, from the bulging lines of the gables and the walls without, to the old gun hanging over the mantel-shelf within doors, or the flitches suspended in the smoke of the capacious chimney-place. He has the art of drawing out the inmates, and getting at their innermost thoughts, with their quaint fancies and prejudices, and their lingering remains of superstition. He does the geography and hydrography of the parishes and chalk-downs, with a careful exactness of touch that would do credit to the Ordnance Survey. And as for the birds that people the overgrown masses of ivy, the clustering creepers on the crumbling brick-walls, the fruit-trees in the old-fashioned orchards, the copses, the hedgerows, and the rushes and sedges that fringe the brooks and half-choke the pools,—he knows every one of them by sight and note, and can not only describe their intimate habits, but seems to penetrate into their individual idiosyncrasies. He should be president of a staff college for gamekeepers and foresters; and the severest stricture we can pass on his books is, that they might be adopted as manuals by intelligent young poachers, were poachers as a rule addicted to literature. In fact, we are rather sorry to say that the new series of articles he has commenced are actually entitled 'The Amateur Poacher.'

Studies in Biography.

THERE are few greater services that can be done to an age, short of living a good and noble life, than that of recording one. And biography is a branch of literary art to which the present generation devotes itself. Scarcely any man of note can get safely out of this world without leaving behind him, already at the easel and with all the necessary tools in hand, a son, or a friend, or a professional man of letters, ready to 'take him off' and set forth his portrait in black and white, in voluminous volumes. It has come to be almost a necessary compliment to a notability. We put up the shutters on our shop windows; we sew a bit of black cloth round our arm; and we write the life of the departed. In some cases the one operation is of little more importance than the other, but it is as inevitable. It is safer to do what some men take the precaution of doing, and provide beforehand against the danger, by leaving behind us something more or less in the shape of an autobiography; but even this only partially mends matters, for it will go hard with our editor if he does not re-shape our personal chronicles, cut out all that is best in them, or else supplement and dilute them by telling the story over again. There is thus a perpetual example going on of that tantalising performance which keeps the word of promise to the ear and breaks it to the heart; and in the same breath with which we declare that the chronicle of a life is one of the best things we can have, we are compelled to add that we get many chronicles of lives which are about the worst things that we can have—pretentious, foolish, and false, chronicles of all the small beer, but of little of that divine elixir which keeps existence going. It is true that small beer, being matter of fact, is always capable of being measured and identified, while there are but a few that can read the meaning in a life, or trace out what its finer issues are and how the spirit is touched to them. Still, the dimmest mirror may give forth something, elsewhere unattainable, in its broken reflections, and we are often able to identify, notwithstanding all the flaws in the glass, the absence of quicksilver, or even the twist in the metal which makes a countenance awry, something, an outline, a gesture, which reveals the original. We are unable to say that there is much of this revelation in the portrait contained in two big volumes with which we have just been presented [1] of Charles Lever. It is a book without insight, without penetration, with neither beauty of style nor force of meaning to recommend it. The letters of the subject of the memoir are systematically and of set purpose

---

[1] *Life of Charles Lever.* By W. J. Fitzpatrick, LL.D., M.R.I.A. Chapman & Hall.

suppressed. We think we remember to have found somewhere an intimation that this is done with the intention of making a separate publication of some of these letters, in which case it is something very like an intended *exploitation* of the public, by dividing into two what was certainly not too much for one issue. Mr. Fitzpatrick is not an artist of merit, but he has evidently adopted the trade of biographer as a tangible handicraft, and in this capacity is diligently on the outlook, and industriously eager to take advantage of every opportunity for its exercise. We have no right to debar him from his chosen work, or even to censure his selection of a branch of industry which is nowise unlawful or dishonest in the ordinary sense of the word. We can only regret that his virtuous and laudable application to his business should have brought him across the path of anyone in whom we are interested. The 'Biographer of Bishop Doyle, Lady Morgan, Lord Cloncurry, &c.,' who is also 'Professor of History in the Royal Hibernian Academy,' and a J.P., with many other letters to his name, the meaning of which we do not profess to be able to decipher, is apparently a kind of national official, and does not therefore threaten the life of any subject who is not Hibernian, which is a consolatory reflection. But it is grievous that a man like Lever, one for whom all the world has a kindness, a man not great enough to bear any tampering with his memory, and full of foibles and eccentricities which need delicate handling, should have fallen into the hands of such a practitioner. This is all the more to be regretted that it can never now be remedied; for Lever's gift, such as it was, was not so great, nor is his recollection so precious, that it should be worth any better artist's while to endeavour to amend the coarse and commonplace portrait which is here supplied. In this way a trade biographer does less harm to a celebrity of the highest class than to one of secondary pretensions. The larger genius will get justice somehow, but for the less there is not much hope of rehabilitation.

Few men have gained so much kindly appreciation from the world as the Irish novelist, to all appearance the last of his race, who did for his country exactly what the general public likes to have done, enlarging and strengthening the conventional idea of it, and leaving us more sure than ever of the justice of all our prejudices and the truth of our scoffs. This is by far the most popular way at least of writing national novels. We hail with lively satisfaction every apparent proof of those generalisations which save us so much trouble in respect to our neighbours. It is more easy to conclude that the Italian is treacherous, the Frenchman fickle and light, the Spaniard proud, the Scot canny and calculating, than it is to realise that the resemblances of human nature are more striking than its differences, and that each member of a race is an individual. Consciously or unconsciously, Lever humoured this general inclination. Nothing can be more conventionally Irish than his Irishmen. They are all constructed on a pattern which we understand and have given in our adhesion to; for does not Ireland contain, as everybody knows, a rollicking, light-hearted, reckless, dare-devil sort of population, madly brave, and wildly witty, totally unfitted for the ordinary pursuits of life, yet quick to apprehend and wise to know everything that is ornamental and amusing and unnecessary? Lever's art, so full of freedom on the surface and so conventional underneath, is as inferior as can be conceived to that of Scott, who never lost sight of the deeper sea of human nature which underlies all local distinctions; and it is needless to point out which of the two is the most true historian of national life. But, notwithstanding, the conventional is always sure of a certain success. We get in it what we look for. We have all our foregone conclusions carried out, and we are pleased to feel that we have been right in our estimate of our neighbours. At the same time we must add that Lever, though Irish only by the accident of birth, was in himself a complete example of the type we accept as Irish. Though he was the son of an Englishman, thrifty and hardworking, he was himself as gay, as reckless, and as extravagant, accepting the pleasures of to-day with as little reference to to-morrow, as any descendant of Brian Boru: and embodied in his own person all those traditions of wit, gaiety, and prodigality which are supposed appropriate to the aborigines of the Emerald Isle. How this trick of nature came about it, it would be difficult to say. The Irish air must have got into his head as a baby, though Saxon by both sides of the house, and intoxicated him from the cradle. He lived a life of wild uncertainty, not knowing often enough what the morrow might bring forth; yet somehow managing it so that the day, which had menaced destruction before it came, generally cleared off into smiles, and justified the light-hearted pilgrim's reliance on his fate. Thus possessing the type in himself, he drew upon it with bold and dashing hardihood, and so long as the first flush of animal spirits and unquenchable gaiety lasted, his gay dragoons and light-hearted adventurers, always daring, always lucky, enjoying alike their dangers and their successes, renewed the old tradition of Irish character, and took the soberest readers by storm.

The task which Mr. Fitzpatrick seems to have set before him in compiling this memoir is to show with how little genius Lever managed to accomplish such a result, how little, in short, he himself had to do with it at all, and how completely he was indebted to casual meetings and social surroundings for his success. We do not say that the 'Biographer of Bishop Doyle and Lady Morgan' has any malignant purpose in this attempt, or even that he is aware that he is doing his best to damage Lever. He writes as a local historian so often writes, with unbounded admiration for the society of which he forms a part, and a little less admiration for the one notable individual who is the only man whom the world cares to know in that society. That there was 'a very social, well-informed set' at Kilrush, and again, 'half a dozen companionable men, some of more than average acumen,' at Portstewart, near the Giant's Causeway, is more important to him than the qualities of Lever himself. He is more anxious to impress upon the reader that Father Malachy and Father Tom were exact transcripts from the life, and that 'the best of the stories in Lever's tales were told round that mahogany,' than to show how Lever's imagination took hold of the racy and primitive country life, and got the flavour and savour of it, with or without the facts which are so much less important. But it is scarcely worth our while to go further into the literary merits, or rather demerits, of this biography. It has no pretension to be criticised at all as a piece of literary work, although, indeed, its pages are full of national eccentricities of an unintentional kind, which are as amusing as if they were meant to be so. The biographer and his obliging correspondents are alike delightful in this respect. One lady, speaking of Lever's mother, informs us that 'she had a brother who one day appeared from India, bearing beautiful presents, but on returning to the East, just as he was about to step on board, he fell into the Liffey and was lost.' Another contributor describes how Lever as a boy 'told stories at school, danced, fenced, laughed, *and then rode off on a pony*,' a charming climax. A little further on Mr. Fitzpatrick indulges in some mildly funny anecdotes respecting a medical authority, explaining that 'these things we give not for their point, but because they reveal on Lever's showing that when a student he received comic grind from the witty doctor, whose sayings, pruned of thorns and slang, had effect upon the mind and character of the subsequently brilliant humourist.' 'He struck me,' says another contributor, 'as a man of most winning manners, which indeed were shared by his wife, to whom in the course of my visit he asked me to give my arm.' When the first book of the series was published, we are told that 'the public clapped, the critics coughed, the cynics hissed. It was not till long after that *the censer swung*;' and here is an account of Lever's performances when a country doctor, which is better still:—

Lever, while dancing at balls, was dancing attendance with bright vigilance by the bedside of suffering humanity; and this his worst Evangelical enemies were constrained to confess. Now whirling in the waltz—a few minutes later by the bedside of danger. Back to the ball again! engaging Miss Dashwood for the Lancers—hurrying away to see the cataplasm renewed, and with his own hand administering relief, or spreading the balm. He arrives just in time to take his place with the Belle of the Ball; but the intermitted pulse of the little sufferer still throbs at his own heart; the glance of its glassy eye is before him; and he is less impressionable than usual to that 'hazel and blue,' which evoked his best lyric. He is back with the sick girl again; gives a stimulant; she rallies. Within ten minutes he is doing the same for himself at the supper-table. Happier now, he is in a state of supreme felicity when dancing that 'Morning Bell' gallop, with which the rout winds up. He goes home, revolving in his mind some tonic wherewith to set up the convalescent.

Lever was the son of a builder in Dublin, to whom Mr. Fitzpatrick has supplied a very pretty pedigree. Let us hope it is genuine: it is, at least, a respectable sort of thing to hang up in the vestibule, though we doubt how far it is consistent with the modest position of the 'English carpenter and builder' who—which is much more to the purpose—established himself comfortably in Dublin, and was able to give his children considerable educational advantages. His family consisted of two sons, one ten years older than the other. The novelist was the younger of the two. We have various accounts of his school days from various old contemporaries, each of whom seems to plume himself on being the last survivor; but among them they do not add much to our knowledge of their playfellow. He was a merry boy, fond of frolic and of story-telling, who played a great many tricks, made a number of jokes, told a number of stories, went to America, where he had sundry (extremely improbable) adventures, and to Germany, where he learned all the odd ways of the Burchenschaft, copying them when he returned to Dublin in a fantastic society, of which he was himself 'the most noble grand.' The survivors of this society fondly declare it to have been one of the wittiest of social assemblies: and Lever himself afterwards pronounced that 'for a witty doggerel on the topic of the hour, a smart epigram, or a clever piece of drollery, all I have ever since met of *beaux esprits* in my own or other countries could not approach comparison;' as, indeed, most survivors of similar youthful companies are ready to swear. Lever's career at college was not a distinguished one; indeed, the very fact of his University education at all seems to have been called in question by contemporary writers; however, we are assured here that he took his degree at Trinity College, Dublin, in 1827, being then, as we guess, about twenty-four years of age. The dates, however, are wildly confused, and it is impossible to make head or tail of them. Thus, we are assured that Lever sailed for America in the spring of 1829, and that he afterwards paid a visit to Germany, the dates being arranged as follows:—'We were at first disposed,' the biographer says, 'to place it (the German expedition) before the Canadian trip; but in his account of Cologne he alludes to the emotions he had previously felt in viewing Niagara. The first part of his "Logbook of a Rambler" appeared in the "Dublin Literary Gazette" for January 16, 1830, and was probably written towards the end of 1829. "In the early part of last year," he writes, "I was waiting in Rotterdam," which fixes the date, namely, 1828. At Göttingen he passed the winter of that year and the ensuing spring,' *i.e.* the spring in which he went to America and saw Niagara, to his emotions on beholding which he has just been said to refer in his account of Cologne. This confused jumble proves that Mr. Fitzpatrick knows very little about the matter, and has not taken the trouble to note that, with true Irish liberality, he has proved his hero to have been in two places at once. The whole story, however, of the American experiences reads much more like a hoax than a record of real adventure.

Lever took, we are told, the degree of Bachelor of Medicine in 1831, but instead of taking his M.D. from his own University, subsequently acquired one from a foreign school—a curious fact, if fact it is. He began his practical work humbly enough, being sent off with a number of other young medical men to meet the outbreak of cholera in the north. He was sent to Kilrush, where, as we have already said, we hear more of the brilliant society which took the young doctor up than of himself. These local celebrities encouraged and brought him out, though they thought him 'retiring and evidently nervous.' 'To Mr. Keane,' says Lever's biographer, 'we owe the introduction of this shy *débutant* to a circle of genial well-informed men. Had not means been taken to draw him out, the genius within might have flickered and sunk.' A footnote to this remarkable statement informs us that 'the feeling finally merged into an involuntary motion of the muscles of the mouth.' We do not attempt to unravel the connection between these sentences. But the fine human vanity of these rural patrons of genius is delightful. Naturally the little country-town coterie identified every character when 'Harry Lorrequer' burst upon them like a thunderbolt. 'Who let the cat out of the bag?' cried the men of Kilrush. They gave themselves the entire credit of the production. The doctor was but a kind of secretary, betraying these good things to the world. Even his own family shared this feeling. 'John Lever told me that he became aware that his brother was the author of "Harry Lorrequer" from the story of Father Darré and the Pope. But ah!' he added, 'how inferior to my father's mode of telling it!' Lever himself could have done nothing more laughable than this serious narrative of his own appearance—wild Trinity College undergraduate, bold and brazen medical student, 'most noble grand,' and Dublin wit as he was—in the capacity of a 'shy *débutant*,' whose genius might have been quenched altogether but for the insight and encouragement of the brilliant circles in Kilrush.

However, the life of a country doctor, laborious and ill-rewarded as it is, was no doubt of great advantage to the young writer full of fun and animal spirits and sympathy, with an eye to see all the humours of the country-side about which he was continually dashing, driving 'a pair of grey bloods,' says one witness, and carrying out, like one of his own heroes, every wild fancy that came into his head. 'Once, when galloping to visit some patient, he came full tilt against a turf cart as it suddenly emerged from a side street, and, not having room to pull in his horse, he "put in" the spurs and lifted him over the load of turf, which feat gained him the name of the Mad Doctor.' On another occasion, in the streets of Coleraine, he is said to have jumped over a horse and cart, perhaps another version of the same heroic incident. Not much less daring is the fact that he married on the strength of that parish doctorship at Portstewart, and sent off his last twenty pounds to buy a ball dress for his wife when an invitation came to them for a dance at a great house, which the gay young couple could not resist. Fortunately other resources were beginning to open up. The 'Dublin University Magazine' was instituted about the time of Lever's marriage, more humbly than any of its contemporaries, 'by six collegians, each of us subscribing ten pounds' —a modest capital with which to start a great literary venture. Lever began to contribute at an early period, sending some unimportant tales, which have not been preserved. But how it happened to him to strike the vein of which he was to make so much we are not informed. He would seem to have fallen by chance and natural fitness into the gay 'Confessions' and erratic career of Harry Lorrequer. His previous writings had evidently not prepared any of his friends for an outburst so characteristic, and so full of dash and daring. Fortunately, however, he found, as most successful writers do, a publisher with imagination and judgment enough to perceive that it was really something genuine in its way, which his new contributor, still unaware that this venture was different from the others, had brought him. They stumbled together, writer and printer, into success. Lever himself, though not naturally diffident, does not seem to have realised for a long time that what had cost him so little could be worth much. He continually demands from his publisher the applauses of the newspapers, probably feeling that nothing but such matter of fact evidence could make him quite sure of the reality of his 'hit;' and altogether, so far as we can see him through Mr. Fitzpatrick's rendering, conducted himself with the caution and doubt of a man still far from sure that the public were not making a mistake. Throughout all his life, though he would puff himself on occasion with a barefaced humour, quite distinct from vanity, we never see any trace of elation over his own powers, or self-admiration of any kind. Perhaps Lever was too reckless, too *insouciant*, too hugger-mugger, if the word may be used in a literary sense, for any of the exhibitions of intellectual self-esteem. He wrote, as he lived, from hand to mouth; feeling himself very lucky when he succeeded, in much the same way as he was lucky when he had good cards at whist, and cast down indeed when he failed, but not with any feeling of personal responsibility. To the end, like many men of greater genius, he never seems to have been clear as to what was his best, but went on boldly, dashing as of old over all obstacles, as ready to put in the spurs and lift his reckless Pegasus over a difficulty, as he was to bolt a pike or clear a cart in Coleraine.

In the meantime he went to Brussels, where, with easy audacity, he called himself Physician to the British Legation, an appointment which it now appears did not exist. Lever's conscience was quite impervious to any blame in respect of such an innocent fib. But though he had no distinct appointment he seems to have got, if not into practice, at least into the best society, always a prime object, and lived expensively as was natural to him, in great gaiety and sociability, interrupted by brief intervals of difficulty and doubt, in which he wished himself back in his dispensary, and persuaded himself that the life of a country doctor was a better passport to competency than that of a popular author. It seems unlikely that a man so fond of society and movement could have had anything like a practice in the gay little capital where he wrote his second book, 'Charles O'Malley,' in the opinion of many people the best of all the brotherhood; but he did continue more or less to exercise his profession. He tells us, on one of the few occasions on which his biographer permits him to speak for himself, that he was 'very low with fortune' at the time 'O'Malley' was begun. 'At the same time,' he says, 'I had then an amount of spring in my temperament, and a power of enjoying life, which I can honestly say I never found surpassed. The world had for me all the interest of an admirable comedy in which the part allotted myself, if not a high or foreground one, was eminently suited to my taste.' 'I wrote as I felt,' he adds, 'sometimes in good spirits, sometimes in bad; always carelessly, for, God help me, I can do no better.'

This, no doubt, was the great secret of his success. Though we agree devoutly with the greatest of living moralists that genius may, at least on one of its sides, be described as an infinite capability of taking trouble, yet there is a charm in the spontaneous, even the careless, when kept alive by a spark of genuine life, which always appeals to the sympathies of mankind. Even genius has to be wary how it shows the signs of taking trouble, and the ease and flow of a stream which is evidently natural, and carries everything along with it in a bold and sparkling rush of constitutional vigour, is always attractive. When Lever's first flush of impulse failed, and he began to take trouble, having no natural instinct that way, the interest of the public failed also. He was wiser, more thoughtful, perhaps on the whole better worth reading; but he had lost the ingenuous fervour, the harebrained impetuosity, the dash and spontaneousness which were his chief attractions. 'The Dodd Family' is a much more elaborate performance than 'Charles O'Malley.' It has far higher moral desert, the virtue of conscientious effort; but it is not to this grave production of his manhood that the reader turns. There is something far more attractive in the disjointed adventures, poured out anyhow, just as they occurred to him, in hearty enjoyment and fullness of life, of the Irish dragoon.

Space will not allow us to follow Lever's life in detail. The reader will receive a vague impression of it, not to be altogether spoiled by any badness of telling from the volumes before us. As he began life, so he went on, save that all the extravagances of his nature increased as time passed, and the young fellow who made himself talked of by practical jokes, or by vaulting over a horse and cart in his way, or by any other mode of harmless display, in early years, went on getting himself talked of all his life long, by extravagances perhaps not less harmless, but creating a greater amount of animadversion. There was too much champagne, too many cards, with the irregularities attendant on both, throughout his gay life. It was not whisky, which would have been degradation; but in the long run it was scarcely less dangerous. And he had all the liberality which belongs to his careless nature; he did not choose always to be entertained, but loved to be in his turn the entertainer, to give the best of wine and cookery, and to lavish his money upon his friends. He kept 'quite a stud of horses,' and rode about with his children round him—a remarkable group, the girls on their ponies, with auburn hair hanging over their shoulders, and wearing fantastic dresses, so that he was not unfrequently taken for the head of a circus, a mistake which amused him greatly. The mixture of tender vanity and fondness, delight in his children's society, and pleasure in showing them off, which appear in this incident, are thoroughly characteristic of the man. He loved to give a sensation to his fellow-creatures in the dullness of ordinary life, as well as to make one, and exhibit his fine horses and his skill in the management of them, and all the beauty and the splendour of his belongings; there was amiability in all his vanity, yet also a love of display and genial self-exhibition in all his kindnesses. As he went on in life these peculiarities formalised themselves, losing the gay dash of youth to which everything is pardonable, and calling forth the remarks of unkind tongues, as the riding, and the swimming, and the card-playing, the late hours, and the luxurious living, and the necessities which now and then interrupted and threatened to break up life altogether, became more and more patent to the observation of the world. Such a life must have huge drawbacks; but perhaps its uncertainties, its hair-breadth 'scapes, its despairs and threatenings of ruin, had not much more effect than the hardship and headlong perils of a campaign such as Lever loved to describe. They gave zest to the brilliant gaiety, the lavish and thoughtless enjoyment; and a man who thus manages to get by hook or by crook all that he most likes in this life—beautiful villas, fine horses, a luxurious table, a variety of excellent society, and the constant company of those he loves—is in reality less to be pitied than the more humdrum individual who denies himself many fine things in order to live tranquilly, without debt or danger, 'within his income,' according to the most respectable ideal of domesticity. He has indeed the best of it in every particular, since, after thus triumphantly getting his own way, he gets the sympathy which his occasional paying of the penalty calls forth, into the bargain.

Lever spent the greater part of his later life in Italy, and was, during his last years, in the diplomatic service, holding the post of vice-consul at Spezzia, and afterwards at Trieste, in which latter place dullness for the first time seized upon him. And there he lost his wife, the beloved companion of all his vicissitudes, whom he had fallen in love with when a boy at school, and to whom he had been always bound by the most tender affection. He did not long survive her, and life was a blank to him after she was gone. He died at Trieste in the spring (so far as can be made out from the want of dates) of 1872. His books have come down from the position they once held, almost abreast of the works of his two great contemporaries, Dickens and Thackeray. It is hard to believe even that there was a time when he was thought a competitor with them for the highest rank in fiction. Few mature readers, we believe, now think of taking up by choice one of those dashing productions which pleased us so much in our youth; but though we are no longer young, there are always others who are, and with them 'Harry Lorrequer' and 'Charles O'Malley' still hold a scarcely diminished place.

It seems a kind of disrespect to Thackeray,[2] after reviewing at length a bad and big book upon the life of his friend and contemporary, who was so greatly his inferior in art, and even in manly dignity and merit in life, to take up the brief and incomplete chapter of biography, which is all the world has had of him. Mr. Anthony Trollope—well qualified as a literary workman and as a friend to give some idea of the attractive figure of a man who, though buried these thirteen years, we can scarcely feel to be dead: but hampered by a hundred reticences and limitations, by the reluctance of Thackeray's representatives to transgress his own wish, and by the very warmth of the jealous love which guards his memory—has produced, we need scarcely say, an interesting study of the author of 'Vanity Fair' and his productions, with something not much more than a frontispiece, a vignette, a sketch softly outlined and lightly tinted, of the man. It is all we have got, and it is all we are likely to have; but it is scarcely substantial enough to justify comment. But there is much reference in Mr. Fitzpatrick's large and loose volumes to the far greater artist, against whom he does not scruple to measure his hero; and the very suggestion of the period in which 'Harry Rollicker' encountered his many adventures, recalls the true and great humourist, who by a touch of happy travesty characterised Lever and his works as he did so many other men and things. There seems a certain impertinence in putting forth the details of a life so sad and so cheery, so bravely gay in courage and endurance, so tender and soft at heart, so 'cynical' to the vulgar understanding, so remorseless to the mean and false. Why it is that we should feel this we cannot tell; it is in itself a tribute to the more delicate, more noble nature of the man. Dickens has been stripped bare to the very inner core of his living, and nobody has minded much; neither do we feel the least compunction in respect to all the details given of Lever, which indeed we knew before. Thackeray has been as long—nay, longer—gone from the midst of us, and we all know dimly the great misfortune that overclouded his life, and the beautiful tenderness with which he was father and mother alike to his children —but it almost wounds us to draw the veil from a career which he accepted so bravely and sweetly, with no crying out against fate. No author of recent times has worked himself so entirely into the love of his readers. It was not so at the beginning of his career, when the virtuous public thought him cynical, and contrasted his

---

[2] *Thackeray.* By Anthony Trollope. (*English Men of Letters*).

unheroical familiarity with the blemishes and weaknesses of human nature with his great rival's sentimentalities, much to his disadvantage. We can ourselves remember, in the fervour of youthful optimism, to have protested with hot indignation against those lowering views of life, those revelations of unconscious vanity, with which he disturbed all our ideas of the perfect; and it is certain that among the mass of ordinary readers, the multitude which must give in its adhesion before any fame reaches its height, there were many who stood fast in this doctrine, refusing to be moved by the noble tenderness and pathos of much they found in his books, on account of the preponderance of that 'cynicism,' to which for the moment we could give no better name. But all this is now over and past. Only a belated person here and there, old-fashioned, and clinging to the rash judgment of a previous generation, speaks of Thackeray now as cynical. We continue to combat the accusation, as people continue to do battle with an old mistake long after it has died a natural death. Mr. Trollope even, who remembers, like ourselves, the fervour with which it was once asserted, pauses to offer a justification—but it is an unnecessary effort. It is no longer the custom to call Thackeray cynical. We have learned to know him better by mere lapse of years.

He was the only great humourist, in our opinion, whom the present age has brought forth. Dickens has been honoured with the name: but to set forth the oddities and eccentricities of life, to pick strange characters out of the mud, and set before us the grotesques of nature, requires a faculty altogether different from that which, putting before us no new types, no exaggerated peculiarities, but people like ourselves, formed of the ordinary metal of humanity, makes us acquainted with all the laughable pranks of human vanity without taking away our sympathy for our foolish brothers. This sympathy runs through and through all Thackeray's work. We are not sure that it is not called forth even for Barry Lyndon; and Captain Costigan certainly, with all his sins upon his head, never gets beyond a certain softening of fellow-feeling. But who would think of regarding Mrs. Gamp with any sympathetic sentiment? In the one case we laugh with an unmoved indifference to the individual, who is odious always, even when most amusing; while in the other we are never without a hope that they may 'tak' a thocht and mend,' as Burns wished that the devil himself might do. But it is not our business to discuss this great quality. Humour is the fashion, the favourite quality of the age; we all like to credit ourselves with its possession, and to claim the power of controlling our own absurdities by means of it, as well as perceiving those of other men.

Mr. Trollope has little to tell us of Thackeray that we do not already know. He was born of a well-connected, well-established family, perhaps with no floating grandeur of a pedigree, but with generations of cultivated lives behind him: and thus had the advantage, not shared by all his rivals, of thorough acquaintance with the inner life of those classes who are the favourites of literature, and among whom the finer problems of civilised life can best be studied. Dickens never possessed this advantage. However elevated the society might be in which he lived, in fiction he was never at home among gentlemen, and had no freedom in handling them. But though thus standing on a higher level than his great competitor, Thackeray had not his immediate success—he had not even the success which attended Lever's easy and dashing sketches: but toiled upward for a long time before his hand touched at a hazard the hidden spring, and the door flew open before him. Up to this time he had lived a struggling life: spending and losing in the first place the little fortune to which he was born, and then for a number of years struggling along with varying degrees of unprosperity, neither happy in his circumstances, nor fortunate in his efforts, but always cheerful, always honourable and self-sustained; a man flung by stress of weather into many out-of-the-way vessels and voyages, but never staining his good name, or leaving shame behind him. Mr. Trollope is disposed to discourse a good deal upon the story which does not furnish him with the details he loves. And indeed we cannot but regret that, having been opened up at all, it should not have been given with more detail, and a more complete revelation afforded us of the life-long sorrows and deprivations, the sweet and gay and melancholy humour with which he faced his troubles, and the purity and honour of the imperfect and diminished life to which he was sentenced from early manhood, and which he lived heroically, seeking no compromises or compensations for the loss which honour and duty called upon him to bear. It was but the other day that a great writer protested against the excuses offered for some offenders against justice, that they were highly moral and devoted to their wives and children: but whatever truth there may be in this protest, it is but right that such a moral hero as Thackeray should have his meed of praise. Society has learned to condone many a doubtful connection formed by those who have genius (or rank or wealth) sufficient to compel its tolerance *quand même*. But here was a man who might have been excused if any could, whom no one could have had the right to judge harshly, but who asked no indulgence, required no tolerance, and lived his half-life with uncomplaining courage. The circumstances are such that perhaps no biographer could yet speak with perfect freedom of this part of Thackeray's life. He was a man of the world, a man full of life and the love of enjoyment, and at the same time of domestic affection and that need of household expansion and the support of love and sympathy which belong to most fine natures; yet he bore without a murmur the desolation of his home, and left not the ghost of any doubtful connection to disturb the adoring devotion of his children. When so many indiscretions are condoned, should not this noble discretion and self-command be told in his praise? There is no more beautiful feature in Lever's life than his faithful love for the wife who was everything to him; there can be no nobler trait in any existence than Thackeray's undeviating fidelity to the wife who, by the saddest of afflictions, was nothing to him, and could not even have felt any pang, had he escaped somehow, as so many men do, from the bond which cut him off from so many of the enjoyments of life.

We have said that Mr. Trollope is a little apt to moralise upon the life which he is not, we suppose, permitted to fill in with fuller particulars. He gives Thackeray credit for irregularity and idleness, and tells us various particulars of his dilatoriness. One, for instance, which ended very pleasantly for Mr. Trollope himself, in the substitution of a hastily written (but admirable) story of his own for the novel planned and intended by Thackeray with which the 'Cornhill Magazine' began its career. This passage, however, is so extremely characteristic, if not of Thackeray, at least of Mr. Trollope, that we are tempted to give it in full.

About two months before the opening day I wrote to him suggesting that he should accept from me a series of four short stories on which I was engaged. I got back a long letter in which he said nothing about my short stories, but asking whether I could go to work at once and let him have a long novel so that it might begin with the first number. At the same time I heard from the publisher, who suggested some interesting little details as to honorarium. The little details were very interesting, but absolutely no time was allowed me. It was required that the first portion of my book should be in the printer's hands within a month. Now it was my theory, and ever since this occurrence has been my practice, to see the end of my own work before the public should see the commencement. If I did this thing I must not only abandon my theory but instantly contrive a story, or begin to write it before it was contrived. That was what I did, urged by the interesting nature of the details. . . . I will not say that the story which came was good, but it was received with greater favour than any I had written before or have written since. I think that almost anything would then have been accepted coming under Thackeray's editorship.

I was astonished that work should be required in such haste, knowing that much preparation had been made, and that the service of almost any English novelist might have been obtained if asked for in due time. It was my readiness that was needed rather than any other gift. The riddle was read to me after a time. Thackeray had himself intended to begin with one of his own great novels, but had put it off till it was too late. 'Lovel the Widower' was commenced at the same time as my story, but 'Lovel the Widower' was not substantial enough to appear as the principal joint at the banquet. Though your guests will undoubtedly dine off the little delicacies you provide for them, there must be a heavy saddle of mutton among the viands prepared. I was the saddle of mutton, Thackeray having omitted to get his joint down to the fire in time enough. My fitness lay in my capacity for quick roasting.

'It was his nature to be idle—to put off his work,' Mr. Trollope says in another place, with all the conscious strength of a man who takes Time by the forelock, does his so many hours of work daily, and has so many novels to the good, all put away in drawers and ready for use, according to the whisper of malicious gossip. Thackeray did not do this; he wrote from hand to mouth, composing part by part as he published them, a mode which, notwithstanding the undoubted advantages of Mr. Trollope's more orderly way, has also something to recommend it, especially for the writer to whom it is essential to be in sympathy with his readers, and to keep up the freshness of his own interest by way of holding theirs. And it was no doubt a method very suitable to the character of Thackeray's work, of which the plot and story are the smallest part, and which, opening up one mind, and soul, and life after another in an apparently capricious, episodical way, fell in very well with the new start of every month, which made it natural and advantageous for the artist to shift the light of his lamp, so that now one little circle, now another, should glow with that complete, minute, and all-pervading illumination which makes every character and every foible of every character, and their goodness and their truth, and their little fibs and deceits, and all the unseen, half-conscious mechanism of their lives, so familiar to us. But perhaps Mr. Trollope does not quite see, being a man of more orderly and industrious ways, how this 'idleness' of his friend's nature chimed in with the conditions of his art.

Working in this way as he lived, his craft no distinct thing to be shelved in so many hours of close labour, and put away from the ordinary course of his existence, Thackeray went on after his first great success, a true spectator, a more graphic and familiar chorus than ancient art ever invented, showing to all beholders how the world wagged. Great passions were not in his way, and he studiously disowned the heroic, notwithstanding that perhaps the most purely heroic figure of modern fiction owes existence to his hand. George Eliot professes a far more serious meaning than Thackeray, and is the possessor of at least an equal genius, but neither has she, nor any other writer of the century, invented for us anything that can stand by the side of Thomas Newcome. But the genius to whom we owe that ideal gentleman went through the world laughing in the face of his countrymen, and protesting that the heroic was not, and that his were novels without a hero. Naturally the public took his art at his own word, not seeing the humour of the protest, nor how the writer was laughing softly, with the tears almost too deep down to be visible, at his own certainty of an ideal and heroic human nature as well as at theirs. One can imagine that he laughed still, but a little ruefully, when he found how entirely he had succeeded in producing the confusion he had worked for, and in getting one of the tenderest of human hearts branded with the name of cynic. But all the same it was his own doing; for how were the unknown masses, who knew nothing of him but what he chose to tell us, to see through the paradox. Happily by this time it has explained itself.

It was Thackeray's name which floated off into full flood of prosperity our able and brilliant contemporary, the 'Cornhill Magazine.' Some of the 'Roundabout Papers,' published in its earlier years, were among the most exquisite chapters he ever wrote; easier, as being a direct communication from himself to his audience, without the intervention of any formal framework of a story to interfere with the flow of his commentary; and full of all the softness and kindness of his real nature. Everything he touched at last turned to gold. One of the enterprises of his life, his lectures, was undertaken greatly against the grain, and with many doubts as to the effect it might have upon his reputation and standing, for the most tender and laudable of purposes. Public opinion has fully pronounced against the idea that public appearances of this kind are derogatory in any case. But we cannot see how they ever could have been derogatory in his, since there was in them no trading upon bygone effort, no reproduction of old work, made piquant by the exhibition of the artist himself to satisfy the curiosity of the public; but a series of original compositions made *bonâ fide* for the object he had in view.

As there is so little opportunity of giving a fair impression of this man, as a man, to the reader who has no other means of knowing, we may quote the end of Mr. Trollope's essay in biography, which shows at least the estimate of Thackeray's character made by those who knew him best.

His charity was overflowing, his generosity excessive. I heard once a story of woe from a man who was a dear friend of both of us. The gentleman wanted a large sum of money instantly—something under two thousand pounds—had no natural friends who could provide it, but must go utterly to the wall without it. Pondering over this sad condition of things just revealed to me, I met Thackeray between the two mounted heroes at the Horse Guards, and told him the story. 'Do you mean to say that I am to find the two thousand pounds?' he said angrily, with some expletives. I explained that I had not even suggested the doing of anything, only that we might discuss the matter. Then there came over his face a peculiar smile, and a wink in his eye, and he whispered his suggestion as though half ashamed of his meanness. 'I'll go half,' he said, 'if anybody will do the rest.' And he did go half at a day or two's notice, though the gentleman was no more than simply a friend. I am glad to be able to add that the money was quickly repaid. I could tell various stories of the same kind, only that I lack space.

He was no cynic, but he was a satirist, and could now and then be a satirist in conversation, hitting very hard when he did hit. When he was in America he met at dinner a literary gentleman of high character, middle-aged, and most dignified deportment. The gentleman was one whose character and acquirements stood very high—deservedly so—but who in society had that air of wrapping his toga around him, which adds, or is supposed to add, many cubits to a man's height. But he had a broken nose. At dinner he talked much of the tender passion, and did so in a manner which stirred up Thackeray's feeling of the ridiculous. 'What has the world come to,' said Thackeray, out loud to the table, 'when two broken-nosed old fogies like you and me sit talking about love to each other!' The gentleman was astounded, and could only sit wrapping his toga in silent dismay for the rest of the evening.

These incidents are almost equally delightful and characteristic of the man, who could not bear to see trouble without relieving it, or pretentious folly without slaying it with swift and penetrating shafts of ridicule. Mr. Trollope concludes his work by declaring with an emotion which does him honour:—

Such is my idea of the man whom many call cynic, but whom I regard as one of the most soft-hearted of human beings, sweet as Charity itself, who went about the world dropping pearls, doing good, and never wilfully inflicting a wound.

We may add that the mere fact of this little biographical chapter having been written, should, we think, incline Thackeray's representatives to reconsider the expediency of giving a fuller picture to the world. As it has not been possible to conform to the letter of his wish, perhaps it would be more according to the spirit of that wish, that he should be made known to posterity in a perfect and complete manner, rather than by slight sketches and broken gleams of revelation. His letters, which we believe have been preserved in large numbers, would of themselves furnish a memorial more worthy, and a record more genuine, than any composition. His works disclose his mind more than his character to the public, and though those who know something of the latter will read a great deal between the lines, yet we can scarcely believe that any completely uninstructed reader would be able to divine the generous, tender, soft-hearted, sweet-tempered, manly and modest and unstained nature of the man from 'Pendennis' or 'Vanity Fair.' To know more about him, to know all that can be known, would be nothing but a benefit to the world.

It is a high testimony to the artistic classes that so many of the most interesting biographies we meet with come from their ranks. Statesmen, and warriors, and philosophers may play greater parts in the world; but for the interest of human character, for glimpses into pleasant homes, and for that friendly intercourse which books sometimes afford us, widening our acquaintance, and enlarging the circle of our sympathies and our capability of friendship—it is in those circles at which almost everybody, not excepting the persons chiefly concerned, permit themselves to scoff, that we find most that is attractive. Literary society has been the subject of the jibes of all its own members, and of many who know nothing of it, since the beginning of time; but, short of the classes who are without distinction altogether, and who are frequently the most interesting of all, but so difficult to obtain a glimpse of, it is in the homes of literature and of its allied arts that we find most pleasure, when they become matters of history. The memoir of Charles Mathews the Younger,[3] which is now before us, is not like that we have been considering, the story, more or less imperfect, of a man of genius. He was, like Yorick, a fellow of infinite jest, of most excellent fancy; in his way an admirable actor, and with unbounded energy, vivacity, and skill, as well as that genial and happy spirit which resembles genius more than

---

[3] *The Life of Charles James Mathews, chiefly autobiographical.* Edited by Charles Dickens. Macmillan & Co.

any other quality; but his claim did not reach beyond this. Everything he did was easy to him, spontaneous, and natural, but it would be doing Mathews injustice to claim for him a higher inspiration. Though he did all that man could do to save himself from his predestined career, he was an actor born; and after that determined struggle against it which filled up his earlier years, he yielded gracefully enough to his fate. The greater part of the two large volumes before us is autobiography, and it is very amusing reading, and gives us the idea, not only of an Admirable Crichton, skilled in all the arts, but of a most bright, lovable, and happy nature. A more accomplished, or amusing, or delightful young fellow scarcely could be than the youth of twenty who went with Lord Blessington to Italy in the year 1823, and kept his noble patrons in amusement with a thousand clevernesses, with his pencil and his voice, and his extraordinary powers as a mimic, and his vivacious and happy presence. The account he gives of himself to his parents at home, with whom he was on terms of the happiest confidence, is of the most attractive kind, and the reader will wish as he reads, that he could be sure of having so lively, intelligent, and agreeable a companion for his next long journey, or country-house visitation. He had his little impetuosities also, sparks of generous temper, and fine flashes of self-assertion; but no more than becomes a high-spirited youth. We do not know when we have come across a more pleasant picture. And this young professor of all the arts showed himself as shrewd and sensible in business as he was brilliant in all the elegances of life. No wonder the parents were proud of him, to whom he writes of all his adventures with affectionate familiarity, yet respect, and whose trust in him, and satisfaction with all he does, give happiness to their lives. There have been various publications lately in which the domestic life of eminent actors has been exhibited to the world. Fanny Kemble, for instance, in her 'Records of a Girlhood,' has laid open to us a home so kindly, so refined and graceful in its homeliness, that the most prejudiced of old-fashioned readers could do nothing but admire; and here is another, not so distinct in all its accessories, but equally decorous, well-ordered, and graceful, in which the good son who has secured the suffrages of all who have had to do with him from his boyhood, is at once the pride and consolation, the object of all hopes and wishes, and the most beloved friend and counsellor of his parents, reciprocating their tender trust and confidence. These are the player-folk, whom we assume to be lawless and irregular by right of their profession. The revelation is a very charming one. There is no teasing of the boy with unnecessary restrictions in this pleasant record, no conflict between parent and child, no impatience on one side or attempt at constraint on the other. All is wise, kind, and mutually considerate in the family relations, and last, and most perfect evidence of their mutual trust and excellence, the parents are liberal and the son economical. Not often, either in the world or in books, is the union and agreement so perfect. The best of fathers mistake their sons, the best of mothers misunderstand them. Here, however, there is neither the one mistake nor the other, but all goes on with perfect harmony—an example to the world.

Perhaps, if there had been a little less perfection of intercourse, the story would have been more moving. As it is, we are introduced to a most excellent family party, using perhaps a little finer language on account of their connection with the stage, and in everything else acting up to the best ideal of their parts. A suspicious recollection, quite unjust and injurious, yet involuntary, of the *père noble*, haunts us when we read the excellent letters of Charles Mathews the elder, who on the stage, as is very well known, never did attempt the line of heavy father. But this is a wicked and improper suggestion, and the group is as dignified and pleasant a group as could be met with. However, it is young Charles's course of pleasant adventure, and all his delightful circle of accomplishments, that chiefly charm us. What so congenial to the recollection of that summer sea, that magical air, those moons and skies of Italy, as the life of youthful enjoyment, all song, all society, all mirth and luxurious pleasure, which the young man lives on the shore of the most lovely of bays, with all these fine people about him, dashing off beautiful sketches, lively songs, and mischievous mystifications and sketches of character with the most lighthearted facility. He was working hard at art in those early days, studying Italian architecture (his profession being that of an architect), measuring every villa he sketched, and knitting his brows over plans and calculations. He was indeed engaged upon the plans of a mansion for Lord Blessington, which was never to be built, but which was then intended to give a beginning to the young architect, who was never to be an architect any more than his sketches were to grow into Lord Blessington's house.

It says a great deal for the wholesome character of the all-accomplished boy, that after this resplendent episode of Naples and the Blessingtons, and all the petting and flattery and *succès* of his early career, he went into the wilds of North Wales with a brave heart as surveyor to a flash company, and wrote as cheerfully from the chaos of the 'Welsh Iron and Coal Mining Company' as from the Italian villa. In the same way, after another long and delightful period of rambling, studying, and adventuring in Italy, and after several chapters of renewed success in society, picnicking with duchesses, and other such piquant amusements, he took, in despair of establishing himself more effectively, a situation as local surveyor at Bow, which he held for three years, journeying to and fro on the top of an omnibus, 'with the Building Act in my hand,' into those wilds of obscure and dingy London which are further from the centre of society than either Naples or Pontblyddyn. 'The only touch of joy I had,' he says, 'was on the discovery of a locality rejoicing in the name of Cutthroat Lane, and in no other place could I make up my mind to fix my office. "District Surveyor, Cutthroat Lane," was something to have on one's card, and gave a spice of romance to the affair.' We are not told, which is a pity, whether the Surveyor of Bow had any time to disport himself among the duchesses while this address was on his card. Immediately afterwards he was driven to the stage by stress of circumstances; his father's affairs having fallen into irretrievable confusion. Short of this supreme reason, it is curious to remark, no actor's son or daughter consents to take up the paternal occupation. This cause drove Macready on to the stage; it led thither the two accomplished Kembles, Fanny and Adelaide; and it transported Charles Mathews from the uncongenial surroundings of Cutthroat Lane. Perhaps things would have gone better had he yielded sooner to the inevitable fate.

The most painful part of Charles Mathews' life occurred after his marriage to Madame Vestris, an episode very lightly dwelt upon, save in respect to the overwhelming embarrassments which the theatre brought upon the pair of actors, embarrassments which culminated in the highly dramatic incident of Mathews' arrest when on the eve of setting out for the theatre, where he was to play some of his favourite parts. Debts and difficulties had so increased upon him that the arrest itself might be natural enough, but the personal hostility that contrived it exactly at the moment when the provincial theatre was crammed, and the appearance of the 'star' eagerly expected, is melodramatic in the extreme; and the attendant circumstances—the pandemonium of the debtors' prison, which it is almost impossible to believe in as having existed so short a time ago, and in which Mathews was almost as incongruous a figure as the Vicar of Wakefield in his not unsimilar imprisonment—and the still sadder unseen figure of the suffering wife, who died a few days after his liberation, give all the features of a tragedy of domestic life to this miserable chapter of Mathews' existence. But it was only a chapter in that long life. His wife's death ended what would seem to have been in more ways than one his grand mistake, and left him still a young man to form new ties, under serener heavens. He lived to seventy-five, always in the exercise of his profession, playing to the last, always popular, always successful. We cannot think that the performances of an old man in broadly comic parts are ever a pleasant exhibition, however wonderful may be his state of preservation: but Mathews' performance in 'The Critic' was without doubt a most finished and fine piece of acting, and his transformation from Sir Fretful Plagiary to Puff something like a miracle. We will not say, however, that we like him as well when he presents himself before us as an old actor, making the little speeches which delighted the public, and a great deal of money to boot, as when he was a young artist, playing a thousand gay parts, not for gain, but for fame and pleasure, in the highest enjoyment of his own faculties and life.

It is rarely enough that a student of the art of biography has it in his power to contemplate together a group which has done so much to lighten up and brighten the age—and there is a whimsical pleasure in contrasting these men so full of genial gifts, and, though in degrees so different, of genius itself, the one unaccountable and supreme endowment which we can neither create nor acquire by cultivation, but which bloweth where it listeth like that Divine Spirit which is the fountain of inspiration—with the excellent artist [*] and good man whose record of his own life and work is so quaintly unlike theirs. Sir Gilbert Scott was, we have every reason to believe, an architect of great powers. No one has left more traces of his progress throughout England. He has embellished his country over all its surface, and left his mark even upon other countries which are supposed to be better instructed in art than England. And this he has done, though with prudent regard, as became a man of sense, to the practical advantages, yet with a great deal of honest enthusiasm and 'feeling' for his art. We took up the one volume to which he and his editor have judiciously confined themselves with feelings of pleasant expectation. An excellent artist, and a good man: what more could be desired? But alas! dear reader, there is something more to be desired. A man may be very good and may not be interesting: it is a quality like another. There are some who are short and some who are tall; some who are dark and some who are fair; and, in like manner, some people are interesting and some are—not. Sir Gilbert did a great deal of excellent work. *Circumspice*, he may say, as a still greater architect did. Look round you, and you will see what he has done; but if you read the book in which his name is enshrined, you must be content to read it for some other purpose than that of knowing him. Just as he says, with excellent brevity and truth, of an art expedition, 'I enjoyed it greatly,' we can but say of him, 'He was an excellent man.' But the interest lies in the details, in a certain kind and choice of details which we cannot teach any man how to make, and which this admirable artist did not know how to make. Otherwise his life might have had sufficient elements of interest in it. He had a struggle in the beginning of his career which almost for a few pages gets to the point of being interesting, and there is a quite unintentional indication of a vigorous rapid figure by his side in the person of Mr. Moffat, his early partner, who catches our eye and seems to possess the necessary human features. But though this gentleman is about the only point in the book which will attract the reader, he did not so well suit the writer, and accordingly he drops very early in the narrative, and we are left to virtuous dullness and Sir Gilbert. The autobiography, we are told, was not meant for publication, but for the instruction of the sons who have very good reason to be proud of such a father. This, however, can only, we feel, be partially true, for it is in fact a long and tedious and detailed defence and explanation of certain incidents in Sir Gilbert's professional career, which his children no doubt were already acquainted with, and of which

---

[*] *Personal and Professional Recollections.* By Sir Gilbert Scott. Sampson Low & Co.

they could not need so elaborate a re-statement. The great architect was both honest and modest, but he does not like it to be said or thought that his work ever fell off or was less than excellent, or that he did not act exactly as he ought to have done in the occasional professional crises which occurred from time to time. How it was that, being a Gothic architect, and having sent in Gothic plans, he should have held fast by his appointment as architect of the new public offices, even though it was necessary to cancel his first designs and execute the work in the Classic style, he is specially anxious to explain. It would have been better taste if in doing so he had not represented Lord Palmerston as entirely under the thumb of Mr. B——, a hostile member of the profession, and the Prince Consort as speaking the sentiments with which Mr. C—— had indoctrinated him. Both these great personages were very capable of, and more than likely to possess, an opinion of their own; but Sir Gilbert evidently felt it necessary to believe that private jealousy must have something to do with any check in his prosperous career. It is not his fault that he has injudicious backers, but it is a pity that it should have been thought necessary to supplement so much explanation as Sir Gilbert has given of special passages in his professional life, with an explanation of Sir Gilbert himself from the somewhat fantastical hand of the Dean of Chichester, to whom we owe an anecdote in the very worst taste, of a confidence which it is to be regretted the good man should have made even to his confidential servant, but which certainly should never have come to print, as to the fervour of his personal devotions. 'No one about,' says Dr. Burgon, 'not even his sons, knew the strength and ardour of those religious convictions which were with him an inheritance, for the Rev. Thomas Scott of Aston Sandford, the commentator, was his grandfather.' It is a little difficult to follow the sequence of ideas here; but if the fact of having a grandfather who has written a commentary is enough to make religious conviction hereditary, we cannot but think that the Rev. Thomas Scott of Aston Sandford would have had a greater difficulty than ourselves in recognising the connection between any ideas of his and the religious convictions which prompted his descendant to breathe a prayer for a beloved companion dead, every time her image recurred to him. We need not, however, dwell upon this book, which is neither literature nor biography. It is a pity that some one who had some acquaintance with these arts, which are different from architecture, should not have had a hand in it. It will confuse the reader's ideas even as to the eminence of Sir Gilbert Scott in his profession, which we for our own part, as a mere lay and uninstructed spectator, believed to be unquestioned, until we saw how many explanations, and what a detailed account of discussions and hindrances, twenty years old, there was to make.

Sincerity in Biography.

THE rapidity of criticism nowadays is a patent evil. For years a number of men, eminent for the special talents required for such a task, has been engaged on a work of national importance, the revision of the New Testament. It appears, and in twenty-four hours the critics are sitting in judgment. Mr. Carlyle's 'Reminiscences' are given to the world and contain such acidities as those who knew this great but rather cantankerous genius were not surprised at. Straightway down come the critics in wrath that Mr. Carlyle's nose was not rubbed off his face. It is open to a critic as a consequence of the publication of the 'Reminiscences' to revise his opinion of Mr. Carlyle, but it is another thing to quarrel with the editor who has given him the means of doing so.

The cue is given generally by some able writer, strongly biassed, or by some audacious young spark, some young man of the clubs, full of animal spirits, and undoubting faith—in himself; and the rest follow suit. "Every one according to his cue." There is no need to go to the opposite extreme of haste and, like one of the weekly papers, a Church one, review a book only when it has become the guardian of the 'best Aylesbury. Bishop Wilberforce said it would be a very good thing if we all had our cooling days. A little decent pause, a little holding of the breath before the shout of ill-informed condemnation, is desirable.

These remarks are provoked by the manner in which Mr. Froude has been hastily assailed for his courageous honesty and faithful adherence to plain duty. When we had occasion in the May number of 'TEMPLE BAR' to regret the picture which Carlyle had painted of himself, we were not of those who blamed Mr. Froude for placing it on view. Had we foreseen the storm of abuse hurled at him, we should have delivered our conscience on this matter for such as it is worth. What is it these people want? These idolators of Carlyle, having first done their best to spoil a noble character by a life-long flattery, want to impose their opinion of Carlyle on the world, and object to Mr. Carlyle's own objections to their fictitious portrait of him. We are not concerned to prove Mr. Carlyle a prophet, a saint, or a particularly good man, but we are concerned in having an honest portrait of him. We do not expect to find him perfect, should be rather disappointed to find him without the necessary shadow, and knowing it to be impossible, should suspect doctoring.

Where would Dr. Johnson be, if Boswell had painted out all his roughness, softened all his rudeness, taken all the bosses out of the old oak, and sent him up a clean poplar to the sky? Where would Byron be if Moore had striven to make a saint of him, and sent all his billings and cooings to the dovecote? How much better if Lockhart had frankly shown the one slight blemish on bright and genial Scott, instead of murdering the reputation of Constable and the Ballantynes, honest men, whose only fault was a blind follow-my-leader, when Scott showed the way. Even the scoundrel Cellini has our sympathies by reason of the truth that is in him, and shrewd Pepys lives in our affections, spite of his love of money, foreign kisses, and occasional opening of the palm to bribes. Carlyle, whilst casting about for the reason of Burns' popularity with every class of life and different forms of mind, settles on sincerity, on "his indisputable air of truth," as the chief cause. Mr. Froude recognises this, and that we want Carlyle the man; we want him as we want Cromwell's wart, Johnson's splutter, and Scott's foxy look; we want him good and bad, brightness and shadow—and it is precisely this we have in the 'Reminiscences.'

The gold in Carlyle must needs have some alloy, but he has done such service to the State, is so far raised above ordinary men by genius and by worth, he is at once too great and too good, to suffer in reputation from the whole truth being told of him. Without unsaying, therefore, a word which we said in May, we repeat what we there said, that we cannot afford to do without the qualifying colours supplied by Carlyle himself to the image erected by his idolators.

We know too much how biographies are sometimes cooked, sometimes from family affection, sometimes from party motives, sometimes from the ignoble reasons of space. Again there are cases where so much more canvas must be covered than the subject warrants; or, editors will not take pains to absorb and assimilate and give out a result, but they must shoot the correspondence into the literary highway. Even this is better than a foregone conclusion to exhibit a preternatural character for holiness, or genius. What melancholy reading most biographies are, wherein the hero is niched up high out of our earthly vision, and aureoled for the family descendants.

Most religious biographies are sufficient to make one a sinner, so dreary are they in their monotonous goodness, so banked out by flattering laurels is the view of any weakness or shortcoming. Lives of Roman Catholic saints have an artificial air about them, and a wooden aspect. We don't believe in them at all, and if theirs is goodness, commend us to a little of this world's ways. More pardonable, but slightly nauseous are widow's tributes to the departed. There are rare cases where an unclouded judgment has perceived that the highest tribute to the memory of a loved one is the truth; but they are rare.

If honesty was more than ever necessary in biography, it was so in the case of Mr. Carlyle. He had been praised not only where he deserved it, but also precisely where he did not, and if his character had been suffered to retain the false colours his worshippers desired for it, a certain support would have been given to all his opinions bad as well as good, of which they are now deprived. Thackeray has told us

"How very weak the very wise,
How very small the very great are."

And even Carlyle had his weaknesses and littleness, for with much rugged and honest protest against all forms of insincerity, Carlyle yet mixed an unhealthy worship of mere force of will and intellect. "God forbid," said he, "that the time should ever come when we shall esteem riches the synonym of good." To which we add, God forbid that will or intellect, or mere force of any kind, should come to be synonymous with good. The deification of mere intellect is probably as dangerous as the deification of wealth, if not so obviously debasing; and Carlyle's notion that intellect was a security for morality is not borne out by the facts of life, whilst the deification of force is the subversion of right by might, and the return of society into savagery. When not employed in this worship of force, he set himself to "hurl forth defiance, pity, expostulation, over the whole universe, civil, literary, and religious," as he wrote to De Quincey, when he proposed to found a Misanthropic Club at Craigenputtoch. It is this hurl of defiance which probably makes people consider Carlyle a democrat, but there was a good deal more of the Tory than the Radical in Carlyle.

We cannot get away from the idea that there were two Carlyles, and that the last was not the better of the two. Whether or no he sympathised with Frederick the Great, and allowing that he really did get disgusted with the imperial robber during the fifteen years in which he was engaged chiselling out a monument to him, yet he has erected this monument with the black flag flying on the top of it. It will not do the harm it might have done had it been more intelligible and more brief. But the harm it must have done Carlyle himself for fifteen years to be trying to make the worse appear the better cause, is evident in the way in which he got soured towards the world and most of his contemporaries.

The difference in style and choice of language between the

magnificent "Essay on Burns" and 'Frederick the Great,' represents the difference between Carlyle unappreciated and condescending to express ideas of great breadth and depth in the ordinary language of the day, and Carlyle bowed to as an authority and dealing out his thoughts just as they came to him with the certainty of imposing the conveyance of the idea as well as the idea itself upon a grateful audience. Where he had been a servant in the service of letters he had become master: instead of seeking fame he had been made dictator. Wordsworth had in much earlier days called him " a pest to the English tongue," but this is an exaggerated method of expressing the natural regret of a man of rhythm at seeing his native language distorted. Like Turner, Carlyle had two styles. As with Turner's early pictures, Carlyle's early essays, whilst having the same force of ideas as his later works, yet had the advantage of a comparatively clear delivery. Like Turner, once known and famous, and able to assert his individuality, Carlyle indulged in every fancy which sported before his imagination. As Turner in his latter pictures gave free scope and what appears to some lay minds unbridled licence to his imagination, as he cast upon the canvas the very dream of a thought, so Carlyle at the last gave out some of his thoughts in the process of formation, and trusted to the intelligence of his reader to find his way to his meaning.

There is a lesson in Carlyle's life, the immense power of the world to ruin a man. That it did not ruin Carlyle, but only stimulated some of his defects, leaving the great truth of his nature untouched, is not owing to the world, but to his early training, and to his communings with himself on the lonely peat moor of Craigenputtoch. Had he continued to live at Craigenputtoch, drank in of the wisdom he there sought, and kept aloof from the flatteries of men, much that horrifies his worshippers in the 'Reminiscences' would have been absent. None the less would he have fought against vice, cant and the decaying patriotism and strength of the nation, but there would have been allied with this more charity to individuals, and possibly less continual reference to self.

But it was not to be, and Carlyle, poor and struggling, and out of the hard earth forcing the violet to bloom, fled from this rough but healthy school, to a London world which secured him as a novelty, and which liked to hear his bitter observations, which drew him out purposely by acting as foil to him, and, marching in the opposite way of his well-known opinions, gave him what he grew to want ever more and more, an audience to listen to his replies. Who can doubt that any vanity there was in the man was stimulated by this incessant flattery? Who does not understand how Wordsworth and Lamb, who did not condescend to this mode of dealing with Carlyle, came to be disliked by him? But this is the least part of the mischief. These very worshippers who were crying aloud in the streets, "A prophet, a prophet," this very world who threw wide open its portals to one who gave it a reflex brilliancy, did with Carlyle as they had done with Irving, checked his progress. They flung themselves across his path, and turned his truth almost into a lie, for can we imagine that Carlyle in his days of wrestling would have placed a whip in the hand of the white man to scarify the black, that he would have idolised force as the ultimate good, and got to look upon his fellow-creatures, " *down upon them* " alas! as " weltering of my *poor* fellow-creatures . . . . stuck in that fatal element."

And now this very world, these very worshippers cry out, "Prophesy smooth things, prophesy deceits." Suppress everything unpleasant, or rough, everything which lowers our idol in public estimation. This injudicious advice has fortunately come too late, although we do not believe it would have deterred Mr. Froude from the course he has taken, for which fifty years hence people will thank him, as we now thank Wraxall for the very truths which in his days were called lies. He has resisted the temptation to palter with the truth of history. It matters little or nothing, in dealing with an ordinary man, which of his opinions you give or suppress, but every opinion of Carlyle is a line or dot in the plate on which the engraver of his portrait is working. Leave it out and you have an approach more or less to *a* portrait, but not *the* portrait Yielding to no one in a love of Lamb, for his grand unselfishness, for the originality of his quaint wit, for his letters equal to any in the English language, yet we will still have Carlyle's estimate of him also, we can see dimly through "the ghastly London wit," of which Carlyle accuses Lamb, Carlyle's difficulty in estimating a subtlety of mind, which his hotter intellect burnt up as cinder.

Seeing that Wordsworth sometimes climbed to the sublime heights and had visions of beauty denied to the many, we yet cannot afford to part with Carlyle's finding him like a rustic fiddle. It is the measure of Carlyle's inability to appreciate a genius which had in it the repose of nature, rather than the vehemence of force. Everything had to be served up hot with Carlyle. So, too, there is a certain limited truth in Carlyle's estimate of Shelley. A defect of Shelley is pressed out to its extreme point, and thus made to be seen. This does not injure Shelley, but slightly mars the catholicity of Carlyle, that he did not see the insignificant relation of this defect to Shelley's merits.

We see some of the results of the opposite method to Mr. Froude's in the Metternich and Talleyrand Memoirs. Taking these seriously, we are called upon to believe that Metternich was nothing short of a pious statesman, and Talleyrand only anxious for the reign of law. The piety of the one and the morality of the other are for the stage, and have a certain dramatic interest, but let some master mind fasten on these men, and throw off the stage properties and the Monmouth street attire, and give us the very men, and whilst we should miss the lofty characteristics claimed by these great actors for themselves, we may find in return human beings with many loveable qualities, standing on pedestals a little more level to the ordinary human eye. Metternich would not then appear as the Pecksniff of politics, nor Talleyrand as the Tartuffe, characters they somewhat resemble when drawn by their own pencil.

The 'Life of Wilberforce' is very ably written from a certain point of view, a definite and consistent picture is obtained, but it is a Wilberforce for the church window, not Wilberforce with his finger on the public pulse nor the brilliant, versatile prelate, affluent of words, with a touch of all things to all men. If biographers will put a mask over their hero they must be content with the consequence of robbing from us the sight of the human face. There was a great deal more to love than to dislike in Wilberforce, for his chief weakness seems a desire for the world's love and approbation, but he is painted as the Roman Catholics paint their saints, in whom one takes infinitely less interest than in the remoter Pagan gods, who went in for their failings along with their more celestial attributes. Naughty as Mercury was in his deception of poor Sosia, grossly wanting in proper morality as Jupiter was towards Alcmena, we see that the poets and dramatists had a better sense of artistic fitness than these painters of the saints, who give us impossible virgins and inhuman saints.

We are inclined to treat any suppression of evidence which goes to the construction of a perfect picture of any great man as a crime. In this light we should almost include the destruction of Byron's autobiography, which, if not all printed, should have been all preserved. It should have been in the power of students to refer to it. We therefore favour the publication even of those criticisms by Carlyle of his friends which show an acerbity and even an insincerity. If there had been insincerity in Johnson, it must have been of the slightest, and we don't think there was much in Carlyle. Give it and all the bad things with it, and time will let them settle at the bottom, and the wine none the worse. No man is the same man all through his life, and there may have been half-a-dozen Carlyles between 1820 and 1880. A man is not necessarily insincere because in an accidental fit of spleen or dyspepsia he sees only the worst side of human nature. If we regret the publication of anything in the 'Reminiscences' it is the essayist's recollections of Smail. Here even our regret is tempered by the fact that it has drawn out from Mr. Ireland a genial and sympathetic defence in the *Manchester Examiner*.

If the world desire an ideal character of Carlyle, it must look for it to the poet, and not to the historian. The business of the latter is with Truth. Carlyle was not an amiable man, apparently, and in reading his 'Reminiscences' he occurred to us as rather a difficult, not to say a cantankerous man, but yet of an essentially kindly nature. He was a man of such originality of mind, and possessed such a command of language, he had such a power of throwing into dramatic form any event, idea, or character with which he was dealing, has so infused his mind into that of the generations which succeeded him, and has thus been so large a factor in the composition of modern thought, that a living picture of such a man is a national want.

To speak of him as we have heard him spoken of, as the Johnson of our time, appears unreasonable. In force of imagination and rapidity of insight alone was he superior to Johnson. In learning, judgment, humanity of mind, in that common sense which is more valuable than genius itself, Johnson was generally the superior of Carlyle. With all his stupendous powers of talking, Johnson could listen as well as talk, a quality in which Coleridge and Carlyle seem to have been lacking. We are not aware whether this applies in anything like the same degree to Carlyle as to Coleridge or Macaulay, but we have yet to see whether we shall have in the forthcoming 'Life of Carlyle,' any conversations equal in interest to those reported by Boswell. Further, there was a touch of the Diogenes in Carlyle, a cynical disbelief in any great amount of human goodness, which grew upon him. From his comfortable tub in Cheyne Row, he barked at his fellow-creatures, whom he thought poor creatures, most part fools. They certainly took his gospel very freely, and saw, or fancied they saw, through the haze of words, and through much uncouth jargon mingled with much poetic thought, great meanings and sublime moralities. The great mist through which his meaning could be discerned enhanced the bigness of the thought, and gave it preternatural value. He was a great preacher and poet; an enemy of all cant and of all insincerity, including biographical insincerity. We are all of us his debtors; and we think there must be something wrong in the man who cannot recognise, under the ruggedness of Carlyle's thoughts, the true nobility which, with his severe sincerity, has given him such a hold over the English people in all parts of the world. But, for all this, we want nothing obliterated or kept back which is essential to a perfect view of Carlyle's character.

Let us suppose that Mr. Froude had acted as those who have attacked him wished him to act, and had cancelled every unkind passage in the 'Reminiscences' in which Carlyle unconsciously describes himself whilst describing his friends and contemporaries. We should then be precisely in the position we were before the 'Reminiscences' were published, and be without the modification supplied by Carlyle himself to the too eulogistic character of him claimed by his worshippers. We should, we now know, be obviously seeing Carlyle in a false light. *Qui vult decipi decipiatur.* We are not of the number.

G. B.

THE ETHICS OF BIOGRAPHY.

THE art of biography is one of the oldest in the world—if not the first, at least a very early form of literary composition. If before Homer and Moses there burst forth into lyrical lament the overburdened soul of the early homicide who " slew a man to his wounding and a young man to his hurt," making, before law began, the discovery that the criminal is always the most miserable of all the sons of Adam—his is, perhaps, the only human utterance which has preceded story-telling : and primitive story-telling is always a kind of biography. The ancient history of the Old Testament is entirely of this description. It concerns itself less even with law-giving, though the first theory of a constitution is involved in it, than with the records of the life of one man after another—Moses, Joshua, David, the leading spirits of their generations. The art of the minstrel takes a somewhat different development, and selects the dramatic incidents which count most in a man's career, but still follows Ulysses through all his wandering course, and leads the reader back through intervening centuries to the footprints of an individual man across an undeveloped world. It is the same in the sacred books of all religions, which are secondarily the storehouse of thought, of moral injunction and teaching, but primarily the records of the life of Brahma, Buddha, Mahomet. And of all religions, that which to us is the one entirely divine, the greatest and purest inspiration of heaven, what does our Gospel mean but the biography of Christ, the most perfect of lives and portraitures, so transcending all others that either the fishermen of Galilee must have been men of a divine genius, before which neither Plato nor Shakespeare could lift their heads, or He whom in their simplicity they knew, such a Man as never man before or after was. These are all biographical works upon which the faiths of the world are founded. And so are those legends of the saints in all ages, to which the affectionate imagination of the simple have lent a thousand embellishing touches beyond the simplicity of Nature, and adorned with garlands of miracles, but which hold every one a living soul of humanity, a human life commending itself to the admiration, the instruction, the following of men.

These are perhaps rather too magnificent examples to be brought down to the experiences of an age which scarcely permits a man to be cold in his grave before it turns forth from his old drawers and wardrobes such relics of his living personality as he may have left there, and displays his vacant clothes, with any twist that attitude or habit may have lent to them, as characteristic of his soul. And yet as the rules that Titian worked by, must still direct the modern art of portraiture, even though descended into the hands of Dick Tinto—and our object is not to gather specimens from present performance, but rather to elucidate the laws by which the workmen in this art of moral portrait-painting ought to be guided—it is scarcely possible to go too high for our examples. The saints and heroes, however, if we believe what is now told us on every side, were neither heroic nor saintly to their valets, and it might have been, for anything we can tell, quite possible to deprive us of every noble name that now gives lustre to humanity, and to leave the past as naked of all veneration or respect as is the present. That fine St. George, who has given an emblem of spotless valour and conquest over the impure image of fleshly lust and cruelty to two great nations—he who tilts against his dragon with such concentrated grave enthusiasm in that little chapel on the Venice canal, which Mr. Ruskin has made one of the shrines to which we all go on pilgrimages—turns out, they say, to have been an army contractor, furnishing the shoddy of his time to the commissariat; and a great deal the better we all are for that exquisite discovery. And St. Francis was a dirty, little half-witted fanatic, and Oliver Cromwell a vulgar impostor with a big wart, and Luther a fat priest, who wanted to marry. How many more could we add to the list? till at the end nobody would be left towards whom we could look with any sentiment more reverent than that which we feel for our greengrocer. That this is not the true sentiment of humanity, nor in accord with any law of natural right and wrong, must be evident to the most cursory observer, and it is worth while, perhaps, to make an attempt to discover what are the tenets on this subject which ought to guide the artist, and which commend themselves to the impartial sense of mankind in general. Though there is a great deal of unconfessed cynicism in the common mind as respects matters within its practical range and immediate vicinity, there is something underlying this of a nobler strain, which does not permit even the man who doubts his neighbour's motives, and thinks the worst of his actions, to refuse a higher justice to those who stand apart on the vantage-ground of age or distance. Man is more just, more charitable than men; and an appeal from the individual to the general is a privilege which we all seek instinctively, and in which, in the majority of cases, our instinct is justified.

In this investigation we are met at once by a rule universally respected and very generally acquiesced in—the first and broadest expression of natural feeling towards our contemporaries who are dead, *De mortuis nil nisi bonum*. Nothing can be more entirely justified by the instincts of human nature than this. In the hush of the death-chamber, by the edge of the grave, there is even a sort of benevolent fiction which comes naturally to our lips and to our thoughts, so that not only do we say nothing that is not good of the dead, but we go further, and during that moment in which judgment is suspended, do actually take the most charitable view of him, and find explanations for what is doubtful in his conduct, which would not satisfy us either before or after. Thus the French custom of a speech over a man's grave becomes necessarily, instinctively, an *éloge*. That it should be anything else would outrage every feeling of humanity. If we cannot praise we are silent, by a law of Nature more strong than any written law, and shrink as from a blow if any unnatural voice is raised in disapproval. This, however, is not a rule which can be applied in any case to biography. The sentiment of the death-chamber is one thing, the judgment of history another. When we speak of the dead we mean our own contemporaries, those who have gone along with us through the conflicts, and probably competed with us in the rivalries, of life. The personages of previous generations are not in this sense the dead at all. They have passed through that period of softened regard, and are now beyond all such temporary courtesies, permanent figures upon the clear horizon of the past. It is one of the mysterious qualities of human nature that, though we all share the natural awe of that extraordinary and unfathomed wonder of death to which we are in our turn universally subject, yet an instinctive appreciation of the effects of it as temporary is equally universal. A man who has been dead twenty days is enveloped in a mystery and solemnity which the most heartless will not disturb. We speak of him with subdued voice, and recognize his right to the utmost stretch of tenderness of which charity is capable, and say nothing of him if not good. But he who has been dead twenty years, has, as it were, emerged from death altogether. He has been, and to our senses is, no longer; but the mystery and awe have departed, and he is restored to the cheerful atmosphere of common day, though of a day that is past. It is probable that we know him better than in his lifetime, when he brushed shoulders with us, and we found him now in one mood, now another, but could not, so near were we, ever get him in perspective, or divine what he was thinking about, even while he walked with us by the common way. We saw the best of him, or we saw the worst of him, but we never saw all of him. By degrees, however, he emerges out of that close vicinity and neighbourhood, and rises greater, smaller, as it may be, but at last complete in the perfection of an atmosphere which no new events can disturb. To say nothing, if not what is good, of a man in this monumental position, would be a foolishness beyond even the foolishness of human kind. Biography would in that case become a senseless series of *éloges*, in which all character and individuality would be lost; for praise is the dullest of all expressions of feeling, just as a round of unbroken happiness is dull, and there is little or nothing to say about those who do well all their lives and neither offend nor suffer. Thus it is at once false in art and in Nature to apply this proverb beyond the immediate period of the conclusion, when all hearts are soft, and every man who is not a monster receives from his race a natural tribute of sympathy at least, if not of regret.

That it continues, however, largely to influence the minds of those to whom it falls to write the records of men's lives, is due to various very simple causes. When this is done by a wife or a child, natural affection and family pride unite to make such a result almost inevitable. They know more about their subject, and they know less, than any stranger. It is a rare gift, indeed, to be able to fathom the characters of those most dear to us, and we doubt much whether it is a very desirable one. They are to us not men and women in the first place, but father and mother, husband or brother, a portion of ourselves. To judge their actions at any crisis of their lives is as difficult as to judge our own, and disturbed by the same perception of all the trifling motives that come in to interfere with the influence of the greater, which confuses us in our own case; and to judge unfavourably would be an act of natural impiety which would outrage the reader as well as the reverence due to the closest ties of humanity. Impartiality is not to be looked for, scarcely to be desired, in such a case; and it would be a greater harm to mankind if a son, much less a wife or daughter, were capable of setting forth the darker shades in the character of the father, than the proportionate gain of a complete and well-balanced picture could be to the world. Such is by far the larger class of biographies; they are written in the shadow of the great event, which has separated from the writer the man from whom, perhaps, he derives consequence, the most notable person of the family, the most beloved friend. He does not attempt to criticize or judge, he records; and as all things small and great are important to his affectionate recollection, he crowds the annals with detail and explanation, or accumulates every scrap of writing which fell from that pen, and every word, however trifling, which dropped from those lips, in fond unnecessary fulness, though skimming lightly over every dubious point, and leaving us without guidance or enlightenment where elucidation is most required. And while we regret we can scarcely censure such a principle; it is not the part of a son to set forth his father's faults, still less that of a wife to unfold the imperfections which, perhaps, she is all the more jealous of revealing because fully conscious of them, and perhaps, more happy, has never discovered. It is not from such witnesses that we can expect the uncoloured chronicle of absolute truth.

Something of the same kind must be said, though with at once less excuse and a better reason, for the disciple-biographer whose enthusiasm for his subject is of a different kind, yet for whom we feel a sympathy almost more strong than that with which we regard the family exposition of a great name. He whom the character and work of another so captivates, that he is ready to be his champion and defender in all the conflicts that may rise around him, and defy the world on behalf of his hero, conciliates our regard for himself in affording us proof of so generous a devotion, and for his subject by making it apparent that one man at least cordially believes in him. The disciple's defence is usually even warmer than the son's; for he is better aware what are the objections, and knows that he cannot be permitted to ignore them, and with the instinct of adoration establishes his strongest bastions where the natural defences are most weak. He who formulated Hero Worship as one of the creeds, adopted this system to its fullest extent, and never is more hot and fiery for his gruesome hero, than at points upon which other writers, less thorough, would give up Frederick. The enthusiast-biographer gives nothing up. If he makes a demi-god of his subject when right, he deifies him altogether when wrong, and forces his errors upon the world as virtues too dazzling to be understood, with a determination which no evidence can shake. Not only does he say nothing if not good, but he turns with the adroitest partizanship the evil itself into a heroic adaptation of the instruments of evil to a good purpose, and will rather affront the world to its face with high scorn, as unworthy to hear of and incapable of understanding a character so elevated, than allow that there is a speck on the sun of his idolatry. Such passionate interest and appreciation carry us away; the warmth, the generosity, the devotion, give of themselves a certain greatness to the subject. We cannot believe of him that he could be put on such a platform without some natural worthiness, some real claim upon our admiration. Neither Cromwell nor Frederick were heroes congenial to the ordinary mind; even those who maintained most strongly the historical greatness of the Lord Protector, were willing to admit that sentiment and romance were on the other side, and that his great figure was not one to charm or attract though it might overawe. And Frederick, called the Great, was a still less likely object of popular admiration. Yet we were all dragged at the chariot wheels of these conquerors, making protests, perhaps, that were scarcely audible in the roar of the royal progress, and, to our astonishment, were compelled to approve of everything so long as the spell lasted, and found that even Drogheda and Wexford, even Silesia, instead of crimes upon which charity itself could do nothing but drop a veil, were but additional glories on the hero's crest, deeds for which our approval, our applause, were challenged, as a sort of test of our own capability of judging. There is something grand in the impetus of such enthusiasm as this. It takes away the reader's breath; it casts dull justice into the shade, as a sort of humdrum and unheroic quality, judging by line and measure, incapable of the greater inspirations of a heroic code. The result may not indeed be permanent, but it is overwhelming while it lasts.

It might afford a cynic amusement to consider upon whom the great contemporary example of an opposite class of biography has been exercised. The enthusiast-biographer passes away, and his system with him. It is not a true system; but there is a large and generous warmth in it which appeals to the universal heart, and, for the moment at least, subjugates the judgment. The opposite plan has no such sympathetic emotion to appeal to; but it has other sentiments less noble on its side. This paradoxical human race, which cannot refuse its admiration, its applause, its adhesion of sentiment, to any generous champion, and whose universal breast thrills at the warm touch of a genuine enthusiasm, is also, and almost at the same moment, pleased to be informed that all goodness is a pretence and all enthusiasms hollow, that the idols are clay and the heroes contemptible. We do not attempt to explain how it is that the two are compatible, nor are we at all concerned for the consistency of mankind. Enthusiasm of the highest and cynicism of the lowest description exist, we are aware, in the same circle, even sometimes in the same mind; and the man who one day puts all his breath into one lusty cheer for the good and true, and acknowledges, with the eloquence of suppressed tears and a voice quivering with sympathy, any noble appeal to his emotions, will send forth peals of laughter the next on the discovery that the hero is a humbug and that he has been cheated out of his sympathy. Perhaps the pleasure there is in finding out that, after all, no one is so much elevated above the ordinary level as the idealist would have us believe, is a more widely-spread sentiment than any other. Even those who are ashamed of so unworthy a feeling are moved by it. We are so conscious of a lower strain ourselves, so well aware that the higher mood is temporary in us, and that even from the height of an occasional elevation we drop into selfishness and stupidity, by some dismal law of gravitation which we have little power and perhaps less will to resist, that it consoles us to find others no better than ourselves. It is from this sentiment, no doubt, that all the developments of scandal-mongering take their origin: we do not say of gossip, which is not necessarily scandal, and may have a kinder source in the inalienable human interest in everything that illustrates our common life. The cynic principle, as applied to biography, is, however, to the credit of human nature, of far more rarity than that of the enthusiast. Perhaps this fact gives it, when it appears, the greater power. But there is a difficulty at the very outset in explaining what motive a writer can have in choosing as his subject a character of which his moral estimate is very low. Friends there are, no doubt, who love without approving; and it cannot be questioned that the prodigal in a family, the black sheep in a group of companions, is very often the individual whom the others regard with the greatest tenderness. But in most cases their faults are those of youth; they produce almost invariably tragic consequences, and they are often compatible with qualities so genial and lovable that the judgment refuses to condemn, and the heart clings to the victims of their own folly, those who themselves are the greatest sufferers by their imperfections. Save in such instances as these, however, it is difficult to understand why a biographer, himself a man of intellect and character, should voluntarily seek the society living, or devote himself to the elucidation of the life when ended, of a warped and gloomy soul, whose temper is odious to him, and whose defects he sees in the clearest light. The meaning of the enthusiast's work is simple, but not that of the detractor. We ask ourselves, What is its motive? Is it a cynic's gratification in proving that to be the "wisest, meanest" of mankind is possible to more than one historical personage, and that no one can be more petty and miserable than he who is most great? Is it a pleasure in associating moral deformity with genius, and showing, in one who has strongly demanded veracity as a condition of life, a character ignoble and untrue? These are questions somewhat apart from the question we set out by asking, Whether a work executed in this spirit can fulfil the true objects of biography? But they are inevitable questions. Impartially, the cynical record is no more biography, in any true sense of the word, than is the enthusiast's; but it is almost impossible to be impartial in such a discussion, and we must add that, according to all our capabilities of judging, it is less so. For the enthusiast by turns justifies himself by discovering the latent nobleness of a man whose motives have been misconstrued, and at all times is likely to serve the ends of justice better by thinking the best, than he can ever do who thinks the worst. For it is more often in performance than in intention that men go astray. Save in the very worst cases there is a certain ideal, a shaping of better things in the mind, which love divines, but which hate, dulling the finest insight, is unconscious of. We all set out with a better intention than our performance comes up to, and our defender is at all times more nearly right than our detractor.

Neither of the two, however, attain the true objects of biography, which are twofold—for the individual and for the world. In both cases the biographer holds an office of high trust and responsibility. In all likelihood, if he is at all equal to his subject, permanent public opinion will be fixed, or at all events largely influenced, by the image he sets before it. It will be his to determine how far the man of whom he writes carried out his own creed, and was worthy of his greatness, or departed from the ideal which he set up for others, yet was indifferent to in his own person. A mere record of facts will not satisfy either the reader or the conditions under which such a writer ought to work. He is expected to enable us to surmount or to correct such momentary impressions as we may have taken up from chance encounter with his subject, and to give guidance and substance to such divinations of character or life as we may have gleaned from the public occurrences in which he was involved, or the works he has left behind. While we stand without, eager to gain a glimpse through an opened door or window of the object of our interest, he is within, in the very sanctuary, free to examine everything; and he is consequently bound to spare no pains in eliciting that truth which is something more and greater than fact, which it is possible even may be almost contradictory in its development, and which is of far greater permanent importance than any mere occurrence. In every portrait the due value of differing surfaces and textures must be taken into account, and we must be made to perceive which is mere drapery and apparel, and which the structure of the individual beneath. If this is true of the pictured history which represents but one movement and one pose, it is much more true of the whole course and progress of a life, which it is the office of the literary workman to set forth, not according to momentary and easily recognized tricks of manner, but according to the real scope and meaning which pervade and inspire it. That which is accidental, and due to the force of circumstances, is thus on a different *plan* from that which is fundamental. The most patient may be subject to a burst of passion, which, seen unconnected with the rest of his life, would give a general impression of it, in reality quite false, though momentarily true. Thus Moses, the meekest of men, might possibly be known to the carping Jew by the one act of scornful impatience which marred his public life, rather than by all the long-suffering with which he endured the continual vagaries of his stiff-necked people. Nor is it less easy to disentangle the character from the little web of petty susceptibilities which often, to the cursory observer, throw a mist over the most generous and noble spirit. The biographer must be in no respect cursory. It is his business to preserve us from being deceived by appearances, and still more to guard himself from superficial impressions. And if he is unfortunately compelled, by evidence which he cannot resist, to form an unexpectedly unfavourable judgment, it is the merest commonplace of honourable feeling to say that the most scrupulous care must be taken in testing that evidence, and that anything that is mere opinion must be discarded and left entirely out of the question.

Towards the world his duties are scarcely less important. To give an erroneous impression of any man, living or dead, to the mind of his country and generation, is the greatest of social sins. But the living may outlive every misrepresentation; and the most unpardonable offender in this respect is the man who persuades a whole community into injustice towards the dead. Without even going so far as this, a biographer has to discriminate between the legitimate and noble interest which mankind takes in every man sufficiently distinct in character or genius as to have identified himself from the crowd, and that prying curiosity which loves to investigate circumstances, and thrust itself into the sanctuaries of individual feeling. The question of how far the world should be allowed to penetrate into those sanctuaries, and to invade the privacy which every soul has a right to guard for itself, is one in which the delicacy of his perceptions and that good taste of the heart, which no artificial standard can supply, will be severely tested.

There is a kind of heroic candour and impartiality belonging to the early ages of history which cannot well be emulated in our more intricate condition of society. The biography of the Old Testament is a model of this primitive method. As soon as the primeval age, in which we see darkly men as trees walking, gigantic figures faintly perceptible, in a dim largeness of existence unlike ours, is over, how clearly and with what complete human consistence does the wonderful history of Israel, the wandering nation, begin in the great figure of Abraham setting out upon his journey in nomadic freedom, not knowing where he is going, his flocks and herds trudging behind, his beautiful wife wrapped in her veil, yet not so closely but that King Abimelech sees her; and the patriarch betrays a weakness, which, had he been a modern, would have been either concealed or excused, or brought against him, with a babble of contending tongues. Neither this divergence nor any other does the ancient Scripture leave out. There is no explanation, no softening down. The man was the Father of the Faithful, a good man, the best man of his time, the friend of God, a most noble human personage; and yet there was a moment when his courage and integrity failed him. The primitive writer does not separate this event from the context, or apologize for it, or represent it as the object of a lifelong repentance. He records it precisely as he records the arrival of the three wonderful guests, whom Abraham, standing in the cool evening at his tent door, perceives to be more than men. The one scene and the other are set before us with equal brevity, without hesitation in the one case or vain-glory in the other, in the clear setting of those Oriental skies and desert scenes. The patriarch had his faults; they stand there as they happened, like his virtues, no one asking pardon or attempting to account for them. Moses, too, the great prophet, the chosen guide and lawgiver, he who talked with God, and brought the shining Tables of the Law out of heaven, and reflected in his own dazzling countenance the glories he had seen, neither of him is there any picture of perfection. Sometimes his heart fails him, sometimes he is presumptuous and arrogant, though the most patient of men. His sudden passion, his brag of that power which is not his but God's, are told like the rest, plainly, without shrinking and without exaggeration. David is made up of faults, a man out of date, belonging rather to the Middle Ages than to that primitive time, full of generosities and chivalrous traits, but also full of guile when necessity or inclination moves him, of hot and undisciplined passions, of love and self-indulgence, redeemed only by that openness to conviction, that self-abasement and impassioned penitence, which are " after God's own heart." Not one word of excuse for all these evil deeds says the primitive impartial record. His crime, his grief, his punishment, are all before us to speak for themselves. There is no moralist to say—" these were the manners of his time." All is set down as it happened, for our judgment. We see the man of impulse moved by a touch, with all his senses keen and unbridled; loving, sinning, repenting, yet with something gracious about him that wins all hearts; letting his enemy go with high generosity, scorning to take advantage of sleep and weariness; pouring out before the Lord, in an outburst of noble and grateful emotion, that pitcher of water from the well of Bethlehem, which had been bought at the peril of men's lives, and was too precious a draught for him. The story is absolutely impartial, nothing hid, nothing unduly dwelt upon, the one part balancing with the other. Such impartiality is incompatible with modern manners. Had such an episode as that of Uriah the Hittite occurred in the life of any modern general, how sedulously would one class of historians have concealed or slurred it over, how bitterly another dragged it forth and put it in the front of every other incident of his life. It would have called forth a little literature of its own; the apologists discovering a hundred reasons why it should not be believed at all, or why it should be considered a just and generous way of dealing with a man who had deserved a worse fate; while the assailants made it the chief incident of his career, and dismissed all public services, all private qualities, as too insignificant to be noticed in comparison with such a crime. The Bible historian does neither; he tells us the tale, the temptation, the retribution, in brief but full detail—the beautiful wanton on the house-top, the doomed soldier in the front of the battle, the king, in all the flush of success, confronted by the stern prophet with his parable. Nothing could be more succinct yet more graphic. The historian will "nothing extenuate," neither will he " set down aught in malice." When the incident is over, he proceeds with perfect composure to the next, without prejudice or prepossession. Such a method is not practicable now-a-days. It was the more robust constitution of the antique mind which could go on again, calmly wiping away the past as if it had not been; but, though we cannot attain to the serenity of this state of mind, there are lessons in it by which we may profit. Who among us stands more evidently before the world than King David? All that is written of him, and all that he himself has written in illustration of the close yet picturesque narrative elsewhere afforded us, would go into a very small volume: yet there is nothing that is important left out. We have the picturesque incidents on which modern art reckons so much, and even, in some respects, an analytical study of his inner being; for when he stands and reasons with himself over Saul's slumbers in the cave, we assist at the processes of thought that go on in his rapid mind, and perceive how much natural piety and magnanimous impulse there is in the young adventurer, yet how truly his romantic generosity serves the best purposes of policy. But all is told without a reflection, without a moral. No doubt this has something to do with the perennial attractiveness of the Old Testament historians. They are never exhausted; for the reflection, the judgment, the analysis, and moral summary are all left to the reader, whose faculties are kept in full play by the very simplicity and primitive straightforwardness of the tale.

"Speak of me as I am," says Othello, "nothing extenuate, nor set down aught in malice." This is an epitome of the code which we have endeavoured to set forth. But the mode of the biographer of the period would, we fear, coincide but little with these instructions were he to set to work to write a biography of the Moor. Such a production could not be other than the work of a partisan. There have been many essays upon Othello, and many critics have endeavoured to explain and account for that extraordinary conversion of the admiring and confiding husband, the dignified and courteous general, whose self-defence is such a model of noble candour and simplicity, into the wild and savage avenger of his supposed shame, the miserable man whose very soul is jaundiced by suspicion. It is a change which will always remain inexplicable; for Iago's arguments, however skilful, are not sufficient to produce such an effect, and but for the glamour of Shakespeare, we should dare to doubt whether such a transformation could have been. The poet does not condescend to argue, nor does he appear even to have foreseen the difficulty. But were Othello a man of to-day he would not leave his character, with so easy a mind, in the hands of his historian. The biographer would be nothing if not a partisan. He would enlarge upon Brabantio's bitter words, till there should not be a vestige left us of the spotless image of that gentle lady, married to the Moor, who has commanded all our hearts. Or, on the other hand, he would make such a picture of the swart savage, half-civilized and dangerous, in whom all tigerish impulses were but suspended, ready to leap into ferocious life, as the critic sometimes fancies in his bewilderment, but Shakespeare never drew. On one side or the other, the consciousness of the catastrophe would colour all his thoughts, and everything would be set down in malice, and strained to account for it. (For malice let us read a theory, for the biographer who destroys a reputation does not necessarily do so out of any evil intention.) And thus the fine problem which supreme genius leaves to us to settle in our own way, and which excites our interest and sympathies more than any other, the never failing mystery by which a group of the innocent and unsuspecting are caught in the meshes of fate, and driven into a tragic complication of crime and misery without any agency of their own—the favourite subject of tragedy—will be worked out into an endless discussion of motives and tendencies, and Othello no longer know himself under the host of imaginary details with which his story is extenuated or unkindly set down.

Such an exercise of the faculties may be harmless in the world of imagination, but it is disastrous when it is employed upon the facts of real life; and we must add that the biographer must use his imagination only as an adjunct to his sympathies, and as giving him the power of realizing the position of his hero, and putting himself in his place; and that he must violate no law of testimony, and call no unfair witnesses, such as are debarred by nature and the common sentiment of humanity. A barrister who has to defend a man's character before the tribunals of the law is not more bound to use legitimate means and approved testimony than the historian, to whom is absolutely committed the care of his reputation, the aspect with which he shall stand and encounter the gaze of coming generations. Were the advocate to call the gossips of a fireside coterie, and bring forward the *disjecta membra* of a wastepaper basket, the judge would call him to order, the jury would make indignant protestations, the omnipotent solicitor banish him ever after from his confidence. But the biographer is all the more deeply responsible, since, in his case, there is no authoritative voice to check his proceedings; the great jury of the public is too vast, too irresponsible, too indifferent, to afford any serious opposition, and the publisher, concerned only for a great sale, is little likely to exercise any controlling influence over a writer who fulfils this first necessity. There remain only his brethren, so to speak, of the bar, the competitors of his own profession, to object or restrain, and their protests are but little effectual, being, as they are, without power or authority, and subject to imputations of rivalry and personal feeling. A successful writer is in this way the most unfettered of all men. The more unjustifiable his revelations are, the more are they likely to amuse and please the public; and he has this privilege besides, that no evidence brought against their justice afterwards can do more than excite a controversy, which the public, more amused than ever, take as a personal question, without in any great measure departing from the first impression which the first speaker has made. In a recent instance there has been a chorus of indignant voices raised against the biographer who has misused his advantages and traduced his subject. To what profit? The great audience, which is the ultimate judge, heard his story first, which was a story told with all the grace and effect of a practised writer; and it is in vain that our objections are made, in vain that the very material he has collected contradicts him at every turn. The general reader is not skilled in the laws of evidence. He accepts what is told him, as he has a right to do. The squabbles of the *cognoscenti* do not move him. If he examines at all it is into the claims of the first speaker to his faith. And who can contest those claims? They are indisputable. The closest of many friends, the most trusted of companions, the executor of his hero's last wishes, is there any one who can shake his position, or assert that he does not know? There is nobody; and the public is perfectly justified when it accepts the original witness, and lets the rest of us rave unheeded. Thus the position of the biographer carries with it a power which is almost unrestrained, the kind of power which it is doubly tyrannous to use like a giant. Not even the pulpit is so entirely master; for we all consider ourselves able to judge in respect to what the clergyman tells us; and we have his materials in our hands, by which to call him to account. If we must let him have his say at the moment, it is only for the moment, and we are always ready to hear all that is to be said on the other side; but the biographer has a far more assured place, and if he is not restrained by the strictest limits of truth and honour, there is nothing else that can control him in heaven or earth.

To those who have stepped out beyond the ranks of their fellows it must thus become a terrible reflection, that they may one day be delivered over helpless into the hands of some one, who, with no power in the world to call him to account, will give what view he pleases of their life and career and all their most private relationships. He may be a man without that power of penetrating beneath the surface into the character of another, which is sympathy, imagination, genius, all in one. He may be one of those who understand only what is spoken, to whom everything has a rigid interpretation, who take *au pied de la lettre* utterances intended for anything rather than that matter-of-fact statement. He may be incapable of appreciating the special conditions of another's education or habits of living, and from his different point of view may find only in the familiar facts entrusted to him material for dishonouring a memory. This may well give a sting to death among those who cannot fail to be aware that their lives will have an interest to mankind.

Nothing, indeed, can be more touching, more pathetic, than the helplessness of the dead in such a case. It is easy to say that it will matter little to them. How can we tell that it matters little to them? A year, a month ago, it would not have mattered little what their country and society, their friends, known and unknown, the world, for which they lived and laboured, thought of them. Had they imagined that the end of this life should also make an end of those friendly thoughts and warm admirations that consoled their concluding days, and the tender respectfulness with which their name was spoken, could we imagine it possible that they should have regarded with indifference this sudden failure of their reputation? A man who is conscious of having left much behind him which the world will not willingly let die, and of leaving at the same time, no duty unfulfilled, no sin to be discovered, no record which can leap to light and shame him, feels himself secure, at least in this, that he will not suffer at the hands of posterity. He may have been misconceived in life, but then he will be righted. Circumstances may have kept him in the background, or obscured his fame, but then there will be justice done. He may smile even, with a melancholy disdain, yet pleasure, to think that the generation to come will build the tomb of the prophet whom their fathers have slain; and who can doubt that if this conviction were taken away, it would take much from the comfort with which men prepare themselves for their exit from the familiar universe and entry into the unknown? He leaves his name to those that come after him with a confidence that is full of pathos. Let them say what they will, he can answer nothing; he cannot explain or defend himself out of his grave; they may kick at the dead lion who will; he who could a little while ago have crushed them with a touch, must now bear everything without the power to ward off a single indignity. But rare indeed are the circumstances in which any alarm is felt on this score. The dying have full faith in the justice that will be done them when they are dead. They are delivered over into the hands of all that have a grievance against them, into the power of their enemies, if they have any; but they have no fear. And to the credit of humanity, be it said, this last touching faith in the goodwill of men is scarcely ever without justification. As a general rule, justice may be calculated upon over a grave.

The biographer alone can interrupt the operation of this rule of natural equity. He stands, in the first instance, in the place of posterity, for those who, with a touching confidence, thus await its decision. He has it in his power to guide the final deliverance, like that judge whose summing up so often decides the verdict. And hence there arises a weighty question in which we think much is involved. If a man, on the eve of so important an undertaking, finds that the idea he has formed of the person whose good name is in his hands is an unfavourable one, and that all he can do by telling the story of his life is to lessen or destroy that good name—not indeed by revealing any system of hypocrisy or concealed vice, which it might be to the benefit of public morals to expose, but by an exhibition of personal idiosyncrasies repulsive to the ordinary mind and contradictory of the veneration with which the world has hitherto regarded a man of genius—is it in such a case his duty to speak at all? Is the necessity of producing another book among many so imperative that the natural reluctance, which any honourable man must feel, to put forth accusations which can only be answered at second-hand, and which the person principally concerned is powerless to reply to, must be disregarded? There are cases of perverted intelligence in which the detractor does not perceive the moral bearing of the statements he has to make, and thus maligns his subject without being sensible of it, with a certain innocence of mind, perhaps even glorying in the shame he originates. But this can scarcely be the case, except in an obtuse understanding and uninstructed judgment. We can imagine that in such circumstances a high-minded man, alarmed by his own discoveries—which we must suppose to have been made after the death of his hero, since it is scarcely possible that any one should love and frequent, and identify himself with, a character of this description— would seek every means of getting rid of the ungracious task set before him; that he would, in the first place, anxiously consult every authority, and test and compare every piece of evidence, and try every method of dispelling the painful shadows which were gathering between him and the object of his trust; and that, finally, rather than be the instrument of ruining a virtuous reputation, and betraying the secret weakness of a man whom the world held in honour, he would retire from the field altogether, and leave with a sad heart the work which he could only execute in this way to some less severe moralist, who might be able to throw upon it a gentler light. This is the view which we believe most good men would take of a position so painful. In private life most of us would rather not hear new facts disadvantageous to our friends who are dead, and would consider the publication of them a breach of every delicate sentiment. To bring a great man, who has lived in the common daylight without reproach during his life, to the bar of this world's opinion after his death, is in itself a painful act. The defendant is, in all cases, silenced by English law; but, at least, he has the privilege of communicating all the facts in his favour to his advocate, and furnishing explanations of his conduct for counsel's use. But the dead have no such safeguard; they have no longer any privacy; their very hearts, like their desks and private drawers and cabinets, can be ransacked for evidence to their disadvantage. Is it in any conceivable case a biographer's duty to do this? If the question, as one of literary and social morals, were submitted to any competent tribunal, or jury of his peers, the answer, we think, would be unanimous. Should something more powerful than any private sentiment demand the performance of so painful a duty; should there exist other and darker accusations that might be made were not these acknowledged and established, an argument which might perhaps have held in the case of Byron, for instance; should the scandal be so great that investigation was imperative—then with patience and care, waiting till the fumes of passion had died away, and every privilege of perspective had been attained, the work should be done. But if there were no such necessity, it is impossible that a man could be compelled to criminate his friend, or to soil an established reputation entrusted to his care. In this case his plain duty would be to refrain.

We have, perhaps, dwelt too long on the graver side of a subject which so many recent publications have brought forcibly under the consideration of all men, and specially of those of the literary profession. But there are also questions involved of less solemnity, which still should not be passed over in any discussion of the duties of a writer of biography. We remember being consulted upon one such work, in which a mass of original letters, in the very autograph of the subject of the memoir, were shovelled up entire into the printer's hands with an inconceivable disrespect, and all the superfluity inevitable in such indiscriminate publication. The writer in this case meant only to do his work with as little trouble as possible, and, as a matter of fact, contrived to make two large volumes thus out of a life with no events in it, which might have been treated advantageously in a small octavo. Such has been the system adopted in another well-known instance, where the careless jottings of a diary have been swept up with hasty hands and thrust into the respectable text, affording a curious and comical reminder to the reader of a former popular conception of the hero, and certain well-known tendencies in his character, which the well-intentioned biographer would have been the last willingly to recall. Such unintentional betrayal arises however, no doubt, from a certain opacity of intellect, and is consequently not a fault so much as a mistake, which would be laughable if it were not so injurious. It is not a mistake, however, but an offence against social morals, which even an obtuse mind cannot make with impunity, that the foolishness thus imported into the record is calculated to wound many living persons besides discrediting the character of the diarist. To appeal to the higher morals in order to condemn such a breach of the simplest social code, seems a waste of force, since society ought to be able to enforce respect for its own rule. There is no more favourite imagination in romance than that of a Palace of Truth, an enchanted place, in which every man is compelled to express his opinion of his neighbours with a candour which at present is used only to third parties. But a book is a dangerous medium for such simple speaking. If the person with whom you are conversing suddenly tells you that you are an empty fool, and he has always thought you so, you have at least the consolation that it is said to you only, and not to all your friends and acquaintances. But there is something bewildering in the sensation, when, through the pages of a hasty biography, we suddenly hear a voice which has been used to talk to us in pleasanter tones, discoursing audibly to earth and heaven in this simple and candid fashion about us and our concerns. The startled victim feels for the first moment as if he were an eavesdropper, one of those proverbial listeners who never hear any good of themselves, and has to satisfy his conscience that this is not a dishonourable action of which he is being guilty before he realizes what it actually is—an action perhaps not very honourable, but without blame so far as he is concerned. It is at all times an odd experience to hear ourselves discussed; not those who are our best friends will do it in a way entirely pleasing to our consciousness. There is a something, a tone, a smile, perhaps even an excuse, when we feel no excuse to be necessary, which jars upon that absolute sense of property which we have in ourselves. And the effect is proportionally stronger when a famous person, on whose words we have often hung, suddenly, and with startling composure, begins at our very ear to publish to the world what our friends say of us. The sensation is still more startling than that with which we should receive the candid remarks of the Palace of Truth. There is nothing in it of the gravity with which we would wish to receive the strictures of a Right Reverend Father in God, translated into a better sphere, who might indeed admonish us for our good with perfect propriety; but it is whimsically like the old notions which a gossiping world once entertained of that well-known personage, and which we had put away, with all untimely smiles and nicknames, when he became a portion of the past. We feel now that being past, he has no right to be so present; the position is ludicrously incongruous. And in the irritation of the sufferers, and the amusement of those who do not suffer, there is an element of irreverence, of disrespect, which annuls all the advantages of death. In this case the biographer has brought back a figure of which we had altogether forgotten the comic side, out of the natural deference and respectful gravity with which we were glad to contemplate him, into the atmosphere of *Punch*, and the familiarity of a most unreverential appellation.

Can nothing be done to prevent this system of desecration? The most bitter of pessimists would scarcely desire that all the softening tenderness which death brings with it should be thus rudely and ruthlessly disturbed. Half of the harm, no doubt, arises from the frantic haste which confounds all broader and larger views, and turns us from any attempts we may wish to make to gain a higher friendship with the spirit, into an enforced contemplation of those tricks of attitude and gesture, those twitches of nervous movement, and little vulgarities of personal peculiarity which do not, whatever may be said to the contrary, make the man. In a language in which there are noble examples of the art of biography, it is curious that we should find so general a callousness to the claims upon our respect, upon even the most ordinary consideration of what their wishes and feelings would have been, of persons so very recently separated from us. Perhaps it is still worse when what is done is in a pretended compliance with their desires, a compliance in the letter and utter contradiction in the spirit. The profound offence which this course of proceeding has given to all who had any personal knowledge of the victims, and almost all whose opinion is worth having on such a subject, makes a curious balance to the unthinking satisfaction of the common public in such revelations of domestic privacy as it could not have hoped for, the crystallized gossip which is always "so interesting" to the crowd. But when a writer chooses this cheap method of success it is perhaps hopeless to attempt to call him to a perception of any higher duty.

M. O. W. OLIPHANT.

Art. VIII.—1. *Biographie Universelle, Ancienne et Moderne.* Nouvelle édition. 45 tomes imp. 8vo. Paris, 1843–1865.
2. *Nouvelle Biographie Générale.* Publiée par MM. Firmin-Didot frères sous la direction de M. le Dr Hoefer. 46 tomes 8vo. Paris, 1852–1866.
3. *Specimen of a 'Dictionary of National Biography.'* Edited by Leslie Stephen. London, 1883.

'THE biographical part of literature,' said Dr. Johnson, 'is what I love the best,' and his remark is echoed daily in the hearts, if not in the words, of hundreds of readers. The lives of men of genius, or even of men of learning, are always of interest, however dead may be their writings. How many are there who care nothing for 'Rasselas,' 'The Vanity of Human Wishes,' or the 'Rambler,' who yet take delight in the biography of Johnson! The writings of Casaubon and Scaliger are so dead that, unlike some of their contemporaries, they could not even be galvanized into the momentary appearance of life; yet we have all read with pleasure Mr. Pattison's admirable monograph on the one, and are looking forward with eagerness to his promised biography of the other. The 'Lives' of Plutarch and Suetonius were the novels of the Greeks and Romans, as the *Gesta*, with their mixture of truth and fable, were of the Middle Ages; and though for the last half-century pure fiction has been in the ascendant, the popularity of biography, if not relatively yet absolutely, seems to be continually increasing. The success of such series as those of 'English Men of Letters' and 'Ancient' and 'Foreign Classics' shows the extent of the interest felt in the lives of men of letters. But not less keen is the desire to know the details of the personal histories of kings, queens, statesmen, soldiers, and churchmen. Lives of the Lord Chancellors, of the Chief Justices, of the Archbishops of Canterbury, of the Archbishops of York, of the Speakers of the House of Commons, of the Queens of England, of the Princesses of England, of more or less (generally we fear *less*) value, and with a success not always proportioned to their merit, find numerous readers, while single lives appear daily in still greater abundance, if not of superior quality. Formerly it was thought that no one deserved a statue or a biography until his death. But Prince Bismarck, Mr. Gladstone, and Mr. Bright (to say nothing of men of less mark), have been the subjects of elaborate biographies (or eulogies) in their lifetime, and the grave of a man of any reputation is hardly filled up before an announcement is made of a speedily forthcoming 'Memoir.'

Of the two classes of biographies—the spiteful and the panegyrical—

gyrical—the latter is by far the more numerous. The long obituaries of men of second, third, and fourth-rate eminence, which fill the columns of the 'Times,' scarce 'hint a fault or hesitate dislike;' while those of men of no eminence whatever, appearing daily in still greater number in that child of the affections of Mr. Bright and Mr. Gladstone, the provincial press, show that 'the prominent citizens' of our great cities possess every virtue and every talent under heaven. Lord Campbell's 'Life of Lord Lyndhurst' is one of the most conspicuous specimens of the spiteful class of biographies, but his misrepresentations have been exposed, and a faithful portraiture given of the great Chancellor and statesman, in Sir Theodore Martin's biography. But we would not be thought to be unmindful of the many excellent biographies which the last few years have produced. To say anything in praise of Mr. Trevelyan's Life of his uncle would be merely to re-echo what has been already said by every one competent to form an opinion. In the biography of Bishop Patteson we have the narrative of an heroic life simply and naturally told; and though the biographers of Bishop Wilberforce have written an elaborate defence of their hero, they have neither indulged in panegyric nor attempted unduly to colour their facts. Whatever indiscretions they—or one of them—may have committed, a true and lifelike picture of the Bishop is set before us, and we have no difficulty in seeing him as he really was.

But while no country, not even France, can rival England in the importance and number of the biographies which have appeared during the last half-century, we are still without an universal Biographical Dictionary—one, that is to say, worthy of the name, or comparable either for value or extent to either of the two works, the titles of which we have placed at the head of this article. The space of more than sixteen years has elapsed since their completion, yet no attempt has been made in this country either to displace them from their position as by far the best biographical dictionaries in existence, or even to provide a biographical dictionary in the English language coming anywhere near to them in merit.

That England, indeed, is capable of planning and carrying out a biographical dictionary on a scale at once extended and well-proportioned, which should rival the merits, while it avoided many of the defects, of the Biographies 'Universelle' and 'Générale,' has been shown by the fragment published under the auspices of the Society for the Diffusion of Useful Knowledge (1842–1844): but the sudden collapse of that work on the completion of the letter A, owing chiefly to failure of obtaining support,

support, shows that in England at that time there was no public which required in a biographical dictionary anything but the most superficial and meagre of compilations.

Nor are there any grounds for expecting that the 'Biographie Universelle' will be deposed from its unquestioned supremacy. The world has grown too vast for anything like a reasonably exhaustive *universal* biographical dictionary. How many men and women have died in the past twenty years for whom a place would be demanded! How great is the number of names, hitherto omitted, of persons who have been, as it were, discovered and written about, and who are entitled to be included! Every year adds to, and will at least for some time continue to add to, the list. Had the Dictionary of the Society for the Diffusion of Useful Knowledge been completed on the scale on which it was commenced, it would have reached at least one hundred and fifty volumes of the same size as the seven actually published, and that without including any names of persons deceased in the last thirty-eight years; while a new edition of the 'Biographie Universelle,' carried out on the same scale as the last, would certainly bring up the forty-five large volumes to at least sixty. The lives, indeed, of the second, third, and fourth-rate French generals and politicians of the Revolution and the Empire, might with advantage be diminished in length. Yet the relief thereby gained would be hardly appreciable, in the face of the number of names constantly and increasingly pressing for admittance into a dictionary of universal biography. Μέγα βιβλίον μέγα κακόν is a maxim which still holds good in England. In Germany, indeed, a book can never be too long. The excellent Encyclopædia of the last century, known as 'Zedler's Lexicon,' though unfinished, reached sixty-eight folios; and that of Ersch and Gruber, commenced in 1818, has now, after sixty-four years, arrived at its hundred and fifty-fourth volume, but has not nearly approached its end. The earlier volumes have become obsolete long before the work is completed.*

But though a general biographical dictionary, on the scale on

* The 'Encyclopædia' of Ersch and Gruber has been carried on in three divisions, commenced simultaneously. The first, A—G, has just reached its ninety-eighth and last volume; the second, beginning with H, has arrived at its thirty-first volume and the end of the letter J; the third, beginning with O, has reached the twenty-fifth volume and the word *Physicos*. In an article on Cyclopædias in the 'Quarterly Review' for 1863 (vol. 113, p. 371), it was compared to 'a gigantic tunnel for the execution of which three shafts are obliged to be sunk.' The 'Encyclopædia' of Krünitz, commenced in 1773, was completed in 1858 in two hundred and forty-two octavos. We may add that both 'Zedler' and 'Ersch and Gruber' include admirable biographical dictionaries. There are names in 'Zedler' which we should seek in vain elsewhere.

which

which such a work ought to be composed, is not to be expected, perhaps not even to be wished for, in England, yet books which may supply its place better than any single work could do, may be expected, and are even in progress. The 'Dictionary of Greek and Roman Biography and Mythology,' edited by Dr. W. Smith, is a book which far surpasses any book of the kind in existence. The 'Dictionary of Christian Biography, Literature, Sects, and Doctrines, during the first Eight Centuries,' edited by Dr. W. Smith and Dr. Wace, and of which the third volume has recently appeared, is a work of still greater merit. Many of the articles in the new volume—notably those on Hippolytus, Ignatius, Irenæus, Jerome, Julian, and Justin Martyr, (as well as many shorter and less important ones)—show a ripeness and depth of scholarship, a thoroughness of investigation, and a power and clearness of expression, which have rarely been found in the contributors to dictionaries and encyclopædias, and which prove that now at least, whatever may have been the case a few years since, England has no cause to fear a comparison with the best and highest German scholarship.

The 'Biographia Britannica,' projected by Mr. Murray under Dr. W. Smith's editorship some years since, unfortunately fell through, but we rejoice to know that the task has been taken up by Mr. Leslie Stephen, and we hope shortly to see the commencement of an adequate and exhaustive 'Dictionary of National Biography.' If, when the 'Dictionary of Christian Biography' is completed, it could be continued by a 'Dictionary of Medieval Literary Biography' on the same scale and equally well done, a grievous *hiatus*, not only in English literature, but in literature generally, would be filled up, and we might point to a series of books in the department of Biography unequalled in Europe.

Nothing in any way resembling our modern Biographical or Historical Dictionary was known to the Greeks and Romans, or even to the Middle Ages. Collections of special biographies, indeed, were not wanting. Those of Plutarch and Suetonius among the ancients, and of St. Jerome and St. Isidore at a later period, are among the most important. But while the Lexicon of Suidas, which combines in one, Grammar, Geography, and Biography, came the nearest to an Historical Dictionary of any work of antiquity, it is altogether a misnomer to describe it as such, as is done by Moreri in the Preface to his 'Grand Dictionnaire Historique.'

The direct ancestor of the 'Biographical Dictionary,' and the earliest that has as yet been discovered, is a small volume compiled by Herman Torrentinus (Van Beeck), and printed at Deventer

Deventer at the end of the fifteenth century, under the title of 'Elucidarius Carminum et Historiarum vel Vocabularius Poeticus, continens Historias Provincias Urbes Insulas Fluvios et Montes Illustres.' It is, as its title implies, and as the author tells us in his Preface, a Dictionary alphabetically arranged of the proper names of gods, illustrious men, provinces, islands, cities, and rivers, which are to be found in the poets. Its object was the assistance of those reading the poets, and among the authors from whom it is compiled are Terentius Maurus, Sallust, Livy, Strabo, Pliny, Justin, Virgil, Perottus, Tertullian, and Craston. The descriptions of the different places named are generally given in a line or two, but many of the biographical articles are longer, extending in two or three cases to more than half a page. The two longest are those on Ulysses and Medea. The book was found to be most useful and indeed indispensable to students, and no less than twenty-four editions of it (before 1537) are enumerated by Panzer, while we have ourselves seen, or found noticed in catalogues, more than seventeen later editions in Latin, besides two of an Italian translation.*

The first step in advance was taken by Robert Estienne, who had in 1530 and 1535 given reprints of the 'Elucidarius.' In 1541 he printed a Dictionary of proper names, incorporating part of the 'Elucidarius,' but with three times as much additional matter. The edition of the book of 'Torrentinus,' put forth by Gryphius in 1540, and which is now before us, contains 214 pages, small 8vo.; that of Robert Estienne—a quarto—has 588 pages, and each page contains more than double the quantity of a page of Torrentinus. The name and preface of Torrentinus have disappeared, and a short preface by Robert Estienne is prefixed, in which, as well as on the title-page, he claims, and justly, that his work is 'plane novum nec antea unquam editum.' A comparison of the two books, which does not seem to have been made by any writer who has spoken of them, shows how erroneous it is to treat the work of Robert

* One of the most interesting articles in the 'Dictionnaire Historique' of Prosper Marchand is that upon Torrentinus (Part II. p. 283), in the notes to which will be found a long dissertation, not only upon the different editions of the 'Elucidarius,' but upon Historical Dictionaries in general, and an account of the first twenty editions of Moreri. The article is the result of careful research in an obscure department of literary history, on which it throws much light. Unfortunately it is disfigured by many errors, especially in the matter of dates and names, each of which should be verified before being relied upon. It also omits many editions as well of the 'Elucidarius' as of the other Dictionaries that it notices. The 'Biographie Universelle,' in its notice of Juigné-Broissinière, refers its readers to this article in Marchand; but by a strange blunder, unpardonable when repeated in the second edition, the article is stated to be *Terentianus*, instead of *Torrentinus*.

Estienne,

Estienne, as has been frequently done, merely as a new edition, with additions and corrections, of that of Torrentinus. A certain number, not one-fourth, of the less important articles of the 'Elucidarius' are, indeed, textually reproduced in the 'Dictionarium,' a certain number are altered, enlarged, and corrected, but the greater part of the 'Elucidarius' has disappeared. All the important articles are new. The names are no longer only those mentioned by the poets, but all the chief names of antiquity, orators, poets, and historians, are inserted. Of Cicero, Livy, and Tacitus, real biographies are now to be found. But a still more important advance is made. Several names not belonging to classical antiquity are included. Though why a distinction should be conferred upon Bede, Benedict, Bernard, and Boniface, which is granted neither to Thomas Aquinas, Gregory the Great, nor Charlemagne, it is not easy to understand, especially in a Dictionary of names occurring only in 'scriptis prophanis,' and which finds no place either for Augustine or Jerome. But, so far as we have noticed, the 'venerable' monk of Jarrow, the founder of the Benedictine order, the great abbot of Clairvaux, and the apostle of the Saxons, are the only post-classical names.

In the twelve years which followed 1541, several editions of the book of Robert Estienne appeared, with some additions, but of no great importance. But the year 1553 is an era in the history of Biographical Dictionaries, of which it may be said to be the birth-year, for in it Charles Estienne printed the first edition of his 'Historical Dictionary,' the first book to which this title was given, and the first that purported to be a universal Dictionary of Biography, modern as well as ancient. The book is really, as Charles Estienne admits in his preface, a new edition of the 'Dictionarium Propriorum Nominum' of his brother Robert, but it is in all respects greatly extended and improved. It forms a thick quarto, and was destined to hold its ground against all comers for upwards of a century, and more than five-and-twenty editions proved its popularity, and attested its merits. Meagre and full of inaccuracies, and absolutely worthless as it seems to us, it was found to be an enormous help to scholars and students. The second edition, published in 1566, two years after the author's death, is greatly improved, while the 'augmentations,' comprising six hundred new articles, besides many corrections, subsequently made (according to Marchand, by Frederic Morel), greatly raised the value and increased the utility of the editions of and subsequent to 1596. According to the Preface, much is added, much corrected, and much rubbish (particularly in the mythological part) omitted.

omitted. But the modern names are still but few and far between, and the information respecting them is most scanty. Notices of a good many emperors and kings, of a few medieval jurists and philosophers — such as Accursius and Bartolus, Averroës and Avicenna — constitute almost the whole of the modern department. A single line is devoted to 'Franciscus Petrarcha.' In 1627 (according to the 'Biographie Universelle,' but in 1644 according to the 'Biographie Générale) it was translated into French by Juigné-Broissinière, with some unimportant and frequently incorrect additions, taken, according to Moreri, chiefly from the works of Magin and Sebastian Munster.

Inexact and superficial as the book seems now, yet, as the only Historical and Biographical Dictionary in the French language, it was found so useful, that it attained an enormous popularity, and eight or ten editions, successively enlarged and corrected, appeared in the next thirty years. In 1670, Nicholas Lloyd published at Oxford an edition of the 'Dictionarium Historicum' of Charles Estienne, but with numerous additions, corrections, alterations, and omissions, a book which gave the author a high reputation, not only in England, but on the Continent, where it was acknowledged as superior to any of the previous editions of the book of Charles Estienne. But Prosper Marchand thinks the praises given to this book by Moreri and others much in excess of its real merits, and considers the alterations made by Lloyd often disfigurements rather than improvements. A second and in many respects improved edition (London, 1686) was published after the editor's death, and was several times reprinted on the Continent. Yet in some important matters the earlier work would seem the more useful. Many English and French kings and German emperors are to be found in the earlier edition, though on what principle they are included it seems impossible to conceive, for the Henries, English, French, and German, are to be found, but neither Francis I. nor Elizabeth. In the second edition, however, all the modern European sovereigns have disappeared, except Charlemagne and Charles V.; yet the preface gives no hint of any article being omitted.

Shortly after the appearance of Lloyd's book a work was printed, the reputation and popularity of which—altogether disproportioned to its real merits—was destined to throw all its predecessors into the shade, or rather to cause their complete and permanent disappearance; a work which has passed through more than twenty editions, the last of which, after a lapse of a century and a quarter, is still an indispensable companion of every student of literary history, and ought to be found

found in every library, but which really owes all its present value to the labours of its successive editors. The original edition of the 'Grand Dictionnaire Historique' of Louis Moreri, in a single folio, was given to the world in 1674. It was received with so much favour, that a new edition was in preparation when its author died in 1680, at the age of thirty-seven, a victim of the labours which he had devoted to the work. The second edition, increased to two folios, appeared in 1681, and far surpassed the first in popularity as in merit. It was received with a chorus of praises. The 'Acta Eruditorum' of Leipsic vied with the 'Journal des Sçavans' in praises of the utility of the dictionary and the learning of its author. It was pronounced the most exact, the most excellent, that had ever appeared. The judiciousness of its criticisms was not less favourably spoken of than its accuracy in matters of fact. It was certainly an improvement on Juigné; it omitted or curtailed some redundancies, it added much, it corrected much. Yet its faults were innumerable, and the words of censure which Moreri used of his predecessors, Estienne and Juigné, might, Prosper Marchand suggests, be more fitly applied to himself. But, in truth, we ought rather to use of Moreri the language of Bayle:—

'I am of the opinion of Horace with respect to those who show us the way. The earliest writers of dictionaries have committed many faults, but they have performed great services, and they ought not to be deprived by their successors of the glory which is their due. Moreri took great pains, his work has been of some use to every one, and to many has afforded sufficient information. It has thrown light into regions to which other books would never have brought it, and where an exact knowledge of details is not necessary.'

Never did a book so completely efface its predecessors as that of Moreri. For a whole century it had the field to itself. The Dictionaries of Bayle, Marchand, and Chaufepié, were merely supplements to it. The care of successive editors, among whom Saint-Ussan, Leclerc, and Goujet should be mentioned with special praise, corrected and enlarged it. An immense number of biographies were added. Many redundancies were cut off, until at last, in the ten huge folios which constitute the last and best edition of Moreri (the 21st or 22nd) it is difficult to discover any traces of the original work of the author whose name is still given to it. The last edition of Moreri is one of the collections still useful and necessary to the literary student. Upwards of half the work is occupied by biographies; among them are numerous names not to be found in any subsequent Biographical Dictionary. They are no doubt mostly obscure ecclesiastics, scholars, and jurists; yet they include not a few names of men
of

of the sixteenth and seventeenth centuries whom we are surprised to find omitted from the 'Biographie Universelle.' Again of many writers a much fuller account is to be found than in any subsequent work, with references to authorities which would be sought in vain elsewhere. Nor are the genealogical articles on the great French historical families of less interest and value. Of the non-biographical part, the geographical has entirely lost its value and interest; but among the miscellaneous articles there are many, such as the lists of Cardinals, of Knights of the Order of the Holy Ghost, those on *Parlements*, on *Lits de justice*, containing information which one would have some hesitation in deciding where else to look for. In short, the last edition of Moreri, easy as it would be to draw up a long list of its errors, is a book which is not likely now to be superseded, though a single folio would probably contain all that gives the book its present value.

But Moreri's Dictionary has a claim to distinction beyond its intrinsic merits. It brought for the first time into a field, which had hitherto been abandoned to compilers and Dryasdusts, a man of real and rare genius, and gave birth to that armoury of obscure learning and acute criticism, whence successive generations of scholars and dialecticians have drawn their choicest and sharpest weapons. Bayle's Dictionary, originally intended merely to fill up the deficiencies and to correct the errors of Moreri, became in the end one of the greatest monuments of erudition and critical acumen which any single scholar has given to the world. The names which occur in the text form so many pegs on which to hang all kinds of recondite and interesting information, acute and profound criticisms, keen and unanswerable attacks on the fallacies of dogmatism and superstition. Never was there a man whose character, equally in its defects as in its merits, so fitted him to be a perfect critic. He is neither creative nor destructive. He doubts, and that is all; or rather he puts forward the two opposing arguments with so much force, so much clearness, and so much impartiality, that they seem to destroy each other and produce doubt in the mind of the reader. As for himself, he is indifferent. He compares himself to the cloud-gathering Jove of Homer. 'Mon talent est de former des doutes; mais ce ne sont que des doutes.' And to 'Peter Bayle' Carlyle has applied the epithet 'stupid!'

We can never calculate with certainty what names we shall find in Bayle; and, as the notes are frequently unconnected with the life to which they are appended, we often find the information we are seeking under the most unlikely heads. 'If Bayle,' says Gibbon, 'wrote his dictionary to empty the various collections

collections he had made without any particular design, he could not have chosen a better plan. It permitted him everything and obliged him to nothing. By the double freedom of a dictionary and notes he could pitch on what articles he pleased, and say what he pleased in those articles.' His critical dictionary first appeared in 1697, in two volumes folio, subsequently amplified into five, and in this century an edition has been published with notes and additions in sixteen octavos. But Bayle's Dictionary is one of the few books which, from its arrangement, can only be read conveniently in folio. The comparatively insignificant text, the long and far more important and interesting notes, and the notes upon notes, make the reading it in any form but a folio an incessant turning of pages backwards and forwards. But while Bayle's plan was admirably suited to his subject matter, it had the misfortune to be taken as a model for all the historical and biographical dictionaries which followed for nearly half a century. Those of Chaufepié and Marchand, and the 'Biographia Britannica,' have all short and meagre texts, with notes and dissertations many times longer, to say nothing of notes upon notes—making it a weariness to the flesh as well as to the spirit to study or even consult them.

The Dictionary of Chaufepié (1750-56), in four bulky folios, forming, as its title-page tells us, a supplement to that of Bayle, acquires an interest for us, not so much on account of its intrinsic merits as because it was derived from an English source. In 1694, there had been published a translation of the Dictionary of Moreri 'by various hands,' all more or less incompetent. The book, however, sold, and a new edition being called for, the preparation of it was entrusted to Jeremy Collier. He re-wrote much and corrected more, and his edition of 'The Great Historical, Geographical, Genealogical, and Poetical Dictionary,' appeared in two folios in 1701, but he was so little satisfied with it that he gave a supplement in 1705, and a further supplement in 1721. These four volumes are known as 'Collier's Dictionary.' Besides what is taken from Lloyd, Bayle, and Hoffmann,* there are a considerable number of original articles relating to England and Englishmen.

Passing

---

* In 1677, John Jacob Hoffmann, a professor at Basle, gave to the world a 'Lexicon Universale Historico-Chronologico-Poetico-Philologicum,' in two closely printed folios. It is based on the Dictionaries of Lloyd, Estienne, and Juigné, though with large additions. A supplement was added in two still larger folios in 1683, and the whole was revised, corrected, and incorporated in an edition issued by the author in 1698 in four folios. It contains an immense mass of information on all the subjects mentioned in the title, and its biographical
articles

Passing by the translation of Bayle's Dictionary, published in 1710, in four folios (of which a second edition was put forth in 1734-7, in five volumes), with the remark that it was made by a company of French refugees, whose knowledge of the English tongue was wholly insufficient for the work they undertook, we arrive at the 'General Dictionary, Historical and Critical,' which appeared in ten folios (1734-1741). The basis of this work is a new and improved translation of Bayle, but it corrects some errors, enlarges many of his brief notices into complete biographies, and, above all, adds more than nine hundred new lives, including a large number of Englishmen, chiefly men of letters, whose lives, though contained in the collections of Pits, Bale, Boston, Fuller, and Wood, had not before been included in any general, historical, or biographical dictionary. J. P. Bernard, Thomas Birch, John Lockman, and, for the Oriental part, George Sale, were the compilers of this book, which, though not wanting in faults, is a most creditable, and in many respects an admirable performance, which may still be consulted with advantage, and should be found on the shelves of every well-stored English library. Of several more or less eminent Englishmen it contains exhaustive biographies; and copious extracts from, and often judicious criticisms upon their writings, are to be found in the notes. But the book is in general eminently unreadable. The English lives are mostly due to Birch. 'Tom Birch,' said Dr. Johnson, 'is as brisk as a bee in conversation, but no sooner does he take a pen in hand than it becomes a torpedo, and benumbs all his faculties.' Soon after its appearance, J. G. de Chaufepié, a Dutch minister of French extraction, translated into French the greater number of those articles which were not themselves translations from Bayle (altering and correcting some few of them), and, with additions compiled from other sources, formed them into the 'Nouveau Dictionnaire Historique et Critique pour servir de supplément ou continuation au Dictionnaire de M. Pierre Bayle,' which was published in four folios, 1750-1756. The bulk of the book, being merely a translation from our own Historical Dictionary, is of little interest; but many of the lives of which Chaufepié was the author, notably those of Postel, G. J. Vossius, and Utenbogaert, are still by far the fullest and best that exist of those learned persons. But the book is intolerably dull reading, and the author's disquisitions are enlivened neither by the wit,

---

articles may still be referred to with profit. Isaac D'Israeli's remark upon it has often been quoted: 'I heard a man of great learning declare that whenever he could not recollect his knowledge he opened Hoffmann's "Lexicon," where he was sure to find what he had lost.'—'Curiosities of Literature.'

the

the sarcasms, nor the acute criticisms, of Bayle. Of about fourteen hundred articles that the book contains, six hundred are simply translated from the English, two hundred and eighty are revised by Chaufepié, and nearly five hundred are entirely new.

Shortly after the completion of Chaufepié, there appeared the last of the 'Historical Dictionaries,' or rather supplements to Moreri and Bayle. The dictionary of Prosper Marchand was compiled after his death, from his manuscript notes written upon loose sheets and scraps of paper. It is a series of literary biographies and dissertations by a man of much reading and of literary taste, written in a lively and agreeable style, always interesting, and containing much matter of literary history not elsewhere to be met with; but, as was to be expected from the manner in which it was compiled, full of errors, especially of dates and editions.

With the last edition of Moreri in 1760 the canon of the 'Historical Dictionary' is complete. The twenty large folios of Moreri, Bayle, Chaufepié, and Marchand, form together a Biographical Dictionary, of fullness, of accuracy, and of general utility, up to that time unknown and not dreamed of half a century earlier. They contain notices of many men whose names do not appear even in the 'Biographie Universelle,' numerous dissertations which may still be read with interest and profit, and lives, especially of men of letters, which remain our chief sources of information respecting them. But the books had grown too unwieldy, and the biographies too long. Like Nares's 'Life of Burleigh,' the 'Dictionary' of Chaufepié might, 'before the Deluge, have been considered as light reading by Hilpa and Shalum'; but life is not now long enough to allow any but professed students to wade through the double columns of his closely-printed folios. To the student the books are still invaluable, but even in the middle of the eighteenth century 'the general reader' had become a person to be catered for, and he required a lighter and more easily digested diet. A short and easy book of biographical reference was needed, and the 'Biographical Dictionary,' properly and strictly so called, though for another half-century generally retaining the old title, was the result.

The 'Historical Dictionary,' though in its final stage of development chiefly biographical, was not exclusively so. Moreri professed to include history, geography, and genealogy; and, even in the last edition, not much more than half is devoted to biography pure and simple. Bayle, Chaufepié, and Marchand, not only occupied themselves to a large extent with literary criticisms, but admitted numerous articles which were not even in form biographical. The dissertations on Anabaptists and Manicheans

Manicheans in Bayle, Adamites and Picards in Chaufepié, and 'De Tribus Impostoribus' and 'Bibliothèques Belgiques' in Marchand, are still, after the lapse of a century and a quarter, not the least interesting or the least instructive of their articles.

The year 1752 saw the birth of the first book strictly entitled to be called a General Biographical Dictionary. Abundance of special collections of lives, and particularly those of men of letters, had existed for centuries, but the 'Dictionnaire Historique portatif des Grands Hommes' of the Abbé L'Advocat was the first book which purported to comprise the lives of all persons worthy of being commemorated, and to comprise nothing else. The book is merely an abridgment of the biographical part of Moreri, with a certain number of additional lives, some taken from Bayle and Chaufepié, but with a few new names, chiefly ecclesiastics. The book (in two volumes, 8vo.) is crowded with faults of every description:—

> 'Men, measures, seasons, scenes, and facts all
> Misquoting, misstating,
> Misplacing, misdating,'

as the 'young gentleman of Oxford' wrote of the 'Memoirs of Sir Nathaniel Wraxall.' Nor could we expect anything better of a work which, as the author says in his Preface, was composed 'pendant les vacances à la campagne par manière de délassement.' Yet that the book supplied a want is proved by its numerous editions, the last so recent as 1821 (in five volumes), and by translations of it into English,[*] Italian, German, and Hungarian. Successive editors enlarged and corrected it, and the orthodoxy of its sentiments in the matter of religion preserved for it a certain reputation for the first quarter of the present century.

The 'Dictionnaire Historique littéraire et critique des hommes célèbres' of the Abbé Barral (1758, six volumes) is a work of a much higher character, displaying far more research and greater accuracy; and is compiled on a scale more proportioned to the importance of its subject. But the pronounced Jansenism of its author, which manifests itself in season and out of season, detracts from its value, and prevented its attaining the success which the learning and research of Barral and his two coadjutors deserved. It has not been unfairly described as 'Le martyrologe du Jansénisme fait par un convulsionnaire.'

Eight years after the publication of the work of Barral, a book appeared, which was destined to eclipse all its rivals, and

---

[*] The English translation, by Catherine Collignon, in four volumes, was printed at Cambridge in 1782. A second edition appeared in 1799-1801.

to reign supreme in Europe as *the* 'Biographical Dictionary' for nearly half a century. The 'Nouveau Dictionnaire Historique portatif' (four volumes, 1766), printed at Avignon, but with the rubric *Amsterdam*, so as to avoid the censorship, was the sole work of Dom Chaudon, a Benedictine of the congregation of Clugny; though—to escape the necessity of submitting it to the approval (and expurgation) of the congregation of which he was a member—his name nowhere appeared, but the title-page announced it as the work of 'une société des gens de lettres.' The book originated in that of L'Advocat, a copy of which Chaudon had corrected and annotated for his own use. The innumerable errors and the meagreness of that work, as well as the prejudice and bigotry shown in that of Barral, from which he had hoped much, determined Chaudon to give an improved 'Dictionary of Biography' to the world, and the remainder of his life was devoted to its revision and extension.

A book must be judged from the point of view of its time, its contemporaries, and its predecessors; and, so looked at, our judgment of Dom Chaudon's work will be favourable. It has neither the prolixity of Moreri, the meagreness of L'Advocat, nor the prejudices of Barral. It is marked by impartiality and good sense. The popularity of the book was great; imitations or translations appeared in English, German, and Italian; and seven editions, with successive improvements, were issued by its author. To the seventh edition—that of 1789—was added an appendix of four volumes by Delandine, which in the eighth was incorporated with the original work. In that edition the two authors' names appeared on the title-page—Chaudon consenting very unwillingly to the addition of that of Delandine—and the book has thenceforth been known as 'Chaudon et Delandine.' In 1810 the copyright was purchased by Prudhomme, and a new edition was published in twenty volumes, to which a supplemental volume was afterwards added. To this edition Chaudon contributed only some notes and corrections. But the editor was furnished with more than four thousand notes by Brotier and Mercier de St. Léger. He received the assistance of men like Haillet de Couronne, H. Grégoire, and P. H. Marron. Materials of every kind were furnished him from different quarters. But, whether from the incompetence of Prudhomme as an editor, or from the haste with which the book was hurried through the press, the edition of 1810–12 is crowded with every kind of fault possible to occur in a Biographical Dictionary. Ginguené called it 'le recueil le plus complet de quiproquos bibliographiques que l'on connaisse.' With this edition the name of 'Chaudon and Delandine' disappears, but the

the 'Dictionnaire Historique,' edited by J. D. Goigeux, in thirty volumes, 1821–1823, is in fact only a new edition of that of Chaudon and Delandine, much corrected and improved.

But Chaudon had not given universal satisfaction. Though a priest, he was not a bigot, and though he had written against the philosophy of Voltaire, he was imbued to some extent with the liberal spirit of the eighteenth century. The *parti prêtre* was alarmed at the popularity of his book, and the Jesuit Feller took the field against him in a 'Dictionnaire Historique,' the first edition of which was printed in 1781, in six volumes. Feller's method of producing his dictionary was simple enough. He took Chaudon's book, and merely altered it as much or as little as he conceived the interests of religion to require. The lives of heretics, Protestants, and infidels, are curtailed in length, their abilities are disparaged, and their merits decried; while the most insignificant Jesuit is lauded to the skies, and genius as well as virtue is shown to be the monopoly of the orthodox.

'In the dictionary of Chaudon,' writes M. Henrion, a recent editor and biographer of Feller, 'the cause of religion is not sustained in a sufficiently marked manner, dangerous novelties are not combatted. A work was needed which should supply these defects. That is what the Abbé Feller undertook to do. He has used the materials of Chaudon, making only such changes as seemed absolutely necessary. Thus, without touching the substance of the work, he has confined himself to supplying omissions, to suppressing blameable reflections, and substituting others more likely to be approved by well-disposed persons, to rectifying the judgments dictated by partiality, to making it, in short, a book which young people may read without risk, and which will be applauded by all pious persons.'

A book compiled on these principles was sure of success. Dom Chaudon and his friends indeed complained of it, and the more so, that Feller never acknowledged those obligations to Chaudon which M. Henrion admits, but put his book before the public as a new and original work, and never mentions Chaudon but to find fault or to sneer. His dictionary he calls 'le moins mauvais de ses ouvrages.' Feller's Biographical Dictionary reached thirteen editions; the last, much improved and enlarged, and edited by the Abbé Simonin, appeared so recently as 1860. It has also had the honour of translations into Italian and Dutch.

The book of Feller completes the list of the French Biographical Dictionaries of the eighteenth century, and its immediate successor was the 'Biographie Universelle.' But we may turn aside for a moment, to enquire what has been done outside France

France in the same direction. Italy and Spain had contented themselves with translations from the French. The ten folios into which Moreri had grown were translated into Spanish and printed in 1753, while both Italy and Germany had translations of L'Advocat and Chaudon. In Germany, while dictionaries of the lives of learned men, and critical or bibliographical accounts of their works abounded, some of them most excellent, witness those of Jöcher and Adelung—no important dictionary of universal biography, except the translations already referred to, has appeared; though the biographical parts of the later Conversations-Lexicon, and of the great Encyclopædias of Zedler and of Ersch and Gruber, have attained a high standard of excellence.

In England the 'Biographia Britannica,' comprising only lives of natives of Great Britain and Ireland, does not come within the scope of this paper, except indeed as the connecting link between the great 'Historical Dictionary,' already mentioned, and the 'New and General Biographical Dictionary' of 1761 (eleven volumes 8vo.). The last-named work, projected by the well-known bookseller Osborne, and published by him and others, deserves special notice as the first book in any language having the title of *Biographical Dictionary.* 'It is sometimes ascribed to Birch,' remarks Hallam, 'but I suspect Heathcote had more to do with it.' We cannot ourselves find any trace of Birch having taken any part in the compilation of the book, or indeed of the 'Biographia Britannica,' with which his name is commonly connected, though many of his lives in the great 'Historical Dictionary' clearly form the basis of the notices in the 'General Biographical Dictionary.' Ralph Heathcote certainly contributed many of the most important articles.

Not content with the humble though useful position of a book of reference, the 'New and General Biographical Dictionary' aimed at affording light and entertaining reading, as the following extract from the Preface shows:—

'And we have also been attentive to the instruction and amusement of the ladies, not only by decorating our work with the names of those who have done honour to the sex, but by making our account of others sufficiently particular to excite and gratify curiosity, and, where the subject would admit, to interest the passions, without wearying attention by minute prolixity or idle speculations.'

Editions, each with improvements, of this useful compilation, in which, as the title announces, special attention is given to lives of persons of the British and Irish nations, appeared in 1784 and 1798–1810. The latter, in fifteen volumes, was edited as to the first five by W. Tooke, and as to the last ten by Archdeacon

deacon Nares and W. Beloe, and contains three thousand four hundred lives, either re-written or wholly new. Much of the additional matter is taken from Chaudon. Early in the present century the book was entrusted to Alexander Chalmers, for a new and improved edition, which was published between 1812 and 1817, in thirty-two volumes. It is still, after sixty-five years, the standard English Biographical Dictionary, and indeed, with the exception of that of Rose, the only one, and is now as necessary a companion for every student of English literature as it was on the day of its completion. It contains many articles valuable for their accuracy and learning, though they are generally among those transferred either from the earlier editions or from some other work. Chalmers's own articles, though not without the merit which characterizes a laborious compiler, are too long and tedious for the general reader, and show neither sufficient research nor sufficient accuracy to satisfy the student. No one would read for pleasure an article by Chalmers. Moreover, they are often marked by a narrow and intolerant spirit. The book contains about nine thousand notices: of these, three thousand nine hundred and thirty-four are entirely new, and of the remainder, which constitute the articles of the preceding edition of the 'General Biographical Dictionary,' two thousand one hundred and seventy-six have been re-written.

A few years prior in date to Chalmers, and far before it in point of merit, appeared the work of Dr. Aikin (ten volumes, 4to., 1799–1815), assisted in the first volume by Dr. Enfield, and in the later ones by others of less reputation; by far the best of the lives being the work of the editor. But, unfortunately, the book does not profess to be a Dictionary of *Universal* Biography. It contains only the lives of the more eminent persons, and, for most of the purposes of a Biographical Dictionary it is therefore almost useless. But while Aikin surpasses Chalmers in learning, accuracy, and criticism, he is nearly, if not quite, as dull and heavy, and hardly less prejudiced, though in an opposite direction. We should not advise our readers to form their judgments of Churchmen from Aikin, or of Dissenters from Chalmers.

The biographical dictionary which passes under the name of Rose, having been planned by Hugh James Rose, and the first volume edited by his brother, Henry John Rose (twelve volumes, 1840–1847), is the only one which has appeared since that of Chalmers,* and is the most useful compilation of the kind which

---

* We do not forget the many meritorious and popular Biographical Dictionaries which have appeared in this country and in America during the past half-century.
'Gorton's

which we possess, containing a much larger number of names than any other English biographical dictionary. Under the earlier letters of the alphabet, more than double the number of names contained in Chalmers are to be found. In general its articles, except as to persons recently deceased, are abridgements; in the case of Englishmen, of those contained in Chalmers, and as to foreigners in the 'Biographie Universelle;' though, especially in the earlier volumes, there are a certain number of original articles of considerable length, and not devoid of merit. The Greek and Roman lives are among the best, and are carefully written. In the later volumes there is a considerable falling-off in every respect, as might be expected from the fact that exactly half the work is devoted to the letters A, B, and C. The book is composed from the orthodox and high church point of view, and abounds in moral reflections and criticisms of the most commonplace character, delivered in a pompous style, which seem inserted rather as being in accordance with the general opinion of the compilers, than as required by the subject-matter. The 'sceptical tendency and objectionable matter of much in Bayle's work,' we are told, 'renders it unfit for indiscriminate use,' and of Alfieri it is said, that 'under due control, and with religious principles, he might have been a shining light; but he is now only a beacon to warn men against his errors and his vices. His works, indeed, have their admirers, but it is chiefly from the boldness of his views and his attacks on the present state of things.' *

It was early in the present century that two French men of letters, the brothers Michaud, conceived the idea, which they subsequently successfully carried out, of a Universal Biographical Dictionary, on a far more extended scale, and on a far superior plan to any that had before appeared. For such a work the co-operation of the foremost men of letters and science then living in France was sought and obtained. The more important articles were entrusted to the most eminent men in their respective departments, and a committee was associated with MM. Michaud, to which each article was submitted for revision before being inserted in the work. The lives of naturalists and geographers were entrusted to men like Cuvier

---

'Gorton's Dictionary' is a closely packed and useful compendium. The Biographical division of the 'English Cyclopædia' contains numerous biographies of a very high degree of merit, but it does not profess to be a Universal Biographical Dictionary. Only names of men of eminence are to be found in it. For a review of this work, and other Cyclopædias, see an excellent article in the 'Quarterly Review' (vol. 113, p. 354), the writer of which was the late Joshua Watts.

* What purports to be an edition of Rose's Dictionary, printed in 1857, is simply the original impression with a new title-page.

and

and Malte Brun. Delambre and Biot undertook the mathematicians, Sylvestre de Sacy the Orientalists. The statesmen of Italy were entrusted to Sismondi, and her poets and artists to Ginguené. Guizot and Benjamin Constant wrote the lives of the public men of Germany, and Lally Tollendal and Suard those of England. And round these chiefs of the undertaking were grouped Madame de Staël, Raoul-Rochette, Boissonade, Charles de Rémusat, de Barante, Nodier, Quatremère de Quincy, and at a later period Chateaubriand, Villemain, Humboldt, Cousin, and numerous less brilliant lights.

The first volume of the 'Biographie Universelle Ancienne et Moderne' appeared in 1811. The elder Michaud soon withdrew from the direction of the work, and confined himself to writing the articles on the Crusaders and others, for which his historic studies especially qualified him; and M. Michaud *jeune* had the satisfaction of completing it in fifty-two volumes in 1828. But completion is not the word. The seventeen years during which the work had been in progress had seen the deaths of numerous men of eminence, including many of the writers in the earlier volumes. In other respects lacunæ had been noticed, and a supplement was immediately commenced. Three volumes were devoted to mythology, and twenty-nine to humanity, bringing up the work in 1857 to eighty-four volumes and to the article 'Vandamme.' Three hundred writers had co-operated with M. Michaud, and had received from him little less than half a million of francs for their articles. But the work needed consolidation, revision, and addition. With its double supplement it was inconvenient for reference.

The lives of many philosophical writers, and especially of the schoolmen, were become wholly inadequate, in view of the great advance made, both in knowledge and in scientific modes of treatment. Numerous errors required correcting, numerous lacunæ filling up; and accordingly, in 1843, the publication of a new edition commenced. M. Michaud *jeune* again undertook the office of editor, though he had disposed of the copyright to M. Thoisnier Desplaces. The founder of this great work did not live to see its completion. He died in 1858, at the age of seventy-five, having retired some time before from the editorship, in which he had been succeeded, after the twelfth volume, by M. Ernest Desplaces. To the second, as to the first edition, the most distinguished men of the time contributed; and among the names of the new writers we find Arago, Barthélemy and Geoffroy St. Hilaire, Brunet, Capefigue, Chaix d'Est-Ange, Philarète Chasles, Dupin, de Falloux, Figuier, Gerusez, Jules Janin, Paul Lacroix, Legouvé, John Lemoine, H. Martin, Mérimée,

Mérimée, Montalembert, Paulin-Paris, Quatrefages, E. Renan, Saint-Marc Girardin, Sainte-Beuve, and E. Thierry. The work was completed in 1865, in forty-five large octavo volumes, each containing as much as four or five volumes of the original edition; and M. Ernest Desplaces could say with truth, and with just pride, that the second edition of the 'Biographie Universelle' was as superior to the first, as the first was to all the biographical dictionaries that had preceded it.

But the progress of the book was neither as smooth nor as rapid as its proprietors and editors had hoped and expected. It had to fight for its very existence in one of the longest, most important, and most interesting actions at law, that have dealt with literary rights.

Hardly had the first volume of the original edition appeared, when an action was commenced against MM. Michaud by the bookseller Prudhomme, as the assignee of Dom Chaudon, who alleged that the new dictionary was a piratical imitation of his 'Dictionnaire Historique.' It was not difficult for the defendants to show that their book was wholly original, and in no respect indebted to that of Chaudon, though it would contain much matter common to both. In the forty years which followed, several imitations of the work of MM. Michaud appeared. One of these, by General Beauvais, was published in 1826, under the title of 'Dictionnaire Historique ou Biographie Universelle Classique.' A second edition was issued by the bookseller Furne in 1833, with the title 'Biographie Universelle, ou Dictionnaire Historique.' An action was forthwith commenced by MM. Michaud against Furne, with the result that judgment was given for the defendant, and the title *Biographie Universelle* was declared to be part of the public domain. In 1852 a new and more formidable rival appeared, which threatened the very existence of the Biographie Michaud. A 'Nouvelle Biographie Universelle Ancienne et Moderne depuis les temps les plus reculés' was commenced by MM. Didot, the eminent publishers, which, as in the case of all new publications, was to have all the merits without any of the defects of the Biographie Michaud. It was to be at once more extensive and more concise. It was to include all living men of eminence, as well as innumerable deceased persons worthy of note who were omitted in the older work. But it would not be half the length of the Biographie Michaud, and this would be accomplished by merely omitting superfluous details, and by substituting condensation for diffuseness. Above all it was to be cheap, wonderfully cheap, 3 fr. 50 c. the volume, which was to contain about two-thirds as much as a volume of the

the new edition of the 'Biographie Universelle,' which cost, and was well worth, 12 fr. 50 c. The MM. Didot were the proprietors of several collections of lives, of the ' Dictionnaire Encyclopédique de la France' of M. Lebas; of the ' Encyclopédie Moderne'; they had also the right of reproducing articles from the 'Encyclopédie des gens du Monde,' a work which contained many excellent biographical notices by men of acknowledged eminence. With these and articles from the 'Biographie Universelle,' and from the dictionaries of Chaudon, Feller, and others, MM. Didot calculated on publishing a complete biographical dictionary on an extended scale, without having to pay, as MM. Michaud had done, for any original articles except such as the editor, Dr. Hoefer, might himself furnish. The book came out in weekly parts, ten making a volume. In the first two volumes, which appeared in 1852 and 1853, no less than 336 articles from the 'Biographie Universelle,' mostly by men of eminence, including Cuvier, Grégoire, Delambre, B. Constant, and Maltebrun, were textually inserted in the Biographie Didot. Sixty-nine articles were appropriated with slight alterations, and a considerable number besides were clearly based on those in the 'Biographie Universelle.' Madame Thoisnier Desplaces, upon whom, by the death of her husband, the copyright of the 'Biographie Universelle' had devolved, hastened jointly with M. Michaud to appeal to the law for the protection of her rights. If MM. Didot were to be at liberty to appropriate the articles of the 'Biographie Universelle' at pleasure, her late husband in purchasing the copyright had bought nothing, and M. Michaud had sold what was not his to sell. On the 19th of May, 1852, the action of Madame Desplaces and M. Michaud, in respect of fifty-nine articles textually reproduced and twenty-two slightly altered, which appeared in the first seven numbers of the Biographie Didot—all that was then published—was brought before the tribunal of the Seine, and the further publication of the 'Biographie Universelle' in the meantime ceased. Unless the copyright could be protected, the continuance of the publication would be utter ruin to Madame Desplaces. No one would buy a book at 12 fr. 50 c. the volume, when all the cream of it could be had in another book for 3 fr. 50 c. The defence of MM. Didot was bold and simple. It was summed up in the formula, *Feci, sed jure feci*. The defendants admitted the fact of appropriation, but alleged that the Biographie Michaud was not a single work, but a collection of isolated lives by different authors, without unity, without connection, and without plan, and they claimed that on the

death

death of any author his article became public property. To MM. Michaud they gave no other position than that of publishers of the work. As to the use of the words *Biographie Universelle*, they relied on the decision in Furne's case. The tribunal of the Seine gave judgment for the defendants, and Madame Desplaces and M. Michaud forthwith appealed to the Imperial Court of Paris. They were again unsuccessful, for, though the court recognized the unity of the work, and acknowledged in MM. Michaud its originators and its editors, yet it held that each writer was to be considered as the independent author of the article to which his name was attached. Again Madame Desplaces and M. Michaud appealed, this time to the Supreme Court, the Court of Cassation. This court confirmed the judgment of the court below so far as related to the title of the book, holding that the words *Biographie Universelle* were public property; but it decided that the Biographie Michaud was a single work, and that MM. Michaud were entitled to the position and to the rights of authors of it. The decree of the Court of Paris was quashed, and the action sent to the Imperial Court of Amiens, to be heard and decided on the principles laid down in the judgment of the Court of Cassation. It was now necessary for MM. Didot to change their line of defence. After the decree of the Court of Cassation, they could no longer contend that M. Michaud was not the legal author of the 'Biographie Universelle,' and they now alleged that, having regard to the proportion which the eighty-one inculpated articles bore to the whole 'Biographie Universelle,' so small an appropriation did not amount to a '*contrefaçon.*' The court took this view, and gave judgment for the defendants. Again Madame Desplaces and M. Michaud appealed to the Court of Cassation: the decree of the Court of Amiens had the same fate as that of Paris, it was quashed, and the action sent for trial to the Imperial Court of Orleans. Here the defendants adopted a third line of defence; they alleged, in their lengthy *mémoire* in answer to the plaintiff's 'statement of claim,' that the MM. Michaud had put themselves out of court by acts of the same nature as were complained of in the defendants; that a large number of articles in the 'Biographie Universelle' had appeared also in the 'Dictionnaire' of Chaudon and Delandine; and that, as this book was anterior in point of date to the 'Biographie Universelle,' these articles must have been piratically appropriated by MM. Michaud. The answer of the plaintiffs was complete and crushing. The whole of the articles referred to in the *mémoire* of MM. Didot appeared for the first time in the edition of Chaudon and Delandine of 1821, and

and were borrowed from the 'Biographie Universelle'! The Court of Orleans held that an attempt to deceive it had been made by the defendants, and judgment on all points was given in favour of the plaintiffs. By two decrees of the Imperial Court of Orleans, of the 10th of July, 1854, and the 12th of February, 1855, MM. Didot were declared guilty of piracy (*contrefaçon*) in respect of eighty-one articles in the first six numbers of their dictionary; they were forbidden to use the title 'Biographie Universelle, *Ancienne et Moderne*,' were ordered to pay the costs of the action, and 45,200 francs damages.

For some time after the commencement of the action, MM. Didot continued to appropriate the articles of the Biographie Michaud, so that in the remainder of the first volume, and in the second volume of the Biographie Didot, no less than two hundred and seventy-seven further articles were textually reproduced, and forty-seven only colourably altered. With the commencement of the third volume MM. Didot changed the title of their book. Henceforth (until the tenth volume) it was called 'Nouvelle Biographie Universelle depuis les temps les plus reculés,' the words *ancienne et moderne* being omitted. And from this time very few articles from the 'Biographie Universelle' were textually reproduced, though it was clear that a large number were really based upon those in the older Dictionary.

In August 1854, MM. Didot announced that the entire impression of the first two volumes was exhausted (a statement to say the least of it, inaccurate) and that they were being reprinted with numerous changes and new articles. In fact, the remaining copies of the first two volumes were withdrawn and reprinted, with important alterations, under the new title, but with not a word in either volume to intimate that it was a new edition, or that it had any alterations. The articles taken from the Biographie Michaud were omitted and replaced by others.

Emboldened by the success of the first action, Madame Desplaces did not hesitate to commence a second, claiming that the new title was not less an infringement of her rights than the original one, alleging the piracy of the two hundred and seventy-seven articles reproduced, and the forty-seven colourably altered in the first editions of volumes 1–2, and of twenty-nine articles textually reproduced in volumes 3–7. The action was commenced on the 2nd of September 1854, by the seizure, on behalf of the plaintiffs, of the whole stock of volumes 1–10 of the Biographie Didot, including as well many copies of the original

original as of the new edition of the first two volumes. The tribunal of the Seine declared MM. Didot *contrefacteurs* so far as the two hundred and seventy-seven and the forty-seven articles were concerned, ordered the confiscation of the volumes containing them, and gave Madame Desplaces 300 francs damages, but acquitted MM. Didot in respect of the other charges, and held that the title 'Biographie Universelle' was common property; decided that Madame Desplaces had been wrong in seizing the remaining volumes; and ordered each party to pay half the joint costs of the action. Madame Desplaces appealed, first to the Imperial Court of Paris, and from it to the Court of Cassation; arguments of great length and of much interest, antiquarian as well as legal, were adduced on each side, as to the right to use the words Biographie Universelle; but the decree of the tribunal of the Seine was in the end upheld, except as to the 300 francs damages awarded to Madame Desplaces. This the Court of Appeal held MM. Didot were entitled to set off against the damage done to them by the illegal seizure of volumes 3–7. Thus terminated the litigation between Madame Desplaces and MM. Didot, which had lasted upwards of three years, during which time the publication of the 'Biographie Universelle' was entirely suspended. It at once re-commenced under the editorship of M. Ernest Desplaces. With the tenth volume of the Biographie Didot, the name of this work was again, and this time definitively, changed to that of the 'Nouvelle Biographie Générale.'*

The forty-fifth and last volume of the 'Biographie Universelle' was published in 1865, and the 'Nouvelle Biographie Générale' ended with its forty-sixth volume in 1866. To a comparison of these two great works, and of their respective merits and shortcomings, the greater part of the remainder of this paper will be devoted.

The 'Biographie Universelle' is in every respect greatly improved in its new edition. Numerous errors of fact, particularly as to names and dates, are corrected. A considerable number of names, to be found neither in the first edition nor in the supplement, are added, and these not only of recently deceased persons, but of those who certainly ought to have found a place in the first edition. Thirty-three new names appear in the first volume, fifteen being of persons recently

---

* At the same time new title-pages were printed for all the copies of volumes i.–ix. still in stock, and a new preface was added to volume i. Of volumes i. and ii. there are thus three varieties: (1) the original edition with the 405 articles taken from the 'Biographie Universelle'; (2) the new edition with the title 'Biographie Universelle'; (3) the same new edition, but with a fresh title-page and preface, and with 'Nouvelle Biographie Générale' for the title.

deceased.

deceased. A considerable number of articles have been in whole or in part re-written, and to a still greater number notes or appendices have been added. In the first volume, 64 articles were thus re-written or completely revised, and the editor tells us that not less than 20,000 new notices (and notes) appear in the new edition. Many of the scientific and literary men—particularly the schoolmen and others of the Middle Ages—could not have been adequately treated in the early part of this century. Many were then thought only worthy of a contemptuous notice, whom the more scientific study of later days has seen to be deserving of far different treatment; and the immense mass of documents brought to light in the first half of this century has shown many men in an altogether different light from that in which they necessarily appeared to the men of the Empire and the Restoration. An article on Abelard written in 1811, however accurately it might narrate the facts of his life, could not give an account of his opinions, his writings, or his character, which would seem adequate or satisfactory to a reader in 1850. But the most serious fault of the earlier edition has yet to be noticed. MM. Michaud, and many of the writers whom they associated with themselves, were pronounced royalists and orthodox Catholics, and in too many of the articles dealing with the men of the revolution and the empire, and with republicans and freethinkers generally, a violence and a party spirit is displayed, such as we are not surprised to find in the journals of a time when party spirit runs high, but altogether inconsistent with a work of the character and pretensions of the 'Biographie Universelle.' And none of the writers in the first edition was a more conspicuous sinner in this respect than M. Michaud *jeune*. He as well as MM. Lally-Tollendal, Suard, and de Bonald, speak with the voice of men to whom the reign of terror had been a living reality, to whom rebellion is as the sin of witchcraft, and to whom scepticism in religion and liberality in politics seem to be trees necessarily bearing as their fruit atheism, immorality, and anarchy. In the volumes which appeared after the fall of the empire (10 *et seq.*),* the violent and unfair party-spirit becomes more and more manifest. On the other hand, in the first nine volumes of the first edition the severe censorship of the empire would allow nothing but what was in harmony with

* Although volume x. bears date 1813, it was not in fact published until after the fall of the empire. The article 'Cromwell' in this volume contained passages not obscurely pointing at Napoleon, and the censure forbad its appearance without modification. The writer, M. Suard, refused to allow his name to appear to the article as modified, and the publication was delayed until the fall of the empire permitted it to appear as originally written.

the Emperor's views, and several articles, particularly those of a certain M. Durdent, seem written with a view of gratifying the personal spite of the Emperor. The life of General Acton is little more than a collection of the calumnies which the French journals had, from time to time, heaped on that well-known enemy of French influence in Italy. Of M. Durdent, it was said by one who knew him, that the same motive, which had engaged him under the Empire to heap up praise on the great man, inspired him under the Restoration to produce royalist writings marked with the same exaggerations. In the new edition, a new life of Acton is inserted.

After the fall of the empire, M. Michaud *jeune* took his revenge for the enforced curtailment of some of his articles, and the necessity of saying in others what would be agreeable to the authorities. In his remarkable article on Napoleon (first printed in the supplement to the first edition, at a time when the Napoleonic legend, fostered by Louis Philippe and M. Thiers, was entwining itself in the hearts of the French, and preparing the way for the second empire), though he has done full justice to the greatness of the Emperor's genius, to the splendour of his achievements, and to the glory which he acquired for France, he has yet set forth with unsparing truthfulness the meanness of the great man, his selfishness, his utter carelessness of truth, justice, and human suffering. He inserts at full length the perhaps exaggerated account, given by Count Waldbourg-Truchsess, of the contemptible behaviour of Napoleon on his way to Elba, and gives verbatim his will, which the Emperor's friends would gladly have forgotten. In the thirtieth volume of the second edition, printed in 1861, though the reprint of a life which had been in free circulation in France for nearly twenty years could hardly be forbidden, it was necessary to make some sacrifices to imperial susceptibilities. A few excisions were made. The narrative of Count Waldbourg-Truchsess is omitted as 'remplie de détails invraisemblables.' The will is also left out. An appendix of sixty-seven columns is devoted to an apotheosis of *l'homme*, and to a bibliography and criticism on his writings; and a running commentary on the text by M. Begin, the author of the appendix, appears at the foot of the page, flatly contradicting M. Michaud's statements wherever the reputation of the Emperor seems to require it. Notes like the following appear at every few pages, and make the article and its commentary most entertaining reading:—' L'exagération vindicative de l'écrivain écraserait peut-être la vérité si,' &c., ' Ce récit n'est pas exact,' ' C'eût été la pensée d'un fou. Jamais l'empereur n'a pu l'avoir,' 'Cette scène n'est pas vraisemblable:'

semblable;' 'Ceci est une exagération;' 'Pourquoi dénaturer ces belles paroles;' 'Ces expressions vulgaires ne sont pas croyables.' *

In the new edition much has been done to remedy the violence and party spirit displayed in the original book. The lives of Diderot, D'Alembert, and of other encyclopedists and philosophers of the eighteenth century have been in some cases modified, in others appendices have been added, and much fairer presentments of the men are given. The same course has been taken in the earlier volumes with the men of the revolution, while in the later volumes most of the lives which disfigured the original edition have completely disappeared, and have been replaced by articles leaving nothing to be desired in point of fairness or accuracy. For M. Michaud's bitter article on Robespierre, which is little better than a caricature, is substituted a life from the pen of M. Ernest Hamel, which is a model of impartiality. Unfortunately in the earlier volumes, of which M. Michaud was the editor, or in which his influence was still felt, the defect we are noticing has not entirely disappeared. At a time when orthodox churchmen in this country were beginning to see the profanity of the comparison between Charles I. and our Saviour, and when the service for the Blessed Martyr was about to be removed from the Book of Common Prayer, the editor of the second edition of the 'Biographie Universelle' finds nothing to modify in M. Lally-Tollendal's life of Charles I., the tone of which will be seen from the following passage:—'On a dit *le martyre*, on aurait pu dire la *passion* de Charles Ier. Tous les cœurs chrétiens sont d'accord avec celui de Clarendon quand on lit dans son histoire: The most execrable murder that ever was committed since that of our Blessed Saviour.'

But unfairness and party spirit are the exceptions, and not the rule. It is only in a small number of lives, transferred from the earlier edition, that these faults are found. The new lives are written with an entire absence of party spirit, and generally with conspicuous fairness. But an article originally written from a violent and party point of view can never be made satisfactory by the mere excision of certain passages, and the substitution of others, or even by corrective or explanatory notes. It is irritating to a reader who goes to a book published in 1859, expecting to find there the result of the most recent investigations, the most authentic documents, and the most accurate nar-

---

* The article Napoléon, with its notes and appendix, extends to 160 pages of the new edition, equal to 350 pages of the 'Quarterly Review.'

ratives

ratives of the life of Louis XVI., to meet with an article prefaced by a note like the following:—

'Le mérite littéraire de cet article, le nom de son auteur, nous ont fait un devoir de le conserver tel qu'il a paru dans la 1re édition de la "Biographie universelle," en supprimant toutesfois les passages qui sont le plus empreints de la violence de M. de Bonald. Il est facile de s'apercevoir que cet article a été composé à une époque de réaction contre la révolution; outre que les principes de l'absolutisme les moins déguisés y servent de *criterium* à l'appréciation des faits, les faits eux-mêmes n'y sont pas toujours exactement rapportés.'

One of two courses ought to have been adopted by the editors in the case of such an article, either to print it in full as originally written, adding corrective notes, or better still, to insert an entirely new biography. If the articles on a certain class of men were all written with a strong party bias, the evil would be less, for when once we knew of the tendency we should be on our guard against it. But we cannot read any of the long and generally able articles on the men of the Revolution, the Empire, and the Restoration, without an uneasy feeling of doubt as to whether we are reading a patched up article from the first edition, or an original article, which really gives the results of the writer's independent investigations based upon the most recent authorities.

In a book to which three hundred writers have contributed, there must necessarily be a great inequality in style, in treatment, and in merit. A large number of the more important articles, written by men of ability and learning, leave little or nothing to be desired, such as those on Fox and Fénelon by M. Villemain, on Buffon and Lavoisier by Cuvier, on Boccaccio by Ginguené, which may be considered as models for articles in a biographical dictionary. On the other hand, we sometimes find meagre and superficial notices where we should least have expected them. Those by M. Durdent are always superficial, and generally inaccurate. But the book, on the whole, has been well edited, and with one exception bears signs of that unity of treatment and sense of proportion and fitness, for which M. Michaud justly claimed credit.

Lives of men of letters form the chief and the most satisfactory part of the work, at least in the earlier volumes. Those of natives of France, Italy, and Spain, are in general excellent, and the same may be said of a large number of those of Germany, England, and other countries. Their lives are narrated with fulness and accuracy of detail, and an adequate account of their writings is given. Nor, except in the case of freethinkers,

freethinkers, is there much fault to be found on the score of unfairness. The bibliography of the work is deserving of great praise, and is due to a large extent to the labours of M. Weiss, to whom the supervision of this department in the first edition was entrusted. No book in any language contains such an amount of bibliographical information, much of it not to be found elsewhere, as the new edition of the 'Biographie Universelle.' For precise details on rare books and rare editions, indeed, we go to Brunet, to Graesse, or to Lowndes. But no single book contains lists so detailed, and on the whole so accurate, of the works of so large a number of writers, and of their principal editions. These alone would make the work invaluable, and indeed indispensable to literary students. But bibliographical information is worse than useless if it is not strictly accurate; and M. Weiss, though a born bibliographer, and possessed of an enormous fund of literary information, shared that carelessness as to accuracy in trifling matters of detail, characteristic of most of his countrymen, which detracts so much from the value of their brilliant generalizations, and makes their admirable literary skill often mislead instead of inform the unwary reader. Nowhere is this failing more mischievous than in bibliography, where accuracy is the one thing needful. It is the extreme care and accuracy of their writings, that has given such deserved pre-eminence as bibliographers to Barbier, Renouard, Quérard, and Brunet, and has placed them on so much higher a level than men greatly their superiors in point of literary skill, like Peignot, Nodier, and P. Lacroix. Unfortunately it is among the latter class of bibliographers that we must place M. Weiss. The bibliographical information contained in the 'Biographie Universelle' abounds in errors, especially of names and dates, many of them no doubt mere misprints, showing (in the first edition) only carelessness on the part of the corrector; but when reproduced in the second edition they are unpardonable, and betray great deficiencies in editorial supervision. The substitution of a 6 for a 5, or an 8 for a 3, may perhaps seem a very trifling and venial offence, but when the result is that an edition of the works of Pomponatius is given as 1625 instead of 1525, it will at once be seen how serious the error really is, and what an amount of inconvenience it may cause the reader.* That two editions of the entertaining journey of Ambrose the Camaldolese, to which he gave the title 'Hodœporicon,' are cited as printed at

---

* The error cited caused us to waste many wearisome hours searching for the book, before we came to the conclusion that no edition of 1625 existed, and that the date was a misprint for 1525.

Florence

Florence in 1431 and 1432, might be supposed to indicate a mere misprint, were it not for the fact that the book itself was not printed until 1678 or 1680, and that 1431 and 1432 are the dates of the journeys which Ambrose took. Nor is there less editorial carelessness shown in the statement that Nicolas Bourdin, who died in 1676, was a son of Jacques Bourdin, who (six lines before) is accurately stated to have died in 1567.

In the article on the celebrated Rabbi Joseph Albo, one of his works is said to have been edited by *Soncino*. The author, M. Durdent, has mistaken the name of the town so celebrated for its Hebrew press, for that of an editor; and this mistake, although noticed in the Preface to Rose's 'Biographical Dictionary' in 1840, was continued in the second edition of the 'Biographie Universelle,' printed three years later. The same book notes an error in the article 'Alberti (Cherubino),' who, though born in 1552, is called a contemporary of the celebrated artist, Marc Antonio, who died before 1550. Nor is this mistake corrected in the second edition. These are only specimens of the kind of mistake that is unfortunately frequent in the 'Biographie Universelle,' nor are blunders wanting that show something more than mere carelessness. In the sixth volume there is a short article devoted to an imaginary Gilbert Cagnati, whom the writer (M. L. M. A. Dupetit-Thouars) describes as an Italian author born at Nocera, in the kingdom of Naples, who lived about the middle of the sixteenth century, and was the author of the treatise 'De Hortorum Laudibus' (Basle, 1546), afterwards printed and inserted by Joachim Camerarius II. in his collection of treatises 'De Re Rustica.' In fact, however, the treatise 'De Hortorum Laudibus' is one of the works of Gilbert Cousin, called in Latin *Cognatus*. At the end of the book of Camerarius, 'Opuscula de Re Rustica' (Norimbergiæ, 1596) is a list of authors and treatises *de re rustica*, among which is 'Gilberti Cognati Nozerani de Hortorum Laudibus,' Basileæ apud Oporinum, 1546. The work itself, however, is not inserted in the Opuscula of Camerarius. M. Dupetit-Thouars clearly knew nothing of the book or its author, but having copied the title from the book of Camerarius, and never having heard either of Gilbert Cognatus or of Nozeray in Burgundy, and knowing there was a town of the name of Nocera in Naples, he made an unsuccessful guess, and then amplified an imaginary fact into a detailed biography.

The English department of the 'Biographie Universelle' cannot, on the whole, be considered as satisfactory. In the treatment of our sovereigns, our leading statesmen and generals, our men of science and our travellers, and a certain limited class of our men of letters of the eighteenth and nineteenth centuries, we have indeed in general nothing to complain of.* Addison and Pope, and other writers of the eighteenth century, to whom Voltaire introduced his countrymen, are amongst the best of the English biographies; but when we go further back, and particularly all through our history in that important department of literature, theology, we find an inadequacy of treatment which would be ludicrous, were it not so entirely to be expected as a matter of course. A Frenchman, unless (if we may be pardoned something like a bull) he is from Geneva or Lausanne, is, whether a Catholic or a freethinker, absolutely incapable, not only of appreciating Protestant theology, but of understanding that any intelligent human being exists to whom it can possibly be of importance or interest. Those of our divines, indeed, who were in the 'Historical Dictionary,' and whose lives were translated by Chaufepié, are treated with sufficient fulness, but the rest and our earlier men of letters generally receive but scant justice.

That the book abounds in a certain class of errors as regards English names and titles, is unfortunately a matter of course in a book written and printed on the other side of the Channel; but it is only just to say that we know of no book where these errors are so few, in proportion to the great extent of the work. An immense number which appeared in the first edition are corrected in the second; yet there still remain many, which a little care and attention would have obviated, besides errors of a more serious character, of which two specimens must suffice. In the life of Samuel Parker, Bishop of Oxford, it is stated that he was eighty-eight years of age at his death. 'His English biographers,' says the author (M. Lefebvre-Cauchy), 'state that shame and chagrin, at seeing himself despised by all right-minded people, threw him into an illness in which he died in March, 1687, in his eighty-eighth year.' Now as M. Lefebvre-Cauchy had written a few sentences before, and as is the fact, that Bishop Parker was born in 1640, he must, one would suppose, have written eighty-eight instead of forty-eight by a mere clerical error, but so careless is he that he founds upon his mistake a reason for distrusting Parker's English biographers. He thus continues, 'La passion perce évidemment dans ce récit : à un pareil âge on peut bien mourir sans les effets du chagrin.'

The 'ever memorable' John Hales is honoured with two notices, one as Ales (Jean), described as originally a Calvinist

---

* There are, however, some notable exceptions, especially in the earlier volumes. The articles Bacon, Clarendon, Cromwell, Melbourne, and Walpole (Robert), are wholly inadequate.

and afterwards a Catholic, author of a tract on Schism; the other as Hales (John), Anglican Theologian, whose works were collected and published under the title of 'Golden Remains.' Each of the notices is most inadequate. It would be easy to give a long list of the errors in English biographies, though in general not so flagrant as those relating to Bishop Parker and John Hales.

But probably few Englishmen will go to the 'Biographie Universelle' for the lives of their countrymen. If, however, any one should desire a piece of most amusing reading, we can refer him to the long and elaborate article, ten pages (equal to about twenty-two of the 'Quarterly Review,' and more than twice the amount of space devoted to Hume or Holbach) on Theodore Hook, written by M. Parisot, an enthusiastic admirer of Hook, of whom he relates many well-known stories paraphrased in a thoroughly French fashion, in order, as we suppose, to suit the received French ideas of English manners and customs. The well-known story of Hook dining at a house at which he was not invited, is related with extraordinary fulness, if not accuracy, of details. It occupies three columns, and its 'vraisemblance' to the original may be judged by the fact that Hook is represented as informing his Amphitryon that he believed the house to be that of ' Le correct et ponctuel Noll Dick Jack Smith!'*

We have said that there is one exception to the unity of treatment and sense of proportion generally to be found in the 'Biographie Universelle.' As far back as 1837, Hallam, in the preface to his 'History of Literature,' remarked, 'there seems a redundancy of modern French names; those, above all, who have even obscurely and insignificantly been connected with the history of the Revolution—a fault, if it be one, which is evidently gaining ground in the supplementary volumes.' The fault has gained enormous ground in the second edition, and has greatly increased in the later volumes. As a rule, before a Biographical Dictionary arrives at its termination, the editor, the publisher, and perhaps the subscribers, become wearied. The book is hurried to its conclusion; important names are crowded out, and those that are inserted are treated in a superficial and perfunctory manner. This, at least, is not a cha-

---

* The 'Biographie Générale' is not less complimentary to Hook, to whom it devotes a long article (eight columns), which, though written in a less absurd manner than that of M. Parisot, contains the following astounding piece of criticism : ' Parmi les romanciers de nos jours, en un mot, nous ne voyons que deux peintres exacts de la vie réelle : Théodore Hook pour la classe élevée et la classe moyenne ; Charles Dickens pour les classes populaires !' Dickens is only honoured with half a column, in which we have remarked five mistakes.

racteristic

racteristic of either edition of the 'Biographie Universelle.' The lives become more and more lengthy and elaborate, the further we advance in the alphabet. The first volume (of the new edition) has 1643 names, the fifth 1376, the twentieth 776, the fortieth 827, the forty-fourth 1100, and the forty-fifth 947.* But each volume is within a few pages of the same length. Thus, in the later volumes, every name has on the average nearly double the amount of space allowed to an article in the first. But though undoubtedly many men of the highest eminence are more adequately treated in the second half of the work than would have been the case had their names appeared in the earlier volumes, it is, unfortunately, the second, third, and fourth-rate men of the Revolution, the Empire, and the Restoration, that crowd the pages of the 'Biographie Universelle,' and have, especially in the later volumes, articles altogether disproportioned to their importance and interest. The *soi-disant* Count de Monbreuil did nothing in his whole life of the slightest interest to any human being, except rob the Queen of Westphalia of her jewels, and slap Talleyrand on the face; yet eight columns are devoted to his worthless life—as much as to Lorenzo de' Medici, and nearly twice as much as to Melanchthon! The latter, is, indeed, most inadequately treated. Forty-six columns may not be too much for Robespierre, or thirty-three for Talleyrand, but surely sixty-eight is too much for Fouché, twenty-six for Marmont, and twenty for Merlin (de Douai), when we find that Wellington has only sixteen columns, Suvaroff six, and Von Stein two and a half. In fact, in the case of French names of the eighteenth and nineteenth centuries, the editors have confused the functions of biographers and historians—two entirely distinct things. The lives of Louis XVIII., Charles X., and Louis Philippe, are histories of France during their respective reigns. Nor has the 'Biographie Universelle' escaped the tendency common to all Biographical Dictionaries, to exaggerate the importance of royal and princely personages, and to devote to them long historical articles, with hardly a single biographical detail.

But with all its shortcomings, no literary student can have any other feeling towards the 'Biographie Universelle' than that of deep admiration and gratitude. It is impossible to pursue any investigation bearing upon literary history or biography, especially of the sixteenth or seventeenth century, without having the book constantly at one's elbow; and although it is to be regretted that the authorities for so few of the lives

---

* In the case of members of the same family several names are frequently included in what at first sight looks like a single article.

are

are specifically stated, yet the articles themselves generally point to the sources for verifying their statements, correcting their errors, and amplifying their details.

Turning now to the 'Biographie Générale,' the first point which must strike every reader is the utter want of proportion in the book, and, in most of the volumes, the want of any guiding principle for the insertion or exclusion of a name, or for the length or importance of the respective articles. We have noticed as a fault in the 'Biographie Universelle' the greatly increased length of the articles in the later volumes devoted to inferior men; in the 'Biographie Générale' the fault is precisely the opposite. Of its forty-six volumes, upwards of thirty-six are devoted to the letters A—M, leaving less than ten for N—Z; and long before the middle of the book is reached, the professions with which it was commenced, as to the insertion of names, are wholly thrown aside, and the evident desire of the editor and proprietors is seen to be to bring the work to a conclusion as speedily as possible, and to omit as many names as can with any decency be omitted. The original intention was to insert, first, all the names in the 'Biographie Universelle,' secondly, a large number to be found neither in that work nor in any other Biographical Dictionary; thirdly, all living persons worthy of note. The first three volumes are devoted to the letter A, and contain more than nineteen hundred and fifty names of deceased persons, chiefly (though with some not unimportant exceptions) obscure Spaniards, Portuguese, and Orientals, omitted from the 'Biographie Universelle,' besides notices of more than one hundred persons then living. But the additions become fine by degrees and beautifully less, until at length, before the end of the work, they wholly disappear, while the later volumes do not include nearly all the names in the 'Biographie Universelle.' Of nine hundred and eighty names in the thirty-ninth volume of the 'Biographie Universelle,' five hundred and thirty-four are omitted, and of eleven hundred in the forty-fourth volume of the 'Biographie Universelle,' more than seven hundred and sixty are omitted from the 'Biographie Générale!' In fact, in the last few volumes it is useless to look for any less important name, and on nearly every page there is evidence of the strongest desire to bring the book to a close.

We have already remarked how many articles are merely abridgments or reproductions of those in the 'Biographie Universelle,' and the mistakes of the original are in many cases left uncorrected. The ridiculous blunder in the life of Joseph Albo, as to Soncino, is duly reproduced in the 'Biographie Générale,'
while

while the error as to the date of the first edition of the 'Hodœporicon' is hardly corrected by being altered from 1431 to 1451. The duplication of John Hales has not been followed by Dr. Hoefer, yet both in the name and in the details respecting *Jean Alès* we have some difficulty in recognizing the 'ever memorable;' while in the article immediately preceding, on the Scotchman Alexander Alès, we have the extraordinary statement that he must not be confounded with *his elder brother who bore the same prænomen of Alexander*, and who published the 'Expositio in xii. libros Aristotelis Metaphysicæ!' But Dr. Hoefer did not always confine himself to copying the errors of the 'Biographie Universelle.' M. Briquet has pointed out in the 'Bulletin du Bibliophile'* several errors in the articles 'Amalthée' and 'Aléandre' in the 'Biographie Universelle,' all of which have been faithfully reproduced in the 'Biographie Générale,' every other error which was possible being added concerning the relationship of the several members of the Amalteo family, besides making of Marc Antonio Amalteo two distinct persons, and devoting to him two articles. So that, as M. Briquet remarks,—

'Dans cette *farce biographique* le plus ancien des Amalthée est classé le dernier; les fils deviennent les frères de leur père et de leurs oncles; le père devient le frère cadet de son fils; le frère devient le fils aîné de son frère cadet. C'est le désordre élevé à sa plus haute puissance.'

The general editing of the book is in fact disgraceful. Of the editor, Dr. Hoefer, we know nothing, except from the laudatory article on himself which he caused to be inserted in the twenty-fourth volume, where twice as much space (nine columns) is devoted to his life as is given to Thomas Hobbes, more than is given to Madame Roland, and, to go to his contemporaries, four times as much as is devoted to Michelet, and eight times as much as is thought sufficient for the Vice-Emperor, M. Rouher. Yet M. de Bellecombe, the author of the article, informs us in a note that 'par un sentiment de modestie et de convenance, à notre avis exagéré, le directeur de la "Biographie Générale" ait cru devoir supprimer une grande partie de notre article!' But though, according to this article, he was a man of universal genius, who 'took all knowledge for his province,' he certainly does not shine as the editor of a Biographical Dictionary. Innumerable are the names, even of persons of eminence, mentioned in the book as to which we are referred to non-existing articles in other volumes.

* 12me série, p. 360.

Under the name 'Liset' is the reference 'voy. Lizet,' but no article 'Lizet' is to be found, nor does a life of this celebrated first President appear in the book. In the article 'Du Pont, sieur de Drusac,' we are referred to the article 'La Borie' for a notice of 'Arnaut de La Borie,' but no such article is to be found, the notice of La Borie being given under 'Arnaut.' For Duplessis-Bellière we are sent to 'Rougé,' but neither under that nor any other name does the life of Jacques de Rougé, Marquis Duplessis-Bellière, appear, nor any other member of that distinguished family; the only Rougé mentioned in the book, being a contemporary professor of philology in the Collège de France. In the article 'Saint-Florentin' we are referred to the article 'Vrillière' for Saint-Florentin's father Louis, but under 'Vrillière' we simply find 'voy. Saint-Florentin et la Vrillière,' but no article 'La Vrillière' is to be found. Under 'Bamboche' is the reference 'voy. Laar,' but on referring to 'Laar dit Bamboche' we find only 'voy. Laer,' and no article 'Laer' is to be found, nor does any notice of this celebrated Dutch painter appear in the book. Polydore Virgil is omitted, though under 'Virgile' we read 'voy. Polydore.' These are merely specimens out of a much larger number, which we have ourselves accidentally lighted upon, and we doubt whether there is a single volume which does not contain many references to non-existing articles.

One of the principal points, upon which the proprietors of the 'Biographie Générale' took credit to themselves for its superiority over the 'Biographie Universelle,' was, that to every life a list of the authorities would be appended; certainly a most useful feature, the absence of which deprives many of the articles of the 'Biographie Universelle' of much of their value. We have ourselves repeatedly found the greatest advantage from these lists of authorities in MM. Didot's book, in many instances when sources of information have been indicated which we might otherwise have been unable to discover without much labour and research. But unfortunately truth obliges us to add, that in many cases authorities are cited which contain no reference whatever to the persons in question. In a large number of lives, particularly those simply borrowed from the 'Biographie Universelle,' the plan seems to have been to refer to Œttinger's 'Bibliographie Biographique,' and to copy his list of authorities, adding the names of any other books the subjects of which made it seem probable that they might contain references to the person in question. We have already mentioned the invention of Gilbert Cagnati, by M. Dupetit-Thouars, in the 'Biographie Universelle.' Dr. Hoefer has simply pitchforked M. Dupetit-Thouars'

Thouars' article textually into the 'Biographie Générale,' adding however (as was his wont, in order to suggest independent research) imaginary authorities to the imaginary biography. The authorities cited in the 'Biographie Générale' for the notice of Gilbert Cagnati are, *not* the 'Biographie Universelle,' but 'Biographie Médicale,' and 'Eloy, Dict. de Médecine,' neither of which, it is needless to say, contains any mention of Gilbert Cagnati, or indeed of Gilbert Cousin or Cognatus. For the life of Nicolas Berauld as a native of Orleans, 'Les Hommes Illustres de l'Orléanais' is cited,' but no biography or notice of him is there to be found, though his name once occurs. For the great architectural Bishop of Limoges, Jean de Langeac, 'La Croix du Maine' is given as an authority, but the 'Bibliothèque Françoise' will be searched in vain for any mention of him. For the life of Gui Breslay, 'Taisand, Vies des plus célèbres jurisconsultes,' is cited, but there is neither a life nor any mention of him in that useful but inaccurate work. It is assumed that the life of every physician is in Eloy, or the 'Biographie Médicale,' and of every jurist in Taisand.

The lives of Englishmen are not in general an improvement on those in the 'Biographie Universelle.' Though upwards of a column is given to Bishop Bonner, there is not the slightest reference to the persecutions with which his name is connected, or, indeed, to any event whatever of his life during the reign of Queen Mary. But this does not appear to have arisen from any desire to screen Bonner from censure, but simply from the carelessness with which most of the lives of the less important persons are written.

But we now turn with pleasure from the shortcomings to the merits, and they are many, of the 'Biographie Générale.' And first let us say that the book seems to us to be perfectly fair, and generally free from any party spirit or party bias. Again, though most of the articles are inferior to those of the 'Biographie Universelle,' the exceptions are numerous and important. Many of the longer articles, written and signed by men of literary eminence, are in every way admirable. The articles on the Aldes, the Estiennes, Dolet, Josse Bade, and other printers, by M. Ambroise Firmin-Didot, and one or two by Gustave Brunet, are far superior to those on the same persons contained in the 'Biographie Universelle.' To the general crowding of the last few volumes, the article on Voltaire, by M. Eugène Asse, is a noteworthy exception. It extends over eighty-five columns, and is the best life of Voltaire of that length which we have met with. A certain number of other literary biographies, not perhaps equal in merit to these, but of a very high character, and

and also occasionally elaborate literary analyses, will be found throughout the work; though it is not easy to say on what principle they have been selected nor where they will be found.* Nothing but praise can be given to those (principally of men of science) written by Dr. Hoefer himself. Again, several of the series of lives of members of the same family, particularly of royal or quasi-royal houses, are of a high degree of merit. The articles on the princes of Condé and of Conti, the families of Sforza and Visconti, are instances which may be cited.

But it would be improper, in a review of the 'Biographie Générale,' to pass over without notice the most remarkable series of articles in the book—those upon Napoleon, his dynasty, and the members of his family. They occupy five hundred and thirty-eight columns† of the thirty-seventh volume, which appeared in 1863, at the time when the second empire was at the height of its glory. Apart from the internal evidence derived from the articles themselves, it is clear from the printing and the pagination that the entire series, as originally printed, has been suppressed, and that the present articles are double the original length. They are all written from the imperialist point of view, and the source of their inspiration is not far to seek. The glories, the talents, and the virtues of the imperial family, are set forth in the most glowing terms, and without even that amount of shade which a judicious portrait painter will always know when to insert. All the men are brave, and all the women (with one exception) are virtuous. The life of Prince Napoléon Jérôme is especially entertaining. Two columns are devoted to his military abilities, and the bravery which he showed in the Crimean War and the Italian campaign; and the like space is given to his oratorical distinctions. Nor is there a single word, in the nine columns occupied by his life, which affords the slightest hint of any of those traits in his character which, ten years after the downfall of the Empire, have occasioned his being left without a single friend or admirer among the party of which he is the nominal head. The single exception to the universal pæan of praise is found in the life of the Empress Marie Louise; but though her heartless conduct to her husband and son are duly censured, and her disgraceful *liaison* and subsequent marriage with her chamberlain, Count Neipperg, are duly chronicled, for some reason her third marriage is not even hinted at, and the reader is left in ignorance

---

* To the lives of Augustine and Jerome are appended long and elaborate analyses of their works (that of Augustine being extracted from Du Pin, and occupying twenty-one columns).

† Equal to 580 pages of the 'Quarterly Review.'

of the fact that the wife of the greatest captain and sovereign of the age died *Madame de Bombelles!* But the articles contain an immense fund of information respecting the Bonaparte family. With the exception of this series of articles, for which clearly the editor must not be considered as responsible, it cannot be said that any particular class of men are treated at too great length or receive undue notice. The long articles are all of persons who may fairly be said to be of exceptional merit, or to deserve exceptionally lengthy treatment. If we are to have articles of a disproportionate length, we at least prefer them to be of Augustine or Voltaire, rather than of Joseph Fouché or Dr. Francia.

Of the larger number of the less important literary men there is very little more than their names, the dates of their birth and death, and the titles of their principal works, without any of that information respecting the contents or subjects of their writings, which adds so much value to the articles in the 'Biographie Universelle.' Nor are these lists so full, or compiled with so much accuracy, as those in the 'Biographie Universelle.' In one point, however, and that of no small importance, the bibliographical information of the 'Biographie Générale' is superior to that of its rival. The titles of books written in Latin, or in any modern European language, are invariably given in the original language. In the 'Biographie Universelle' there is no fixed rule on this subject. In general, the titles of books written in English, Italian, or German, are translated into French, while those written in Latin are given in that language; but as this rule is not universally followed, it is often impossible to guess whether the title of the book is accurately given by the 'Biographie Universelle,' or in what language the book was in fact written. Another excellent feature in the 'Biographie Générale,' which may appear trifling, but which is really important, and of great convenience to the reader, is that each article begins with the date, and in most cases the place, of the birth and death of the person in question. This ought never to be omitted in a biographical dictionary. In many of the longer articles of the 'Biographie Universelle' we have to spend some time before we can discover the date of the death of the subject of the article.

We have thus noticed at some length the merits and the defects of, and the differences between, the two great biographical collections. Giving the preference in general to the 'Biographie Universelle,' we have seen that there are points, and those of no small importance, in which the 'Biographie Générale' is superior. In the letters A–M we are more likely to find any obscure name in the 'Biographie Générale,' under N–Z in the 'Biographie Universelle.' In fact, the two books are complements of each other; each is necessary for the student. But, alas! how many hundreds of names there are, which ought to be included in a biographical dictionary, which are to be found in neither! In the case of a large number of lives, the greater conciseness of the 'Biographie Générale' is an improvement. But, perhaps, this is hardly ever so in the case of literary men, where we generally seek in a biographical dictionary more details than we want in the case of great historical or political characters.

We end as we began, by saying that there is little prospect of an English universal dictionary of biography on anything like the scale of either of the two French dictionaries, still less of one upon a scale which we should now consider satisfactory, nor do we think that such a work is, on the whole, to be desired. Special biographical collections, such as those edited by Dr. W. Smith, to which we have before referred, are better for the scholar and student, while for the ordinary reader compilations like that of Rose are perhaps sufficient. We look forward with the greatest possible interest, and with some anxiety, to the new 'Dictionary of National Biography,' about to be edited by Mr. Leslie Stephen, which we hope may prove a worthy companion of the two dictionaries of National Biography now in course of publication, the 'Biographie Nationale de Belgique' and the 'Allgemeine Deutsche Biographie.'

The first question which the editor will have to decide, and certainly one of the greatest importance, is what names are to be included; and we cannot but express regret that, to judge from the tentative list of names proposed to be inserted under the letter 'A,' it is not intended to include nearly so many names as were contemplated in the 'Biographia Britannica' formerly announced by Mr. Murray under Dr. W. Smith's editorship.

'I exclude names,' Mr. Stephen has written in the 'Athenæum,' 'which are only names, because otherwise I should have to publish (amongst other things) all the parish registers. A biographical dictionary should surely consist of biographies, however brief; and this circumstance seems to me to define the point at which the province of such a dictionary divides from mere catalogues of books and lists of names. . . . I hope to have as many thousands of obscure names as possible, so long as they are not merely names. If nothing is known of John Smith except the bare fact that he published a pamphlet, he belongs, in my opinion, to the bibliographer, and not to the biographer. As soon as anything more is known of him he has some claim to a place in a biographical dictionary.'

Now

Now while we are glad to have the promise of as many thousand obscure names as possible—for these, in our judgment, form the most valuable part of a biographical dictionary—we think Mr. Stephen cannot have fully considered the effect of the rule here laid down. It would exclude the John Smiths of the sixteenth century, about whom the student wants to know something, and would include the John Smiths of the nineteenth century, about whom no one wants to know anything. Innumerable are the John Smiths of the nineteenth century, about whom there is much more known than the fact that they published pamphlets, yet whom, to judge from his tentative list, Mr. Stephen does not intend (and, in our judgment, rightly) to include in the new Dictionary. Of nearly every one of the many thousand deceased persons of this century, and of most of those of the last, who have written nothing but insignificant pamphlets, much may be known by any one who takes the trouble to enquire; yet in the tentative list many writers, not of insignificant pamphlets but of substantial books, are omitted, of whom copious biographical details exist. Indeed, when we examine this list, we are altogether at a loss to discover any principle upon which some names, which are little more than names, have been inserted, and many others which are much more than names omitted. In the printed specimen of the Dictionary is a notice of John Angus, a Dissenting minister (whose name did not appear in the tentative list), whose sole claim to distinction appears to be the publication of several funeral sermons. If any persons who in the eighteenth or nineteenth centuries have printed funeral sermons or pamphlets are to be considered merely as names, we should have thought that this worthy minister was one, and we are altogether at a loss to conceive on what principle he is inserted, unless several hundred others, of whom just as much is known, and who have published sermons just as interesting and important, are also added. We are far from complaining of the insertion of a memoir of Mr. Alchin, the late librarian of the Guildhall, and the compiler of several indices and calendars of wills, but we fail to see on what principle he is included, and innumerable other writers of more or less useful and successful books, which have appeared during the past century, are omitted.

Whether every writer of a meritorious book ought to be noticed is a question which we have not space to discuss, but we are satisfied that the point requires more consideration than Mr. Stephen has given to it, and that the rule as laid down by him in the 'Athenæum' must be withdrawn, or materially modified. Up to a certain (or uncertain) period, every one who has written the most insignificant pamphlet deserves some notice, if the Dictionary is to be of real use to the literary or historical student. If nothing more can be discovered of a John Smith who lived in the reign of Henry VII. than the fact that he wrote a pamphlet, his name and the title of his pamphlet, and the fact that nothing more can be discovered, ought to be recorded. But there may be many writers of substantial volumes in the eighteenth or nineteenth centuries, who do not deserve this—or rather who, as Mr. Stephen suggests, must be relegated to books like Lowndes, Watt, or Allibone. To include them, however briefly, would be to extend the book beyond practicable limits. The date before which every writer is entitled to a notice is not easy to fix; we should ourselves place it towards the end of the seventeenth century. The Revolution synchronizes with the commencement of an enormous increase in the publication of pamphlets and other ephemeral literature. From this time, and for a century onwards, Mr. Stephen's rule not to insert names that are only names, may be fairly applied. But from somewhere about the latter part of the eighteenth century, a different rule from that of nothing more being known about an author than the fact of publishing a book must be adopted, unless the length of the Dictionary is to be enormously extended. For this period no rule can be laid down. The editor himself must wade through the titles of innumerable worthless books and tracts, and weigh the claims of their authors to a niche in his Dictionary.

The question as to the length of the respective articles, and the maintenance of a due proportion, is one of no less difficulty. No fixed rule can be laid down, but the inconsistencies of the great French collections in this respect will at least afford suggestions of what is to be avoided. At the same time it must be borne in mind, that the length of the article ought not in every case to be proportionate to the importance or interest of the person treated of. It is not the most important persons to whom the longest and most elaborate articles should be devoted. For an account of our great writers and chief historical characters we naturally go to special biographies or literary and civil histories. Few readers turn to an article on Shakspeare or Milton in a biographical dictionary for any other purpose than that of being reminded of names and dates. Marvell and Prynne demand fuller and more elaborate treatment; while the articles on Dr. Dee and Hugh Speke should be still more nearly exhaustive.

A word of caution may be added as to modern and contemporary lives, which there is always a tendency in biographical dictionaries

dictionaries to treat at too great length, so difficult is it to have a due regard to historical perspective in painting those who are close to us—especially those to whom accidental circumstances have given a temporary and wholly factitious notoriety. Above all things, the editor must impress upon his contributors, in reference to the lives of royal, political, or military persons, that they are to write biography, and not history. What is wanted are commonplace biographical details illustrating personal character, concisely stated, duly marshalled in order, and accompanied by dates and authorities. The presentment of the person, and not military or political disquisition, is what we seek in the case of a general or statesman. We do not go to a biographical dictionary for a narrative of the campaigns of Marlborough or Wellington, or for the political history of the reign of George III., but to have the *men* and their lives and characters brought before us. So much history as is necessary for a connected view of their lives, in the briefest possible form, must indeed be stated. The reign of George III. is one of the most important in our annals, but the King's biography is comparatively uninteresting and unimportant, and requires no extended treatment. Political affairs must indeed be touched upon so far as they were affected by, or had an influence upon, his personal character, and so far as is necessary for a connected narrative of his life, but the political history of his reign would be quite out of place.

In the lives of literary men, while the account of their writings and the bibliographical information must be full and accurate, anything like elaborate and detailed criticism must be avoided, nor should any place be found for critical theories and general views such as are now so much in fashion.

Turning to the specimen of the Dictionary which has been printed, we have nothing but praise to give to the life of Addison by the editor, which occupies nine out of the fourteen pages. It is a model of what an article on a writer like Addison ought to be; it is full of details, yet clear and concise. The criticisms, though brief, are sufficient and satisfactory, and to nearly every statement is appended its authority, and a reference to the page whence it is taken. If Mr. Stephen will induce his contributors to follow this model strictly, we shall have no fear for the result so far as the lives of the more important characters are concerned. But when we come to the bibliography, and the statement of the authorities at the end of the article, we are unable to give the same measure of praise. Six collected editions of the works of Addison are enumerated, without a word to suggest which is the best, the

most

most critical, or the most nearly complete. One of the principal editions is omitted, and, strangest of all, Bohn's is simply described as a reprint of Bishop Hurd's edition, without any reference to the fact that it contains a great number of elucidatory notes, many letters never before printed, and upwards of one-fifth more matter than is in Hurd's edition. In fact, whatever shortcomings there may be in the editing, it is the most nearly complete, the most useful, and the most accurate, of any English edition of the works of Addison.* Moreover, in the list of authorities, the letters in Bohn's edition, and the life of Addison in the General Dictionary, Historical and Critical, ought to have found a place. 'It is of primary importance,' as Mr. Stephen has himself remarked in the 'Athenæum,' 'to give in all cases, and upon a uniform plan, a clear reference to the primary authorities, and in the case of literary biographies it is important to give a bibliographical notice.' But a bibliographical notice is worse than useless, unless it is the result of the writer's personal examination of the books referred to, or states where the information it purports to give is derived. Judging, however, from internal evidence, we should say that the writers of several of the articles in the specimen have not personally examined nearly all the books to which they refer, while in more than one article important primary authorities are omitted, and modern compilations alone cited.

If we have noticed what seems to us faulty, either in Mr. Stephen's design or, so far as the specimen goes, in its execution, it is with the view, before it is too late, of indicating some points which may deserve reconsideration by the editor, and of making suggestions which we believe, if adopted, would tend to enhance the value and promote the success of the book. We cannot doubt either the ability or the special qualifications of Mr. Stephen; and while we are sure that in each department of English literature and English history he will receive the assistance of those who are most competent to afford it, it will principally depend upon the editor himself whether a national biography is produced, to which Englishmen may point with pride as a monument no less worthy of the men whom it commemorates than of those by whom it was written; or whether a mere commonplace book is produced, a little better than Chalmers and Rose, and a little, or even more than a little, worse than the 'Biographie Universelle.'

---

* We say English edition, because Mr. Stephen cites an edition edited by G. W. Green, of New York, which we have not seen.

ART.

On Biography and Biographies.

THERE is probably no reason for the existence of antiquity except to instruct posterity, and it does this in two ways—either by making discoveries in science and leaving records of such discoveries for us to use, or by solving in some measure the practical problems of life. The writers of all ages have recognised the paramount importance of leaving on record a history of such partial solutions, and here we have the true motive and only justification of biography. From the Book of Exodus down to the Biographical Dictionary, literature has been mainly occupied with biography. It was the first form of literature to arise; it was the first to come to perfection; and inasmuch as the gods loved it, it died young. Though much good work has been produced in many departments of literature in modern times, we can find nothing in the department of biography to compare with that life of David, King of Israel, where each act and thought, each fault and virtue, so consistent in their inconsistency, is as comprehensible to us as if we ourselves had lived and acted so. But in these latter days a curiosity other than healthy has crept in, to serve at first as an apparent aid to the birth and growth of such records: a misbegotten zeal for bringing all the facts of a man's life into harmony with some ill-considered theory of unnaturally consistent action, helped in the work of corruption; and an unconscionable desire to force others to accept this theory bids fair to complete the work.

The biographer must be prepared to find his subject full of contradictions. "Die Welt ist voller Widerspruch," says Goethe; but nothing in the world, we may add, is so self-contradictory as man's action. We are all saints, and we are all hypocrites—heaven and earth—a mystery; and the biographer's eye must, like the poet's, glance from heaven to earth, from earth to heaven in a moment of time—must see the devil and the angel at work in the same act. Even this is only to see through a glass darkly; the motives that determine such actions must also be understood, although in the ideal biography the reader should be able to discover the motive in the act without explicit statement on the part of the biographer.

Human life may be said to be the product of the interaction of character and circumstance, which is only a more exact way of saying that our nature oscillates between good and evil. If, then, the biographer tells us truly everything of importance that a man has said or done, if he tells us also what were the outward conditions of his life, which influenced him, but over which he had on control, it seems a simple sum in subtraction to find what part of such sayings and doings was the product of the man's character; and hence we may gain some conception of the nature of the man himself.

Stated thus, the task seems simple enough, but it seems more simple than it is. For to the biographer is left the task of deciding what is important and what is not, and perhaps, after all, this is the whole problem of biography. It would be more satisfactory, if it were possible, that we should know all that a man said or did, for no action and no utterance can rightly be called unimportant; and in this sense biography is impossible. But we love to read of our fellows; and so, for our own comfort, we tell ourselves that this complete statement is unnecessary; and we hug to ourselves, with something like thankfulness, what scraps of facts are thrown to us; and we say to ourselves, with quite unfounded exultation, on reading some story that we in our wisdom think typical: "Here is a characteristic action;" and we flatter ourselves that now we know the man. But no action is characteristic of the whole man; and a patient scepticism and diligent adherence to all the facts are always required. Indeed, these two traits—love and a patient disbelief in himself—are the things most necessary for any one who would be a true biographer. There must be love, for without love there can be no sympathy, and without sympathy there can be no understanding. There must also be a patient and persistent scepticism as regards his own conclusions. The biographer must not consider any verdict on his patient's character as absolute and final; but must always hold himself in readiness to change or remodel it, on discovery of new facts that seem to open up new traits of character, or to modify the old.

But although it is fairly easy to propound general rules for biographers, it is more difficult to descend to particulars, and to see how these rules are to be applied in detail. Is the biographer to edit letters as he finds them, or is he to cut out those portions that are *unimportant* or *not characteristic?* Is he to announce theories that might explain actions, or is he merely to report the actions? How much is he to suppress? Is he to be idealistic or realistic in his treatment of the subject? Questions such as these are hard to answer, and, indeed, must be left in great part to the individual biographer. Every answer to them has its difficulties. An epigrammatic friend of mine went so far as to say: "There is no biography but autobiography; and autobiography does not exist. You bring me," he continued, "a brick from your house, and you ask me to form an opinion on the house; you bring a few shells, a few pebbles, and a bucket of salt water to one who has never seen the sea, and you ask him to appreciate Byron's Address to the Ocean." His words are, of course, unconvincing to a generation whose village debating-clubs nightly grapple with the question whether society should know all the facts of the lives of its great writers; and we must try to see whether no answer can be given to our questions.

Perhaps the best answer will be found by examining the work of some typical biographers, and seeing how they succeeded in applying to practice the universal rules of their art. We may select as fairly representative Boswell's 'Life of Johnson,' Froude's 'Life of Carlyle,' and Trevelyan's 'Life of Macaulay,' and the last, first. These three biographies, one of them admittedly the best biography known to exist, agree in one point—they were all written by personal friends of the hero. Trevelyan, being Macaulay's nephew and his intimate friend in the closing years of his life, had, of course, every opportunity of learning the virtues and the faults of Macaulay while alive, and every facility for examining his private letters and journals for information after his death. And so he has given us an excellent biography, with the requisite atmosphere of priggishness clinging to it. He has painted Macaulay well, because he was in such perfect sympathy that he understood the faults of his hero's character without knowing that they were faults. He has extenuated nothing, because to him there was nothing to extenuate; and yet his biography does not for a moment hide the blemishes in this somewhat spoiled child of this century. We find his vanity and his pedantry set down side by side with pictures of his charity and domestic love; his unwearied industry and philanthropic zeal are not more clear to us than his superficial omniscience. And through the whole biography we have the necessary dead-level of a calm prosperity and monotonous success that could afford to laugh at the world, but would not, because the world was kind to it. Even the conversation of Macaulay, which is only sparingly reported, is the ordinary conversation of respectability that is in the habit of dining well. With all its defects, the work reaches a high decree of excellence. So great is the power of perfect sympathy; so true it is that the biographer's attitude towards the hero is half the problem.

Froude's 'Life of Carlyle' suggests the answer to another of our questions—how far is a biographer justified in exhibiting the frailties and defects of those whom the world has been led to look on as heroes? The answer it suggests is one that Carlyle himself would have approved—we must have the whole man or none at all. We are not to be put off with a picture that has no shade but all sunshine; and if you present one such to us, we frankly tell you that it is unnatural, that we have no reason for believing that any such life was ever lived, and that we have every reason for believing that such a life and such a character is an impossibility.

In the case before us, even if we judge Carlyle from his own reminiscences, we find him not far from what we should expect him to be from the contents of his published works, and not unlike the portrait given us in the set biography of Froude. We find him querulous, unsympathetic, and apart—one to whom his fellow-creatures are for the most part fools—one who despises Wordsworth, pities Southey, and brutally (no other word will suffice) scoffs at Charles Lamb for the one failing which Lamb was absolutely powerless to remedy—for the hereditary taint of madness which made Lamb's life a more heroic tragedy than that of Hamlet. It is not the perfect man who calls the rest of mankind fools, and persists in calling them fools not once but often; but weaker souls who shrink from the necessary work of iconoclasm think that he who stands on a pedestal must needs be a hero, and are impotently angry at those who point to the spots on the sun.

These two biographies—of Macaulay and of Carlyle—are works concerning which various opinions may be held; concerning the third—Boswell's Johnson—there is one opinion, that if not the best possible, it is undoubtedly the best existing. It is curious to find what an excellent conception of biography Boswell had, and with what show of commonplace, and what eighteenth-century solemnity he expresses it.

"Indeed," he says, "I cannot conceive a more perfect mode of writing any man's life, than not only relating all the important events of it in their order, but interweaving what he privately wrote, and said, and thought: by which mankind are enabled, as it were, to see him live, and to 'live o'er each scene' with him, as he actually advanced through the several stages of his life. . . . I profess to write, not his panegyrick, which must be all praise; but his life—which, great and good as he was, must not be supposed to be entirely perfect. *To be as he was, is indeed subject of panegyrick enough to any man in this state of being.*"

As a matter of fact, Boswell has so succeeded in interweaving conversation and outward fact, that there is no one who can be better known than Dr. Johnson. His uncouth bearing, his savage gesticulations and mutterings, his meditatively-tentative moving of the feet in a room, which caused an old gentleman to assure him that though the room was old, the timbers were quite safe—all these are better known to us than our own mannerisms. On the other hand, his mind is as readable as an open book. His piety, his independence, his intolerance, his systematic mode of thought, are plain and intelligible to us. And all this has been accomplished because the biographer was at once an admirer and a truthful person. This, then, is the essence of biography, and the only thing needful. Without this there is no biography, but only a make-believe; with this, there cannot fail to be some picture, true at least, however imperfect.

Now that we have seen wherein lies the excellence of biographical work, we may notice briefly two species of biography that are written on false lines, and that lead us either to false conclusions, or to nothingness and mere inanity of meaningless incident. The latter form of composition is perhaps the most futile and inept mode of uttering himself that is possible to fallen man. It has been characterised by innumerable writers as "Biography fallen into anecdotage," and the high-priest of it is Isaac Disraeli. His books are the most vacuous pabulum that ever made believe to nourish the heaven-sent curiosity of much-enduring mortality. They pretend to give us some idea of the lives of various men of letters, but they give us none. The work is merely antiquarian, and has even less interest than most antiquarian studies, for all through it we feel that we are viewing the men in a false light, or more properly "no light but rather darkness visible," thick darkness that covers the land, and prevents us from seeing the highways to and fro. It is easy to see that the faults of anecdotage-biography spring from an implicit want of belief on the part of the writer in the seriousness of his subject, and a consequent failure to understand it. We may find a parallel to such work in the misbegotten and misguided efforts of one nation to understand another. The contempt of Greek for barbarian has not yet died out, only now the great middle-class of each nation believes itself the Hellenic section of the world, and all the rest outsiders. This mistaken belief is taken advantage of by some writers, and works like 'Friend Macdonald' have been known to sell. We do not complain that such works are caricatures. We complain that they have no character whatever, that nothing binds the parts together but contiguity in printed space, which, after all, is a poor substitute for a rational conception.

But while the biographer must be careful to avoid the Scylla of anecdotage, he must be no less careful to avoid the opposite danger—of setting out with a too definite conception of a man's life, into which all the facts, known and unknown, must be made to fit. It may sometimes seem to be necessary to overstate a case in order to gain a hearing for it, but any such over-statement takes away from the permanence of the work, and brings it into the dust of common-day controversy.

This species of biography, though not so bad as anecdotage, is bad enough; and when we see one, it makes us almost long for a return to dry, hard facts, into which we ourselves might put some colouring not quite false. The return to true biography must indeed be by this way of facts; and perhaps the best biographies soon will seem to be those "little lives" that open with a pedigree, and are rounded with the date of death.

BIOGRAPHY.

THE most amusing book in the language is *The Dictionary of National Biography*. If anyone doubts what appears to me to be a self-evident proposition, he has only to buy the work and to dip into it at odd moments. He must be hard to please if he is not interested in a collection of all that is known about our countrymen of all ages, including the dim personages who "flourished" in an uncertain century and the last M or N whose obituary notice is in last year's newspapers. Many volumes full of interesting anecdotes, every word of which is true, must surely fascinate every intelligent reader. As I had the fortune to be closely connected with this undertaking for some years, and was bound therefore to read every article, I ought to speak with some authority, as I can now speak with impartiality. An excellent friend of mine, who inferred that I must be overflowing with the knowledge so imbibed, asked me the other day whether I had not become a profound psychologist. Possibly I ought to have acquired what is called "a knowledge of the human heart." But, in the first place, I find that I forget all about the A's before I have got well into the C's. In the next place, the chief part of an editor's duties consists in acting as Dryasdust. Questions as to whether a date is given in the old style or the new, or as to whether two different titles refer to the same book or to two different books, or to two different modifications of the same book, cannot be said to throw much light upon problems of psychology. And, finally, to say nothing else, one has to study not life at first hand, but what has been said about lives by biographers, which is a very different thing. A study of biographies by the dozen, though it often leaves one pretty much in the dark as to the people biographized, ought perhaps to give one some views as to the art of biography. It is difficult, indeed, to say much that is true and that is not perfectly obvious about any art whatever, and I feel that the few remarks which my experience has taught me will be neither original nor profound.

Biography in the dictionary form has certain peculiarities of its own. The dictionary-maker stands in awe of Dryasdust. He must try to satisfy the genealogist and the bibliographer. He must, therefore, give a number of details which often have little bearing upon the life of his hero. It is impossible to say what minute fact may not have some incidental interest for the historian, and a good deal of dry information must be recorded which the reader for amusement must be trusted to skip. Still more has the dictionary-maker to trust to the reader to supply the flesh and blood to his dry bones. He must restrain his rhetoric and sentiment and philosophical reflection within the narrowest bounds. Our critics—it is the only fault I can find with them—sometimes do us too much honour by comparing us with literature of a more ambitious class. They take the show-lives—the Shakespeare or William the Conqueror—and ask whether they have been adequately written, and whether the writers show a sound judgment in their literary or historical theories. Now, we cannot afford to expatiate about Shakespeare: we have to make room for the less conspicuous people, about whom it is hard to get information elsewhere. The real test of the value of the book is in the adequacy of these timid and third-rate lives. Nor, again, will a reader of sense look to a dictionary to tell him (if he wants to be told) what he ought to think of Shakespeare's plays, or of William's position in the world's history. There are plenty of philosophers who will gladly supply him with ideas on those subjects. The dictionary-maker can at most give a brief indication of the opinions held by good authorities and a reference to the books where they are discussed; and, possibly, may intimate summarily his own conclusions. But to discuss or expound those conclusions at length is impossible, and the critic, if he chooses to take the article as a peg on which to hang his own theories, must not complain if it pretends to be no more than a peg.

I have given these hints because they may indicate the true nature of the problem to be solved. The dictionary-maker writes under the strictest limitations. But art, as is often observed, may show itself best under such limitations. The writer of a sonnet, if the comparison be not too ambitious, knows that his success is due to the difficulties which he has surmounted. His gems are imperishable if he has fitted his thought precisely to the prescribed form. Now, the writer of an ideal dictionary life would achieve a somewhat similar task. He would manage to say everything while apparently saying nothing; to give all the facts demanded from him; to give nothing but the facts; and yet to make the facts tell their own story. If he is not allowed to comment or to criticize, he may put the narrative so that the comment or criticism is tacitly insinuated into the mind of his reader. By skilful arrangement of his story, by condensation of the less important parts, by laying due stress on the most essential, he should set the little drama of a human life in the right point of view and reveal its most important aspects. A smart journalist knows how to beat out a single remark into a column of epigrams and illustrations. The dictionary-maker should aim at the reverse process he should coax the column of smoke back into the original vase; he should give the very pith and essence of the case, and, like the skilful advocate, appear to be simply relating a plain narrative, when he is really dictating the verdict. "Thou hast convinced me," as Rasselas says, that nobody can write such an article. That is perfectly true; but to produce such an article may be the dream of the writer, however conscious he may be that ideals are rarely attainable in this world.

I say this from the dictionary-maker's point of view; but it applies to biographers in general, and now more than ever. The modern biographer is not content to be silent when there is nothing to be said. If facts are wanting, he fills up the gap with might-have-beens. He tells us that when Robinson was born Brown was on his deathbed and Jones prime minister, and speculates upon what would have happened if they had all been contemporaries. When the poor dictionary-maker has to say briefly, is, "John Smith was educated at the grammar school of his native town" the writer of a graphic biography talks of the Renaissance and the early system of scholastic training, and Dr. Bushy and corporal punishment, and the influence of classical culture upon the human mind in general as well as upon Smith in particular. The dictionary-maker must trust that his reader will see all this between the lines; take the philosophy and the pathos for granted, and make his own picture of the small Shakespeare creeping like a snail to the Stratford school, instead of repeating the well-known paragraph which begins, "The imagination loves to dwell." When I have had to read some of these exuberant biographies I have wished that I could have had the writer under my charge for a time. Firmly, if benevolently, I would have drilled him; cut out all his fine things, condensed his sentiment by a little cold water, and squeezed his half-dozen pages into half-a-column. I have tried the experiment, and it should be recorded, for the credit of human nature, that a writer was once good enough to express gratitude for my surgery. Others mildly remonstrated; yet surely, if I did not use the knife very clumsily, the discipline was a good one. In these days, when we have decided, as it seems, that nothing is to be forgotten, two things are rapidly becoming essential—some literary condensing machine, and a system of indexing. Our knowledge, that is, requires to be concentrated and to be arranged. When I have been in the library of the British Museum I have been struck with a not wholly pleasing awe. I went one day to the manuscript-room, and there was invited to regale myself with three thick volumes of closely-written letters by the London agent of certain foreign booksellers, filled, in an illegible hand, with the smallest literary gossip of the days of George II. I extracted from it, after much pains, the name of the University at which Des Maiseaux had taken his degree, for which I hope my readers will be thankful. I went to the reading-room, and discovered there a college exercise printed in the seventeenth century at Leydon, which enabled me to reveal to an inquisitive world the name of Bernard Mandeville's father. It is bewildering to think that a lad cannot print a declamation in Holland without the thing being preserved for the benefit of Englishmen two centuries later. The mass of matter preserved on the shelves of that invaluable Museum is the externalized memory of the race. There is nothing too petty or contemptible to be preserved. When one thinks of all the records preserved up and down Europe in the archives of various States, of all the materials in private hands, of the infinitesimal portion which any reader could get through in a lifetime, and then of the enormously accelerated rate at which information is now being compiled and amassed in safe repositories, one stands aghast. If a fire should take place at the Record Office or the British Museum I would give all the strength I possess to working the engines. But if fire were a discreet element, which could be trusted to burn only the rubbish, I could find it in my heart to applaud a conflagration.

This is a digression; but it gives the reflection which is constantly before the dictionary-maker. He is a toiler among those gigantic piles of "shot rubbish" of which Carlyle complained so bitterly when he too was a slave of Dryasdust. He is trying to bring into some sort of order, alphabetical at least, the chaos of materials which is already so vast and so rapidly accumulating. To write a life is to collect the particular heap of rubbish in which his material is contained, to sift the relevant from the superincumbent mass, and then try to smelt it and cast it into its natural mould. His first operation is, of course, to take the lives already written, and to boil them down into the necessary limits. Many lives must contain as much history as biography, and of the historical aspects I do not propose to speak. The life with which I am concerned is the record of what happened to a single human being between his birth and his death; and the purpose of the narrator is to show what he was and how he came to be what he was. It is only in a few cases that these questions can be said to have been adequately treated. The most really interesting problem —that of the development of the human character—is generally the most inscrutable. If, as has been frequently said, any man

even the most commonplace, could be adequately explained ; if we
could be told with what qualities he started, and what influences
really moulded and developed them, we should have a book of un-
surpassable interest. But it is rare to find any approach to such
an account. Few facts are preserved till a man has become well-
known, and by that time his character is generally formed. Nothing
is more striking to the biographer than the rapidity with which all
possibility of satisfactory portraiture vanishes. Nobody, as Johnson
somewhere says, could write a satisfactory life of a man who had
not lived in habits of intimacy with him. Now, it is rare for a man
to preserve the intimates of his early years ; school friendships are
transitory, and schoolboys are not generally keen psychologists.
All they can generally remember is the best score made in a cricket-
match or the prize at an examination. They generally see nothing
of their schoolfellow's real life, and they are divided between the
wish to show that they recognized genius early, and the pleasure of
supporting the paradox that the genius was originally stupid. If
the father or mother or schoolmaster survive, the schoolmaster
has an eye to the merits of his school ; the father probably thought
more of the school-bills than of the boy's work ; and the mother—
was a mother. The friends who survive are generally those who
have been attracted in later years ; and even if they are keen of
penetration and of power of telling what they have perceived—both
rare qualities and frequently disjoined—they only tell us of the
finished product. The few biographies which give a really instructive
account of mental and moral growth are autobiographies. After
making obvious allowances, they are always instructive, and they
generally dwell with natural fondness upon the early years, in which
the critical process was undergone. Without such a narrative or
letters or diaries which are in some respects a better, because
a more unconscious and less modified, autobiography, the life of
a famous man is often an insoluble problem even at his death.
I could mention men whom I have known, who were known to very
wide circles, and who were survived by many contemporaries, whose
early history, except so far as the bare external facts are concerned,
must remain purely conjectural, simply because no competent
witness has survived them. Those who were in a position to know
were unobservant, or stupid, or dull, or forgetful.

We can now generally ascertain—it is a rather melancholy
reflection—all the external facts ; but whatever cannot be inferred
from them vanishes "like the smoke of the guns on a wind-swept
hill !" School registers and the like will supply us with an ample
framework of dates ; but the history of the mind and character
evaporates, and is vaguely supplied by conjecture. Do we even
remember our own history, or did we even know at the time

what was really happening to us? Some people with powerful memories seem to preserve a detailed map of the past; but in my own case, which is, I suspect, the commonest, I should be reduced to mere guessing as to my motives and the influences which affected me almost as much as though I were writing of a stranger. And yet, with all such necessary imperfections, biographies have a fascination, even when they are of the scantiest. They stimulate the imagination to realize one of the hardest of all truths to accept—that the existence of a "Hamlet" now proves that there must actually have once been a William Shakespeare. The lives written in that period, indeed, seem to leave the case almost doubtful. They are so vague, perfunctory, and unsubstantial, that we are half inclined to regard the heroes as mere phantoms, vague X's and Y's who never trod the solid earth. The actors upon the great stage of politics here, of course, come down to us with sufficient vividness. A man who has cut off other men's heads, or had his own cut off, has impressed his reality upon the world; but the mere author, philosopher, or poet, has vanished, like Aubrey's famous spirit, leaving nothing behind but a "twang" and a sweet, or perhaps, not sweet, savour. The biographers at most were content to amplify the conventional epitaph; or at times, like the excellent Izaak Walton, they wrote most charming little idylls, beautiful to read, but curiously empty of facts, and tinged with a rose-colour calculated to rouse suspicions. For some biographies the main authority is a funeral sermon; and the typical funeral sermon is one which an eloquent divine constructed out of an elaborate parallel between the characters of King David and George II. If we had only known of George the points in which he resembled the Hebrew monarch, our information would obviously have been defective. A writer to whom all readers of seventeenth-century biography often owe their fullest knowledge is Anthony à Wood, one of the most thorough and satisfactory of antiquaries. His inestimable collection is charming not only from its good workmanship within its own limits, but also for the delightful growls of disgust extracted from the old High-Church don at every mention of a Nonconformist or a Whig— especially if the wretch claims to possess any virtues. But Wood can only give, and only professes to give, data for lives, not the finished product. As time goes on we get the biography which serves as a preface to collective works. The author is haunted by the modest conviction that his readers are anxious to get at the author's own writings, and is content with pronouncing a graceful *éloge*, without defiling his elegant phrases by the earthy material of facts. Toland wrote a life of Milton, when a dozen people were extant who could have described for him the domestic life of his hero. He felt, however, that to go into such details would compromise his dignity, and leave no room for his judicious observations upon epic poetry. Of Toland himself we are told by a biographer that he was forced to leave the Court at Berlin " by an incident too ludicrous to mention." We vainly feel that we would give more for that incident than for all the other facts mentioned. This dignified style survived till the end of the last century, and we have a grudge against Dugald Stewart, otherwise an excellent person, for writing a life of Adam Smith in the spirit of a continuous rebuff to impertinent curiosity. The main purpose of such biographies seems to be to prevent posterity from knowing anything about a man which they could not discover from other sources. There is a biography famous for not giving a single date, and an autobiography in which the hero apologizes for once using the word " I." The biographer of modern times may be often indiscreet in his revelations; but so far as the interest of the book goes the opposite pole is certainly the most repulsive. We want the man in his ordinary dress, if not stripped naked; and these dignified persons will only show him in a full-bottomed wig and a professor's robes. Johnson changed all this as author and subject of biography.

In the *Lives of the Poets*, we have at least a terse record of the essential facts seen through a medium to shrewd masculine observation. The writer is really interested in life, not simply recording dates or taking a text for exhibiting his own skill in perorating. He is investigating character, and, with obvious limitations, investigating it with remarkable insight. Of the immortal Boswell, it is happily needless to speak. Since his book, no writer has been at a loss for a model; and many most delightful books are its descendants, though none has eclipsed its ancestor. Boswell founded biography in England as much as Gibbon founded history and Adam Smith political economy. He produces that effect of which Carlyle often made such powerful use, the sudden thrill which comes to us when we find ourselves in direct communication with human feeling in the arid wastes of conventional history; when we perceive that a real voice is speaking out of " the dark backward and abysm " of the past, and a little island of light, with moving and feeling figures, still standing out amidst the gathering shades of oblivion. Perhaps there are no books in which the imagination is so often stimulated in that way as in Carlyle's own *Cromwell* and Spedding's *Bacon*. The *Bacon* is to me a singularly attractive book, to which, indeed, the only objection is that it is not properly a book, but a collection of documents. It is therefore the mass of raw material from which I hope that a book may some day be constructed. Such a book might be a masterpiece of applied psychology. It would give the portrait of a man of marvellous and most versatile intellect, full of the noblest ambitions and the most extensive sympathies, combined with all the weaknesses which we are accustomed to class as "human nature." Spedding's hero-worship led him to apologize for all Bacon's errors; and, though the very ingenuity of the pretexts is characteristic both of the hero and his biographer, we are sensible that a more disengaged attitude would have enabled Spedding to produce a more genuine portrait. He has provoked later writers to air their virtuous indignation a little too freely. We want the writer capable of developing the character in the Shakespearian spirit; showing the facts with absolute impartiality, not displaying his moral sense, if that be really the way to display a moral sense, by blackening the devil and whitening the angel. We should then have a pendant to Hamlet with the advantage of reality; the true state of a man of the highest genius, but without enough moral ballast for his vast spread of intellectual sail.

This case represents the great crux of the biographer. Is he to give a pure narrative of his own, or to let his hero talk to us face to face? In some cases the raw material is better than any comment. No biographer could supersede the necessity of reading Pepys' own diary. The effect is only producible by following Pepys to his own closet and overhearing all his most intimate confessions to himself. Indeed, if we had time, we should generally get a far more perfect picture by studying all a man's papers than by reading his life. But that means that we are to cook our own dinners and write the life for ourselves. I say nothing of the vast rubbish heaps which would have to be sifted. Many such collections, again, Walpole's letters, for example, are really interesting for the side-lights thrown upon other persons or the general illustrations of the period; and a life which only showed us Walpole himself would miss the interest of all that Walpole saw. Everything must, of course, depend on the particular circumstances, the nature of the hero's career, and of the materials which he has left. The life proper, however, is that in which the main interest is the development of the man's own character and fortunes. Now, as a fairly working principle, I should say that the main purpose of the writer should be the construction of an autobiography. Boswell's felicity in being able to make Johnson talk to us is, of course, almost unique. Only the rarest combination of circumstances can produce anything approaching to such material. But the next best thing is the autobiography contained in letters. The question of whether a really satisfactory life can be written is essentially the question of whether letters have been preserved. It is a general belief that the art of letter-writing has been killed by the penny post. Your correspondent, you know, will pick up all the gossip from the papers, and a Horace Walpole is therefore an anachronism. Cowper's delightful letters, again, presuppose an amount of leisure, a power of sitting down quietly to compose playful nothings for a friend, which has now almost vanished. Your author can put his good things, if he has any, to better account. But the general statement is, I think, disputable. The letters of the day must always appear to be bad, simply because few are yet published. Our grandsons will first be in a position to judge of us. Many of the best letters of the last generation were written by busy men, already exposed to many of our difficulties, and yet were, I think, equal to any of the past. I do not know a much pleasanter course of reading than is to be found in the letters of Scott, Southey, Byron, Macaulay and Carlyle, to mention no others. The very fact that we have not to act as newswriters often gives us a better opportunity of expressing our feelings about the events of the day. We may take for granted that our correspondent has read the debates, and may confine ourselves to blessing or cursing Mr. Gladstone or Mr. Balfour. One can hardly bless or curse without displaying one's own nature. While letters become less important as records of events, they preserve their full significance as revelations of character; and that is what the biographer chiefly requires. It should therefore be regarded as a duty (it is one which I systematically transgress) to keep all letters written by a possible biographee; and I think that we shall be surprised, not that they have so little merit, but rather that the amount of passion and feeling with which they are throbbing has allowed them to lie quiet in their dusty receptacles.

Be this as it may, letters in the main are the one essential to a thoroughly satisfactory life. From them, in nine cases out of ten, is to be drawn all that gives it real vividness of colouring. Everybody knows the strange sensation of turning over an old bundle of letters, written in the distant days when you were at college, or falling in love. Your memory has ever since been letting facts drop, and remoulding others, and colouring the whole with a strangely delusive mist. You have unconsciously given yourself credit for deliberately intending what came about by mere accident; and, in giving up youthful opinions, have come to forget that you ever held them. I found out once from an old letter that I had taken a decision, of great importance for me, upon grounds which I had utterly forgotten, and of which I had unconsciously devised a totally different (and very creditable) account. I burnt the letter and forgot its contents, and I now only know that my own story of my own life is somehow altogether wrong. A writer of an interesting autobiography tells us how he refused a certain office from a chivalrous motive; and then adds, with charming candour, that, though he has always told the story in this way, he has found from a contemporary letter that one of his motives was certain natural but not chivalrous fears as to his own health. His memory had kept only the agreeable recollection. Such incidents represent the ease with which the common legend of a life grows up; and the sole corrective for good or for bad is the contemporary document. To know what a man said at the moment is of primary importance, even if he was lying or acting a part. The letter which shows what a man wished to appear generally tells a good deal as to what he was. Even if we take a hero in active life, one of Nelson's letters or phrases shows more of the man than the clearest narrative of the battle of Trafalgar. His signals enlighten us as much as they appealed to his crews, and show what lay behind the skilful tactics and the heroic daring. A biographer has, of course, to lay down his framework, to settle all the dates and the skeleton of facts; but to breathe real life into it he must put us into direct communication with the man himself; not tell us simply where he was or what he was seen to do, but put him at one end of a literary telephone and the reader at the other. The author should, as often as possible, be merely the conducting wire. Some biographies are partly intended to show the merits of the biographer; but even the most undeniable hero-worship is often self-defeating. The writer shows his zeal for a friend's memory by treating him as the antiquaries treat Shakespeare. It is pardonable, in our dearth of information about Shakespeare, that, no real biography being possible, we should hunt up all the trivial details which are still accessible. We cannot know what he thought of his wife or his tragedies, or what realities, if any realities, are indicated by the sonnets; and we may therefore be thankful for a beggarly account of facts from a few legal documents and registers. But when a man's memory is still fresh and vivid, when the really essential documents are at hand, biographers display their zeal too often by preserving what would be useful only in the absence of the genuine article. There is some interest now in reading Goldsmith's tailors' bills and noting the famous bloom-coloured garment; but a biographer need not infer that the tailors' bills of his own hero should also be published at length. We have to learn the art of forgetting—of suppressing all the multitudinous details which threaten to overburthen the human memory. Our aim should be to present the human soul, not all its irrelevant bodily trappings. The last new terror of life is the habit of "reminiscing." A gentleman will write a page to tell us that he once saw Carlyle get into an omnibus; and the conscientious biographer of the future will think it a duty to add this fact to his exhaustive museum.

The ideal biographer should in the first place write of some one who is thoroughly sympathetic to him. Excessive admiration, though a fault, is a fault on the right side. As Arbuthnot observes in the Recipe for an Epic Poem, the fire is apt to cool down wonderfully when it is spread on paper. Readers will make deductions enough in any case; and nothing can compensate for a want of enthusiasm about your subject. He should then consider how much space his hero undeniably deserves, divide that by two (to make a modest denominator), and let nothing in the world tempt him to exceed the narrower limits. Sam Weller's definition of good letter-writing applies equally to biography. The reader should ask for more and should not get it. The scrapings and remnants of a man's life should be charitably left to the harmless race of bookmakers, as we give our crumbs to the sparrows in winter. If there are any incidental facts with which the hero is connected, but which have no bearing upon his character, consign them to an appendix or put them into notes. I have myself a prejudice against notes, and think that a biography should be as independent of such appendages as a new poem. But there are people, perhaps, of better taste than mine, who like such trimmings, and have a fancy for trifling with them in the intervals of reading. The book itself should, I hold, be a portrait in which not a single touch should be admitted which is not relevant to the purpose of producing a speaking likeness. The biographer should sternly confine himself to his functions as introducer; and should give no more discussion than is clearly necessary for making the book an independent whole. A little analysis of motive may be necessary here and there: when, for example, your hero has put his hand in somebody's pocket and you have to demonstrate that his conduct was due to sheer absence of mind. But you must always remember that a single concrete fact, or a saying into which a man has put his whole soul, is worth pages of psychological analysis. We may argue till Doomsday about Swift's character: his single phrase about " dying like a poisoned rat in a hole " tells us more than all the commentators. The book should be the man himself speaking or acting, and nothing but the man. It should be such a portrait as reveals the essence of character; and the writer who gives anything that does not tell upon the general effect is like the portrait-painter who allows the chairs and tables, or even the coat and cravat, to distract attention from the face. The really significant anecdote is often all that survives of a life; and such anecdotes must be made to tell properly, instead of being hidden away in a wilderness of the commonplace; they should be a focus of interest, instead of a fallible extract for a book of miscellanies. How much would be lost of Johnson if we suppress the incident of the penance at Uttoxeter! It is such incidents that in books, as often in life, suddenly reveal to us whole regions of sentiment but never rise to the surface in the ordinary routine of our day. Authors of biographies come to praise Cæsar, not to bury him; but too often the burial, under a mass of irrelevance, is all that they really achieve. It requires, indeed, a fine tact to know what is in fact essential. A dexterous use of trivialities often gives a certain reality to the whole. St. Paul's cloak at Troas, I fancy, has often interested readers by a suggestion of certain human realities; though commentators hesitate about its inspiration of the allusion. Mason, who deserves credit for being the first (or one of the first) to see what use could be made of letters, thought himself at liberty to manipulate Gray's correspondence so as to make it suit his notions of literary art. The stricter canons of later times have led us to condemn the falsification of facts which was involved. But too many modern authors seem to think that Mason's fault consisted not in attributing to Gray things which he did not write, but in omitting anything that he did write. Mason would have been fully justified in making a selection, with a clear statement that it was a selection. Even so admirable a letter-writer as Gray wrote of necessity a good deal which the world could perfectly well spare. In these days many men write several volumes annually, of which nine-tenths is insignificant, and the remainder consists in great part of repetitions. To choose what is characteristic, with just enough of the trifling matter in which it is embedded to make it natural; to avoid the impression that the writer was always at the highest point of tension, is the problem. I wish that more writers achieved the solution.

Every life, even the life of Dr. Parr, has its interest. We want to know what was under the famous wig. Many modern lives are especially charming in spite of excesses; and in the briefest and driest of dictionary lives I have always found something worth reading. I have only ventured a mild protest against a weakness which naturally grows upon us. My protest comes simply to suggesting that a biography should again be considered as a work of art; the aim should be the revelation, and, as much as possible, the self-revelation, of a character. Everything not strictly relevant to that purpose should be put aside. Some of our ancestors were so anxious to be artistic that they wrote mere novels and mere essays, with occasional allusions to the chief events of their hero's life. We are too apt to fall into the opposite error of simply tumbling out all the materials, valuable or worthless, upon which we can lay our hands; and making even of a life, which has a most natural and obvious principle of unity, a chaotic jumble of incoherent information. The ideal of such writers seems to be a blue-book in which all the evidence bearing upon the subject can be piled like a huge prehistoric cairn over the remains of the deceased, with no more apparent order and constructive purpose than the laws of gravitation enforce spontaneously. Let us have neither the blue-book nor the funeral oration, but something, with a beginning, middle, and end, which can cheat us for the time into the belief that we are really in presence of a living contemporary.

LESLIE STEPHEN.

CANDOUR IN BIOGRAPHY

"PUBLISH everything. To suppress is to falsify history. The frank, manly, honest, straightforward biographer knows that he would do small service to the character he is portraying by omitting anything. The timid or cunning friends who ask that documents should be suppressed are calling on the biographer to be untruthful. If I bowdlerise, I shall idealise and give a false picture. I will brave the anger of surviving friends. I will have the courage to speak out." This and a great deal more of the same quality is (in effect) what we have been hearing during the past six weeks in defence of a recently published biography. The biography itself, though unquestionably a vivid and graphic work, is, I believe, open to criticism, which it is gradually receiving, of a kind that would carry us far beyond the considerations above alluded to. But as these considerations have a force of their own, and open a question interesting beyond the special occasion, I shall attempt to make a few suggestions on the theory of biography which they imply. I will examine the theory on its own merits and without reference to any existing exemplification of its possible consequences.

I begin by entirely admitting that the careful student who wishes to form an accurate judgment of a given character should see the whole available evidence. The suppressions of the "astute" or the "timid" are so far prejudicial to perfect truth and accuracy. I go a step further, and do not care to dispute that, apart from letters unintelligible or misleading without explanation of their circumstances, the public may, in the long run, form a truer impression of a man from a very liberal publication of his letters. No doubt the judgment of the public is far more superficial and liable to bias than that of those deeply interested in forming a true judgment. But in the long run the evidence will be sifted by the more careful students, and their verdict will obtain with the majority.

Here, be it observed, a more or less true impression may be gained at some cost. Feelings may be hurt; failings may be brought into prominence, which friends would prefer to forget; faults may be placed in such relief as to give quite an erroneous impression—from the accidental preservation of an undue proportion of letters in which they are vividly disclosed. Still, if choice is to be made between two inaccurate versions of a man's character, one due to the suppression of letters in which faults are exhibited, the other to their over-free publication, the less pleasant is likely to be the nearer to the truth. Whether, having regard to the sacredness of a dead man's reputation, it is right to give the world what is slightly unjust rather than what is considerably too favourable is a further question.

Be this as it may, the biography of a man is on an entirely different footing from the mere publication of his remains. It is not a collection of documents, but a narrative, illustrated by documents. The process of sifting the evidence is supposed to have been already gone through by the biographer. The reader takes him as a guide. He knows that the publication of *all* documents is an impossibility. No biography could be endurable which attempted it. Selection there must have been; and he trusts to the biographer's judgment, to his personal knowledge of his subject, to his opportunities of seeing *all* the evidence, that the selection has so been made as to give the various elements of the character justly. The reader does not, in the first instance, sit as a judge or sift critically. He knows that material for so doing is largely inaccessible to him. He takes in the character as it is depicted by the biographer, with the aid of the materials of his choice.

And the writer obviously chooses from his mass of material that which will exhibit the conception of the character which he has been led to entertain by the conscientious study of *all* the evidence available. Two biographers who have formed different conceptions would not choose the same material. If Carlyle and Macaulay had adhered to their respective estimates of Boswell, after reading all his papers and letters; and if each had then proceeded to write the life of Boswell, the letters which would strike each as characteristic would be largely different. To one writer he was a toadying busybody, with a touch of reverence, to the other a reverent disciple with an element of the prying busybody. Both many of the letters chosen and the suggestion in the text of their relative significance would differ accordingly. And the impression left on the reader—who, be it ever remembered, does not study the matter as a critic at first, but takes in the general effect of the book as a whole—is likely to be determined by the biographer's own **judgment.**

In other words, a biography is *not* primarily an accumulation of evidence. It is a picture.

Now nothing is more striking in painting a likeness than the minute changes which may alter the whole expression. One finishing touch is added to an excellent picture. The casual observer may still say, "Like, very like. The long nose, the lanky limbs, the big eyes—just what I remember." But the intimate friend groans and says, "That line has spoilt the whole picture. It gives a sinister look which tells of a wholly different nature."

This may happen from a momentary lapse in the painter's art. But if so minute a change has so considerable an effect, how extensive must be the powers of the caricaturist, whose aim it is to paint an unmistakable likeness, which shall nevertheless have certain features so exaggerated as to produce a ridiculous result. His art consists in delineating what is true, but out of proportion. He fascinates by his vividness, and it is often waste of time in the ordinary onlooker to hunt out the secret of the false impression produced. Every feature can be defended as corresponding with the original. And it is an endless task to trace in detail the numerous changes in relative proportion which in combination produce so startling an effect. No better caricatures are made than by the mechanical process of reflecting a figure in a convex or concave mirror. Here the laws of nature ensure a real correspondence between the reflection and the object reflected. And yet a comparison between the two reflections will show what absolutely opposite effects can be produced from the same "material" by the reversal of its proportions.

It is obvious that a similar result may be obtained in biographical narration. All human characters are made up of the same primary affections and passions; just as all human faces have eyes, nose, mouth, and chin. It is in minute varieties of form and in the proportion they bear to one another that the difference lies. And here is the opportunity for the biographical caricaturist. Turn a man's occasional weakness into a besetting sin, by accumulating instances of it without reminding the reader that five occasions may be spread over fifteen years; depict an odd mannerism as though it were of the essence of his manner; dwell on three instances of resentment and leave barely described twenty cases of generosity—this is the kind of treatment which may manufacture from true items of evidence a grotesquely false representation of a man, both of his bearing and of his character.

And there is another tempting method of caricature. It used at one time to be the fashion in schoolroom histories to make the characters embodiments of some leading quality, of some characteristic marked out, it may be, beforehand, by political or religious prejudice. Becket has been the proud and ambitious Churchman; Queen Elizabeth has been Good Queen Bess; Mary, Bloody Mary. And on the other side Luther has been little more than an insincere sensualist.

A biography on such broad lines would carry its inaccuracy on the face of it. But the temptation remains to make one quality the characteristic to which all others are subordinate. And this is a common means of effective caricature either in painting or in writing. The Jew is caricatured as being the embodiment of a nose. The vacant fop may be typified by want of chin. And in literature it is often tempting to give the typical miser, the typical spendthrift, the typical hypocrite. To do so enables the author to be more graphic and leave a more definite impression on the reader's mind than by observing the true proportions and giving fully the complex web of human character. You may even give forcibly a perfectly true aspect. But such pictures as a whole are utterly untrue to the original. They stand out in the memory as Dickens's Harold Skimpole, or Jingle, or Fagin, or Pecksniff, or Micawber, as vivid and never-to-be-forgotten sketches of certain aspects of men who, if they ever lived, were something so much more, that the sketches are not real representations at all.

A caricaturist, then, seizes true aspects and develops them out of proportion. A literary caricaturist does the same for some salient features of character, or external mannerism in a creation of his own. The biographical caricaturist does it for the subject of his biography. And as Dickens was all the more effective because, as his friends tell us, he used in real life only to see the peculiarities he depicted, and to be so fascinated by them as to neglect looking further, so the biographical caricaturist is the more vivid and effective if he writes with conviction, if he sees in the character he is describing almost exclusively the peculiarities he is led to dwell on and to depict out of proportion. He gives the man as he sees him; instinctively selects material illustrative of the aspect which fascinates him by attraction or repulsion; interprets everything by the leading feature; makes a Macchiavelli, or a Mephistopheles, or an Iago, of one who had in reality many human qualities very evenly balanced.

In fact, he commits precisely the same offence against true art as the idealising biographer, with the addition of an offence against kindliness

The idealiser takes the good traits, chooses instinctively by preference material illustrative of them, neglects weaknesses or faults. The other takes the special characteristics which have amused or struck him; notes a trace of them in every letter he prints; seizes with delight and places in boldest relief such documents as really bring these characteristics out; achieves a result similar to that of the born caricaturist in art, who has from the first *seen* in his subject mainly suggestions of the giraffe, or the peacock, or the hawk; who concentrates his attention on the features to which such suggestion has been due—the prominent nose or chin, the long neck, the strut, the lanky legs—develops them with fascinated amusement, until the other features appear to have scarcely any connexion with the general character of the face—to be mere appendages, or a necessary background for the significant excrescence. The conviction grows upon the artist that the features which have struck him are the key to the whole face, that he is more and more inclined to treat reduction to proportion as suppression of truth. He defends his sketch with perverse ingenuity. He has done full justice to the other features, he declares. He enlarges on their beauty and significance, though he has, in point of fact, traced them hastily and faintly in the actual picture. He will not reduce by a hundredth part of an inch the uncomely mouth and chin which he has made so large and distinct. They are there in the original man, and on no account will he rob his picture of its realistic details which he has so carefully elaborated. And the chief offence against accuracy being a change of proportion, it is waste of time to argue with him in detail. The inaccuracy cannot be adequately measured in words or figures. No broad statement can be commensurate with the far-reaching error. A tenth of an inch too much here and too little there is only in all two tenths; the faint colouring or blurred outline elsewhere cannot be described in its exact degree; yet the untrue effect of the whole is grotesque.

All this holds good of biography. The caricature, which is due mainly to a one-sided view of the character, held with conviction, is likely to be at once the most vivid and the most misleading. A memoir of Dr. Johnson is, we will suppose, to be written, shortly after his death. The writer who undertakes to deal with his remains and write his life (Boswell by hypothesis being non-existent) has barely known Johnson. The only time he met him he was the worse for liquor, and was extremely rude to one or two of the writer's friends. He has adopted

Horace Walpole's estimate of Johnson, that "he may be a very good man at bottom, but is a most disagreeable man at top." The sight of him with his swollen veins after excess in eating and drinking has made an indelible impression. Of his brilliant conversation he knows only by hearsay. He does not deny or doubt it. But all he heard and saw was rudeness obviously joined with drunkenness. He reads Johnson's papers and diaries, noting as most significant the confessions of excess in eating and drinking, the slothfulness, the other faults liberally owned to. The picture takes shape and grows vivid in his own mind. " Here is a man who, from his great talent and reputation, has been idealised by his friends. I have no such prepossession. I will depict the man as I saw him myself. I will extenuate nothing." And the writer is as good as his word. He gives the picture of a drunken sot, an uncouth bear, rude to every one, hardly human, without sense of propriety. He does not deny that Johnson reformed and gave up drink, that there were better traits in his character; nay, having read the diaries and letters, he says that the character was in some respects a noble one—when he was sober. But such admissions are addenda and appendices. The book is, on the whole, a protest, full of righteous indignation, against idealisation. It is a picture "of the man as I saw him, as I knew him." It is not the Johnson whose piercing perceptions, vigour of mind, moral elevation of judgment, wonderful brilliance and wide information, commanding force of will and intellect, have made us almost forget that such a scene as impressed this biographer may have really occurred. It is a picture drawn from that one evil hour, by one to whom that evil hour is a living fact, and the rest a matter of hearsay or reading.

The friend of Johnson is indignant. "Where," he asks, "is Johnson's piety?" The author triumphantly shows in a footnote the words "in spite of his religious feeling." "Where is his constant charity?" The author has set down twenty lines in the seven hundredth page of Vol. II which give a long eulogium of his charity and goodness of heart. "But you represent him as unkind in the great bulk of the text, and even in this passage you do not convince the reader that you believe in his kindness, or give instances of it." Here, indignation is the effectual retort: "When I acknowledge the faults of the man I am accused of telling lies, yet when I speak in admiration of him I am told that I do not say enough. Because I do not give a set of goody-goody stories suitable for a saint's life, I do not satisfy you." "How about his tender love for his wife?" Two whole pages on it in the seventeenth appendix.

"I had not observed these pages. Still, the general effect is contrary to the drift of such passages. You do not give his good qualities due proportion. Take, for example, his real sense of the fitness of things, quite inconsistent with this picture of a mere boor—take his interview with George III, his visit to the Duke of Argyll?" Five pages, including both episodes, in the twenty-seventh appendix. The biographer here becomes effective and even triumphant. "False proportion," he exclaims, "is now your criticism. How could I emphasise such a quality more than by concentrating the instances of it, collecting them together and giving it as a salient feature in his character? The fact is you want me to suppress his excesses and sottishness. This I will never do. His was a noble character and will not be served by such unworthy subterfuges. He was a downright and truthful man, and would be the last to sanction such suppressions himself."

We have our Boswell, and such a book would do Johnson no harm. But had it given to Englishmen their first idea of Johnson, I venture to say that it might have taken years for the proportions to be set right— for the *evidence* in the book itself to have corrected the *picture* in the book. Appendices seventeen and twenty-seven would eventually be reached by some literary Columbus, would be enlarged upon in their bearing on the rest. A fresh key would be thereby supplied to letters hitherto read for their incidental illustrations of blunt rudeness. Confirmation of the new view of Johnson would come from the book itself, read under the influence of this new suggestion. Further confirmation would be given by the anecdotes and letters supplied by surviving friends. The current of opinion would be changed, and the secret of the one-sided biography analysed.

But, meanwhile, the unpleasant picture of the original biographer may have been reproduced by reviewers without the favourable admissions which even his own text supplied, to qualify the painful effect of the whole; and for a generation Johnson would have lived for the popular mind a vivid figure, painful to his surviving friends from the very authenticity of the anecdotes against him so carefully collected, and the rude letters preserved. The picture would remain as the true Dr. Johnson, whom his friends had invested with a halo which the evidence produced had for ever removed.

I will only add that, such being the power of the biographer from his own erroneous or prejudiced judgment to turn the picture derivable from a man's writings into a caricature, in which the proportions are distorted, it has naturally been the custom to leave private papers to be dealt with by a friendly hand. To obtain a true likeness is difficult. It is nearly impossible that one who is not a friend should so far understand those remarkable traits which make a man worth writing about as to execute a true likeness. And though many a friend will give an idealised portrait, it is certainly juster to the dead that the selection and description should be carried out on the principle of illustrating good qualities at the cost of giving insufficient space to bad, than of illustrating faults in such lengthy detail as to leave little space for anything else. The latter method can give no real picture of those qualities but for which the biography should not be written at all. Neither course is satisfactory; but if omissions are to be called "suppressions," and to be regarded as uncandid, it is hard to understand how a biography is more candid which goes on the principle of omitting nothing which tells against a man, than on that of leaving nothing unsaid which would tell in his favour. Luckily the latter class is the commoner. The fault of ignoring weak points is popularly criticised; while that of giving them the most prominent place is less commonly considered, because fortunately we have not yet reached the time when many persons are ready to publish the remains of a good or eminent man, without feeling before all things interested in depicting those qualities to which his goodness or eminence has been due.

WILFRID WARD.

ON THE ETHICS OF SUPPRESSION IN BIOGRAPHY

In his *Historical Sketches*, Cardinal Newman wrote as follows in reference to omissions in great histories :

> Here another great subject opens upon us, when I ought to be bringing these remarks to an end; I mean the endemic perennial fidget which possesses us about giving scandal; facts are omitted in great histories, or glosses are put on memorable acts, because they are thought not edifying, whereas of all scandals such omissions, such glosses are the greatest.
>
> But I am getting far more argumentative than I thought to be when I began, so I lay my pen down and retire into myself. (Vol. ii. p. 231.)

Cardinal Newman in his own person had a painful experience of the effects produced by the 'endemic perennial fidget' which he so aptly describes. They, who in his day managed Catholic affairs in England and at Rome for a long period of years, were possessed by this endemic fidget in regard to John Henry Newman himself. It broke out by fits and starts. Now, it was feared lest the illustrious Oratorian, by making admissions imposed upon him by a sense of justice and love of truth, or by accepting documents which, though impugned, he knew to be authentic, or by refusing to put the required glosses on historical facts, might give scandal to Protestants. Now, lest scandal to Protestants might be given by independence of judgment in criticising, on occasions, the policy pursued by ecclesiastical authorities ; or in objecting to the unreasoning prohibitions imposed, at times, on legitimate freedom of action on the part of the laity. The mere mention of the name of Newman, or of his writings, or of advice given to his friends and disciples sent a shiver, as it were, through the letters which, for ten years or more, passed between Archbishop Manning and Monsignor Talbot of the Vatican. This endemic fidget in regard to Cardinal Newman endured to the end.

On the first appearance of the *Life of Cardinal Manning* the endemic perennial fidget of giving scandal to Protestants fell on the sudden, like a shiver penetrating marrow and bones, upon some effeminate or mistrustful Catholics among us. Many for a time lost their heads or their tempers, or both.

Fear of giving scandal to Protestants in matters which seem, however remotely or relatively, to touch the Catholic Faith, amounts in men of over-sensitive temperament or of limited capacity almost, in its acutest form at any rate, to mania. In their fear and fidget such men are incapable of discerning the distinction between the human agencies, which play their subordinate part and which in their nature are fallible and open to criticism, and the divine elements which sustain the Church in its infallible teaching-authority, and in its spiritual life.

Fear of giving scandal to Protestants was the cardinal element in the outcry which was raised against the publication of Cardinal Manning's letters, diaries, and journals. To take one instance only as an illustration: Fear accounted for the almost insane desire for the suppression of the now famous correspondence between Archbishop Manning and Monsignor Talbot. What wringing of hands, what gnashing of teeth, what lamentations were not uttered by good but timid Catholics lest scandal should be given! These pious people, happily but few in number, are mistrustful of their Protestant fellow-countrymen; mistrustful of the effect of simple historic truth; know not, or have forgotten, that in all ages the Church at times has had to bewail or reprove or condemn the human agents to whose hands the divine work had to be entrusted. The pure springs were, alas! but too often defiled. In the divine constitution of the Church such risk of evil was not excluded.

Even if in the diplomatic correspondence between Archbishop Manning and Monsignor Talbot at the Vatican, human motives may have obtruded themselves, or human weaknesses be at times detected, the guiding motive of Archbishop Manning's action was not, according to the evidence recorded, personal antipathies or a desire for self-advancement, but a deep-rooted determination to safeguard in a critical transition period, and at all costs, no matter who suffered in the conflict, the interests of the Catholic Church in England. Even if Manning's action had been a corrupt intrigue; even if the Pope, by Monsignor Talbot's secret and underhand influence, in 'making,' as he himself declared, 'every other candidate impossible,' had been cajoled into an unrighteous nomination—what then? Are corrupt intrigues at the Vatican to be suppressed lest scandal be given to Protestants, or is the truth to be told?

That is the vital question raised in the controversy of the last few months. It concerns not Catholics only, but non-Catholics. It concerns the British reading public, which loves truth and hates suppression of facts and documents, no matter what the motive, as almost a lie. The question touches nearly the honour and honesty of the literary world, and not of England only. The question has been taken up on both sides of the Atlantic: Is it a virtue to suppress historic truth or no? The broad issues once raised cannot now be evaded. The advocates of the art of suppression, in great histories or biographies, of historical facts, or of documents on which such facts are based, are now trembling in their shoes. They cannot lay the Frankenstein's monster they have raised.

By force of circumstances, by its candour and outspokenness, and, perhaps, still more by the blunderings of its Catholic critics, the *Life of Cardinal Manning* is become a test-book, as it were: a criterion of the rival methods in the art of writing history or biography. In all the lands where the English tongue is spoken, the question of the hour is asked: Is the publication of historical facts based on authentic documents 'almost a crime' or a virtue?

By a careful estimate it is computed that the Life has already been read in England and the United States, in the Colonies and India, by well-nigh 200,000 persons. As a consequential result of the unprecedented circulation of such a book, or rather as the result produced by action and reaction, it has been criticised over and over again by more than 200 writers in the daily and weekly press, in monthly reviews and magazines on two continents. And yet the authenticity of no single document has been impeached or imperilled.

In regard to this test-question the all but unanimous verdict is in favour of candour and truthfulness in biography as well as in history. They who run may read; unless it be those who elect to walk through life blindfold.

What readers at home and abroad are, perhaps, most concerned to learn from me is the opinion of Catholics, first in regard to the Life, and, secondly, as to whether truthfulness and candour in biography is a virtue or no. In the nature of things I am in a position to learn many opinions on the subject from various quarters which find no public expression. Numerous letters from Catholics come to my hands; many more from Anglicans and others. Many of the former indignantly complain of the suppression of their letters. Catholics of position and experience maintain that Catholic opinion on the *Life of Cardinal Manning* is not fairly represented in *The Tablet* or the *Weekly Register*. They draw a broad distinction between those Catholics who have read the Life and those who have only read criticisms in the Catholic papers. They who have read the Life as a rule, in the teeth of its many faults, approve of it; those who have only read Catholic reviews of it denounce it. I will give two typical instances: a priest only the other day denounced it as 'an abominable book,' but admitted he had not read it. This was in England. A nun in Australia refused to read the Life, which was within her reach, because she had heard it was a 'bad book.' Both priest and nun were honest. They took the opinion of their pet newspaper as gospel truth. They are types of fortunately not a numerous class. On the other hand, fervent and loyal Catholics of independent judgment, who far exceed both in numbers and capacity these good people who believe implicitly what is told to them, have read the book and find it neither bad nor abominable. Quite the contrary. I might justify this assertion by many quotations from letters sent to me by personal strangers, if space and modesty permitted.

Still more convincing, perhaps, than the opinion expressed in private letters is the judgment given in conversation by literary people, and at clubs, and in general society. One personage, a Catholic of high ecclesiastical position, of wide experience and knowledge of men, recently expressed the following opinion: 'The *Life of Cardinal Manning* justifies itself by results. By common consent it is acknowledged that a higher estimate has been formed alike by Catholics and Protestants of Cardinal Manning's character and career than was held before the publication of his Life.'

From the other side of the wall of separation which unhappily divides the Church of Rome and the Church of England—a wall, it is devoutly to be hoped, destined sooner or later, in the inscrutable designs of Providence, to be removed—I am enabled by the kindness of Lord Halifax to recite the following testimony given by his Grace the Archbishop of York: 'I always had a high opinion of Manning's powers, but since reading his Life I look upon him as a saint. The chapter on "Hindrances" is the most attractive and edifying record in the book.'

Such testimonies, however valuable as coming from representative men on either side, are in the nature of things dwarfed by the following words spoken a short time ago by his Holiness Pope Leo the Thirteenth. Though, of course, unofficial, these weighty words will be received with all the more reverence and gratitude inasmuch as they touch upon the test-question raised to-day in all the lands where the English tongue is spoken—namely, whether in great histories or biographies truth is a virtue or a crime?

Someone in the presence of the Pope was regretting that Manning's character should have been so hurt by what had appeared in his biography, and Pope Leo the Thirteenth spoke as follows: 'Truth is the only thing that matters. What would the Bible have been if the writers had considered the effect of what they wrote? What would have become of Mary Magdalene and her sin; what of Peter and his fall?'[1]

Such a verdict is in keeping with all the known acts and utterances of his Holiness. It is not so long since that the well-known author of *The History of the Popes*, before recording the life of Alexander the Sixth, consulted Pope Leo. His Holiness's advice to the eminent German priest was in substance : ' Tell the truth and the whole truth, no matter though the reputation of a Pope should suffer thereby.'

[1] The correspondent—a personage of honour and truthfulness—who conveyed to me the above words of the Pope writes as follows: 'This is, as far as I can remember, what I heard, but of course it was spoken in Italian, and I cannot vouch for the accuracy of every word.' The accuracy of this statement is confirmed by another witness of equal authority.

In the face of the verdict of public opinion in England and America, all but unanimous, as already recorded, in favour of candour and truthfulness in biography, his Eminence Cardinal Vaughan ought to look to it lest he come to be regarded as a sort of *introverted* 'Athanasius,' standing alone, *contra mundum*, in defence of an almost condemned proposition.

At the beginning of this brief article I quoted an effective passage from Cardinal Newman's *Historical Sketches* on the endemic perennial fidget among Catholics of giving scandal. I cannot do better in bringing my remarks to a close than to recite Cardinal Newman's judgment on the true method of writing a biography. The authority of the illustrious Oratorian on ethical and literary questions is recognised to-day by the world at large. Even they who in their haste suggested the suppression of contemporary letters will, I am persuaded, in deference to such a judgment, be only too eager to abandon, or at least qualify, an ill-considered opinion.

In a letter addressed to his sister, Mrs. Mozley, John Henry Newman wrote as follows:—

> It has been a hobby of mine, though perhaps it is a truism and not a hobby, that the true life of a man is in his letters. . . . Not only for the interests of a biography, but for arriving at the inside of things, the publication of letters is the true method.
>
> Biographers varnish, they assign motives, they conjecture feelings, they interpret Lord Burleigh's nods; but contemporary letters are facts.

In these pregnant sentences Cardinal Newman touched by anticipation the heart of the controversy which was raised by the publication of the *Life of Cardinal Manning*. Even before publication I was urged, with singular vehemence and pertinacity, to adopt the policy of suppression. What would have been the result of such a disastrous policy? Contemporary letters, which Newman says are facts, would have disappeared from an emasculated Life. The relations between Manning and Newman would never have been known in their truth and fulness had I consented to the suppression of their letters. The disclosure of those relations was absolutely essential, not only for the sake of historic truth, but for the real manifestation of Manning's character in one of its most salient aspects. In like manner, the suppression of the Manning and Talbot correspondence, out of fear of giving scandal to Protestants, would have been in itself the greatest of all scandals.

In a word, had I in writing *Cardinal Manning's Life* not followed Newman's leading, but had regarded, according to the suggestion of men of faint heart, the suppression of letters, not their publication, as the true method of biography, the world would never have arrived 'at the inside of things' in regard to the character and career of Cardinal Manning. Happily, I was inspired to follow Cardinal Newman's precept and example. Unfairness in controversy or in writing history is a detestable practice. I can conceive little or nothing more prejudicial to Catholic interests, especially to-day in England, than the policy of suppressing historical facts and documents. In his *Essay on the Development of Christian Doctrine*, page 185, John Henry Newman uttered the following warning, which Catholics of the timid and mistrustful sort might well take to heart to-day :—' If the Catholic hypothesis is true, it neither needs nor is benefited by unfairness. Adverse facts should be acknowledged, explained if but apparent, accounted for if real ; or let alone and borne patiently as being fewer and lighter than the difficulties of other hypotheses.' In like manner, in his preface to the *Life of St. Chrysostom*, Newman points out the virtue of letters as forming the best sources or materials of biography. The personality of the saints is known to us, he says, not by their learned treatises, but by their letters. Nothing is known of the personality of St. Thomas Aquinas, called by his contemporaries the ' Dumb Ox,' though his learned works extort the admiration of all men ; whereas, on the other hand, the letters of St. Augustine bring his personality home to our hearts. Speaking of Cicero, John Henry Newman said, ' Cicero is personally known to us, not by his Orations, but by his letters.'

What should we have really known of the personality of Cardinal Manning from his sermons and lectures had his letters, journals, and diaries been suppressed, or such portions of them as revealed his real character or mind in its most salient features ?

Let the robuster faith and trust of Cardinal Newman prevail over the wave of mistrust and timidity, over ' the endemic perennial fidget of giving scandal' which for the moment possesses the heart of a small minority, at all events, of the educated Catholics of England. The old English proverb, ' Honesty is the best policy,' has come true in regard to *Cardinal Manning's Life*. His character, public and private, as Archdeacon of Chichester, as Archbishop of Westminster, as Father of the Vatican Council, as Cardinal and champion of the Holy See, has been brought in its true light and colour to the knowledge of all men. The crowning labours of his later life as Father of the Poor, as social reformer, as champion of the oppressed ; his incessant work, his mental vigour displayed to the end without the remotest trace of ' senile decay '—a cruel slur cast on his closing years which Mr. Sydney Buxton, his fellow-labourer to the last, indignantly repudiates—endeared Cardinal Manning, as no man of his generation was endeared, to the hearts of the toiling masses of London. The upshot is that without an attempt to conceal his faults and weaknesses, the character of Cardinal Manning is held to-day in higher esteem than ever ; his personality—the real Manning as he lived and breathed—is known far and wide ; honoured and appreciated by all men, Catholic and Protestant alike ; honoured all the more because his whole nature stands revealed, and because no gloss is put on human frailties, which were indeed overshadowed by the virtues of his higher spiritual nature. After the experiences of the last few months, it would be politic, to say the least, on the part of the advocates of suppression to forego their fears and their folly, and take to heart the words of Pope Leo—' Truth is the only thing that matters.'

To the biographer of Cardinal Manning, truth was indeed the only thing that mattered. To me it is a supreme and singular satisfaction that it fell to my lot to be called upon to stand up before the world against the faint-hearted or craven advocates of suppression in defence of the cause of historic truth : to write, if I may say so, my name on the annals of the day as a champion of candour and outspokenness, at all events in biography.

Before concluding this brief survey there are two special points to be noted.

It is curious as a psychological study to examine for a moment the mental attitude of Catholic critics in regard to the *Life of Cardinal Manning*. Not one of them has ventured to utter a word on Cardinal Manning's change of front in regard to the Temporal Power of the Pope. This conspicuous and startling change has been absolutely suppressed in the Catholic newpapers; not one of those pious Catholics, whose knowledge of the Life is derived solely from what is told to them in their newspaper, is aware to this hour that Cardinal Manning, not long after the death of Pope Pius the Ninth, declared that the policy of upholding the Temporal Power was bringing spiritual ruin and disaster on the Catholics of Italy. The motives of this suppression on the part of Catholic newspapers was not fear of giving scandal to Protestants, for, as a fact, Protestants were not scandalised by such a change of principle. The habit of suppressing what they regard as awkward facts seems to come naturally to these light-hearted papers. Cardinal Manning's inconsistency about the Temporal Power, it was considered, would give scandal to pious but weak-kneed Catholics. What easier, then, than to suppress the fact?

On the other hand, Cardinal Manning (which is the second special point I wish to note) was consistent from beginning to end in his opposition to the Jesuits. But consistency on this point was also regarded as an ugly fact, and therefore to be kept out of sight.

Cardinal Manning's opposition to the Jesuits came too near home to the hearts of Catholics, was too prolonged and obstinate, to be altogether concealed even by the adroit handling of the astute suppressors of things that be. From Protestants, Cardinal Manning's relations with the Jesuits were, even during his lifetime, carefully concealed. It was feared that if Manning's disputes with the Jesuits got abroad, Catholics would be taunted with suffering just as much as Protestants from the plague of internal dissensions. Catholic quarrels, however, are not on theological questions, but on matters of policy or

Church government; but if otherwise, in either case suppression of facts is almost a fraud. Protestants have no doubt often looked with interest on Jesuit colleges and schools in the neighbourhood of London. But it never occurred to their minds that the Jesuits, with all their teaching apparatus, were exiles from London, that their colleges at Beaumont, near Old Windsor, and at Wimbledon were, as far as his own diocese was concerned, under Cardinal Manning's ban ; that the Diocese of Westminster was guarded, like the Garden of Eden, by two flaming swords against the intruding Jesuits.

Cardinal Manning has put on record his rooted antipathy to the Jesuits. In one of his latest autobiographical notes, written in the year 1890, he said :

> There is only a plank between the Jesuits and Presbyterianism. . . . They are Papal by their vow, but in their spirit they are less Papal than anti-episcopal. The claim of special dependence on the Pope breeds everywhere a spirit of independence of local authority. This is a grave danger to them, and few of them escape it. Their anti-episcopal spirit shows itself in their treatment of their own men when they become bishops. . . . They are like the Low Church Evangelicals in the Anglican Church, who look upon their bishops as 'enemies of vital godliness.'

Cardinal Manning could not endure—it was not in his nature—to be looked upon by the Jesuits as an 'enemy of vital godliness.' They fell under his ban. Metaphorically he 'cursed them with bell, book, and candle.' In a laughing fashion, their retort came quick :

> Cardinals may come, Cardinals may go ;
> But we go on for ever.

Cardinal Manning, as is known of all men, regarded the suppression of the Society of Jesus in 1773 as the work of God's hand ; he likewise looked upon its restoration in 1827 as God's work. But his abiding hostility to the Jesuits, based, as he declared, on their corporate action in England and Rome, was testified by the prediction which he uttered on various occasions : 'I foresee another 1773.'

EDMUND S. PURCELL,
Author of the 'Life of Cardinal Manning.'

Postscriptum.

Some months ago, in reply to Mr. Gladstone's refutation in a letter to me of the charges brought against him in the *Month*, Father Smith addressed a letter to the editor of this Review. Instead of frankly withdrawing his misrepresentations, whether with or without an apology matters but little, Father Smith, in spite of Mr. Gladstone's absolute contradictions, reiterated his charges under cover of putting a gloss on Mr. Gladstone's words. For instance, in regard to Mr. Gladstone's conversation with Manning in the summer of 1848 in St. James's Park, Father Smith suggested that Manning had likewise spoken of his difficulties and perplexities. Mr. Gladstone's denial was plain and positive: 'According to my recollection, not a word.'

Again, in regard to Mr. Gladstone's statement that, speaking of Newman and his fellow-converts of 1845, Manning had said, 'Their common bond of union is their want of truth,' Father Smith suggested that, 'owing to a failure of memory, Mr. Gladstone had inverted the respective parts taken by himself and Manning, and put his own words into Manning's mouth.'

When compelled by Mr. Gladstone's unanswerable evidence to back out of this charge, Father Smith excused himself for his misstatement by saying that his 'suggestion was pleasantly rather than seriously meant.' After such treatment, no one would have been in the least surprised had Mr. Gladstone not condescended to expend another word on such a special pleader. But in his kindness Mr. Gladstone placed 'at my free disposal' the following letter, with the liberty of making use of it when a fit opportunity occurred:

Hawarden: April 1896.

Dear Mr. Purcell,—I do not know how far you may desire to follow up the question which Mr. Smith, S.J., discusses in the new *Nineteenth Century*. I am, however, glad to say that I have found here the collection of my letters to Anglican Manning, which he gave me (a reluctant party to the exchange) in return for his letters to me, of which the destruction has created an irreparable loss. In this collection I find two important letters. In the first, of November 6, 1850, I recite to him the conversation (which, indeed, in substance was all on his side) of 1848. The second is of December 20, 1850, I having heard from him in the interval. In this letter I say 'we are sadly, strangely at issue on the facts of the conversation,' and then go on to specify in what way he contested my narrative:

'If I have any one clear recollection in my mind, it is that your assurances then did not relate at all to God's mercy to those who faithfully follow their light, be it what it may, but to your perfect sense of security in the Church of England from its objective character.'

It is, therefore, plain to me that the way in which he contested my narrative was not by any direct denial of the propositions I had put into his mouth, but by contending that I misconstrued him, and that he meant to refer to Divine mercy for the invincibly ignorant.

In other words, all the evidence we possess exactly agrees with my recollections, though Manning's unfortunate destruction of his own letters has cancelled the best evidence of all.

I also find that the cessation of intercourse was not so entire as we had all supposed. He wrote a letter to me in the latter part of 1852, and I replied to him referring to the great gap between us, but entirely in terms corresponding with our old relations.

[After thus dismissing Father Smith, Mr. Gladstone, referring to the *Life of Cardinal Manning*, said:] The importance of your work rather grows upon us than loses in weight with the passage of time. I do not think any of us exaggerated the importance of the Life as an *event*.

I remain, sincerely yours,
W. E. Gladstone.

In corroboration of the statement in the above letter regarding the now famous conversation in St. James's Park, 'which, indeed, in substance was all on his (Manning's) side,' I may fitly recite a passage from an earlier letter, dated Biarritz, the 2nd of February, 1896, written before Mr. Gladstone knew even of the existence of Father Smith, far less that he had been betrayed into the folly of misrepresenting Mr. Gladstone's letters and conversations given in the *Life of Cardinal Manning*. The passage is as follows:

'I have just been looking into a point which you might have emphasised more strongly: the utter contradiction between the spontaneous declaration to me in St. James's Park, in June, I think, or July, 1848, and the letter he had written in March to Robert Wilberforce'

E. S. P.

THE LIMITS OF BIOGRAPHY

For many years in England the follies of great men have been held the property of the fool. No sooner is genius laid upon its bier than the vultures are ready to swoop, and to drag from the dead bones two (or more) volumes of what were once most worthily described as 'remains.' Neither cancelled cheques nor washing-bills are discarded, and if research may uncover a forgotten scandal the bird of prey is happy indeed. With an energy amazing only for its misdirection the 'collector' wanders abroad that he may purchase the secrets of poets he never knew, and may snatch a brief notoriety from the common ridicule, wherein he involves an unapproachable talent. Thus, by a curious ingenuity, Shelley has become a hero of intrigues. The amateur of letters overlooks the poet, the intrepid champion of lost causes, the fearless fighter of other men's battles. Nor does he interest himself in the gay, irresponsible, pleasure-seeking adventurer, quick to succour others and to imagine fantastic plots against himself. No, he merely puts him in the dock upon a charge of marital infidelity, and constituting himself at once judge and jury, condemns him (in a lecture) to perpetual obloquy. Thus, too, the gimlet glance of a thousand Paul Prys pierces the letters which John Keats destined only for the eye of Fanny Brawne. Thus, too, through the indiscretion of pretended friends, Rossetti has been pictured now as a shivering apostle of sentiment, now as an astute, even an unscrupulous, driver of hard bargains.

To multiply examples were easy, if unprofitable. Nor is it difficult to discover the motive of this restless curiosity. An interest in letters is necessary to a world compelled to read by Act of Parliament. But compulsion does not imply understanding, and gossip is far easier of digestion than poetry. The revelation of a poet's intrigue lacks no element of attraction; it appeals directly to that spirit which confounds printed matter with literature; it flatters the ambition of those who without toil would feign an intimacy with the great; and before all things it seems to impart in the guise of culture a knowledge of life, as it is lived in a sphere of large ideals and liberal courage. What wonder is it, then, that the tragedy of Harriet and the misery of Fanny Brawne are familiar to many who never read the *Ode to the Skylark*, and who could not repeat the first line of Keats's *Endymion*? Such a study of literature is a pleasant relief from the hungry consumption of illustrated magazines and of dextrously assorted snippets. It pampers the same appetite with a furtive show of refinement, and in England at least the greed of irrelevant information has no serious rival save the football field. But it is with a sincere surprise that you note an increasing taste for literary revelation on the other side of the Channel. Hitherto France has preserved a suitable disdain; she has declined to confuse poetry with adultery; she has refused most honourably to tear open the letter-bags of the great; and her appreciation of literature has been in consequence all the more dignified and single-minded. But the austerity of French criticism has yielded at last, and its very persistence in well-doing intensifies the disgrace of its ultimate surrender.

Reticence being at an end, you may note everywhere the same fury of detection. The reviews fatten upon the dead with a ghoulish ferocity; it is almost impossible to discover a journal free from the prevailing frankness; no man's letters are thought too insignificant for print; and the Bibliothèque Nationale will soon be too small to contain the vast array of books and pamphlets which disclose hitherto inviolate secrets. The prime heroes of revelation are, naturally, Alfred de Musset and George Sand. And they were already the common talk of the market-place; they were France's solitary indiscretion before the present epidemic of curiosity. Musset, in fact, is the Shelley of France. His poems may be forgotten; it may need the genius of Sarah Bernhardt to revivify his plays; but his journey to Venice is still discussed in railway train and omnibus. Nor can it be said that either he or his accomplice is blameless in the matter. Even before they had left Italy behind they both displayed a desperate zeal in the open washing of their dirty linen. No sooner had the disconsolate Musset been dismissed by his Lélia than all the world was in his confidence, and Lélia was composing masterpieces of sentiment that Sainte-Beuve and the rest might be furnished with the last bulletin. But gossip, however industrious, was insufficient to proclaim the intimate sentiments of these twin souls. First Musset was inspired to make a public confession of his love, whereupon George Sand was compelled, in self-defence, to a counter demonstration. The scandal once awaken could not easily be put to rest, and M. Paul de Musset, with finer zeal than wisdom, rushed in to champion his brother. So that no detail in this picnic of love and hate, this orgie of fever and hysteria, is withheld from the curious. Indeed, it is not the fault of the actors if we do not know every scene of the tedious drama. Alfred, on the one hand, roamed Venice up and down, while George was dying of fever; George, on the other, began her flirtation with the ineffable

Pagello when the poet lay on the verge of madness, and even threatened the lover who had broken her heart with the terrors of a lunatic asylum. So much was already whispered in the ear of a confiding public when Madame Colet came, with the added result of her investigation; then there followed a mob of curious physicians, who held each his hand at his victim's pulse, and registered every change of temperature which afflicted the sensitive ardour of those unhappy lovers, until at last Musset, the refined and elegant, became the hero of half a dozen cheap novels, and was forced through the mask of an actor to recite bad verses in a provincial theatre.

Yet indignity lives in cycles, and for a while the scandal of Venice was forgotten, only to be revived with fiercer energy and a flood of *documents inédits*. And to-day the war rages more briskly than ever. The Sandistes, led by M. le Vicomte de Spoëlberch de Lovenjoul, are prompt in the attack, while M. Maurice Clouard, with an eager band of Mussetistes at his back, is inexorable in defence. Blame and praise are awarded with a liberal hand, and it does not occur to any single one of these critics that no one may be an arbiter of another's love or hate. A man and a woman engage in an equal duel; now he, now she receives the deeper wound; but each is free to retire from the combat at pleasure, and it is an idle justice which should find a condemnation of either after sixty years. However, French literature is occupied for the moment with the *Amoureux de Venise*, and in M. Paul Mariéton these unfortunates have found their historian. In his recently published *Histoire d'Amour* (Paris: Havard), this writer has investigated the mystery with the diligence of an ancient scholiast. Moreover his impartiality is above suspicion; he has put George Sand in one scale, Alfred de Musset in the other, and he has held the balance with an equal hand. The work is well done; but that is not so wonderful as that it should be done at all. Another flood of rhetoric overwhelms us; once more we are invited to contemplate the love letters which passed between two persons who, apart from their printed works, are complete strangers to us. Once more we are present at a triangular duel which concerns no living man except the amiable and amazing Dr. Pagello.

Now of Dr. Pagello there was many a dark hint in the ancient controversy. But, since he had not yet rushed into the fray with his own little bundle of 'copy,' he alone of the actors in the drama was enveloped in a mysterious atmosphere of reticence. However he too has broken silence at last; in fact, he first broke silence in 1881, and M. Mariéton finds his restraint remarkable. Yet a sin grows no lighter for keeping, and the reflection of half a century might, with the wisdom of old age, have counselled prudence. Call no man happy, said the Persian king, until his life is finished; call no man discreet until death takes away the opportunity of betrayal. And yet how shall we be angry with Dr. Pagello? For, though he is beyond the hope of pardon, though he has revealed another's secret, he has added a new character to fiction and experience. We have no right to contemplate him, but he himself cries for attention, and assuredly his own Italy, rich in farce, provides no more amusing figure. The one surprising event of his life occurred more than sixty years ago. George Sand, his lover, Alfred de Musset, his defeated rival, have long since won death and immortality; but Dr. Pagello remains unknown to the world and constant to his profession. Had he only been able to hold his tongue, he might have smiled at the past with infinite satisfaction. He might have become the Man in the Iron Mask to the amateurs of tittle-tattle. Unhappily temptation proved irresistible. He too, as well as his betters, had kept a record of his love, some fragments of which found their way into print fifteen years since, and, not content with a single revelation, he has now surrendered himself a willing subject to the interviewer. And here he shows himself a true character of comedy. Anxious to create an impression of sublime indifference, he is yet found mumbling over the cup from which 'the Sand' (as he styles her) was wont to drink the tea of her inspiration. He is eager to display to the interviewer's admiring eye the declaration of love written by the love-sick lady and addressed 'au stupide Pagello.' Meanwhile his son is present to extol the broad shoulders of his father—there at least he was Musset's superior—and to applaud prudence which would risk nothing even for Lélia's love. Also he seizes the occasion to throw ridicule upon 'the Sand's' beauty, whereof, says he, his uncle Robert had but a poor opinion. It is all very comic, despite its provincialism, and while you are willing to believe that the Italian knight errant had no comprehension of 'the Sand's' temperament, and that he was never so happy as when he shook the dust of Paris from his shoes, and hastily returned to the practice of medicine at Venice, you are not surprised that he remembers with the suspicion of a smirk the guilty intrigue of sixty years ago.

But the interest in the Venetian fugitives is in no wise exhausted; the aged doctor promises fresh revelations, and half a dozen other monuments of research will presently be erected. Meanwhile Alfred de Musset does not wholly engross the interest of those who prefer gossip to literature. It is but a few months since the *Correspondance Intime de Marceline Desbordes-Valmore* (Paris: Lemerre) was thrust upon the world. Now Madame Desbordes-Valmore is a poet who is admired far more widely than she is read. Verlaine has given her a place among his 'poètes maudits;' Sainte-Beuve, with his inevitable surety of judgment, has told us precisely what we have a right to know of her unhappiness. Her poems remain to produce the true impression of her sorrow and of her patience, and to present such a revelation of self as she chose to make. But the world is not content; it cares not that her verses ring with melody and are quick with passion; it must know the tragedy of her life; it must look over her shoulder as she takes her intimates into her confidence; it must discover the lover who ignobly deserted her, and whose name, she said, should never be betrayed. (The critics have decreed otherwise.) And the publication of her correspondence has won for her the title of 'poor Madame Valmore,' in which the pity is very near to contempt. Now, any one who will may know that her career was one long fight with poverty, and that her spirit, born for freedom, was chained until her death by the lack of money. There is not one of the miseries besetting the provincial actor wherewith she was not familiar—jealousy, uncertainty, and the lack of bread. Reserve is no longer possible, since it is now set down in print that she cherished the memory of her betrayer in old age, and yet was none the less loyal to her fond, incompetent husband. Had her worshippers been sincere in their desire to do her honour they might have published her poems at a modest price; they might even have reprinted the selection of Sainte-Beuve. But no, it is more interesting to tear away the curtain of respect and to reveal to those who know not the pathos of her poems the deeper pathos of her life. And she, of all poets, should have escaped the penalty of her talent. 'What biography can I have,' she once wrote, ' I, who have spent my whole life in a cupboard?' At last the cupboard is open, and all are free to inspect the empty shelves.

The editors of Victor Hugo's *Correspondance* (Paris: Calmann Lévy) had a far better excuse for publication, and they at least are free from the charge of wanton revelation. For Victor Hugo was something besides a poet; he belonged for half a century to the life of France. He fought the battles of his country and of her literature. The public history of modern Europe cannot be written without his aid, and without a due recognition of his influence. But his letters have no other quality than dulness. They tell us that in his youth he was a prig; they hint at a quarrel with Sainte-Beuve, who had a finger in every pie, and they enhance the seriousness of the quarrel, for the very reason that they leave it vague and unexplained. Beyond this they are silent: they reveal neither his political opinions nor his literary predilections: they neither illustrate his character nor comment upon his poetry. In brief, they might have been written by a nameless advocate or a forgotten journalist. And, since they are all untouched by the Olympian quality of their author, they should have been left to slumber in manuscript.

Hard upon the heels of Victor Hugo comes Sainte-Beuve, whose correspondence, if complete, would implicate the whole world, and Sainte-Beuve is followed hot-foot by Mérimée and De Vigny, each with his sheaf of letters. And so profound is the general curiosity that in the interest of life literature is forgotten. Nor is literature likely to recover its readers until the present fashion of gossip is overpast. Meanwhile a thousand excuses are contrived to palliate the recklessness of editors. 'I resurrect the secrets of the dead,' says one, 'that I may throw light upon their work.' Never was a flimsier argument advanced. A writer makes a certain presentation of himself; he sets his talent in such a light as befits his temperament. His poem, his novel, his essay is, in a sense, himself, but himself as he deliberately chooses to appear before the world. It is, in brief, an expression less of his life than of his art; and though his art may be insensibly modified by his life, an elaborate analysis is no part of the biographer's business. The chemical resolution of a diamond into its component parts does not enhance the diamond's brilliance, and no poem becomes more easily intelligible because you are told that its author was wont to fortify his absinthe with white wine. In truth, the greater the artist the more resolutely is he separate from his work; his own virtue may find expression in the presentment of vice; or, being vicious, he may sing a reverential poem to the Virgin. In either case it is a sure means of confusion to illustrate his achievement by a chance intrigue, and some other excuse must be found for the zeal of discovery.

Is it, then, out of respect that secrets are divulged? Hardly: respect does not show itself in the wanton advertisement of unimportant frailty, in the reckless publication of letters which the writer would have given his hand to suppress. If the thousands who assume a fervent interest in the love affairs of Shelley or Musset were sincere in their respect, they would avoid eavesdropping and devote themselves to the study of the poet's works. Nor is the lust of truth a sufficient excuse for these chafferers in private scandal. The result of their research is, and must ever be, falsification. Their zeal and energy are of no account, since the more they collect the more helpless becomes their confusion. They set their idol in a hideous light, and perforce destroy the proportion of his career. Having crowded a brief year with inglorious strife, they leave a decade blank, and so provide a perfect opportunity to mislead the envious. Musset's life is focussed (so to say) in his sojourn at Venice. He goes down to posterity as the lover of George Sand, and the facts that he parted from his Lélia, and that he wrote plays and novels and poems, do not touch the common imagination. 'I tell you he was in love with George Sand,' says the student of literature, and there's an end of it. Above all the authority of letters is suspect. Printed long after the occasion which prompted their composition, read with the cold eye which takes no account of the preceding tumult and excitement, they lose the meaning which once was theirs and become the easiest instrument of falsehood and distortion. It is idle, therefore, to attribute the modern madness for biography to knowledge, or loyalty, or truth. It is not by the heedless accumulations of biography's raw material that truth is established or art is prospered. It is only the general curiosity which prompts the opening of drawers and the glance over the shoulder that demands satisfaction, and satisfaction it finds in half-digested memoirs and unselected correspondence.

Biography, none the less, is the most delicate of the arts, and its very delicacy renders interesting some definition of its limits. But the definition is difficult, because it must be framed with an equal regard to art and to behaviour. If the subject exacts a frank and free discussion of his foibles, his biographer is guarded against reproach, and succeeds or fails merely by his workmanship. Carlyle, for instance, desired an open exposition of his life, and it is hypocrisy to condemn Froude on any other than an æsthetic ground. So, also, memoirs are exempt from the censorship of manners. Every writer is justified in taking his own life as the material of his art, and Pepys no less than Saint-Simon may be credited with a perfect masterpiece.

Byron, on the other hand, shows the reverse of the medal. His strength and weakness alike demand description. He represented not only the poetry but the character of his age, and so openly was his life given to the public that his smallest action was criticised by thousands who knew him not. He was, in fact, a social problem made concrete, even in his lifetime, and thus he anticipated the vogue of Shelley. For him a frank biography is not an indiscretion; it is the necessary response to past libels. That he felt this necessity is evident from the studied Memoir composed by himself and most treacherously destroyed by Moore, whose sin upon the side of caution is less easily pardoned than the clumsiest revelation. Moreover Byron lived a life of energy and action outside his poetry, and his adventures are admirably characteristic of his romantic epoch. So that not only is his career memorable for its fancy and excitement, but every effort should be made to atone for the heedless crime of Moore. This truth has been realised by Mr. Henley, Byron's latest editor, who has undertaken in his commentary no less a task than the portraiture of Byron's 'dissolute yet bigoted' contemporaries.

The irresponsible biographer, then, must pass before this double tribunal, nor can he be acquitted until he satisfy it that his performance is excellent on both counts. He must prove first that he is guiltless of indiscretion, that he has betrayed no secret which his hero (or his victim) would have chosen to keep. He must exercise to the dead the same courtesy and reticence which he owes to the living, and from this prime duty no ingenuity shall absolve him. It is irrelevant to plead love of truth in excuse for betrayal, since truth (were it possible) is not of supreme value, and since truth which is half told (and it is seldom wholly told outside heaven) is indistinguishable from malice or falsehood. And then he must prove that he has fulfilled the æsthetic aim of biography, which is portraiture with a retrospect. He must ·prove that he is capable of suppressing his documents, and catching from a thousand letters a vivid, separate impression. For literature transmutes experience, and takes no account of unimportant facts, and, alas! it is the workman's habit to sweep his raw material into a heap and call it biography.

The man of genius is above and beyond criticism; he is exempt from punishment, and enjoys the free and undisputed privilege of lawbreaking. Boswell's *Life of Johnson* is magnificent, because for once in the world's history genius seized its opportunity with singlehearted devotion. The result is obtained by the most laborious method. The general impression is contrived by an infinitude of details, which in less skilful hands would inevitably have destroyed the portrait. But Boswell escaped triumphantly from the failure which had awaited a man of lesser talent, and his book remains a masterpiece not only of biography but of literature. So also Lockhart defies censure; yet his example is not for the herd, since to few men is given the tact or the occasion which carried his *Life of Scott* to perfection. These two transcend the rules of art, but for the rest the biographer's first necessity is invention rather than knowledge. If he would make a finished portrait of a great man, he must treat him as he would treat the hero of a romance; he must imagine the style and habit wherein he lived. He must fill in a thousand blanks from an intuitive sympathy; should he use documents in his study he must suppress them in his work, or pass them by with a hint; thus only will he arrive at a consistent picture, and if he start from an intelligent point of view he is at least likely to approach the truth.

A quick understanding may divine what a thousand unpublished letters would only obscure. When Mr. Pater drew his imaginary portrait of Watteau he excluded from the perfected work all the sketches and experiments which had aided its composition. There was no parade of knowledge or research, and such research as discovered the quality of the artist was held severely in reserve. This, then, is the ideal of biography: an imagined portrait stripped of all that is unessential, into which no detail is introduced without a deliberate choice and a definite intention. Thus it were possible to write a veritable biography of Shakespeare or of Homer. There is no need to illustrate their work from the casually gathered episodes of their career; it is in their work that you will find the best and truest commentary upon their life, various as the moods of poetry and intimate as the most familiar lines. Here are no facts to prejudice the judgment, no shameful revelations to cast ridicule upon the great. If Homer were unhappy in love we know it not, and the uncertainty of his birthplace will hardly be deemed disgraceful even by those for whom literature is a means of interviewing the dead. Shakespeare is less fortunate, since perversity has fixed more than one scandal upon him. Yet ignorance prevails, and it is no paradox to say that we know more of Homer and Shakespeare because they are less besmirched with falsehood than of those whose misdeeds were notorious fifty years ago. But the industrious persist in the collection of documents, and would make biography perform the duty of the archives. And if you are in doubt as to their motive here is M. Jules Lemaître to enlighten you—M. Jules Lemaître, a member of the Academy and a promising victim to the biographical zeal of the next generation. 'Without the publication of intimate correspondence,' says he, 'the immortality of the dead would be somewhat lethargic, for we have not the leisure to read their works every morning.' And so, with the encouragement of 'intimate correspondence,' Alfred de Musset and George Sand are involved in two posthumous lawsuits, and are compelled to masquerade every night at a music-hall in a brand-new ballet pantomime entitled *Les Amoureux de Venise*. Such is immortality!

CHARLES WHIBLEY.

STUDIES OF A BIOGRAPHER

NATIONAL BIOGRAPHY

MR. SIDNEY LEE has recently (February 1896) delivered at the Royal Institution a lecture upon National Biography. No one has a better right to speak upon the subject. He has been sole editor of the later volumes of the *Dictionary of National Biography*, and, as I can testify, had a very important share in preparing every previous volume. He spoke, therefore, from considerable experience, and if I were to deal with his subject from the same point of view, I should have little more to do than say 'ditto' to most of his remarks. I would not contradict even his statistics, although, as a matter of fact, they differ to some extent from my own calculations—I put that down to the known perversity of arithmetic in general. But I also think that in dealing briefly with a large subject, he left untouched certain considerations which are a necessary complement to his argument. I shall venture from this point of view to say something of a matter in which I have some personal interest.

When the old *Biographia Britannica* was coming out, Cowper made the unpleasant remark that it was

> A fond attempt to give a deathless lot
> To names ignoble, born to be forgot.

If that was a fair judgment, what are we to say to the modern work, which includes thousands of names too obscure for mention in its predecessor? When Mr. Lee speaks of the 'commemorative instinct' as justifying his undertaking, the enemy replies that a very small minority of the names deserve commemoration. To appeal to instinct is to repudiate reason and to justify monomania. Admitting, as we all admit, the importance of keeping alive the leading names in history, what is the use of this long procession of the hopelessly insignificant? Why repeat the familiar formula about the man who was born on such a day, was 'educated at the grammar school of his native town,' graduated in such a year, became fellow of his college, took a living, married, published a volume of sermons which nobody has read for a century or two, and has been during all that time in his churchyard? Can he not be left in peace, side by side with the 'rude forefathers of the hamlet,' who are content to lie beneath their quiet mounds of grass? Is it not almost a mockery to persist in keeping up some faint and flickering image of him aboveground? There is often some good reading to be found in country churchyards; but, on the whole, if one had to choose, one would perhaps rather have the good old timber crosspiece, with 'afflictions sore long time he bore,' than the ambitious monuments where History and its attendant cherubs are eternally poring over the list of the squire's virtues and honours. Why struggle against the inevitable? Better oblivion than a permanent admission that you were thoroughly and hopelessly commonplace. I confess that I sometimes thought as much when I was toiling on my old treadmill, now Mr. Lee's. Much of the work to be done was uninteresting, if not absolutely repulsive. I was often inclined to sympathise with the worthy Simon Browne, a Nonconformist divine of the last century. Poor Browne had received a terrible shock. Some accounts say that he had lost his wife and only son; others that he had 'accidentally strangled a highwayman,'—not, one would think, so painful a catastrophe. Anyhow, his mind became affected;

he fancied that his 'spiritual substance' had been annihilated; he was a mere empty shell, a body without a soul; and, under these circumstances, as he tells us, he took to an employment which did not require a soul: he became a dictionary-maker. Still, we should, as he piously adds, 'thank God for everything, and therefore for dictionary-makers.' Though Browne's dictionary was not of the biographical kind, the remark seemed to be painfully applicable. Browne was only giving in other words the pith of Carlyle's constant lamentations when struggling amidst the vast dust-heaps accumulated by Dryasdust and his fellows. Could any good come of these painful toilings among the historical 'kitchen middens'? If here and there you disinter some precious coin, does the rare success repay the endless sifting of the gigantic mounds of shot rubbish? And yet, by degrees, I came to think that there was really a justification for toils not of the most attractive kind. When our first volume appeared, one of our critics complained of me for not starting with a preface. A preface saves much trouble to a reviewer—sometimes the whole trouble of reading the book. I do not, however, much regret the omission, for the real utility of our undertaking, as it now presents itself to my mind, had not then become fully evident. I am not about to write a preface now, but I wish to give a hint or two of what I might or ought to have said in such a performance had I clearly perceived what has been gradually forced upon me by experience.

The 'commemorative instinct' to which Mr. Lee refers has, undoubtedly, much to do with the undertaking; but, like other instincts, it requires to be regulated by more explicit reason. The thoroughbred Dryasdust is a very harmless, and sometimes a very amiable, creature. He may urge that his hobby is at least a very innocent one, and that we have no more call to condemn a man who has a passion for vast accumulations of dates, names, and facts than to condemn another for a love of art or natural history. The specialist who is typified in O. W. Holmes's *Scarabee*, the man who devotes a lifetime to acquiring abnormal familiarity with the minutest peculiarities of some obscure tribe of insects, does no direct harm to his fellows, and incidentally contributes something, however minute the contribution may be, to scientific progress. We must respect the zeal which enables a man to expend the superabundant energy, which might have led to fame or fortune, upon achievements of which, perhaps, not half a dozen living men will appreciate either the general value or the cost to the worker. Dryasdust deserves the same sort of sympathy. He has, no doubt, his weaknesses. His passion becomes a monomania. He spends infinite toil upon work which has no obvious interest, and he often comes to attach an absurd importance to his results. Such studies as genealogy or bibliography have but a remote bearing upon any of the vital problems suggested by the real historian. We shudder when we read that the excellent Colonel Chester spent years upon investigating the genealogy of Washington, and accumulated, among many other labours, eighty-seven folio volumes, each of more than 400 pages of extracts from parish registers. He died, it is added, of 'incessant work.' The late Mr. Bradshaw, again, a man of most admirable character, and very fine intellectual qualities, acquired, by unremitting practice, an astonishing power of identifying at a glance the time and place of printing of old books. He could interpret minute typographical indications as the Red Indian can read on a dead leaf or blade of grass the sign of the traveller who made it. Certainly one is tempted to regret at first sight that such abilities were not applied in more obviously useful fields. What do we care whether one or another obscure country squire in the sixteenth or seventeenth century had the merit of being progenitor of Washington? Can it really matter whether a particular volume was printed at Rotterdam or at Venice—in the year 1600 or ten years sooner or later? I will not discuss the moral question. At any rate, one may perhaps urge, it is better than spending brain-power upon chess problems, which is yet an innocent form of amusement. Such a labourer may incidentally provide data of real importance to the political or literary historian: he reduces, once for all, one bit of chaos to order, and helps to raise the general standard of accurate research. He is pretty certain to confer a benefit, if not a very important benefit, upon mankind; whereas, if he fancied himself a philosopher, he might be wasting his labour as hopelessly as in squaring the circle. He is at least laying bricks, not blowing futile soap-bubbles.

The labours of innumerable inquirers upon obscure topics have, as a matter of fact, accumulated vast stores of knowledge. A danger has shown itself that the historian may be overwhelmed by the bulk of his materials. A century or two ago we were content with histories after the fashion of Hume. In a couple of years he was apparently not only to write, but to accumulate the necessary knowledge for writing, a history stretching from the time of Julius Cæsar to the time of Henry VII. A historian who now does his work conscientiously has to take about the same time to narrate events as the events themselves occupied in happening. Innumerable sources of knowledge have been opened, and he will be regarded as superficial if he does not more or less avail himself of every conceivable means of information. He cannot be content simply with the old chroniclers or with the later writers who summarised them. Ancient charters, official records of legal proceedings, manor rolls, and the archives of towns have thrown light upon the underlying conditions of history. Local historians have unearthed curious facts, whose significance is only beginning to be perceived. Calendars of State papers enable us to trace the opinions of the great men who were most intimately concerned in the making of history. The despatches of ambassadors occupied in keenly watching contemporary events have been partly printed, and still lie in vast masses at Simancas and Venice and the Vatican. The Historical Manuscripts Commission has made known to us something of the vast stores of old letters and papers which had been accumulating dust in the libraries of old country mansions. When we go to the library of the British Museum, and look at the gigantic catalogue of printed books, and remember the huge mass of materials which can be inspected in the manuscript department, we—I can speak for myself at least—have a kind of nightmare sensation. A merciful veil of oblivion has no doubt covered a great deal. Yet we may feel inclined to imagine that no fact which has happened within the last few centuries has been so thoroughly hidden that we can be quite sure that it is irrecoverable. Over two centuries ago a lad unknown to fame wrote a thesis in a Dutch University. I stumbled upon it one day and discovered a biographical date of the smallest conceivable interest to anybody. But it gives one a queer shock when one realises that even so trumpery and antiquated a document has not been allowed to find its way to oblivion. Happily some University theses have been lost, but as the process of commemorating proceeds with accelerated rapidity, it almost seems as though we had made up our minds that nothing was ever to be forgotten.

It may be doubted whether this huge accumulation of materials has been an unmixed benefit to history. Undoubtedly we know many things much more thoroughly than our ancestors. Still, in reading, for example, the later volumes of Macaulay or Froude, we feel sometimes that it is possible to have too much State-paper. The main outlines, which used to be the whole of history, are still the most important, and instead of being filled up and rendered more precise and vivid, they sometimes seem to disappear behind an elaborate account of what statesmen and diplomatists happened to think about them at the time —and, sometimes, what such persons thought implied a complete misconception of the real issues. But in any case one conclusion is very obvious, namely, that with the accumulation of material there should be a steady elaboration of the contrivances for making it accessible. The growth of a great library converts the library into a hopeless labyrinth, unless it is properly catalogued as it grows. To turn it to full account, you require not only a catalogue, but some kind of intelligent guide to the stores which it contains.

You are like a man wandering in a vast wilderness, which is springing up in every direction with tropical luxuriance; and you feel the necessity of having paths carried through it upon some intelligible system which will enable you to find your way to the required place and tell you in what directions further research would probably be thrown away.

Now it is to this want, or to provide the means of satisfying one part of this want, that the dictionary is intended in the first place to correspond. It ought to be—it is not for me to say how far it has succeeded in becoming—an indispensable guide to persons who would otherwise feel that they were hewing their way through a hopelessly intricate jungle. Every student ought, I will not say to have it in his library, but to carry it about with him (metaphorically speaking) in his pocket. It is true that, in a physical sense, it is rather large for that purpose, though fifty or sixty volumes represent but a small fragment of a decent library; but the judicious person can always manage to have it at hand. And then, though in its first intention it should be useful as an auxiliary in various researches, I shall venture to assert that it may also be not only useful for the more exalted purpose of satisfying the commemorative instinct, but—I do not fear to say so, though my friends sometimes laugh at my saying—it may turn out to be one of the most amusing works in the language.

I will start, however, by saying something of the assertion which is more likely to meet with acceptance. The utility of having this causeway carried through the vast morass of antiquarian accumulation is obvious in a general way. The remark, however, upon which Mr. Lee has insisted, indicates a truth not quite so clearly recognised as might be desirable. The provinces of the historian and the biographer are curiously distinct, although they are closely related. History is of course related to biography inasmuch as most events are connected with some particular person. Even the most philosophical of historians cannot describe the Norman Conquest without reference to William and to Harold. And, on the other side, every individual life is to some extent an indication of the historical conditions of his time. The most retired recluse is the product at least of his parents and his schooling, and is affected by contemporary thought. And yet, the curious thing is the degree in which this fact can be ignored on both sides. If we look at any of the ordinary collections of biographical material, we shall constantly be struck by the writer's unconsciousness of the most obvious inferences. He will mention a fact which in the hands of the historian might clear up a political problem, or which may be strikingly characteristic of the social conditions of the time, without, as Mr. Herbert Spencer would say, noting the 'necessary implication.' A contemporary of course takes things for granted which we see to be exceptional; or he may supply, without knowing it, evidence that will be useful in settling a controversy which has not yet come to light. In the ordinary books such facts, again, have often been repeated mechanically, and readers are not rarely half asleep when they look at their manual. Thus I have sometimes noticed that a man may be in one sense a most accomplished biographer; that is, that he can tell you off-hand a vast number of facts, genealogical, official, and so forth, and yet has never, as we say, put two and two together. I have read lives giving minute details about the careers of authors, which yet prove unmistakably that the writers had no general knowledge of the literature of the period. A man will know every fact about all the people mentioned, say, in Boswell, and yet have no conception of the general position of Johnson, or Burke, or Goldsmith in English literature. He seems to have walked through a great gallery blindfold, or rather with some strange affection of the eyes which enabled him to make a catalogue without receiving any general impression of the pictures. The great Mr. Sherlock Holmes has insisted upon the value of the most insignificant facts: and if Mr. Holmes had turned his mind to history instead of modern criminal cases, he would have found innumerable little incidents which only require to be skilfully dovetailed together to throw a new light upon many important questions. More can be done by the man of true historical imagination—the man who appreciates the great step made by Scott when he observed that our ancestors were once as really alive as we are now—and who finds in those countless neglected and apparently barren facts, vivid illustrations of the conditions of life and thought of our predecessors. We all know how Macaulay, with his love of castle-building, found in obscure newspapers and the fugitive literature of the period the materials for a picture which, with whatever shortcomings, was at least incomparably brilliant and lifelike. Now, the first office of the biographer is to facilitate what I may call the proper reaction between biography and history; to make each study throw all possible light on the other; and so to give fresh vitality to two different lines of study, which, though their mutual dependence is obvious, can yet be divorced so effectually by the mere Dryasdust. And this remark supplies a sufficient answer to one question which has often been put to me. What entitles a man to a place in the dictionary? Why should it include 30,000 instead of 3000 or 300,000 names? Mr. Lee has given an answer which is, I think, correct in its proper place; but, before referring to it, I must point out that there is another, and what would be called a more 'objective' criterion which necessarily governs the solution in the first instance. In order, that is, to secure the proper correlation between the biographer and the historian, it is plainly necessary to include every one who is sufficiently noticed in the ordinary histories to make some further inquiry probable. To give the first instance that occurs, Macaulay tells a very curious story about a certain intrigue which led to the final abolition of licensing the Press in England. The fact itself is one of great interest in the history of English literature. The two people chiefly concerned were utterly obscure: Charles Blount and Edmund Bohun necessarily vanish from Macaulay's pages as soon as they have played their little drama. But it is natural to inquire what these two men otherwise were, who were incidentally involved in a really critical turning-point. A reference to the dictionary will not only answer the question, but help to make more distinct the conditions under which English writers won a most important privilege. The historian can only deal with the particular stage at which an obscure person emerges into public, but the significance of the event may start out more vividly when we can trace his movements below the surface. Now to help in this search the biographer has before him an immense mass of material already partially organised. Nobody who has dipped into the subject is ignorant of the immense service rendered by Anthony a Wood in the famous *Athenæ Oxonienses.* It gives brief, but very shrewd, accounts of all men connected with Oxford, and records the results of a laborious personal inquiry during his own period, which, but for him, would have been forgotten. For the same period we have all the collections due to the zeal of various religious sects; the lives of the

Nonconformists ejected in 1662; the opposition work upon the 'sufferings of the clergy' under the Commonwealth; the lives of the Jesuits who were martyred by the penal laws; and the lives of the Quakers, who have always been conspicuous for preserving records of their brethren. Besides these, there are, of course, many old biographical collections, including the dictionaries devoted to some special class—the artists, the physicians, the judges, the admirals, and so forth. The first simple rule, therefore, is that every name which appears in these collections has at least a presumptive right to admission. An ideal dictionary would be a complete codification or summary of all the previously existing collections. It must aim at such an approximation to that result as human frailty will permit; in other words, it is bound first to include all the names which have appeared in any respectable collection of lives, and, in the next place, to supplement this by including a great many names which, for one reason or another, have dropped out, but which appear to be approximately of the same rank. The rule, it is obvious, must be in part the venerable 'rule of thumb,' but it gives a kind of test which is a sufficient guide in discreet hands.

The advantage of this does not, I hope, require much exposition. I will only make one remark. Every student knows the vast difference which is made when you have some right to assume the completeness of any research. I may look into books, and search libraries on the chance of finding information indefinitely. But if I have a book or a library of which I can say with some confidence that, if it is not there, the presumption is that it does not exist, my labour has a definite, even though it be a negative, result. That, for example, is the sufficient justification of the collection of every kind of printed matter in the British Museum. It is not only that nobody can say beforehand what bit of knowledge may not turn out to be useful, but that one has the immense satisfaction of knowing that a fact not recorded somewhere or other on those crowded shelves must be, in all probability, a fact for which it is idle to search further. No biographical dictionary can be in the full sense exhaustive; an exhaustive dictionary would involve a reprint of all the parish registers, to mention nothing else; but it may be approximately exhaustive for the purposes of all serious students of any of the various departments of history. In a great number of cases, moreover, this can be achieved with a tolerable approximation to completeness. We take, for example, any of the more important names around which has been raised a lasting dust of controversy. A dictionary ought, in the first place, to supply you with a sufficient indication of all that has been written upon the subject; it should state briefly the result of the last researches; explain what appears to be the present opinion among the most qualified experts, and what are the points which seem still to be open; and, above all, should give a full reference to all the best and most original sources of information. The most important and valuable part of a good dictionary is often that dry list of authorities which frequently costs an amount of skilled labour not apparent on the surface, and not always, it is to be feared, recognised with due gratitude. The accumulation of material makes this a most essential part of the work; for we are daily more in want of a guide through the wilderness, and a judicious indication of the right method of inquiry gives often what it may be hard to find elsewhere, and is always a useful check upon our unassisted efforts. When you plunge into the antiquarian bog you are glad to have signposts, showing where previous adventurers have been engulphed; where some sort of feasible track has been constructed, and who are the trustworthy guides. Moreover, for a vast variety of purposes, the dictionary, though only second-hand authority, may be quite sufficient for all that is required. In following any of the countless tracks that may lead through history, you meet at every step with persons and events intruding from different regions. The man of letters may be affected by a political intrigue; a soldier may come into contact with men whose chief activity belongs to literature or science. The most thoroughgoing inquirer has to take a vast number of collateral facts upon trust; and it may save him infinite trouble to get the results of special knowledge upon what are to him collateral points.

This, to which I might add indefinitely, corresponds to what I may call the utilitarian aspect of a dictionary: the immediate purpose to which it may be turned to account by students in any historical inquiry. It should be a confidential friend constantly at their elbow, giving them a summary of the knowledge of antiquaries, genealogists, bibliographers, as well as historians, upon every collateral point which may happen for the moment to be relevant. But, so far, however well done, it must be admitted that it is bound to

be rather dry. To be reduced to a specimen put
in a museum is not a very cheering prospect, and
offers little satisfaction for the commemorative
instinct. Now I have to add that within certain
limits the dictionary may be of importance in that
direction too. I do not expect that a future
Nelson will exclaim, 'Victory, or an article in
The Biographical Dictionary!' I have never
found my own appetite for labour stimulated by
the flattering hope that I might some day be the
subject instead of the author of an article. If I
thought that my posthumous wishes would be
respected, I should beg to be omitted from the
supplement. But, for all that, the dictionary
article may do much to keep alive the memory
of people whom it is good to remember. Nobody
will expect the poor dictionary-maker to be a
substitute for Boswell or Lockhart. The judicious
critic is well aware that it is not upon the lives
of the great men that the value of the book
really depends. It is the second-rate people—the
people whose lives have to be reconstructed from
obituary notices, or from references in memoirs
and collections of letters; or sought in prefaces
to posthumous works; or sometimes painfully
dug out of collections of manuscripts, and who

really become generally accessible through the dictionary alone—that provide the really useful reading. There are numbers of such people whom one first discovers to be really interesting when the scattered materials are for the first time pieced together. Nobody need look at Addison or Byron or Milton in a dictionary. He can find fuller and better notices in every library; and the biographer must be satisfied if he has put together a useful compendium of all the relevant literature. The conditions of his work are sufficiently obvious, and of course exclude anything like rhetoric or disquisition in criticism. He may indicate but cannot expatiate. He has before him an ideal which he very well knows is never quite realised. Condensation is not only the cardinal virtue of his style, but the virtue to which all others must be sacrificed. He must be content sometimes to toil for hours with the single result of having to hold his tongue. I used rigidly to excise the sentence, 'Nothing is known of his birth or parentage,' which tended to appear in half the lives, because where nothing is known it seems simpler that nothing should be said; and yet a man might have to consult a whole series of books before discovering even that negative fact. The poor biographer, again, has to compress his work even at the cost of much clumsiness of style. I am painfully aware of the hideous sentences which I have constructed in trying to say in ten words what, as I fancied, might make quite a pretty passage if spread over a hundred. I have groaned over some charming anecdote which seemed to beg for a few little dramatic accessories, and wedged it remorselessly into its allotted corner, grievously perplexed by the special difficulty in our language of making the 'he's' and 'she's' refer to the proper people without the help of the detestable 'latter' and 'former.' Perhaps — so one thinks when looking at some modern biographies—the training in condensation is not altogether bad. But the problem is to condense without squeezing out the real interest. The dictionary-writer cannot dilate; but he is bound so far as he can to make the facts tell their own story. He is not to pronounce a panegyric upon heroism, but he ought so to arrange his narrative that the reader may be irresistibly led to say bravo! It is possible to make a story more pathetic by judicious reticence, though the writer who depends upon such a method needs especially appreciative readers. He must tell a good story so as to bring out the humorous side without indulging in open hilarity, though he knows painfully that many readers will not take a joke unless it is labelled 'funny,' and some will not take it till it has been hammered into their heads by repeated strokes. It follows that the ideal article should not be condensed in the sense of being reduced to the bare dates and facts capable of being arranged in mechanical order. The aim should be to give whatever would be really interesting to the most cultivated reader, though leaving it to the reader to put the dots over the i's. The writer must often make the sacrifice of keeping his most important reflections to himself; but it is not the less important that they should be in his mind. Imagine a mere antiquary and a competent student to tell within the same limits the life of some eminent philosopher or divine. The difference may be enormous between the writer who sees what are the really cardinal facts and the writer to whom any and every fact is of the same importance: and yet both narratives may appear at first sight to be equally dry and barren. I remember how a life was ridiculed by a literary critic because it explained a certain vote at the Salters' Hall Conference. The critic, who probably knew all about

Denis and Curll and the pettiest squabbles of authors, had never heard of Salters' Hall, and asked who cared for such trifles, or what it could possibly matter how anybody had voted on the occasion? Yet the conference marks a very important point in the religious history of the day, and to know how a man voted may be to define his position in a very serious controversy. The writer, that is, must give the significant facts, but has often to leave the discovery of their significance to the reader. But in order that he should appreciate their significance, he must have far wider knowledge than he can expound. The dry antiquary will often omit the vital and insert the merely accidental: he will fail to arrange them in the order or connection which makes them explain their meaning. He will resemble the witness who should fail to mention a bit of evidence which may be incidentally conclusive of a case because he is not able to appreciate its bearing. And, therefore, though the two lives might be in appearance equally dry, one may teem with useful indications to the intelligent, while the other may be as barren as it looks. The life of the divine, for example, should be given by one who has studied the theology or ecclesiastical history of the day, and who therefore knows the significance conferred upon a particular action or expression of opinion by time and place. He must abstain from exposition beyond narrow limits, and, of course, from controversy. He must not expatiate upon the bad influence of the heresy; or attempt to show that it was a heresy. He must content himself with a pithy indication of its historical position on the development of the time; give a sufficient summary to show how the doctrine is to be classed in its relation to the main currents of thought; and indicate the way in which it has since been judged by competent writers, and what is the view now taken by experts. All this, which might, of course, be illustrated in other departments of biography, shows that the writer ought to be full of knowledge, which he must yet hold in reserve, or of which he must content himself with using to suggest serviceable hints. He will show incidentally why, and in what relations, certain books are worth reading or certain events worth further study; and often, no doubt, will feel the restraint decidedly painful.

Lives well written under these conditions may, I hold, really satisfy the commemorative instinct. For the great names we shall look elsewhere: the minute names, the mere rank and file of the great army, are constantly of great use; but rather because they come into the narratives of other lives or supply data for broader histories, than because of the intrinsic interest of the story itself. But there is also an immense number of second-rate people whose lives are full of suggestion to any intelligent reader. The life in such cases should have the same kind of merit as an epitaph, though under less exacting conditions. The epitaph should give in the smallest possible number of words the very essence of a man's character and of his claims upon the memory of posterity. The life which may spread over two or three pages should aim at producing the same effect: and very frequently may give adequate expression to everything that we can really afford to remember of the less prominent actions. I will venture one illustration. There is no class of lives which has a more distinctive character than the lives of our naval heroes, from the Elizabethan days to our own. As I am not criticising the execution of the dictionary, but only indicating its main purpose, I will say nothing in praise of the particular contributor who has imbedded in its pages something like a complete naval history of the country. But

I may say this : to the mere literary reader, the ideal of a sailor is represented by such books as Southey's *Life of Nelson* ; or still more vividly perhaps by the novels of Captain Marryat or Smollett, or by Kingsley's *Westward Ho!* or possibly Miss Austen's *Persuasion.* We are all supposed to know something of the great admirals, upon whom R. L. Stevenson wrote a charming article. But any one who is attracted by the type, would do well to turn over the dictionary and look up the long list of minor heroes, who stood for their portraits to Marryat and his fellows ; the men who cut out ships in harbour, and fought men-of-war with merchantmen ; and lay in wait for galleons and suppressed mutinies, and had desperate single combats with French or American frigates : the Trunnions and Amyas Leighs and Peter Simples of real life, who certainly are to the full as interesting as their imaginary representatives. Many of them have hitherto only existed, as it were, in fragments: their lives have to be put together from despatches and incidental references in memoirs and histories ; but when reconstructed, these lives form a gallery more interesting than that at Greenwich Hospital. They have got into a little Walhalla ; and I think that no one will doubt who makes the experiments either as to their deserving their places, or as to the fact that the commemoration gives a very real satisfaction to our desire to keep the memory of our worthies in tolerable repair.[1]

And, finally, this may help to justify my daring remark that the dictionary is an amusing work. This, of course, is true only upon certain conditions. The reader, as I have intimated, must supply something for himself; he has to take up the dry specimens in this great herbarium, and to expand them partly by the help of his own imagination till they take something of the form and colouring of life. Perhaps, too, it must be added, that he should know the great art of skipping, though some excellent friends of mine have told me that they read through every volume as it appears. Their state is the more gracious. Yet no man is a real reading enthusiast until he is sensible of the pleasure of turning over some miscellaneous collection, and lying like a trout in a stream snapping up, with the added charm of

---

[1] I am glad to see that, in this observation, I coincide with the author of *Admirals All*, who has been good enough to say a word for the dictionary in this respect. I am happy that the poetic has confirmed the prosaic judgment. Only I must add that the compliment which he pays to the editor of the dictionary is rather due to Professor Laughton, the author of the lives in question.

unsuspectedness, any of the queer little morsels of oddity or pathos that may drift past him. The old *Gentleman's Magazine* is charming in that way, but I do not know that one can find a much better hunting-ground than the dictionary. I take down a volume—honestly at random—and simply dip into it to see what will turn up. I range, as it happens, over all the centuries from Caradoc (Caractacus, the Romans called him), who fought against a Roman army backed by an elephant corps, before A.D. 50, to a gentleman of the same name, who became Lord Howden, and died in 1873; from Carausius, who was a bit of a pirate and something of an emperor, in the third century, and whose biographer pathetically observes that the exact dates of his life and adventures are 'not absolutely certain,' to Carlyle, in whose case the full blaze of modern biography has left not even the minutest detail untouched. There is Canute, who is not here introduced to the tide—the biographer finds out, by the way, that an anecdote is simply the polite name of a lie —and mediæval churchmen, like the admirable Chad, thanks to whom, according to Scott, the fanatic Brooke got his deserts at Lichfield, and William de St. Carilef, whose character, we regret to say, is still puzzling, though exactly eight hundred years have passed since he became a fair subject for discussion. Let us hope that it will be cleared up in time. We have that Catesby who to most of us is known by that famous doggerel so much more impressive than the orthodox historical phrases about 'the cat, the rat, and Lovel our dog,' and the other Catesby who wished to try what would certainly have been a most interesting philosophical experiment of blowing King and Parliament into the air and seeing what the country would think of it. In Tudor times are the three Catherines who had the satisfaction of calling Henry VIII. husband, and three Carolines to match them in the eighteenth century. There is the Elizabethan statesman Cecil, the great Lord Burghley, and the Robert Carr (Earl of Somerset) who introduces us to the darkest tragedy of the time of James I., and Lucius Cary (Lord Falkland), who still goes about 'ingeminating peace' to remind us of the great civil war; and John Carteret (Earl Granville), who, in the jovial Hanoverian days, was at the head of the 'drunken administration.' Though some of these are sufficiently celebrated figures to be set forth in the standard histories, they have all, I think, a personal interest which repays a visit to them in their homes. At the opposite end of the scale we have the names which, though they primarily represent mere oddities, incidentally light up odd social phases. Here is Margaret Catchpole, a real heroine of romance, who stole a horse and rode seventy miles to visit her lover, and after being transported for an offence which excited the compassion of her judges, became one of the 'matriarchs' to whom our Australian cousins trace their descent. There is Bampfylde Moore Carew, the volunteer gypsy, who anticipated Borrow in the previous generation, and gives us a passing glimpse into the vagrant life in old English lanes and commons. There is John Case, astrologer, who, as Addison tells us, made more money by his poetry than Dryden had done in a lifetime. It consisted of the couplet,

'Within this place
Lives Doctor Case,'

and is apparently an early triumph of the great art of advertising. There is the worthy Cat, who had an 'educated and thoughtful mind,' whose story illustrates the early growth of clubs, and whose name has been preserved by the new style of portraits. There is the modern hero, Ben

Caunt, to illustrate the halo which lingered round the last days of prize-fighting. I venture to contribute a fresh anecdote to his life. I once made a pilgrimage to the place where Milton wrote the *Allegro* and *Penseroso*. The name of the poet seemed to have vanished, but a bust of the great Ben Caunt showed that the spirit of hero-worship was not extinct. Its possessor told us the story with legitimate pride. A son of the hero had brought it in a cart to an admirer after the original's death. He stopped at an inn to refresh himself 'with a bottle of soda-water,' with the result that he upset the cart at the next turning, and the bust fell upon him and killed him on the spot. The bust happily survived, and remains to kindle the enthusiasm of the villagers. Should not a Caunt be remembered as well as a Milton? He represents a type which had been characteristic, at least, of the days of the men of Trafalgar and Waterloo. A more respectable memorial of that time was the sturdy Carew (Hallowell was his name at the time) who gave to Nelson a coffin made from the mainmast of the *Orient*, to remind the great man (it was suggested) that he was still mortal. The reminder was hardly needful, one would think, just after the battle of the Nile.

Perhaps a more interesting glimpse of the same period is given by the history of Richard Carlile, the freethinker, who suffered over nine years' imprisonment for spreading opinions offensive to most of his neighbours, but of whom it is said—and, I think, justly—that he did more than any man of his time to promote the freedom of the Press. His career, at any rate, is curiously illustrative of the final struggle in that cause. If you prefer a martyrdom in a different cause, you may look at the life of Edmund Castle, who made 'an epoch in Semitic scholarship.' He was a man of property who chose to labour eighteen or nineteen hours a day at a lexicon—a dictionary-maker again! He lost his health, suffered (it does not quite appear how) fractures and contusions of his limbs, almost lost his sight, and spent all his money. He published his immortal work by subscription, and had to wait for months at the place of sale before he could get a small part of his edition sold. The poor man got a little preferment at last towards the end of his life; but certainly scholars will not grudge him some sympathy. I will, however, go no further. I see many more suggestive names. The Cartwrights, for example, include an important inventor of machinery, a famous dentist, a great Puritan divine, a Romanising bishop, the Colonel Newcome of the old reformers, and a once brilliant dramatist. I do not think that my dip into one volume has produced a result differing much from the average. My readers must judge whether it goes to justify my statement. To me it seems that at every haul one finds some specimens which, though they require the reader to do his part, are full of suggestions to the moderately thoughtful reader. 'What a knowledge of human nature you must have acquired! has been said to me, with a touch, I know, of sarcasm. Perhaps I might, if the B's had not tended to turn the A's out of my head, and if a succinct record of a man's main performances were the same thing as a knowledge of the man himself. But this I may say ; that I have received innumerable suggestions for thought, and had many vignettes presented to my imagination, which to a man of any thought or imagination should have been full of interest. If, that is, I had been a Macaulay, I should have approximated to that vivid perception of the historical panorama which he had to construct by assimilating the raw materials of history. Macaulay had faults which have been so frequently exposed, that the critic should perhaps be now chiefly anxious to insist upon his astonishing power in his own province. And certainly, I think that, though we should wish to see many aspects of history to which Macaulay was blind, nothing could be more delightful than to see the past as clearly, brightly, and graphically as Macaulay saw it. Nothing but a prodigious memory and a keen imagination could enable us to do that. But the dictionary well used, read thoughtfully, with the constant attempt to put flesh and blood upon the dry skeleton of facts, will, I believe, be the best help to enable any one to get as near as his faculties will permit to that desirable consummation. And, though the commemorative instinct may not be fully gratified, I think that no one can ramble through this long gallery without storing up a number of vivid images of the lesser luminaries, which will have the same effect upon his conceptions of history as a really good set of illustrations upon a narrative of travels. And, finally, I will say, what has often been a comfort to me to remember, that great as is the difference between a good and a bad work of the kind, even a very defective performance is immensely superior to none at all.

THE CUSTOM OF BIOGRAPHY
BY EDMUND GOSSE

VARIOUS nations have diverse ways of building the tombs of their prophets. The Americans endow institutions — usually styled 'universities' — and give to them the names of the deceased. The French, believing with Goethe that the best memorial of a man is his effigy, fill the squares of their country towns with bronze statues. We in England bury our dead under the monstrous catafalque of two volumes (crown octavo), and go forth refreshed, as those who have performed a rite which is not in itself beautiful, perhaps, but is inevitable and eminently decent. The custom has now grown into an institution, almost without our perceiving it, until it has become like the Christmas plum-pudding or the Oxford and Cambridge boat-race. We certainly have not realised that we are the only nation in the world that has adopted the big-biography habit, as part of our recognised convention, to such an extent that the 'life' of the deceased begins with the day of his 'death.' The newspapers now combine the one announcement with the other: 'We regret to state that the eminent taxidermist, Viscount Beeswax, passed away after a long illness at ten o'clock last night. The funeral will take place on Friday next, and the biography will be undertaken by the Bishop of Bodkin, a life-long friend of the remains.' The two great solemn volumes, with copious correspondence, and a special chapter (in the case of free-thinkers) on 'Lord Beeswax in his Relation to Religion,' follow the coffin as punctually as any of the other mutes in perfunctory attendance. The man may have lived a life obscure, austere, sequestered; but society absolutely demands some public decency when all is over. There must be a pall, two volumes of biography, and a few wreaths of elegant white flowers.

It is difficult to know how it is that we have slipt inperceptibly into such a strange convention, of which a foreign writer—more lively than exactly accurate—says: 'In the old Albion there never dies a costermonger or a veterinary surgeon, a prime minister or a prize-fighter, but, behold! the bookshops are burdened with his memoirs, in many volumes, with portraits, correspondence, and the sources of his national objection to foreigners, the whole detailed at a length so enormous that only those connected with him by marriage can read so much as a single chapter.' Thus are we sedulously misjudged abroad; yet when indignation has done its work, the monstrous army of biographies remains. There they rise behind the glass fronts of our bookcases, in funereal splendour, serried, undisturbed, making of this portion of the library a sort of solemn Kensal Green. And still in battalions they advance. Since I began to write this page, no doubt, the memoirs have been published of a

THE CUSTOM OF BIOGRAPHY

bishop, a hospital nurse, three railway inspectors, two botanists, and a military man. How did we, as a nation, fall into the biographical habit? What led us to cultivate it with such astounding indifference to form, purpose, and proportion?

Some young man of ambition and energy, looking about for a subject on which to exercise his pen, might do worse than devote himself to the History of Biography in England. It is, I believe, a virgin theme, and it would offer to the conscientious critic a great many interesting and not a few entertaining chapters. The difficulty, I foresee, will be for the historian to arrange its component parts in a satisfactory sequence, for until he reaches the middle of the eighteenth century he will really find very little to relate. The Englishman of the old type had a grounded suspicion of the veracity of memoirs. He feared that, 'with their blasphemous trump, they spread abroad innumerable lies, without either shame or honesty,' as if the personal column of the Yellow Press existed in the reign of Henry VIII. He felt, moreover, very little interest in the life of an individual: such a person, even of great parts and quality, was but a trifling factor in the running chronicle of the times. In the vast flight of locusts, when the general tread of their devastating army betokens life and death, how can one care to take up a solitary insect and study its legs and wings? Consequently, until the ages settled down to some personal comfort, and the movements of kings began to be regulated, there was no chance that biographies of private people should be very largely written.

But about the year 1557 biography was born in England in the shape of a little masterpiece, the true value of which has only of late years been observed—the 'Life of Cardinal Wolsey,' by George Cavendish. It is, however, to be noted, in passing, that this delightful book was so wholly outside the temper of the time that it did not find its way into print at all, and hung, indeed, between life and death, in the limbo of manuscript, for nearly a hundred years. Cavendish, in fact, was a freak of nature: he did not belong in spirit to the literature of the sixteenth century. His interests were all personal and individual. While other writers tried to fix their eyes, as well as they could, on the movement of living history, and saw it very dimly and uncomfortably, Cavendish contemplated the one man of his devotion, and saw him clearly and saw him whole. In George Cavendish there was something of the clairvoyance of Boswell, of the penetration of Walpole: he perceived life—the small square of it which alone interested him—arrayed in clear soft colours, as his great contemporary Holbein saw it. Taste was not yet delivered from the rhetorical bondage of the Middle Ages, and the wonder is that Cavendish was not ashamed to write so well as he did. It is his lack of scholarly affectation, his ability to put out of mind whatever he has not witnessed with his own eyes and ears, that gives him the courage to produce his unique and charming volume.

It is unfortunate that Cavendish has not been allowed to strike the key-note in English biography. Perhaps, if his proper text had been printed earlier, and before the national biographical manner had become so settled, he might have done this. Even now, however, it may not be too late to point to the 'Life of Cardinal Wolsey' as in many respects the type of what the memoir of an important man should be, and as the model of the proper treatment of a subject. We should have little just cause to complain of modern biographers if they were followers of Cavendish. It is obvious, of course, that—as such a pioneer was bound to be—he was ignorant of art. We want to know something about the parentage, childhood, and youth of a hero; and over all these Cavendish goes galloping in twelve lines. We demand the mile-stones of dates, and we shall hardly discover one from cover to cover. We have learned to expect a certain neatness of execution, and the 'Life of Cardinal Wolsey' is often roughly sewn together and shows the seams. Still, when we have read the little book we feel as though we had ourselves watched the triumphant Legate in his chequered progress, as he tasted of the sweet and of the sour.

Cavendish has the root of the biographer's matter in him. His eye is fixed, not on the course of European politics, not on the struggle between England and Rome, not on the course of arbitrary government, but on the single human being whom he worshipped. He is like Agave in the weird Cadmean forest, 'gazing, an insatiate bride, on [Wolsey's] form from every side.' The result is that he loses, with an enchanting carelessness, any sense of proportion: whether Wolsey determines to accept the principle of Papal supremacy or leaves his red buckram bag lying in his chamber, the attention of Cavendish is equally arrested. Sometimes he hunts mice which seem almost too small for a sportsman: as when he says, 'The Bishop of Carlisle, being with him in his barge, said unto him, wiping the sweat from his face, "Sir, it is a very hot day,"' or as when we read that, 'talking with Master Norris upon his knees in the mire, he would have pulled off his under cap of velvet, but he could not undo the knot under his chin; wherefore with violence he rent the laces and pulled it from his head, and so kneeled bareheaded.' No doubt, to contemporary readers of the MS., these things seemed dangerously and irreverently trivial; but more and more, as time goes by, we learn to value them, and to come back to them for that clear-coloured portrait of the man set against the dim background of his age which is the real essence of the art of biography, and should be the sole aim of the biographer.

The more closely we study Cavendish's 'Life of Cardinal Wolsey,' the more we shall be impressed by its vivid merit of portraiture.

THE CUSTOM OF BIOGRAPHY

The story of the degradation of Wolsey, led up to by that strange omen of the great silver cross falling upon Bonner and cutting his head, and culminating in the mysterious visit of the Earl of Northumberland, up to the fatal moment when that trembling envoy said, 'with a very faint and soft voice, laying his hand on Wolsey's arm, "My lord, I arrest you of high treason,"' is a piece of personal description so lively, so poignant, drawn with such an economy of strokes, that it has, in its own sort, never been surpassed. What makes Cavendish the more surprising is the uniqueness of his performance. No one showed him the way to go: he had no precursor: he is our first biographer, born full-grown. There can be no doubt that if his book had been published when, or soon after, it was written, it must have produced a good effect, and have been imitated to some purpose; but political prejudice made it dangerous to print it while a Tudor monarch sat on the throne, and when, at last, in a garbled text, it was published in 1641, it was too late.

We remained, therefore, as a nation practically without biography for another century. It is very strange, if we come to think of it, that the vast concerted blaze of literary talent under Elizabeth should not have included some rocket or catherine-wheel of personal narrative. The miscellanies of discovery and navigation, of which the folios of Hakluyt are the types, contained a good deal of floating biographical matter, and many rapid silhouettes of piratical voyagers, drawn sometimes with infinite spirit and skill. But these were in no sense biographies, and the object of the writers in all such cases was not the psychology of the individual navigator, but where he went, what he saw, and what additions he made to general information. With all his imagination and his curiosity, the Elizabethan was not interested in the little traits and personal characteristics of individuals. He was occupied a good deal with ideas, but more with images and the embroidery of life, and not at all with single specimens of humanity. The curious reader who will take a stroll or a turn in Raleigh's 'History of the World' (no man now living can perform the whole of that dread pilgrimage) will easily divine the mode in which the noblest subjects of Elizabeth and James regarded the personal history of men and women. They were interested in it if it formed part of the magnificent pageant of public manners, and also if it illustrated 'the enterprises of eminent virtue.' Beyond this, the idea of biography never seems to have occurred to them. It is remarkable that even such an event as the murder of Sir Thomas Overbury, which moved Jacobean society to its very core, and led to the publication of innumerable sermons, poems, pamphlets, 'apologies,' and 'sheets,' resulted in nothing which even by courtesy could be called a 'Life of Overbury.'

The most notable biography of the Elizabethan age, and indeed almost the only one which deserves comment, is that 'Life of the Renownèd Sir Philip Sidney' which was published by Fulk Greville, Lord Brooke, in 1625, three years before his servant so mysteriously stabbed him. Everything about Lord Brooke is dim and spectral, and we do not know why he had kept back this book from publication for nearly forty years. He had been one of the most intimate of Sidney's friends; he was a man of high dignity and learning; he had enjoyed the confidence of his Sovereign in delicate conditions both abroad and at home. It might have been supposed that he was the ideal biographer of Sidney; and readers in many generations must have gone to the little book in the hope of finding a neglected masterpiece, a storehouse of good things unrifled. Still, the fact is that Lord Brooke's 'Life of Sidney' is one of the disappointments of literature. In the first place, whether in prose or in verse, Fulk Greville was the Stéphane Mallarmé of the seventeenth century: he used language with such an extraordinary determination to twist it to his private ends that the most attentive and patient reader may study page upon page of what he writes without forming any definite impression of what it is he means. In the second place, profoundly as he admired his friend, it is not mainly of Sir Philip Sidney that he is thinking: it is mainly of how to restore the image of the ancient vigour of the world in this decrepit age—as usual, ideas and imaginative aspirations driving mere homely human features out into the cold. Thus, as a specimen of biographic art, in the proper sense, the 'Life of the Renownèd Sir Philip Sidney' is negligible, and again English literature had missed possessing a biography of real merit.

The reader who is fond of coincidences, however, may be interested to note that a single year saw the beginning of published biography in this country. With all its shortcomings, Lord Brooke's 'Sidney' was a notable production, and it appeared, in 1641, simultaneously with the first edition of Cavendish's 'Wolsey.' But the preceding winter had seen the issue of Izaak Walton's 'Life of Donne,' which preceded the first folio edition of the Dean's Sermons. This year, 1640–1, is, therefore, epoch-making in the history of English biography. If we exclude Cavendish, as a mere portent, the first English biographer is Walton, whose famous 'Lives' have taken a place from which they can never be ousted. These 'well-meant sacrifices to the memory of five worthy men' have a charm, a delicate perfume, which renders them almost as unique as they are delightful. Walton perceived many things which the most artful modern biographer has not seen more clearly than he did; on the other hand, it is mere Waltonolatry to deny that his aim was pre-eminently edification, and that his prime object in writing was to preserve the memory of 'acts and virtues' which might otherwise have been neglected, and to 'present them to the imitation of those

THE CUSTOM OF BIOGRAPHY

that shall succeed us.' This was in every case Walton's design; and it must be acknowledged that this is still far from the biographical purity of a Boswell, who faithfully records every manifestion of the character of his subject, believing that character, in its nudity, to be a perfectly worthy theme for our respectful attention. If fact, it is probably to a survival of the disadvantages of Walton's convention that many of the worst errors of recent English biography are due.

It is curious that Walton, although he seems to have been widely read, was not ably imitated. We should have expected a flock of such lives as those of George Herbert and Sanderson; but they do not occur. As a matter of fact, the seventeenth century, after the Restoration, affords us only two biographies of particular note; and it is interesting to observe, as a sign of want of public interest in this kind of literature, that one of these was not published at all, and the other only as the preface to the Works of its subject. Each of these adds something to the national conception of biography. There have been warm admirers of the 'Life' of her husband, composed by Mrs. Hutcheson, of Owthorpe, about 1670, but not printed until 1806. It has curious merits: as we read it, something in the prim, prejudiced, and narrow, but stately and honest, Puritan lady of quality fascinates us. We listen to her even voice, recounting, at a dead level, without a touch of humour, such things as befell her great and good 'Colonel,' as she invariably designates him; and if we do not, in defiance of good manners, fall into a deep sleep, we have to confess that her austere narrative is impressive and convincing. We may say that Lucy Hutcheson adds to English biography the element of a precise and even sequence of events.

In almost every respect the other important biography of the seventeenth century was a contrast to the 'Life of Colonel Hutcheson.' Bishop Sprat's celebrated 'Life of Cowley,' long the model of elegant obituary, was printed first in Latin, in 1668, and then, at particular request, in English in 1669. Dr. Johnson's denunciation of it is well known, and is on the whole not ill-deserved. But the great critic exaggerates: it is not quite fair to say of Sprat's 'Cowley' (as it is perfectly fair to say of most other English biographies written before the reign of George III.) that 'all is shown in it confused and enlarged through the mist of panegyric.' Sprat, it is true, is desperately afraid of realism, and constantly draws back out of discretion when he is at the edge of a diverting confidence; but it is not just to deny that he does manage to give us a fairly clear portrait of Cowley. The form of his biography—it is addressed as a colossal epistle to a certain Martin Clifford—astonishes the unwary reader by sudden references to 'you, Sir,' and to 'your Unkle, Mr. Fotherby,' and there is a distasteful parade of clerical obsequiousness, that ugly feature of the age; but, when all is said and done, and the ghost of Dr. Johnson is appeased, Sprat's 'Life of Cowley' is a very graceful and pleasing memoir. Not easily will the writer of these lines forget how, as a schoolboy, he bought for a trifle one of the huge early folios of Cowley in the market of Exeter (then a rich hunting-field for such old books), and how he lost himself with joy among the stately parentheses and periwigged circumlocutions of Sprat's sonorous eulogy.

It might have been expected that biography would flourish in the reign of Anne, when the habit of close and graceful observation of character and manners had become paramount, but, for some reason which escapes us, this department of letters fell into deep disgrace. It was abandoned to the lowest class of scribblers, and we find the life of Milton written by Toland, and that of Congreve by Charles Wilson. The composition of personal memoirs was abandoned to 'virulent party hacks who wrote for hire,' and it was not consistent with the dignity of any recognised man of letters to collect, before it was too late, a series of particulars regarding such giants of the preceding age as Dryden and Locke. What was written, if it had a value, as in the case of the 'Life and Actions' of Bunyan, owed it wholly to the rarity of the facts recorded, not to any art or tact in the narrator. By an odd chance, some of the wretched efforts of early eighteenth-century biography have been preserved for us, as flies or the members of flies, in the amber of Dr. Johnson's 'Lives of the Poets.' Oldisworth's 'Life of Edmund Smith,' which Johnson's indolence persuaded him to annex entire, is the most important of these fossil remains. The reader may, without the fatigue of research, turn to this typical specimen of biography in the golden age of Anne. It will hardly tempt him to make further explorations.

In 1741, exactly a hundred years since the birth of English biography, an important experiment was made in the art which had practically slumbered since the days of Izaak Walton. This was the 'Life of Cicero,' by Dr. Conyers Middleton—what we should now call 'a library book'—in two large volumes. It is worth notice that the modern biography, in its solemn conventional shape, lineally descends from Middleton's 'Life of Cicero,' which invented the fashion. This book, moreover, is the earliest example of the species called 'Life and Times,' which has since been so constantly made the vehicle of the history of an individual, set in an elaborate landscape of political or social chronicles. Conyers Middleton tells all he knows about Cicero, not merely as a person but in relation to the Roman history of his day. This very remarkable book, which long ago became obsolete, but should never have been quite forgotten in the history of our literature, enjoyed at the time of its publication an immense success. It was reprinted many times, and it was read by all educated people in England, in spite of the unpopularity of its

THE CUSTOM OF BIOGRAPHY

author, and in spite of the many and not ill-founded attacks brought against its veracity and originality. I do not think that the importance of Middleton's 'Life of Cicero' from the social point of view has ever been properly perceived. It first made biography a respectable independent branch of the literary profession; it first gave the lettered public an appetite for this order of books; and it first set the type which has in measure been followed ever since of the sort of publication which we have known in Mr. Masson's 'Life and Times of Milton' or Sir John Seeley's 'Life and Times of Stein.'

The last remarkable biography in the old, dim manner, written rhetorically, with forcible passages, and a wide disregard for dates, was Dr. Johnson's 'Life of Savage,' published in 1744. But for the inherent excellence of writing in this piece, it might have been composed by any one of the hacks to whom the despised province of biography was abandoned. In general design it showed no advance whatever. But the next step was taken by a man who holds no highly-honoured place in literary history, yet was, in this solitary respect, a remarkable innovator. He was the Rev. William Mason, who, in 1775, issued his 'Life and Letters of Gray.' This was the first attempt seriously made in English to let the subject of a memoir tell his own story. Mason printed Gray's correspondence, and tied it together by means of a slender running thread of narrative. Sprat had laid it down that private letters were not 'full-dress' enough to be presented to the public eye. This dictum of Sprat had hung over the biographer for more than a hundred years. Mason first had the courage to defy it, and to turn the correspondence of Gray into the chief attraction of his memoir. This was an idea of genius, and Mason deserves credit for it, in spite of the indolent way in which he carried out his design and the liberties which he took with his material.

When we glory in the 'Life of Dr. Samuel Johnson,' the greatest and best of all biographies, we ought not to grudge a thought of thanks to the 'Life of Gray,' since, without Mason as a model, Boswell would scarcely have dared to adopt the present form of his incomparable work. It is true that between 1775 and 1791 considerable progress had been made in what was now becoming the reputable art of biography; but Mason's 'Gray' was still the model, and Boswell, while infinitely improving upon it, everywhere shows that it inspired and guided him. His two quarto volumes—so handsome in type and *format*, with the beautiful frontispiece after Reynolds—did credit to the enterprise of Charles Dilly, of the Poultry, and they removed for ever, in their magnificent celebrity, the stigma that until then had never ceased to rest upon biography as a kind of literature not quite worthy of a gentleman. It is certain that down to near the end of the eighteenth century this prejudice against biography as somewhat indiscreet and even ill-bred—as, in fact, almost a sin against good manners, a thing to be relegated at best to the 'virulent' hacks of Grub Street—survived in the minds of the British public. Even the biographies of Goldsmith and Mallet were looked upon with indulgent consideration of the wants of those authors. One must not be hard on a man of genius, who is starving, if he is driven to write a 'Life of Beau Nash'; but one is justified in hoping that he will soon come into a competence and be saved from such drudgery. This is, in fact, the word: until the success of Boswell's 'Life of Johnson,' biography was considered work fit for a drudge only.

This had, no doubt, a great deal to do with the difficulty which Boswell has met in coming into his intellectual estate. After the passage of more than a hundred years, it is by no means universally that proper respect is shown to Boswell. To Macaulay, steeped in all the intellectual prejudices of the eighteenth century, it was impossible to be quite fair to a mere biographer. Boswell might be this or that, might have preserved this one matter of value, or have shown penetration on another question of importance; none the less was he to Macaulay, and to thousands of educated persons at the beginning of the nineteenth century, nothing better than a footman in the house of literature. His coat might be smarter than Oldmixon's, his manners more polished than Toland's; but essentially he was a lacquey, a low fellow, a writer of the life of a great man whom he had toadied. That Boswell might himself be a writer of independent distinction, that he might be destined to live in the history of literature on his own merits, could never occur to a man trained in the school of Macaulay.

But, at all events, if the glory of Boswell was delayed, the fashion for biographies was established. It was no longer to be 'low' to write the life of an individual. Lord Sheffield promptly followed with his little memoir of Gibbon, and the biographies became too many for us to chronicle here, or even to summarise. The curiosity of the public was now fully awakened, and with the opening years of the nineteenth century biography suddenly began to take its place as one of the most fertile branches of current literature. At first, however, the size of these works was still modest, and their scope was confined to subjects which offered a legitimate opportunity for the indulgence of a wide public demand. For example, few books have been awaited with so much impatience as Southey's 'Life of Nelson'; but when it appeared, in 1813, it was apparent that the author had found it possible to say all that was requisite in two small volumes. Let us ask ourselves what number of bulky tomes the career of such a popular hero would be expected to swell into to-day?

Sir Walter Scott, indeed, was one of the earliest offenders. It is melancholy to have to relate that it is his 'Life of Napoleon

THE CUSTOM OF BIOGRAPHY

Buonaparte' which seems to deserve the credit of being the precursor of those monster biographies which have become the curse of our shelves. It was doubtless the least successful of his productions, and even when it was new, and while the aura of romance hung over both author and subject, few readers were found patient enough to read its nine huge diffuse volumes right through. The floodgates were now opened, however, and for the last seventy-five years the funereal tributes have poured over us in a steadily mounting wave,

> Till they cover the place of each sorrow,
> And leave us no Past and no Morrow,
> For what man is able to master
> And stem this great fountain of tears?

It has seemed well, at all events, to point out that the bondage of huge, perfunctory biography does not come down to us from limitless ages, but was the creation of a time relatively recent. It may roughly be said to date from about the year 1830. Perhaps this may encourage some reformer to rise and smite a habit which has not even the dignity of age to support it.

It would be mere affectation, let me hasten to say, in a writer who has himself made various experiments in biography, and knows both its difficulty and its delicacy—it would be mere affectation if I pretended to denounce the writing of lives as a useless or undignified part of literature. It is precisely because I hold it to be one of the most valuable that I would fain see it practised with judgment and common sense. In the seventy years which divide us from the Southeys and the Campbells and the Moores, the pioneers of popular biography, we have seen our language enriched by many lives of eminent men which have been perfect in taste and entirely acceptable in size and proportion. Perhaps the most important single publication of the last twenty years has been a work in this particular department. I mean, of course, the stately 'Dictionary of National Biography.' Mr. John Morley, whose 'Diderot,' 'Rousseau,' and 'Voltaire' were already models of what a monograph should be, performed a most beneficent act when he conceived his series of 'English Men of Letters,' each closely confined within set limits and regulated by the wholesome discipline of compression. These volumes were sneered at as 'little books about great men,' as though it were a merit in a book to be big. It is to be hoped that no one ever thought of reversing the reproach, and of stigmatising our too-frequent 'great books about little men.'

If I had space at my command, it would be a pleasure to enumerate others of the 'Lives' which, during the last seventy years, have afforded English readers pleasure of a very high kind, and have taken a permanent place in history. But that is not possible here. I can only speak of what strike me as some of the

EDMUND GOSSE

abuses of biography as it has now come to be practised in England. These are abuses which, if they are not checked, will make this section of English books a dust-heap which no one will dare to disturb, a vast receptacle of useless matter irremediably devoted to oblivion. It is because I think biography, when properly directed, one of the most delightful of all branches of reading, that I feel drawn to protest against our treatment of it.

In the first place, the popular idea seems to be that no one is too great a fool, or too complete an amateur, or too thoroughly ignorant of the modes of composition, to undertake the 'life' of an eminent person. This I believe to be a survival of the old ignominy under which biography so long suffered. We have seen that for many generations to write a great man's life was considered the work of a 'hack.' The biographer was a pariah; he was not in the inner circle of letters; his dirty trade was only excused because he wanted bread. This conception of the biographer, as a being outside the pale, has so entirely disappeared that everybody seems to have forgotten that it ever existed. But it has left us as a legacy the popular conviction that any one can write a 'Life.' It is still understood that to be a philosopher a man must have made a study of thought, that a historian must have given some years to documents and to their synthesis, that a man is not a dramatist until he has mastered the conditions of the stage. But a biography is supposed to need no skill, no art, no experience of any kind. Here is a dead man, we say: when he was alive no one took much notice of him; but, as he is dead, the national convention insists that we should publish a 'life' of him (two volumes, crown octavo). Who shall write this? O! rush out into the street and stop the very first person who passes, for anybody in the world is as fit as any other body to write a biography. Thus, at least, the people responsible for 'Lives' appear to argue.

Of the untrained persons who step in, or are brought in, to perform this inevitable and perfunctory task, the worst is the Widow. This may be taken as a generic term for the class of life-writers whose only claim is that they are 'on the spot,' that arrogate to themselves the duty of biography merely because they are in possession of the documents. The Widow is the worst of all the diseases of biography. She is the triumph of the unfittest. Others may have little art, little experience, little sense of proportion; but she exceeds them, for she has none at all. Her object is to present to the world an image of the deceased, which shall be deliberately although unconsciously false. The man had his humour, his eccentricities; he had a rough side to his tongue; he had frailties; he was a picturesque and human being. It is the determination of the Widow to hide all this. She desires to show that he was perfect, with that waxy absence of all salient feature which she takes for

THE CUSTOM OF BIOGRAPHY

perfection. She paints him quite smooth and plump, with a high light on his forehead and a sanctimonious droop of his eyelid. She expatiates on his having been humble in spirit, when it was his special function to be ambitious and keen. She dwells on instances in which he was 'a help to others,' and a 'wonderful example to the young.' Above all, she carefully suppresses all evidence of his being unlike other men, or having any oddities, because to admit these would be to lower him from his pedestal, to scratch the flawless pinkness of his wax. It is to the Widow that we owe the fact that a very large section of recent biography might pass for an annex to Madame Tussaud's gallery. For, it must be remarked, the Widow does not always boldly appear on the title-page: she often lurks behind the apparently unprejudiced name of some docile author. Her function, however, always is to stultify and misrepresent the life and character of the deceased; and the more devotion she thinks she is paying to his memory, the more completely she carries this out. I know of only one instance in modern biography where the influence of the Widow has not been disastrous.

Questions of proportion and selection are apparently never considered by the English biographer. Yet, if he did not start with a contempt for his own business, a series of problems would present themselves at the threshold of his work. He would ask himself, Is the subject I propose to write about worthy of separate biographical treatment? To decide this in the affirmative, it should be necessary to satisfy one's self that the subject possessed qualities, moved in conditions, assumed characteristics, so unlike those of other men as to justify his being raised from their ranks. When this primary test has been passed, it should then be for the biographer to ask, What were the extent and the value of his uniqueness? what—in short—is his relative bulk? If he was a small, but quite interesting and curious, biologist or soldier or artist, he must not be treated on the same scale as Darwin or Wellington or Turner. There should be a certain proportion between the size of his portrait and the effect which he produced in public life. (This, it may be broadly said, is never taken into consideration.) The question of proportion, then, being met or evaded, there comes before the biographer the question of material; and this is so important that it requires separate attention.

In the days when biography was first attempted, material was extremely scanty. For a long time—except by such hermit artists as Cavendish and Walton—personal detail was rejected altogether. Until the time of Mason, private correspondence was not looked upon as material at all. Sprat refers, as we have seen, to a collection of Cowley's familiar letters in his possession, and positively takes credit to himself for not using them: he lies, indeed, under some suspicion of having destroyed them. With Mason, however, this superstition disappeared. It became recognised that letters form a rich source of information, richer than even diaries. During the second half of the nineteenth century the difficulty was no longer lack of material, but excess of it. There is hardly a life printed nowadays that does not offend by the publication of too much of everything—too many letters, too many extracts from diaries, too many 'impressions' contributed by unobservant people, too much undigested material of every description. Hardly a 'Life and Letters,' however ably selected, however full of intrinsic value, which would not be improved by a process of heroic shrinkage; no book of the kind in three volumes which would not be better in two; very few in two which would not be better in one.

In offering an example of this excess, I would point not to one of the worst but to one of the best of recent lives. It is not to be questioned that the most valuable purely literary biography published in 1900 was Mr. Basil Champneys' 'Memoirs and Correspondence of Coventry Patmore.' I shall not be accused of a wish to disparage a book which has given us all so much pleasure and profit. But even in this work there is much of a subsidiary and therefore superfluous character. It is not until the third chapter that we meet the subject of the memoir at all, delayed as we are by his ancestry and parentage. He was married three times, and of two of the wives elaborate lives have to be introduced. A whole chapter must be given to one of his daughters; another, to one of his sons. Five long appendices must deal with incidents in the career of his father. It is not to be alleged that all these side-growths are without interest; but it is undeniable that they interrupt the reader, distract his attention, and divert him from the real subject of the book to themes which are only faintly related to it. They swell out the book with about 150 unnecesary pages. In another and earlier biography of extreme interest, the 'Life of Archbishop Benson,' the burden of elephantic bigness has been found intolerable, and, although the book was only published in 1899, it is already boiled down into a memoir of hardly half the size. If this difficulty about the condensation and rejection of material is found to be insuperable in books of this importance, what shall we say of the ephemeral and perfunctory memoirs that issue every day from the press? Surely, this: that their compilers show a just sense of their uselessness by issuing them in such a form as precludes the possibility of their ever being read.

Exaggerated respect for the conventions and tenderness lest the susceptibility of survivors should be wounded are constant causes of biographical failure. There is much to be said, of course, in favour of decency and reticence; but, from the point of view of the general reader, these are matters which are now far too sedulously cultivated. Hardly any biographer dares to present his subject 'in his habit, as

THE CUSTOM OF BIOGRAPHY

he lived.' The best anecdotes, the most illuminating traits, are never recorded in print at all. Tennyson, for example, was, in real life, infinitely more racy and reckless than the authorised portrait gives the public the slightest reason for supposing. Is this wonderful figure of a wayward genius to be successfully hidden from posterity by a misplaced and too-cautious piety? Why should not we be permitted to know Tennyson as we know Pope and Burns and Byron? Why should not we possess of nineteenth-century worthies such seed-pearl of portraiture as Aubrey set down so unreservedly in his invaluable 'Minutes of Lives'? But when a really sincere biography, like Purcell's 'Cardinal Manning,' manages to be written, the welkin rings with screams of 'disloyalty' and 'sacrilege.' One of the most perfect pieces of biographical art issued in our time was the *first edition* of Mr. Baring Gould's 'Memoir of Hawker of Morwenstow'; but it was both candid and humorous, and therefore had to be promptly withdrawn. What would this thin-skinned generation say to J. R. Smith's 'Life of Nollekens'? Smith was Nollekens' assistant, and had always been led to believe that the great sculptor had remembered him very handsomely in his will. This, however, proved not to be the case. Smith, a man of deliberate habits, looked about him for a means of vengeance. He finally determined to write 'Nollekens' Life,' and a most entertaining production it is. But the cultivation of biography as a form of revenge is, I admit, not to be seriously recommended.

If I could venture to hope that these remarks might have some effect, I should wish that it might be in the direction of increasing our sense of responsibility with regard to a delightful, invaluable, and at the present most cruelly abused, department of literature. The art which has supplied us with such masterpieces as Lockhart's 'Scott,' Southey's 'Nelson,' Mrs. Gaskell's 'Charlotte Brontë,' and Carlyle's 'Frederick' in narrative, and has presented us with the correspondence of Lamb, of Walpole, of FitzGerald, and of Stevenson, deserves to be treated with more respect than is usual at the present day. It is not an art which ought to be relegated to amateurs. It should not be taken for granted that it requires no skill or tact or experience in its execution. On the contrary, there is no species of writing which requires the exercise of a finer sense of proportion, of a keener appreciation of the relative value of things and men, or of a deeper sense of literary responsibility.

PRINCIPLES OF BIOGRAPHY [1]

I

I APPRECIATE very highly the honour which the electors have done me in conferring on me the office of Leslie Stephen Lecturer in this University. A word of respectful admiration seems due to the liberality of the electors in bestowing this dignity for the second time in succession on a graduate of the sister University.

I propose to deal broadly with a very familiar ambition—the ambition to record in written words, on the printed page, the career of a man or woman. My design is to consider in the first place the essential quality of the theme which justly merits biographic effort, and in the second place to discuss the methods of presentment which are likely to serve the true purpose of biography to best effect. Some paths which the biographer should avoid will also call for notice. I hope to suggest causes of success or failure in the practice of biography.

II

It is outside my scope to deal in any detail with the biography of particular persons. But I think I may without impropriety venture at the outset on a few words about the man in whose memory this lectureship has been founded, and whose name it bears. I am conscious that I lack many of the qualifications which my two predecessors in this honourable office [2] enjoyed. But I believe I may without immodesty claim one advantage in this post, which neither of them shared with me. Leslie Stephen was the master under whom I served my literary apprenticeship, and it was as his pupil that I grew to be his colleague and friend. He

[1] The Leslie Stephen Lecture, delivered in the Senate House, Cambridge, on 13 May 1911.
[2] [Professors A. C. Bradley and W. P. Ker].

gave me my earliest lessons in the writing of biography, and in speaking of its principles I am guided by his teaching. I am expressing views coloured by the experience for which he trained me.

There still happily survive members of this University and literary friends in London who knew Leslie Stephen in days far earlier than those of my first acquaintance with him. Compared with the companions of his youth or early middle age I have small right to speak of him. My association with him only concerned the last twenty-one years of his life. Yet I may plead that outside the ranks of his family I owe him debts of knowledge and encouragement which have not, I think, been excelled.

Stephen belonged to a notable generation, a generation the heroes of which seem to have been cast in a larger mould than those of my own. Stephen was the affectionate disciple of Darwin, the admiring acquaintance of Tennyson, the frequent but rather critical companion of Froude, the close friend of Henry Sidgwick, of George Meredith, of James Russell Lowell. He was personally known to Browning, Ruskin, Fitzgerald, and Carlyle. With such men as these he would be the first to disclaim equality, but he belonged to their orbit.

It was Stephen's habit to depreciate himself, and to underestimate the regard in which others held him. His qualities did not make for wide popularity. He did not seek what Tennyson calls 'the blare and blaze of fame'. Yet he established a reputation which his greatest coevals acknowledged—a reputation which came of the virility and perspicuity of his work in ethics, in literary criticism, and, above all, in biography.

Justly may the University claim some share in his fame. To Cambridge Stephen owed mainly the greatest blessing of life—health, as well as a large stock of his intellectual equipment. In Stephen's case Cambridge made of a weakly boy an athletic man. His training as an undergraduate turned him into an athlete in body no less than in mind. Not that his physical health was ever obtrusively robust, but the physical exercise of his undergraduate days, in which he engaged with a wholly spontaneous zeal, clearly helped him to measure a span of life exceeding the psalmist's three score years and ten. Even more notable is the influence which this place exerted on his intellectual temper. The ideal of dry common sense, which dominated thought here in his youthful days, was his guiding star through life. He was always impatient of rhetoric, of sentimentality, of floridity in life or literature. His virtues as man and writer were somewhat of the Spartan kind. It was his life here in youth and early middle age that chiefly bred the terseness, the frankness, the dialectical adroitness which give his literary work its savour. Although he severed his connexion with his University before he was forty, and though to some extent his sympathies with Cambridge afterwards decayed, its beneficent influences were never obliterated in him.

To the world at large as years advanced he seemed reserved and melancholy. I have heard him groan for hours together over the verbosity and blindness of biographers. But his seasons of depression, save in sickness, were passing moods. No man found richer solace than he in the early friendships which he formed in his University. His enthusiasm for his college while undergraduate, fellow, and tutor, always kept alive happy memories, which helped to assuage sorrow, as I can testify from some evenings spent with him, when heavy domestic grief bowed down his spirit. 'I love the sleepy river,' he said in his last days, 'not even the Alpine scenery is dearer to me.'

Often a gladiator wielding unsparingly the sword of plain speech against orthodox beliefs, he dealt his strokes fairly and squarely, and few of his adversaries cherished lasting resentment. Wary of enthusiasm and impatient of insincerity or incompetence, he admired without reserve all greatness in deed or thought. Every honest endeavour won his sympathy. His tenderness of heart was without any uncharitable leaven. There was always abundance of affectionate interest in those with whom he worked. Notably in his case is the style of the author the character of the man. 'I think', wrote Robert Louis Stevenson, 'it is always wholesome to read Leslie Stephen.' The dictum is in too minor a key to sound the whole truth, but it is the unpretending sort of language which Stephen would have appreciated about himself, especially from such a quarter.

III

Biography exists to satisfy a natural instinct in man—the commemorative instinct—the universal desire to keep alive the memories of those who by character and exploits have distinguished themselves from the mass of mankind. Art, pictorial, plastic, monumental art, competes with biography in preserving memories of buried humanity. But Jacques Amyot, the great prose writer of the French Renaissance—Amyot who, by his French translation of the works of Plutarch, first made the Greek master of biography an influence on modern thought and conduct—wrote these wise words on the relative values of biography and art as means of commemorating men's characters and achievements: 'There is neither picture, nor image of marble, nor arch of triumph, nor pillar, nor sumptuous sepulchre, can match the durableness of an eloquent biography, furnished with the qualities which it ought to have.' 'Furnished with the qualities which it ought to have'—there is the problem which we are met to face. Biography is not so imposing to the general eye as pyramids and mausoleums, statues and columns, portraits and memorial foundations, but it is the *safest* way, as Thomas Fuller wrote, to protect a memory from oblivion. Plutarch, Tacitus, and Suetonius' biographical memorials of distinguished men have worn better than the more substantial tributes of art to their heroes' fame.

The aim of biography is, in general terms, to hand down to a future age the history of individual men or women, to transmit enduringly their character and exploits. Character and exploits are for biographical purposes inseparable. Character which does not translate itself into exploit is for the biographer a mere phantasm. The exploit may range from mere talk, as in the case of Johnson, to empire-building and military conquest, as in the case of Julius Caesar or Napoleon. But character and exploit jointly constitute biographic personality. Biography aims at satisfying the commemorative instinct by exercise of its power to transmit personality.

The biographic aim implies two constant and obvious conditions. Firstly, the subject-matter, the character and achievement out of which the biography is to be woven, must be capable of moving the interest of posterity. Secondly, the manner or style of the record should be of a texture which is calculated to endure, to outlive the fashion or taste of the hour. In other words, biography depends for its successful accomplishment on the two elements of fit matter and fit manner, of fit theme and fit treatment.

Good treatment will not compensate for a bad theme, nor will a good theme compensate for bad treatment. Theme and treatment must both answer equally a call of permanent distinction. There are cases in which a good subject is found in combination with a bad form. That indeed is no uncommon experience. In the result, the commemorative instinct remains unsatisfied and biography fails to perform its function. The converse association of a bad theme with good treatment, of bad matter with good manner, is rarer, and may kindle some literary interest, although not an interest of biographic concern. For the life of a nonentity or a mediocrity, however skilfully contrived, conflicts with primary biographic principles. Unless subject-matter and style be both of a commensurate sufficiency, biography lacks 'the qualities which it ought to have', the qualities which ensure permanence, the qualities which satisfy the commemorative instinct.

What constitutes fitness in a biographic theme? The question raises puzzling issues. The commemorative instinct which biography has to satisfy scarcely seems to obey in its habitual working any one clear immutable law. The Italian poet Ariosto imagined, with some allegorical vagueness, that at the end of every man's thread of life there hung a medal stamped with his name, and that, as Death severed life's thread with its fatal shears, Time seized the medal and dropped it into the river of Lethe. Yet a few, a very few, of the stamped medals were caught as they fell towards the waters of oblivion by swans, who carried off the medals and deposited them in a temple or museum of immortality. Ariosto's swans are biographers: by what motive are they impelled to rescue any medals of personality from the flood of forgetfulness into which they let the mass sink?

Perhaps the old Greek definition of the fit theme of tragedy may be usefully adapted to the fit theme of biography. A fit biographic theme is, in the Aristotelian phrase, a career which is 'serious, complete, and of a certain magnitude'. An unfit biographic theme is a career of trivial aim, incomplete, without magnitude, of or below mediocrity. The second clause in this definition, which prescribes the need of completeness, offers no ambiguity. It excludes from the scope of biography careers of living men, careers which are incomplete, because death witholds the finishing touch. Death is a part of life, and no man is fit subject for biography till he is dead. Living men have been made themes of biography. But the choice defies the cardinal condition of completeness. There is usually abroad an idle curiosity about prominent persons during their lifetime. It is not the business of biography to appease mere inquisitiveness. Its primary business is to be complete. The living theme can at best be a torso, a fragment. There clings to it, too, a savour either of the scandal or of the unbalanced laudation which living men rarely escape. Politicians, while they are yet active on the political stage, are often panegyrized or vilified by biographical partisans. The efficient commemorative instinct, which sets little store by such panegyric or vilification, craves, before all things, the completeness which death alone assures. No man's memory can be accounted great until it has outlived his life.

At the same time there is danger in postponing indefinitely biographic commemoration in cases where it is rightly due. There are insuperable obstacles to writing the lives of men long after their relatives and associates have passed away. Even the life of Shakespeare has suffered through the long interval which separates the date of his death from the first efforts of his biographers, and there are some of Shakespeare's literary contemporaries, whose biographic commemoration has been postponed to so distant a date after their career has closed that the attempt to satisfy the just call of the commemorative instinct has altogether failed.

But the theme of biography must be far more than 'complete'. It must be, in addition, both 'serious' and 'of a certain magnitude'. By seriousness we may understand the quality which stirs and firmly holds the attention of the earnest-minded.

What constitutes the needful 'magnitude' in a biographic theme? It is difficult to set up a fixed standard whereby to measure the dimensions of a human action. But by way of tentative suggestion or hypothesis, the volume of a human action may be said to vary, from the biographer's point of view, with the number of times that it has been accomplished or is capable of accomplishment.

The magnitude of human action is necessarily of many degrees; the scale ascends and descends. The production by Shakespeare of his thirty-seven plays is an action of the first magnitude, because the achievement is unique. The victory of Wellington at Waterloo is an action of great but of lesser magnitude, because deeds of like calibre have been achieved by other military commanders, and are doubtless capable, if the need arise, of accomplishment again. As we descend the scale of achievement, we reach by slow gradations the level of action which forms the terminal limit of the biographic province. Actions, however beneficent or honourable, which are accomplished or are capable of accomplishment by many thousands of persons are actions of mediocrity, and lack the dimension which justifies the biographer's notice.

The fact that a man is a devoted husband and father, an efficient schoolmaster, an exemplary parish priest, gives him in itself no claim to biographic commemoration, because his actions, although meritorious, are practically indistinguishable from those of thousands of his fellows. It follows further that official dignities, except of the rarest and most dignified kind, give *in themselves* no claim to biographic commemoration. That a man should become a peer, a member of parliament, a lord mayor, even a professor, and attend to his duties, are actions or experiences that have been accomplished or are capable of accomplishment by too large a number of persons to render them in themselves of appreciable magnitude. At the same time office may well give a man an opportunity of distinction which he might otherwise be without; official responsibility may well lift his career to the requisite level of eminence.

In appraising the magnitude—the biographic capacity or content—of a career, one must needs guard against certain false notions—εἴδωλα or idols in Baconian terminology—which prevail widely and tend to distort the judgement. Domestic partiality, social contiguity, fortuitous clamour of the crowd—such things frequently cause mediocrity to masquerade as magnitude. The biographer has to forswear the measuring rods of the family hearth, of the hospitable board, of journalistic advertisement. A kinsman or a kinswoman, an intimate companion, is easily moved by private affection to credit undiscriminatingly a man or woman's activity with the dimensions that justify biographic commemoration. A newspaper records day by day the activities of some seeker after notoriety, until his name grows more familiar to his generation than that of Shakespeare or Nelson. Evanescent repute may very easily, through journalistic iteration, be mistaken for that which will excite the commemorative instinct hereafter.

In estimating the magnitude of human action, there is need of some workable measure or gauge which shall operate independently of mere contemporary opinion. Contemporary fame is often withheld as arbitrarily as it is bestowed. Posthumous fame at times comes into being with strange suddenness, without any contemporary heralding at all. How suggestive to the student of biography is the fact that the name and work of Gregor Mendel, the Austrian monk and biological inquirer, who died nearly thirty years ago 'unwept, unhonoured, and unsung', should fill ten columns of the new edition of the *Encyclopaedia Britannica*,[1] a space in excess of that devoted to any one of the numerous heroes of science who enjoyed repute in their own lifetime. Current fame is no sure evidence of biographic fitness. The tumult and the shouting die and they may leave nothing behind which satisfies the biographic tests of completeness, seriousness, and magnitude.

IV

The biographer having found his fit theme is faced with the problem of its treatment. His aim is to transmit personality, to satisfy the commemorative instinct. He may learn something of the lawful processes from a preliminary study of the processes which are unlawful. The main path which he should follow may gain in clear definition if he be warned at the outset against certain neighbouring paths which are easily capable of leading him astray. Biography must resolutely preserve its independence of three imposing themes of study, which are often seen to compete for its control. True biography is no handmaid of ethical instruction. Its purpose is not that of history. It does not exist to serve biological or anthropological science. Any assistance that biography renders these three

[1] [The eleventh edition, 1910-1. Later editions have appeared since that date].

great interests—ethical, historical, and scientific—should be accidental; such aid is neither essential nor obligatory. Biography rules a domain of its own; it is autonomous—an attribute with which it is not always credited.

It was an amiable tenet in the orthodox creed of an ancient biographic school, that the career destined for biographic treatment should directly teach morality, should be conspicuously virtuous. The biography should, before all else, 'show virtue her own feature', or at any rate hymn her worth. Gentle Izaak Walton, like many biographers who wrote before and after him, regarded biography as 'an honour due to the virtuous dead, and a lesson in magnanimity to those who shall succeed them'. In Walton's demure judgement, dead men who are morally unworthy lie outside the scope of biography. It speaks well for the goodness of the world that good men have occupied more biographic pens than bad men, and that biographers have always cherished a charitable preference for benefactors over malefactors. But therein lies no proof that the merits of biography depend on its powers of edification.

It is with very large qualifications that Walton's ethical presumption can pass current. Sinners excite the commemorative instinct as well as saints. The careers of both Napoleon I and Napoleon III satisfy all conditions of the biographic theme, in spite of their spacious infringements of moral law. Suetonius defied no biographic principle when he treated of Roman emperors, many of whom were monsters of infamy. Biography is a truthful picture of life, of life's tangled skein, good and ill together. Biography prejudices its chances of success when it is consciously designed as an ethical guide of life.

Candour, which shall be innocent of ethical fervour or even of ethical intention, is a cardinal principle of right biographic method. It is often the biographer's anxious duty to present great achievements in near alliance with moral failings. Coleridge was a great poet and an illuminating thinker. But he was deficient in the moral sense, and justified himself for his offences by 'amazing wrigglings and self-reproaches and astonishing pouring forth of unctuous twaddling'. Byron, Porson, Nelson, Parnell, and many more for whom the commemorative instinct assuredly demands biographic commemoration combined great exploits with notorious defiance of virtue.

The ethical fallacy of biography has sanctioned two evasive methods of handling such perplexing phases of life—a method of suppression and a method of extenuation. The method of suppression has found distinguished advocates. Tennyson asked 'what business has the public to want to know about Byron's wildnesses? He has given them fine work and they ought to be satisfied'. Here indeed we are advised, either to dispense with all biography of Byron, or only to accept a biography of him from which his 'wildnesses' are excluded. The cravings of the commemorative instinct which Byron's career has already excited render both these counsels futile.

The alternative method of extenuation has been adopted by an eminent man of letters of our own day in treating of an illustrious poetic contemporary of Byron—of Shelley. Writing Shelley's life under the admiring eyes of surviving relatives, the biographer has made other people responsible for most of Shelley's flagrant errors of conduct and has credited the poet's personality with an unfailing beneficence. In view of the biographer's true goal it is difficult to speak of the whitewashing method more indulgently than of the method of suppression. The biographer is a narrator, not a moralist, and candour is the salt of his narrative. He accepts alike what clearly tells in a man's favour and what clearly tells against him. Neither omission nor partisan vindication will satisfy the primary needs of the art.

At the same time the biographer is likely to miss his aim of transmitting personality truthfully if he give more space or emphasis to a man's lapses from virtue than is proportioned to their effects on his achievement. Although he may not fill the preacher's pulpit, a touch of sympathy with human frailty, of charity for wrongdoing, will the better fit him for his task.

There is a French proverb: *Tôt ou tard, tout se sait*—'Sooner or later everything comes to light'. There is another French proverb: *Tout comprendre, c'est tout pardonner*—'To understand all is to pardon all'.

Both apophthegms make appeal to the biographer, and the second is quite as relevant to his work as the first. Lives written in a hostile spirit may not be wholly untruthful. But they tend to emphasize unpleasing features and thereby give a wrongful impression. Scurrility is not candour. To pander to a love of scandal is a greater sin in a biographer than in anybody else. Lord Campbell wrote lives of lawyers, which satisfy many of the conditions of biography. But their depreciatory tone, which prompted the epigram that biography lends a new sting to death, suggests malignity and distorts the true perspective. The competent biographer may fail from want of sympathy even when his skill is not in question. Like the portrait painter who is fascinated by forbidding aspects in a sitter's countenance, he may, even without conscious intention, produce a caricature instead of a portrait.

All gradations of moral infirmity, from serious crime to mere deviation from accepted codes of good manners, will from time to time claim the biographer's notice and call for presentation in due perspective. Downright offences are not his only sources of embarrassment. Perhaps more often is he confronted with inconsistencies of conduct or opinion, with sudden changes of beliefs, religious or political, which are currently suspected of dishonesty. Defective sympathy or partisan hostility is here as harmful as any resolve to point a moral. 'That conversion', says the moralist, 'will always be suspected which concurs with interest.' The suspicion is inevitable, but is conversion invariably dishonest? May not increase of knowledge or a greater concentration of thought on the questions at issue induce a natural and an honest process of development? Was Wordsworth a lost leader who left the revolutionary companions of his early years for the orthodox Tories just to receive a handful of silver and a bit of ribbon to stick in his coat? Was Disraeli's early abandonment of a radical programme the act of a self-seeking adventurer? Was Gladstone's unexpected adoption of the policy of Irish Home Rule prompted by impulses of reckless ambition, by the hope of stealing meanly a march on political rivals? The biographer must hold the scales even. He must look before and after, and close his ears to party resentments of the hour. He must abide by the just and generous principles which move a critical friend's judgement. Wherever he honestly can, a friend allows the benefit of the doubt; he extenuates nothing, nor sets down aught in malice. Brutus claimed that the record of Caesar's life in the Capitol presented the dictator's 'glories wherein he was worthy' by the side of the dictator's 'offences wherein he was unworthy'. Neither were the merits under-estimated nor were the defects over-emphasized. Brutus's simple words suggest the nicely adjusted scales in which the moral blemishes of great men should be weighed by the biographer. The aim of biography is not the moral edification which may flow from the survey of either vice or virtue; it is the truthful transmission of personality.

V

The pursuit by the biographer of the historian's aims may prove as disastrous as any competition with the austere aims of the moralist. The historical method is as harmful to biography as the method of moral edification. History encroaches on the biographer's province to the prejudice of his art. Bacon, in his survey of learning, carefully distinguished the 'history of times' (that is, annals or chronicles) or the 'history of action' (that is, histories in the accepted sense) from 'lives'. Bacon warns us that history sets forth the pomp of public business; while biography reveals the true and inward sources of action, tells of private no less than of public conduct, and pays as much attention to the slender wires as to the great weights that hang from them.

The distinction between history and biography lies so much on the surface that a confusion between them is barely justifiable. History may be compared to mechanics, the science which determines the power of bodies in the mass. Biography may be compared to chemistry, the science which analyses substances and resolves them into their constituent elements. The historian has to describe the aggregate movement of men and the manner in which that aggregate movement fashions political or social events and institutions. The historian has only to take into account those aspects of men's lives which affect the movements of the crowd that co-operates with them. The biographer's concern with the crowd is quite subsidiary and secondary. From the mass of mankind he draws apart those units who are in a decisive degree distinguishable from their neighbours. He submits them to minute examination, and his record of observation becomes a mirror of their exploits and character from the cradle to the grave. The historian looks at mankind through a field-glass. The biographer puts individual men under a magnifying glass.

It goes without saying that the biographer must frequently appeal for aid to the historian. An intelligent knowledge of the historical environment—of the contemporary trend of the aggregate movement of men—is indispensable to the biographer, if he would portray in fitting perspective all the operations of his unit. One cannot detach a sovereign or a statesman from the political world in which he has his being. The circumstance of politics is the scenery of the statesman's biography. But it is the art of the biographer sternly to subordinate his scenery to his actors. He must never crowd his stage with upholstery and scenic apparatus that can only distract the spectators' attention from the proper interest of the piece. If you attempt the life of Mary Queen of Scots, you miss your aim when you obscure the human interest and personal adventure, in which her career abounds, by grafting upon it an exhaustive exposition of the intricate relations of Scottish Presbyterians with Roman Catholics, or of Queen Elizabeth's tortuous foreign policy. These things are the bricks and mortar of history. Fragments of them may be needed as props in outlying portions of the biographical edifice, but even then they must be kept largely out of sight.

On these grounds I am afraid that that mass of laborious works which bears the title of 'the life and times' of this or that celebrated person, calls for censure. These weighty volumes can be classed neither with right history nor with right biography. Most of them must be reckoned fruit of a misdirected zeal. One would not wish to speak disrespectfully of the self-denying toil which has raised a mountain of stones on however sprawling a plan to a great man's memory. But when one surveys that swollen cairn *The Life of John Milton narrated in connexion with the political, ecclesiastical and literary history of his time* which occupied a great part of David Masson's long and distinguished career, I accept in spite of the varied uses of the majestic volumes that plaintive judgement of Carlyle: 'Masson has hung on his Milton peg all the politics, which Milton, poor fellow, had never much to do with except to print a pamphlet or two.' Masson has hung on 'his Milton peg' not only 'all the politics which Milton, poor fellow, had never much to do with' but also all the ecclesiastical and literary history with which Milton had even less concern. Biography is not a peg for anything save the character and exploits of a man whose career answers the tests of biographic fitness.

I should hardly be bold enough to speak of the relations of biography and science, and of the peril to biographic method of bringing the two studies into too close a conjunction, had not the late Sir Francis Galton and several living correspondents urged on me, in my capacity of editor of *The Dictionary of National Biography*, the general advantage of adapting the biographic method of the

Dictionary to the needs of the scientific investigation of heredity and eugenics.

Biography, it has been argued, should serve as handmaid to this new and absorbing department of biology and anthropology. The biographer should collect, after due scrutiny, those details of genealogy, habit, and physiological characteristics which may help the student of genetics to determine human types, to diagnose 'variations from type', to distinguish acquired from inherited characteristics, and to arrive by such roads at a finite conception of human individuality. If biography, without deviating from its true purpose or method, can aid the scientific inquiry into the origin and development of ability or genius, all is well. But, if biographic effort is to be swayed by conditions of genetical study, if it is to inquire minutely and statistically into the distant ramifications of every great man's pedigree, with the result that undistinguished grandfathers, grandmothers, fathers, mothers, even second cousins, shall receive almost as close attention as the great man himself, then dangers may be apprehended. Whether the secret of genius will ever be solved is for the future to determine. The biographer has no call to pursue speculation on the fascinating theme.

VI

Like all branches of modern literature, biography was efficiently practised by Greece and Rome, and it is to classical tuition that the modern art is deeply indebted. It was Amyot's great French translation of Plutarch which introduced the biography of disciplined purpose to the modern world, with lasting benefit to life and literature.

Plutarch's method is in one respect peculiar to himself. He endeavours to emphasize points of character and conduct in one man by instituting a formal comparison of them with traits of similar type in another man. He writes what he calls 'parallel lives' of some twenty great Greeks and Romans. Having written of Alexander the Great, he gives an account of Caesar; having written of

PRINCIPLES OF BIOGRAPHY

Demosthenes, he gives an account of Cicero. In every instance he adds to his pair of lives a chapter of comparisons and contrasts. The parallel method enhances the vividness of the portraiture, but it is not the feature of his work which gives it its permanent influence. His individual themes, and his detached treatment of them, deserve chief scrutiny.

Plutarch's subjects are all leaders in politics or war. Heroes of literature and art lie outside his sphere. From the modern point of view the range is arbitrarily limited. But his limitation of theme does not prejudice the value of his example. His guiding principles of treatment are of universal application. He collects authorities in ample store. His materials included not only written books and documents, but also experience and knowledge gathered in converse with well-informed persons. He bases his narrative on contemporary evidence wherever it is accessible, but he is watchful of the lies and fables of hearsay accretions. Where two conflicting versions of one incident are at hand, he selects the one which is in closer harmony with his hero's manners and nature.

But wide as is Plutarch's field of research, he is discriminating in his choice of detail. He knows the value of perspective. He did not, he tells us, declare all things at large. At times he wrote briefly of the noblest and most notorious achievements. He preferred to concentrate his attention upon what to the unseeing eye looked insignificant—upon 'a light occasion, a word or some sport'. 'Therein,' he adds, 'men's nature, dispositions, and manners appear more plainly than the famous battles won, wherein are slain 10,000 men.'

Personality was Plutarch's quarry. It was therefore needful for him to bring into due prominence the singularity of each human theme. His studies inevitably acquainted him with many unhappy or ungracious features in great men's lives, which asked admission to his canvas. The frailties were neither suppressed nor extenuated. Yet a sense of what he called 'reverent shame' deterred him from enlarging on men's frailties beyond the needs of his art. He was a just biographer who was not distracted from his proper aim by ethical fervour or by partisanship. Nor were the purposes of history or science within his scope.

None of Plutarch's biographic principles can be ignored with impunity. Very efficiently does his example warn the biographer against two faults to which biography of more modern date has shown itself peculiarly prone—the fault of misty sentimentality or vague rhapsodizing and the fault of tediousness. The value of rhapsodical or sentimental biography is commonly over-estimated when it is credited with any method at all. In a few instances an eloquent piece of literature is the outcome. But it is literature which belongs to another category than that of biography. Boccaccio's rhapsodical account of Dante is a favourable specimen of its class. We learn there much of the effect of love on youthful hearts. There is a fiery denunciation of the city of Florence for her guilt in banishing her greatest citizen. But Boccaccio's impassioned rhetoric leaves the story of Dante's life untold.

The rhapsodical or sentimental mode of biography will always have its votaries. It often makes a powerful appeal to the hearts of the ingenuous kindred of a departed relative. But the vapour of sentimentality is usually fatal to biographic light. I have already suggested how liable domestic partiality is to err in the choice of the biographic theme. It is no less harmful in ordinary conditions to biographic treatment or method. Very rarely will domestic sentiment recognize the limitations of the biographic art, or obey the cry for candour and perspective. Whether the theme be fit or no, the pen which is guided by domestic enthusiasm will, as a rule, flow to satiety with sentimental vagueness and inaccuracy. The advantage of intimate knowledge which might seem to come of a kinsman's personal propinquity to the biographic hero counts, save in a few notable instances for very little or for nothing. The domestic pen is too often innocent of literary experience.

The faculty of selection and arrangement is wanting, or is at any rate lost in the stream of cloudy panegyric. There are tendencies to emphasize the immaterial and to ignore the material. The sentimental image has to be protected at all hazards. How often has one found in biographies of distinguished men, which are compiled under the domestic eye or by the domestic hand, that youthful struggles with sordid poverty or suffering, that irregular experiences of budding manhood are ignored or half told from a misguided fear of disturbing sentimental bias. I may not reveal the secrets of my own prison-house. But I could recall many a surprising example of domestic anxiety to gloss over or misrepresent truthful and pertinent details in careers of immediate ancestors, because domestic illusion, which is often bred of the blindest conventions of propriety, scents an unedifying savour in facts which are quite harmless but quite necessary.

Domestic sentimentality has been known to exert pressure on the biographer who stands outside the domestic circle. He at times lacks the nerve to resist all its assaults. The peril is indeed ubiquitous. It is perhaps some consolation that Shakespeare's life was written after all his descendants were dead; for who knows, had they been alive, that such a detail as that his father was a village shopkeeper and went bankrupt would have been dismissed to oblivion by an invertebrate and conciliatory biographer, at the call of an ill-balanced domestic pride.

VII

Leslie Stephen said of a recent biography—which enjoyed some vogue—that it was 'too long and too idolatrous'. Those epithets 'too long and too idolatrous' indicate the two worst faults in biographic method, which Plutarch's teaching condemns. Of the biographic vice of idolatry, which springs largely from domestic partiality, I have already spoken enough. The vice of undue length is equally widespread and its prevalence stands in little need of illustration. It is a failing against which Plutarch's example warns us even more loudly than against idolatry. Yet it flourishes luxuriantly in spite of the master's warning. The lineal measurement of biography has no single, fixed scale. There is a threefold graduation answering in the first place to the importance of the career, in the second place to the gross amount of available material, and in the third place to the intrinsic value or biographic pertinence of the surviving records. The correspondence or the journals or the reports of conversation out of which the biographic web is to be woven vary immensely in biographic service. Lack of the raw material would make it impossible to write a life of Shakespeare of the same length as Lord Morley's *Life of Gladstone*. But brevity may be enjoined, in the case of men of the first eminence, not solely on the ground that the raw material is scanty. Even where the raw material be abundant, it may be deficient in the quality which illumines personality and may prove useless for biographic purposes. Among men of action especially, the faculty of self-expression in letters and papers is often crude and ill-developed. Diaries are filled with formalities of daily experience, with excerpts from travellers' guidebooks, or with commonplace reflections. The intrinsic interest for the biographer amounts to little more than proof of the writer's inability to transmit his individuality through his pen. Here drastic summarizing is alone permissible. In citing diaries the half or much less than half is very frequently more valuable than the whole. Rigid selection and lavish rejection of available records are processes which the biographer has often to practise in the sternest temper.

It may be needful for the biographer to examine mountainous masses of manuscript, but he must sift their contents in the light of true biographic principles. The balance has to be kept even between what precedes and what follows. No digression is permissible from the straight path of the hero's personality. The mode of work, which was adopted by one of the most skilful artists in black and white of our time, Phil May, may well offer the biographer suggestion here. Phil May in his drawings presented character with admirable fidelity. In the finished result the fewest possible lines were present. But the preliminary draft was, I understand, crowded with lines, the majority of which were erased by the artist before his work left his hand. Let the biographer note down every detail in fulness and at length. But before offering his labour to the world, let him excise every detail that does not make for graphic portrayal of character and exploit. No mere impressionist sketch satisfies the conditions of adequate biography. But personality is not transmitted on the biographic canvas through overcrowded detail. More than ever at the present day is there imperative need of winnowing biographic information, of dismissing the voluminous chaff while conserving the grain. The growing habit of ephemeral publicity, the methods of reporting the minutiae of prominent people's daily life, not merely by aid of the printing-press, but by the new mechanical inventions of photograph, phonograph, and even cinematograph, all accumulate raw biographic material in giant heaps at an unprecedented rate. The biographer's labours will hereafter be immensely increased; but they will be labours lost, unless principles of discrimination be rigorously applied.

VIII

A discriminating brevity is a law of the right biographic method—a brevity graduated by considerations on the one hand of the genuine importance of the theme or career, and on the other of the genuine value and interest of the available material. Instances of biographic failure, owing to infringements of this law of brevity, are legion, and one or other recent examples will leap to the minds of every one who subscribes to a circulating library. But every law is liable in uncovenanted conditions to a temporary suspense. To every rule there are exceptions, which prove its normal justness. The longest biography in the English language is also the best. Boswell's *Life of Johnson* is indeed reckoned the best specimen of biography that has yet been written in any tongue. Critics agree that life on a desert island would be tolerable with Boswell's biographic work for companion. That verdict may be a metaphorical flight. But it has not been risked in comment on any other biography, and only in comment on two other books in English, the English Bible and Shakespeare.

To what is attributable Boswell's unique triumph, in spite of its challenge of the law of biographic brevity? The triumph is primarily due to an unexampled confluence of two very unusual phenomena. A biographic theme of unprecedented breadth and energy found biographic treatment of an abnormally microscopic intensity. The outcome is what men of science might well call a 'sport'.

There is no precise parallel to the episode of which Boswell's biography was bred. Dr. Johnson, a being of rare intellectual and moral manliness, draws to himself, when well advanced in years, the loyal and unquestioning adoration of a rarely inquisitive young man, whose chief virtues are those of the faithful hound. Boswell's personality, save in his aspect of biographer, deserves small respect. Self-indulgent, libidinous, drunken, vain, he develops in relation to Johnson a parasitical temper which makes him glorious. Boswell pursues Johnson for twenty years like his shadow, and takes note of all that fell from the great man's lips, the tones of his voice, the expressions of his countenance. It is fortunate for us that he should have done much which self-respecting persons would scorn to do. The salt of Boswell's biography is his literal reports of Johnson's conversation, reports in the spirit of the interviewer, which run to enormous length and account for the colossal dimensions of the book.

No other biographer has sought or obtained the like opportunity of interviewing his hero and reporting his conversation. It is doubtful if any hero save Johnson could have come through the ordeal satisfactorily. It is fallacious to suggest that a mediocrity would, if submitted to the pertinacious scrutiny of a Boswell, give occasion for a biographic *tour de force* comparable with Johnson's life. There was a singular union of two exceptional human forces which, despite dissimilarity, proved to be mutually complementary. That miracle is responsible for the supreme effect. Until such a conjunction be repeated, Boswell's work will stand alone, quite out of the sphere of normal biography.

Boswell's book defies all traditional biographic scale; its flood of reported talk is biographic license, not law. Yet it is the paradoxical truth that Boswell's work illustrates to perfection many features of first importance to right biographic method. In spite of its unconscionable length and diffuseness, Boswell's biography always keeps with admirable tenacity to the fundamental purpose of transmitting personality. Every page makes its contribution to this single end. There are no digressions, no superfluities, no distracting issues. All the meticulous detail makes for a unity on which Plutarch could hardly improve.

In the second place, Boswell is the supreme champion of the great principle of biographic frankness; his native candour robs his tendency to idolatry of its familiar mischiefs. He declines to suppress anything that helps his reader to realize Johnson's personality. He bluntly refused Miss Hannah More's request 'to mitigate some of the asperities of our most revered and departed friend'. He would 'not cut off the doctor's claws nor make his tiger a cat to please anybody'. He was so faithful to the biographic law of candour that the frequent snubs which the doctor administered to the writer himself find a due place in the record.

Boswell's presentation of himself in the biography offers a third piece of valuable instruction to the biographer. It was not in Boswell's nature to efface himself. Yet it cannot be said of him, as of some other biographers, that he brings himself on the stage at the expense of his subject.

There are biographies which fail helplessly because the writer is always thinking as much, or perhaps more, of himself than of his theme. He is seeking to share in the honours of publicity. Boswell does not efface himself, but he envelops himself in the spirit of his theme; he stands in its shadow and never in its light.

Lastly, Boswell was an industrious collector of information. It may be objected that for the fifty-four years of Johnson's life which preceded Boswell's introduction to him, something more than Boswell knew has come to light since he wrote. It may be admitted that Boswell neglected a few sources of information from petty personal grudges against those who controlled them. The cry has indeed been lately raised, that some pigmy contemporary biographers of Johnson reveal a few phases of the doctor's character which Boswell either wilfully or unwittingly overlooked or minimized. Spots have been detected in the sun, but the sun's rays are undimmed. Boswell's achievement glows with a steadier and more expansive radiance than any other star in the biographic firmament.

There is yet another biography in the English language which transgresses the law of brevity without marring its effect, nay, with enhancement of its effect. There is a second exception to the principle of brevity which fails to impugn the normal rule, if on grounds quite different from those which Boswell pleads with security. Lockhart's *Life of Scott* is the second best biography in the language, Boswell's biography being the first. But Lockhart's merit is mainly due to the excellence and the abundance of the raw material provided for him in Scott's ample journals and correspondence. He was spared Boswell's toil of reporter and collector of information; almost all was ready to his hands, and he had merely to apply to his vast store those faculties of selection and arrangement which came of his literary efficiency and experience. It is very rare for a man of Sir Walter Scott's supreme genius, whose career and character, too, are free of dark places or mysteries prompting suppression or extenuation, to leave to a competent biographer an immense mass of fit biographic records penned by his own hand. So happy an event seems as unlikely to recur as a second meeting of a Johnson with a Boswell. Lockhart's challenge of the law of brevity is justified, and the justification barely touches normal experience.

IX

Encyclopaedic or collective biography is a special branch of biography which has not been infrequently practised, both in classical and modern times. To collective biography, in the form of national biography, Leslie Stephen dedicated immense energy, and to it I, in succession to him, have devoted almost all my adult life. The methods of collective or national biography clearly differ from those of individual biography in literary design and in the opportunity which is offered of literary embellishment. But there are points at which the method of the two biographic kinds converge. Collective or national biography, which brings a long series of lives within the confines of a single literary scheme, presses the obligations of brevity and conciseness to limits which individual or independent biography is not required to respect. Facts and dates loom larger in collective or national biography than in other biographic forms. The object of national as of all collective biography is Priestley's object in scientific exposition—'to comprise as much knowledge as possible in the smallest compass'. Indulgence in rhetoric, voluble enthusiasm, emotion, loquacious sentiment, is for the national biographer the deadliest of sins. Yet his method will be of small avail if he be unable to arrange his bare facts and dates so as to indicate graphically the precise character of the personality and of the achievement with which he is dealing—if he fail to suggest the peculiar interest of the personality and the achievement by some happy epithet or brief touch of criticism. There are instances in which a miniature memoir thus graced has given a reader a sense of satisfaction almost as great as any that a largely planned biography can give—the feeling, namely, that to him is imparted all the information for which his commemorative instinct craves.

The methods of national biography are Spartan methods heartlessly enforced by an editor's vigilance. It might perhaps be doubted if any of the Spartan methods of collective biography could be adopted with advantage by independent biographers who are free of the collective biographer's shackles.

Yet the virtue of liberty may be overvalued. The collective biographer submits from the outset to a strict discipline. Without underrating the dissimilarity of the conditions in which the independent biographer works, one may often impute to him without injustice a lack of any such training as is required of his humbler brother-craftsmen. In the absence of disciplinary control, an untrained biographer has been known to fling before his readers a confused mass of irrelevant and inaccurate information, to load his page with unimpressive sentiment, with the result that the hero's really eminent achievements and distinctive characteristics are buried under the dust and ashes of special pleading, commonplace gossip, and helpless eulogy. Occasionally, at any rate, nothing would be lost by an exchange of a shapeless and woolly effigy from the unchartered workshop of a free and independent biographer, for a skeleton of facts and dates from the collective biographer's law-ridden factory.

X

None the less, from the purely literary point of view, a contribution to collective biography however useful and efficient cannot rank with a thoroughly workmanlike effort in individual biography. It is individual biography which gives unrestricted opportunities of literary skill. Where the theme is fit, the independent biographer has scope for the exercise of almost every literary gift.

Varied qualities are demanded of the successful biographer. He must have the patience to sift dust heaps of written or printed papers. He must have the insight to interpret what he has sifted, and the capacity to give form to the essence of his findings. A Frenchman has said that the features of Alexander ought only to be preserved by the chisel of Apelles. The admonition implies that magnitude in a career demands corresponding eminence in the biographer. No doubt the ideal partnership is there indicated. But like all counsels of perfection, this ideal union shrinks from realization. Did the precept prevail, the field of biography would be very circumscribed and few biographers would find employment. It is more workaday counsel to bid the biographer avoid unfit themes and to treat fit themes with scrupulous accuracy, with perfect frankness, with discriminating sympathy, and with resolute brevity. Not otherwise is one of ordinary clay likely to minister worthily to the commemorative instinct of his fellow men and to transmit to an after-age a memorable personality.

Titles in This Series

Criticism: General, Poetic, and Dramatic

1. Alfred Austin. THE POETRY OF THE PERIOD. 1870

2. Robert Buchanan. A LOOK ROUND LITERATURE. 1887

3. John William Cole. THE LIFE AND THEATRICAL TIMES OF CHARLES KEAN, F.S.A. 1859. (In two volumes)

4. E. S. Dallas. POETICS: AN ESSAY ON POETRY. 1852

5. E. S. Dallas. THE GAY SCIENCE. 1866

6. H. Buxton Forman. OUR LIVING POETS: AN ESSAY IN CRITICISM. 1871

7. Walter Hamilton. THE AESTHETIC MOVEMENT IN ENGLAND, third edition, 1882

8. R. H. Horne, editor. A NEW SPIRIT OF THE AGE, second edition. 1844. (In two volumes)

9. Madge Kendall. THE DRAMA. 1884. with DRAMATIC OPINIONS. 1890

10. Joseph A. Knight. A HISTORY OF THE STAGE DURING THE VICTORIAN ERA. 1901

11. Lord William Pitt Lennox. PLAYS, PLAYERS, AND PLAYHOUSES AT HOME AND ABROAD. 1881. (In two volumes)

12. Robert James Mann. TENNYSON'S "MAUD" VINDICATED: AN EXPLANATORY ESSAY. 1856

13. Mowbray Morris. ESSAYS IN THEATRICAL CRITICISM. 1882

14. Henry Neville. THE STAGE: ITS PAST AND PRESENT IN RELATION TO FINE ART. 1875

15. "Q" [Thomas Purnell]. DRAMATISTS OF THE PRESENT DAY. 1871

16. Walter Raleigh. STYLE. 1897

17. William Caldwell Roscoe. POEMS AND ESSAYS (volume two, ESSAYS, only). 1860

18. Clement Scott. THE DRAMA OF YESTERDAY & TODAY. 1899. (In two volumes)

19. James Field Stanfield. AN ESSAY ON THE STUDY AND COMPOSITION OF BIOGRAPHY. 1813

Parody, Satire, Literary Controversy, and Curiosa

20. Edward Bulwer-Lytton. THE NEW TIMON. 1846. with Algernon Charles Swinburne. SPECIMENS OF MODERN POETS. THE HEPTALOGIA, OR THE SEVEN AGAINST SENSE. 1880. with Algernon Charles Swinburne. "DISGUST: A DRAMATIC MONOLOGUE." 1898

21. [William E. Aytoun and Theodore Martin.] THE BOOK OF BALLADS: EDITED BY BON GAULTIER. 1845. with [William E. Aytoun.] FERMILIAN: OR THE STUDENT OF BADAJOZ: A SPASMODIC TRAGEDY BY T. PERCY JONES. 1854

22. James Carnegie. JONAS FISHER: A POEM IN BROWN AND WHITE. 1875. with [A. C. Swinburne.] THE DEVIL'S DUE: A LETTER TO THE EDITOR OF "THE EXAMINER." BY THOMAS MAITLAND. 1875

23. Philip James Bailey. THE AGE; A COLLOQUIAL SATIRE. 1858

24. [W. C. Bennett.] ANTI-MAUD. 1865. with [Eustace Clare Grenville Murray.] THE COMING K———. 1873. with [W. H. Mallock.] EVERY MAN HIS OWN POET. 1877

25. [John Burley Waring.] POEMS INSPIRED BY CERTAIN PICTURES AT THE ART TREASURES EXHIBITION, MANCHESTER. 1857. with [Anon.] THE LAUGHTER OF THE MUSES. 1869

26. Robert Buchanan. THE FLESHLY SCHOOL OF POETRY AND OTHER PHENOMENA OF THE DAY. 1872. with Algernon Charles Swinburne. UNDER THE MICROSCOPE. 1872

27. J. Rutter. THE NINETEENTH CENTURY, A POEM, IN TWENTY-NINE CANTOS. 1900

Collections of Critical Essays

28. William E. Fredeman, editor. VICTORIAN PREFACES AND INTRODUCTIONS: A FACSIMILE COLLECTION. 1986

29. Ira Bruce Nadel, editor. VICTORIAN FICTION: A COLLECTION OF ESSAYS FROM THE PERIOD. 1986

30. Ira Bruce Nadel, editor. VICTORIAN BIOGRAPHY: A COLLECTION OF ESSAYS FROM THE PERIOD. 1986

31. John F. Stasny, editor. VICTORIAN POETRY: A COLLECTION OF ESSAYS FROM THE PERIOD. 1986

32. William E. Fredeman, editor. THE VICTORIAN POETS: AN ALPHABETICAL COMPILATION OF THE BIO-CRITICAL INTRODUCTIONS TO THE VICTORIAN POETS FROM A. H. MILES'S "THE POETS AND POETRY OF THE NINETEENTH CENTURY." 1986